INTERMEDIATE
MICROECONOMICS

INTERMEDIATE MICROECONOMICS

John H Hoag
Bowling Green State University, USA

 **World Scientific**

NEW JERSEY · LONDON · SINGAPORE · BEIJING · SHANGHAI · HONG KONG · TAIPEI · CHENNAI

Published by

World Scientific Publishing Co. Pte. Ltd.

5 Toh Tuck Link, Singapore 596224

USA office: 27 Warren Street, Suite 401-402, Hackensack, NJ 07601

UK office: 57 Shelton Street, Covent Garden, London WC2H 9HE

British Library Cataloguing-in-Publication Data
A catalogue record for this book is available from the British Library.

INTERMEDIATE MICROECONOMICS

ISBN 978-981-4322-72-0

In-house Editor: Wanda Tan

Typeset by Stallion Press
Email: enquiries@stallionpress.com

Printed in Singapore.

For students who suffered through Intermediate Micro with me
And Caroline, who was my guide

Preface

For the Instructor

Another intermediate microeconomics text? Please! Surely all that could possibly be said about the topic has already been said, and said in ways that are far better than what you find here. What possible reason can there be for another?

Bear with me as I try to make a case. What you will find here is different. Different how? I started teaching intermediate micro some 40 odd years ago as a graduate student. On the final exam, I asked a question about utility maximization that involved indifference curves that went the "wrong" way. Students overwhelmingly told me the tangency was still utility maximum. One of the courses I first taught as an Assistant Professor was Intermediate Micro, and I continued to ask this question. The fact that students insisted on the conclusion of the tangency, when the assumptions underlying that conclusion were not true, befuddled me. Maybe they just did not see what the assumptions are. So I started writing my own notes and tried to make the course as axiomatic as I could, but not so that heavy mathematics would be needed. In fact for years, I did not explicitly use calculus. But I was pretty sure that if students carefully did what I asked, they would find their way through. My aim was to get students to pay attention to the hypothesis of the proposition. If the hypothesis is not true, there is little reason to think that the conclusion is true. What we teach as intermediate micro is really not a settled set of conclusions, but rather a reasoning process. I also assumed that they would learn some micro.

But because of this text's axiomatic framework, it is surely different from most others. Now I have included calculus, but oddly, the calculus is almost always in a section by itself near the end of the chapter. For those who want the calculus integrated into the main part of the text, please look elsewhere.

I am aware that this text is dense and that the focus is on the ideas. I have tried to do four things to break up the reading. First, while the chapters are sometimes a bit long, I have tried to make the sections in the chapters fairly short. Most sections are not more than five pages, and many are fewer. Second, I have also put in quick one-line summaries of important ideas in a cloud shape.

Third, I have included some line drawings that are attempts at humor. Fourth, I have included a "From the Literature" box in each chapter where students can go to find applications of the ideas we have been studying. You will see that the book is largely devoted to the theory, and there are not a lot of applications. I assume that you have applications you like to bring, so these "From the Literature" boxes are brief, but hopefully suggest ways the ideas can be used. These four items are efforts to address the concern that texts need to be approachable.

This book is relatively short, around 500 pages. You might wonder if there is enough here for a semester. In candor, I have never covered all that is here in a semester. Much depends on the students in any given term, but I rarely get to the chapter on uncertainty. The chapter on the long run and sometimes the chapter on labor get short shrift. I believe there is plenty of material here. I would also say that I have been parsimonious with regard to the topics covered. There are a variety of topics you might find in a traditional text that are not here. I have tried to keep a fairly tight focus on what I think are the core concepts, with the idea that most of the other topics are applications. I have put some of the applications in the workbook (available on the book website at http://www.worldscibooks.com/economics/7893.html).

The workbook includes the consumer as a supplier of labor, choice over time, and the discriminating monopolist, among others. There is plenty to do.

The opening chapter, "Some Building Blocks," is really important. The main tools that are used in the text are presented here. The logical tools and the ideas of convex sets are ideas that students rarely know coming into this class. It is important to discuss them. I have also tried to reserve the term "tangent" for the case where differentiable curves touch but do not cross. If non-differentiable curves touch, I do not call this a tangency. Students need to know that special meaning is given to this term. A number of important issues can be overcome if careful attention is given to the ideas in the introductory chapter. I email students before the first class to tell them to read that material and the first class is devoted to starting the discussion of these ideas.

You will see that questions are sprinkled throughout the text, and are not at the end of each chapter. There are nearly 280 of these questions. I have done this because many of the questions are questions that ask the student to engage the ideas that are at hand, leading, I hope, to a deeper understanding. Answers to about one-third of these questions can be found at the end of the text. There is also a workbook that goes with this text. There are more questions in the workbook than can be assigned in a semester, though it is not unusual for me to assign 25 to 30 of these as homework in a semester. Often the homework is an application of an idea we have been working on. So choice over time is an application of utility maximization. Labor supply can be used to illustrate income and substitution effects. Some homework exercises are near-repeats of earlier homework. So the homework where the budget line involves an endowment of goods that can be bought or sold comes up several times, in different guises. These homework questions force the student to confront the ideas and to work with them. Often the homework pushes the student to see that what we learned in the text may not hold in all applications. Some homework builds on earlier homework, and I have tried to indicate the links in the chapter overviews for the homework.

I have also generated PowerPoint slides for the course (see book website). The main complication is that I do not use them myself, so I do not know what works well and what does not. Mary Ellen

Benedict has looked through them and made significant suggestions. If you have suggestions along these lines, I would be most happy to hear your thoughts.

To write a textbook is primarily an advertisement of vanity. Frankly, I can think of few other reasons for me to write this book. I surely know that the market for intermediate micro is pretty small, and a fortune will not be mine even if the book sweeps the market. If the book were full of new results or novel presentations, that might be different, but my guess is the novel ways have been pretty much exhausted — or if not, the chances that I will find them are few. I am left with the vanity of the effort.

The one thing I would say is that perhaps by the writing of this book, I have better learned the micro that I was supposed to have learned in graduate school. It is amazing the number of times that as I write a sentence I can hear the voice of my graduate micro professor saying those very same words. I did not understand at the time that he had chosen those specific words as they were precisely the words needed. Now I better understand.

So who to thank? I have been exposed to a substantial number of excellent faculty teaching micro. As an undergraduate, I had Cliff Lloyd at Purdue University. As a graduate student, I had James Henderson at the University of Minnesota, and Jim Quirk at the University of Kansas with follow-up from Dick Ruppert and Mohamed El-Hodiri. In most ways, I am not like any of them, and I do not think that any of them would see this book as something they would consider useful. Three of those faculty have written their own micro books (Lloyd and Henderson at the graduate level, and Quirk at the undergraduate level), and if you look, you would not see much similarity between what I have done and what they did. They cannot be blamed for what happened here.

At the same time, when I went to Kansas, I did not like micro and thought it just hard and not very interesting. But it was when I took the course from Jim Quirk that I saw the logical structure, the way that what seemed like divergent thoughts were in reality connected; after that I was hooked. I have never been able to do micro at that level, but the study of it is just the most fascinating thing I can imagine. What was more, my graduate student friends shared this interest and passion, and provided an opportunity to discuss what we had learned. Dave Whipple, Katchan Terasawa, and Doug Hale were the primary culprits in this dimension.

As for the cartoons, yes, I drew them. But I had some advice and direction. Both Jory Griffis and Ken Probst were kind enough to have a look and recommend ways to improve them (actually, almost anything would have improved them). Their support in this effort was important; I would not have included these drawings if they had not been so kind.

The other thanks goes to students who, over a large number of years, taught me more about how to make the course stronger, clearer, and better. The number of students willing (and able) to take up this challenge has been substantial, and they have given me comfort. They seem to appreciate that they were asked to do something more, something harder.

I wish to thank Rachel Childers who read the entire manuscript and made significant comments on the presentation and accuracy of the ideas. I have had two semesters of students who used the book pretty much as you see it here, who also made comments and suggestions ("Didn't you read this after you typed it??" "OH! Is that what you meant?").

I also wish to thank the editors and staff at World Scientific starting with Tai Wei Lim, Juliet Lee, and Sandhya Venkatesh. I have had excellent support from the copy editor Wanda Tan, and appreciate her willingness to work through this text and improve the product! It has been a very pleasant and productive working relationship.

But my very best friend and reader was Arleen, who has suffered through more of my prose than any human being should have to. I would tell her that I owe her, but I am already so deeply in her debt that I will never get out.

Intermediate micro has been one of two courses (the other is mathematical economics) I have loved teaching over my career and have always looked forward to. Trying to share the kind of experience I had in Quirk's class — to bring the wonder, the discovery, and the power of the thought process — is what I have aimed to do. Could there be any greater vanity?

For the Student

Prepare for fun! You are about to engage microeconomics, a topic of incredible power and interest. In many ways, it is like a puzzle that you cannot quite complete. It may become clearer as we move along, but it will never be completely clear; take it from me. I do not assume that you will ever take more microeconomics, but if you do, this course will prepare you well. But what you can, and should, gain from this course is not a bunch of conclusions that you can apply willy-nilly, but a thought process that leads you toward conclusions. My interest is as much in how one comes to a conclusion as what the conclusion is. In that sense, the course is not a course in microeconomics, but a course in clearer thinking applied to microeconomics.

Now to be fair, the text is challenging. Got that?! But it is only through hard work that you will reap the benefits of the mental skills I am promoting. You simply have to get your hands dirty, draw some graphs, and work out the arguments. Memorization will be an element, but not the only one. Start by reading the text. You will need to engage the text as you go along. If you skip the graphs or the argument, you will not learn what you should. There are questions embedded in the text rather than at the end of each chapter so that you have a chance to work with the book and the ideas.

There is a homework book that goes with this course. It is not your standard homework. Here I will ask you to go beyond what is in the text and to do some application or some added feature. The homework exercises are not easy, and will not be something you can do in ten minutes. You need to be prepared to devote some time to them. And when done with the homework, you should ask yourself how the homework fits into the chapter where it is assigned. The homework questions are placed as they are for a reason.

When I first started taking economics, micro was my least favorite. But when in graduate school, I saw how exciting and fabulously interesting the puzzles were. I was hooked. It may not be your cup of tea and the approach here may not be one that works for you, but if you persevere, you will learn some microeconomics, and a whole lot more.

Contents

List of Propositions

Mathematics and Maximum

A.13 First-Order Condition
If $f(X)$ is differentiable and has a maximum or minimum at X_0, then $f'(X_0) = 0$.

A.15 Second-Order Condition
Suppose that a function can be differentiated twice and that the function has a zero derivative at X_0. If $f''(X_0) < 0$ (the second derivative of $f(X_0) < 0$), then X_0 is a maximum for the function. If the second derivative of $f(X_0) > 0$, then we have a minimum. If the second derivative of $f(X_0)$ is zero, the test fails.

Preference and Indifference

2.11 *If the consumer has preferences, R, and if both BT_W and WT_W contain their boundary, then continuous indifference curves exist.*

2.15 *If R is a preference relation with continuous indifference curves and more is preferred to less, then indifference curves have a negative slope.*

2.17 *If R is a preference relation and more is preferred to less, then indifference curves cannot cross.*

Utility Maximization and Demand

2.21 Utility Maximization Given the Budget
If   a. *assumptions 2.1 hold,*
          b. *the consumer has differentiable indifference curves,*

c. BT_W is strictly convex for each W,
d. more is preferred to less,
e. at (X_0, Y_0) utility is maximum given the budget, $X_0 > 0$, $Y_0 > 0$,

Then   f. at (X_0, Y_0) all income is spent,

g. at (X_0, Y_0) an indifference curve is tangent to the budget line.

Income and Substitution Effect

3.6 For a consumer satisfying the utility maximization proposition where both X and Y are goods, then the substitution effect is strictly negative.

Elasticity

3.10 If demand is a negatively sloped straight line, then the elasticity falls as quantity rises.

3.15 If, as we move down demand, the expenditure on X rises, then demand is elastic.

Least Cost

4.11 Least Cost Combination

If   a. assumptions 4.1 hold,

b. the firm has isoquants that are differentiable,

c. the set of bundles producing at least X units of output is strictly convex for each X,

d. the expenditure on variable inputs to produce X_0 units of output is minimum at (L_0, K_0) with $L_0 > 0$ and $K_0 > 0$,

Then   e. at (L_0, K_0) there is an isocost tangent to the X_0 isoquant.

Average–Marginal

4.17 If the ATC has a minimum at X_0, then the line from the origin to the TC must be tangent to the TC at X_0 (see Figure 4.14).

4.18 If the ATC has a minimum at X_0 and TC is differentiable, then at X_0 the MC must equal the ATC.

4.19 The Average Marginal Fact

If the total and the average curves are differentiable, then for X > 0, the average curve falls if and only if the marginal curve is below the average curve.

Fundamental Theorem

4.21 The Fundamental Theorem

Given outputs X_1 and X_2 with $X_1 < X_2$, the area under the marginal cost between X_1 and X_2 is $TC(X_2) - TC(X_1)$.

Profit Maximization, Competition

5.6 Profit Maximization for the Competitive Firm

If   a. *the assumptions of least cost hold,*

        b. *the MC and MR are continuous,*

        c. *at $X_0, 0 < X_0 < \infty$, profit is maximum for the competitive firm,*

Then   d. *at X_0, MR = MC.*

5.8 Shutdown Condition

If the competitive firm has a price above the AVC at profit maximum, then the firm will stay in business to at least the end of the short run. If the competitive firm's price is below the AVC at profit maximum, then the firm will shut down and produce zero in the short run.

Average Revenue, Marginal Revenue for Monopoly

6.1 *If we solve the monopolist's demand for P, then the resulting equation is AR.*

6.3 *If the average revenue slopes down, then the marginal revenue will lie below the average revenue.*

Profit Maximization, Monopoly

6.5 Profit Maximization for Monopoly

If   a. *the assumptions of least cost hold,*

        b. *the MC and MR are continuous,*

        c. *at $X_0, 0 < X_0 < \infty$, profit is maximum for the monopoly firm,*

Then   d. *at X_0, MR = MC.*

Compare Monopoly and Competition

6.7   *If the demand under competition would be the same as the demand under monopoly, and if the MC for the monopoly would be the same as the sum of the individual competitive firms' MC curves, then the profit-maximizing monopoly produces less output and charges a higher price than would occur under competition.*

7.9   *If assumptions 7.7 hold and the satisfaction to society is maximum, then for each pair of goods X and Y, we must have $\frac{P_x}{MSC_x} = \frac{P_y}{MSC_y}$.*

7.12 (Converse of proposition 7.9) *Assume that assumptions 7.7 hold, that the MSC is positively sloped for all goods, and that $P_x/MSC_x = P_y/MSC_y$. Then, resources are allocated to maximize social satisfaction.*

Nash Equilibrium

8.3   *If (X_1^0, X_2^0) is a Nash equilibrium, then (X_1^0, X_2^0) is the solution to the best reply functions for firm 1 and firm 2.*

8.5   *If (X_1^0, X_2^0) satisfies both firms' best reply functions, then (X_1^0, X_2^0) is a Nash equilibrium.*

Short-Run–Long-Run Costs

9.4   *If the SRTC and LRTC are differentiable and at X_0 we are on the LRTC, then at X_0 there is a SRTC for some scale of plant tangent to the LRTC.*

9.7   *If both $SRTC_1$ and LRTC are differentiable, and if $SRATC_1$ is tangent to LRATC at X_0, then LRMC must equal the $SRMC_1$ at X_0.*

Profit Maximization, Long-Run Competition

9.9   Long-Run Profit Maximization
      Suppose that LRATC and LRMC are derived as shown above, and that we have a competitive firm. If LRMC is continuous and there is a profit-maximizing output between 0 and infinity, then at the profit maximum, LRMC = LRMR.

9.13 *The long-run equilibrium for the competitive firm maximizing profit will be where the firm earns zero profit (but a normal return).*

Profit Maximization, One Variable Input

10.6 Profit Maximization for One Variable Input

If   a. *there is one variable input, L,*

        b. *technology is given,*

        c. *the* MRP *and* MIC *are continuous,*

        d. *profit is maximum at* $L_0, 0 < L_0 < \infty,$

Then   e. *at* $L_0,$ MRP $=$ MIC.

Equilibrium in Crusoe

11.3 *If* (P^*, w^*, C^*, L^*) *is a competitive equilibrium in the Crusoe economy, then an indifference curve for Robinson must be tangent to the production function at* $(L^*, C^*),$ *and the tangency has slope* $w^*/P^*.$

11.5 *If in the Crusoe world we have an indifference curve for Robinson tangent to the production function at* $(L^*, C^*),$ *and the tangent has slope* $w^*/P^*,$ *then* (P^*, w^*, C^*, L^*) *is a competitive equilibrium.*

Pure Trade Competitive Equilibrium

11.10 *If assumptions 11.6 hold and if, for R,* (C_R^*, F_R^*) *is utility maximum given the budget, then an R indifference curve must be tangent to the budget line at* $(C_R^*, F_R^*).$

11.12 *If assumptions 11.6 hold, and if the prices* (P_C, P_F) *together with the* PTES $\{(C_R^*, F_R^*), (C_Z^*, F_Z^*)\}$ *form a pure trade competitive equilibrium on the inside of the Edgeworth box, then an indifference curve for R must be tangent to an indifference curve for Z at* $\{(C_R^*, F_R^*), (C_Z^*, F_Z^*)\}$ *and this point must also be on the budget line.*

Competitive Equilibrium with Production

11.19 *For the quantity of fish,* $F_1,$ *the maximum quantity of coconuts that can be produced will be the quantity of coconuts of the coconut isoquant tangent to the* F_1 *fish isoquant in the production Edgeworth box.*

11.21 *If assumptions 11.15 hold and if prices* (P_C^*, P_F^*, w^*, r^*) *and an allocation of resources* $\{(C^*, F^*), (C_R^*, F_R^*), (C_Z^*, F_Z^*),$

$(L_C^*, K_C^*), (L_F^*, K_F^*)\}$ *are a competitive equilibrium with production, then:*

a. *the (negative of the) slope of the production possibilities at* (C^*, F^*) *is equal to the (negative of the) ratio of the price of coconuts to the price of fish,* (P_C^*/P_F^*).

b. *at* (C_R^*, F_R^*), (C_Z^*, F_Z^*), *an indifference curve for R must be tangent to an indifference curve for Z, and* $C_R^* + C_Z^* = C^*, F_R^* + F_Z^* = F^*$.

c. *at* (L_C^*, K_C^*), (L_F^*, K_F^*), *the* C^* *isoquant is tangent to the* F^* *isoquant and* $L_R^* + L_Z^* = L_C^* + L_F^*, K_R^* + K_Z^* = K_C^* + K_F^*$.

Pareto Optimum and Pure Trade

12.4 *If assumptions* 11.6 *hold and S is a Pareto optimum on the inside of the Edgeworth box, then an indifference curve for R is tangent to an indifference curve for Z at S.*

12.6 *If assumptions* 11.6 *hold and at S an indifference curve for R is tangent to an indifference curve for Z, then S is Pareto optimal.*

12.9 *If* $\{(P_C^*, P_F^*), (C_R^*, F_R^*), (C_Z^*, F_Z^*)\}$ *is a pure trade competitive equilibrium on the inside of the Edgeworth box and assumptions* 11.6 *hold, then* $(C_R^*, F_R^*), (C_Z^*, F_Z^*)$ *is Pareto optimal.*

12.11 *If* $\{(C_R^*, F_R^*), (C_Z^*, F_Z^*)\}$ *is Pareto optimal on the inside of the Edgeworth box and assumptions* 11.6 *hold, then there is a set of prices* (P_C^*, P_F^*) *and an initial endowment* $\{(C_R^0, F_R^0), (C_Z^0, F_Z^0)\}$ *so that* $\{(P_C^*, P_F^*), (C_R^*, F_R^*), (C_Z^*, F_Z^*)\}$ *is a pure trade competitive equilibrium.*

Efficiency

12.16 *If assumptions* 11.15 *hold, and S is an efficient input state on the inside of the Edgeworth box, then at S, an isoquant for the coconut producer will be tangent to an isoquant for the fish producer.*

12.18 *If assumptions* 11.15 *hold and at S, an isoquant for fish is tangent to an isoquant for coconuts, then S is efficient.*

Pareto Optimum and Production

12.21 *Given assumptions* 11.15, *if* $\{(C_R^*, F_R^*), (C_Z^*, F_Z^*)\}$ *is a Pareto optimal combination of coconuts and fish, and* (C_1, F_1) *is a* *point on the production possibilities where* $C_1 = C_R^* + C_Z^*$ *and* $F_1 = F_R^* + F_Z^*$, *and* (C_1, F_1) *is an efficient mix of outputs, then the slope of production possibilities at* (C_1, F_1) *is exactly equal to the slope of R and Z's indifference curves at* $\{(C_R^*, F_R^*), (C_Z^*, F_Z^*)\}$.

12.23 *Given assumptions 11.15, if we have a competitive equilibrium with production, then the resulting input state and pure trade economic state constitute a Pareto optimum, an efficient allocation of resources, and an efficient mix of outputs.*

List of Figures

Chapter 3

Chapter 4

Chapter 5

Chapter 6

Chapter 7

Chapter 11

Chapter 12

Chapter 13

Some Building Blocks

Key Concepts:

- Slope
- Tangent
- Differentiable
- Derivative
- Maximum
- Minimum
- Convex set
- Strictly convex set
- Contrapositive
- Converse

Goals:

- Provide a review of basic ideas needed for the course.
- Introduce some ideas that will be important for what follows:
  - Theory and its elements
  - Slope
  - Tangent
  - Convex sets
  - Contrapositive and converse.

Economics humor? Not your normal humor!

In this chapter, we will introduce most of the tools we will need in the remainder of this text. One may think that this chapter is not very important, but in fact it lays the foundation for what follows. You will often need to look back at this material to review what was introduced here. While a good part of the material in this chapter is mathematics, the emphasis is not strongly on computation. That is not to say that computation does not matter, as it will matter at least in some settings, but it is not the primary focus of this chapter or this book. We have assumed that you have had calculus before this course. However, there is really only one concept from calculus we need, the derivative, and this concept will be discussed below. There are parts of the text where the calculus is used, but it is rarely more than one-variable calculus. For faculty who wish to avoid finding derivatives entirely, there is enough material here that a substantial course can be offered without recourse to the actual taking of a derivative. This chapter has six sections: introduction, slope, derivatives, maximum and minimum, convexity, and contrapositive and converse. We will start with the introduction.

A.1 Introduction

A couple of other organizational matters should be mentioned. First, there are some particular statements that have central importance in a course on theory: definition, statement of assumptions, statement of propositions, proof of propositions. These will often be numbered with the chapter number and a number for the place in the sequence of argument. Between these we will have explanation, discussion, and construction. The course should remind you, in some ways, of a course in geometry. Second, we will also have space in the margins. This is done on purpose. The space is there for you to make notes and to add any details that are not included. The other item of importance is that exercises are scattered throughout the text, not at the end of each chapter. It is also true that there are substantial exercises offered in a separate workbook.

Given what was just said, one might wonder about the material. What are we about to study? The primary focus of this text is the logic and structure of microeconomics, the theory of micro. While we will offer applications of the material from time to time, our primary interest is in the theory. One should not worry that something so seemingly abstract does not have any use. In fact, microeconomics is all around us. But before making the application, it is more than just useful to understand a bit more about the underlying theory itself.

So what is theory? Theory is an effort to understand the world by constructing worlds that are simpler than the world actually is: model worlds. The reason to do this is that the world is complex and difficult to understand. To begin the process of understanding, we need to simplify, to construct worlds that are (relatively) easy to understand. This process starts by defining terms, but definitions do not provide understanding. So we then begin the process of simplification by making assumptions. Assumptions have the impact of reducing or simplifying the world we are examining. They set the bounds for this model world; the assumptions tell us where we expect the model to work and where it will not work. Once we have some assumptions, we then begin to examine what the assumptions imply. This is accomplished by stating a proposition. A proposition is a statement that starts out with "if [something]," and ends with "then [something else]." The statement is only the beginning. The next piece is the proof of the proposition, the idea that we have to provide some logical steps linking the "if" and the "then." The proof is that set of logical steps. Finally, we should (but we will not always do so) check to see if the proposed behavior, the "then" statement, is actually found in the real world. Can the theory be applied and does it lead to better understanding? Thus, we have that the elements of a theory are definition, assumption, statement of a proposition, and proof of the proposition. When we say we have a theory, we could have just as easily (and correctly) said that we have a model.

The process of creating theory is a difficult task, and one that is often ridiculed. The primary reason for ridicule is that people sometimes insist on making bad assumptions. The fact is that bad assumptions lead to bad conclusions, conclusions that cannot be verified in the real world. The problem is to find assumptions that are simple enough to provide some conclusions that are useful in promoting our understanding, and at the same time also yield useful and powerful conclusions. When we state assumptions, we will try to ask if the assumptions are likely to be true and to what extent we might find the world is consistent with those assumptions. But we will also sometimes plow ahead with assumptions we are not that happy with on the grounds that to more accurately account for the nuances of the world, we generate outcomes that do not lead to understanding.

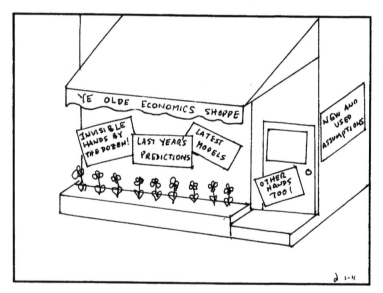

The other fact is that it is incredibly common for people to reason from models. Often we just do not recognize that we are doing so.

There are several key phrases that suggest a model is being used, such as "suppose that," or "what if." When you hear phrases such as those, you know the speaker has some kind of model in mind. What we need is to understand the model and to decide if it is a model we can use. A good part of this course is devoted to the idea that to properly understand a model, we need to understand the assumptions, and we also need to know what the model implies.

With that rather extended introduction, we can get on with the development of the tools we will need. If you have the impression that some mathematics might be useful, you would be right. We start with some ideas about sets.

Definition A.1: *A **set** is a collection of elements with a common feature.*

Definition A.2: *The **union** of two sets A and B is a set whose elements include all the elements of set A and all the elements of set B.*

Definition A.3: *The **intersection** of two sets A and B is a set whose elements are all the elements that are in both set A and set B.*

Exercise 1. Suppose that A includes all even positive integers and B includes all odd positive integers. Find the union of A and B. Find the intersection of A and B.

Exercise 2. Suppose that we consider sets in the plane. Say set A is a circle with center at the origin and with radius 2. Set B is a circle with center at the point $(2, 0)$ and with radius 1. Draw these sets. Shade in the union of these sets. Now draw the graphs again and shade in their intersection.

Another concept is important for us — that of a function.

Definition A.4: *A **function** is a relationship between two sets of variables — X, the domain, and Y, the range — where, for each element in the domain, there is one and only one corresponding element in the range. We write $Y = f(X)$.*

It is important to note that a function, generally, starts with an X and generates a Y. There is an order to this process: X comes before Y. However, that is not to say that we cannot start with Y and find X. But just because $Y = f(X)$ is a function, it does not mean that if we start with Y and generate X we will have a function. It could be that for each Y there is more than one corresponding X. If there is a function starting with Y and going to X that can be obtained from $Y = f(X)$, we call this "reverse" function the inverse function and denote it $f^{-1}(Y) = X$.

While we will normally be clear when we mean a function, we can also use other terms that mean the same thing, "line" or "curve" for example. So if you see the terms "line" or "curve," you know we have a function in mind.

In the above equation, we have $Y = f(X)$. The symbol "=" means that Y is defined as $f(X)$. We can also write an equation $D(P) = S(P)$ by which we mean that at the equilibrium value of P, the quantity demanded, $D(P)$, is the same as the quantity supplied, $S(P)$. This latter "=" is only true for one value of P. This "=" is different from the earlier "=" in that the earlier "=" was true for all X. The equality of $D(P) = S(P)$ is only true for one value of P. This is a significant difference between the two meanings.

> **Section Summary:**
> In this section, we have introduced the idea of a set, the intersection and union of sets, and the idea of a function. We have also suggested that there is a "reverse" function, the inverse function. Finally, we also suggested that the equal sign could mean two different things, and we will need to be clear about the difference. In the next section, we will look at what we mean by the slope of a function.

A.2   Slope

You probably recall the general equation of a straight line, $Y = mX + b$, where X is the variable on the horizontal axis, Y is the variable on the vertical axis, m is the slope, and b is the Y-intercept. Both m and b

are constants, and do not depend on X or Y. This is one of the most important and useful equations we will encounter.

Definition A.5: *The **slope of a straight line**, m, is the rise over the run.*

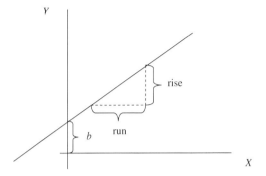

Figure A.1   The slope of a straight line, and the Y-intercept.

In Figure A.1, you can also find the number b, the Y-intercept. It is the value on the vertical axis where the line crosses the vertical axis, where $X = 0$.

There are two observations that are important at this moment:

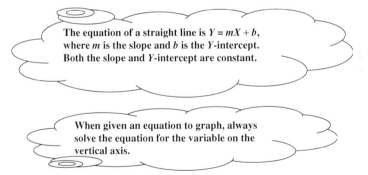

The equation of a straight line is $Y = mX + b$, where m is the slope and b is the Y-intercept. Both the slope and Y-intercept are constant.

When given an equation to graph, always solve the equation for the variable on the vertical axis.

These two rules are essential for you to remember and use. If all else fails, have them tattooed on your arm.

The second observation has the added requirement that in order to solve for the variable on the vertical axis, you need to know which variable is on that axis (and which variable is on the X-axis, too!).

For the purpose of this text, there is only one way to determine if one has a linear equation (that is, the equation of a straight line). The way to do this is to match up the equation (once we have it in slope-intercept form) with the equation $Y = mX + b$, where m and b are constants. Hence the observation: solve for the variable on the vertical axis! You will have plenty of opportunities to exercise this skill in this class.

Exercise 3. On an X, Y plane, graph the following equations:

    a. $Y = 6X - 4$.
    b. $Y = -2X + 3$.
    c. $Y = (-2/3)X - 1$.
    d. $Y = (4/3)X + 12$.

Exercise 4. On an X, Y plane, graph the following equations. First put them in slope-intercept form.

    a. $5X + 2Y = -3$.
    b. $2X - 3Y = 4$.
    c. $-3X + 4Y = 2$.
    d. $-X - Y = 2$.

Sometimes we will need to consider an inequality and sometimes the inequality will be inserted into a linear equation. So we might have something that looks like this:

$$Y \geq mX + b.$$

What does this mean? The essential fact is that a line (straight or not) essentially divides the space (that is, the plane) into two parts — the points on one side of the line and the points on the other side of the line. We start by graphing the line in its equality form. Those points on one side of the line all satisfy one of the inequalities. The points on the other side of the line satisfy the opposite inequality. To tell which side is which, we can take a point not on the line, put it into the equation of the line, and see which way the inequality goes. Then, all points on the same side of the line as that point satisfy the same inequality. The points on the other side satisfy the opposite inequality. If the inequality is weak (that is, greater than or equal to), we know to include the line as it is the points where $Y = mX + b$, equality holds.

Exercise 5. On an X,Y plane, determine the set of points satisfying each inequality.

    a. $5X + 2Y \geq -3$.
    b. $2X - 3Y \leq 4$.
    c. $-3X + 4Y < 2$.
    d. $-X - Y > 2$.

Exercise 6. Suppose that set A is the set of points (X,Y) so that $5X + 2Y \geq -3$ and set B is the set of points (X,Y) so that $2X - 3Y \leq 4$.

    a. Find the union of A and B.
    b. Find the intersection of A and B.

The important defining element of a straight line is that the slope is a constant. That is, the slope does not change depending on where we are on the line. This is the only type of curve for which this is true (we will reserve the term "line" for a straight line, whereas a "curve" could be straight or not). The question is, then, what do we mean by the slope of a line which is not straight? To start, there is some ambiguity in the question. Suppose we have a specific curve in mind. In general, as we move along the curve, the slope will change. So we must first identify a point at which we wish to find the slope and ask: *what is the slope at that point?* To address this question, we begin with the concept of a line tangent to a curve.

Definition A.6: *We say a straight line is **tangent** to a curve at a point where that straight line is the only straight line that touches the curve at the point, but does not intersect the curve at that point.*

The key fact is that there is **only one** such line at the point. If there is more than one such line, then there is no tangent. An example of a tangent is shown in Figure A.2. It is often a good idea to ask what it means for the definition to be not true. In this case, what does it mean to say that we do not have a tangent line? One interesting case is shown in Figure A.3 where we have a curve (actually two straight-line segments that meet) without a tangent at X_0. What happened? The problem is that there is more than one line that touches the curve at

X_0, but does not intersect the curve at that point. Thus, there is no tangent to this curve at the point X_0, because for there to be a tangent, there can only be one such line.

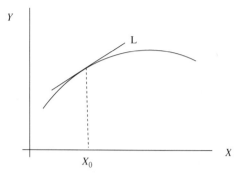

Figure A.2   Here the line L is tangent to the curve at the point X_0.

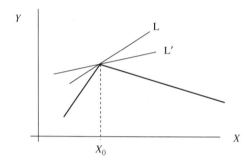

Figure A.3   There is no tangent to the curve at X_0. There is more than one line that could touch the curve and not intersect at X_0. Both L and L′ touch the curve at X_0 and neither intersects the curve.

Now that we have the idea of a tangent line, we can define the slope of the curve.

Definition A.7: *We say a curve has a **slope** at the point X_0 if there is a straight line tangent to the curve at X_0, and the slope of the curve at X_0 is the slope of the straight line.*[1]

_____

[1]The experienced reader will know that we could have defined the derivative of a function first, and then defined the tangent. This would have been a cleaner way to

There are two things to note about this definition. First, we have used what we already knew, the slope of the straight line, to define the slope of the curve. Second, there are curves for which the slope is not defined. In fact, in Figure A.3 we have a curve without a slope at the point X_0. If a curve has a slope, that slope is the derivative of the curve at that point. We extend our idea of slope in the next definition.

Definition A.8: *We say a curve is **differentiable at X_0** if the curve has a slope at X_0. Furthermore, if a curve has a slope at each point, we say that the **curve is differentiable**.*

In short, when we say that a curve is differentiable, that means that it has a slope at each point, that there is a tangent line at each point. Every non-vertical straight line is differentiable.

Definition A.9: *When we say that two curves (or a line and a curve) are **tangent**, we mean that the curves (the line and the curve) touch at a point and have the same slope at that point.*

One other thought: For the curves we will study, the idea of differentiability is that the curve does not have a corner. Note in Figure A.3 where the curve has no unique tangent line at X_0, no slope. The lack of differentiability happens where the curve has a corner. So if a curve is to have a slope, be differentiable, then it cannot have a corner at any X.

Look at Figure A.3 again. Because the curve has no unique tangent line at X_0, you can see that we could have two curves touch each other and not cross. Figure A.2 shows a case where we have two curves, both having the same slope, that are equal at X_0 and do not cross. If two differentiable curves touch at a point and have a different slope at that point, they must cross. This will be an important fact we will use in later chapters.

Definition A.10: *If a function has a slope at a point, we say the slope is the **derivative** of the function at that point, and we note the derivative as $f'(X)$.*

---

proceed, but there is little reason to take a side trip into limits to generate the definition of the derivative.

This definition simply renames the slope as the derivative. So when you see the term "derivative," you know we are talking about slope.

A concept that is related to differentiability is continuity. We will define that concept next.

Definition A.11: *We say a function is **continuous** if the curve can be drawn without lifting our pencil from the paper.*

All of the curves we have drawn so far (Figures A.2 and A.3) are continuous. To be not continuous, we have to have a gap in the function or a point missing. You will see an example in Figure A.4.

Note that a function can be continuous but not differentiable; Figure A.3 shows such a case. On the other hand, if a function is differentiable, it is also continuous.

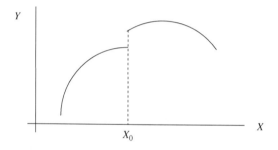

Figure A.4   Here the function is not continuous at X_0.

Section Summary:

We have defined two closely related concepts:

a. the tangent to a function at a point; and
b. the slope of the curve (or the derivative of the curve) at that point.

In the next section, we explore finding the derivative.

A.3   Derivatives

There will be occasions in the text when we will want to find the derivative of a function. There are some well-known rules for finding the derivative, and we will review a few of them here.

Rule 1: Suppose that $f(X) = X^n$. Then, the derivative is $f'(X) = nX^{n-1}$.

Exercise 7. Suppose that $f(X) = X$. Can we write this as X^n? What value would n have to take to make this work? What would the derivative of $f'(X) = X$ be?

Rule 2: Suppose that $f(X) = C$, where C is a constant. Then, $f'(X) = 0$.

Rule 3: Suppose that we have a function $f(X) = h(X) + g(X)$. Then, $f'(X) = h'(X) + g'(X)$.

This says that the derivative of a sum is the sum of the derivatives.

Rule 4: Suppose that we have $f(X) = h(X) \times g(X)$. Then, $f'(X) = h(X) \times g'(X) + h'(X) \times g(X)$.

This is the product rule. Note that the derivative of a product is not the product of the derivatives!

Exercise 8. Find the derivative of the following functions. Assume π, C, and m are constants.

a. $f(X) = X^2$.
b. $f(X) = X^5$.
c. $f(X) = X^{1/2}$.
d. $f(X) = \pi$.
e. $f(X) = \pi X^2$.
f. $f(X) = CX^{3/2}$.
g. $f(X) = 6X + 4$.
h. $f(X) = mX + b$.

There will be times when we wish to find the derivative of somewhat more complicated functions. Suppose, for example, we had the following function and we wished to find the derivative.

$$f(X) = (100 - 7X)^4.$$

What should we do? We could multiply the expression out, $(100 - 7X)$ times itself four times. But that would be a lot more work than we need do. There is a rule for this kind of case, called the chain rule. Suppose we have the following situation:

$$f(X) = g(X)^n.$$

We recognize that this is essentially the same expression as we were dealing with above, where $g(X) = 100 - 7X$. The derivative of $f(X)$ is as shown in Rule 5.

Rule 5: $f'(X) = n \times g(X)^{n-1} \times g'(X).$

In our case, we would have $n = 4$, $g(X) = 100 - 7X$, and $g'(X) = -7$. Hence, the derivative would be the following:

$$f'(X) = 4(100 - 7X)^3(-7).$$

Another example? What if $f(X) = (230 - 3.5X)^{1/2}$? Here, $n = 1/2$, $g(X) = 230 - 3.5X$, and $g'(X) = -3.5$. So we would have $f'(X) = (1/2)(230 - 3.5X)^{-1/2}(-3.5)$.

Work on these exercises!

Exercise 9. Find the derivative of the following functions:

   a. $f(X) = (100 - 5X)^7$.
   b. $f(X) = (1.5 - 3X)^{1/2}$.
   c. $f(X) = (22 - 7.2X)^{-1/2}$.
   d. $f(X) = (143 - 9.2X)^{2/3}$.

We now combine some of the rules we have already learned. Consider the derivative of the following function. Suppose we have

$$f(X) = X^{1/3}(25 - 7X)^{1/2}.$$

What is the derivative? Well, this is a product, so the product rule applies.

$$f'(X) = (1/3)X^{(1/3)-1}(25 - 7X)^{1/2}$$
$$+ X^{1/3}(1/2)(25 - 7X)^{(1/2)-1}(-7)$$
$$= (1/3)X^{-2/3}(25 - 7X)^{1/2} + X^{1/3}(1/2)(25 - 7X)^{-1/2}(-7).$$

Try your hand at these.

Exercise 10. Find the derivative of the following functions:
a. $f(X) = X^{1/2}(45 - 10X)^{1/2}$.
b. $f(X) = X^{1/4}(200 - 48X)^{1/3}$.
c. $f(X) = X^{3/4}(148 - 17X)^{1/8}$.

Section Summary:
In this section, we have reviewed finding derivatives. Derivatives have significant uses in economics. For one thing, they can be used to find the maximum of a function. To that end, we need to define what we mean by a maximum, which we do in the next section.

A.4 Maximum and Minimum

In this section, we will explore the use of derivatives to find a maximum or minimum of a function and ways to distinguish a maximum from a minimum. These tools have significant use in microeconomics, as you will see. We start by defining the maximum.

Definition A.12: *We say that a function $f(X)$ has a **maximum** at the point X_0 if for all X near $X_0, f(X_0) \geq f(X)$. We say that a function $f(X)$ has a **minimum** at the point X_0 if for all X near $X_0, f(X_0) \leq f(X)$.*

This definition is for a local maximum, that is, for X near X_0. If the maximum is a maximum for all possible X, we call it a global maximum. For the most part, we will confine our attention to the local maximum. It turns out that derivatives have a key role in finding the maximum (and the minimum) of differentiable functions. Here is the relevant proposition.

Proposition A.13: First-Order Condition
If $f(X)$ is differentiable and has a maximum or minimum at X_0, then $f'(X_0) = 0$.

This is a first-order condition because the focus is on the first derivative. Note what this proposition says. It says that if we have a maximum, then the derivative is zero. It does not say that if the derivative is zero, then we have a maximum. In fact, that latter statement is not generally true.

There is a way to tell which of the points are maxima and which are minima. The test needed depends on the second derivative. What is the second derivative?

Definition A.14: *Suppose $f(X)$ is a function. The **second derivative of** $f(X)$, denoted $f''(X)$, is the derivative of the first derivative of $f(X)$.*

The second derivative is the derivative of the first derivative. For example, if we have a function $f(X) = 3X^2 - 7X + 4$, we know the first derivative is $f'(X) = 6X - 7$. The second derivative is the derivative of the first derivative, which we will denote by $f''(X)$. In this case, $f''(X) = 6$. The second derivative is just an application of the derivative to a function that is itself a derivative, and the rules of differentiation apply.

Exercise 11. Find the second derivative of the functions in Exercise 8.

Exercise 12. Find the second derivative of the functions in Exercise 9.

Exercise 13. Find the second derivative of the functions in Exercise 10.

We can now use the second derivative to distinguish maxima from minima. To motivate the discussion, we will resort to some graphs. We start with the maximum.

In the upper graph of Figure A.5, we have shown a function with a maximum at X_0. We see that the derivative of the function is positive for X less than X_0. That means that the derivative function must lie above the X-axis. We show this in the lower graph. Now for X greater than X_0, the derivative is negative. Hence, the derivative function must lie below the axis as shown in the lower graph. We can see that the derivative function has a negative slope. In other words, the slope of the first derivative must be negative. But the slope of the first derivative is the second derivative of the function, so the second derivative must be negative if we have a maximum.

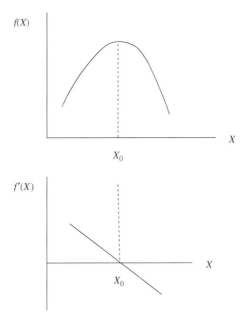

Figure A.5   In the upper graph, we show a function with a maximum at X_0. We see that the derivative of the function is positive to the left of X_0. In other words, the derivative is positive above the axis to the left of X_0 as shown in the lower graph. The derivative is negative to the right of X_0, and lies below the axis in the lower graph. Hence, the graph of the derivative will look as shown in the lower graph.

What about a minimum? You can see that the argument will be similar for a minimum. If the minimum occurs at X_0, the slope of the function will be negative to the left of X_0 and the derivative will be positive to the right of X_0. That means that the derivative function will be positively sloped. Hence, if we have a minimum, the second derivative must be positive. We state this result next.

Proposition A.15: Second-Order Condition
Suppose that a function can be differentiated twice and that the function has a zero derivative at X_0. If $f''(X_0) < 0$ (the second derivative of $f(X_0) < 0$), then X_0 is a maximum for the function. If the second derivative of $f(X_0) > 0$, then we have a minimum. If the second derivative of $f(X_0)$ is zero, the test fails.

We will not prove this proposition, but clearly the above graph provides reason to believe that it is true. Just to be clear, the notation $f(X_0)$

means the function f evaluated at the point X_0. The above proposition says that if $f''(X_0) < 0$ (and $f'(X) = 0$), then X_0 is a maximum for $f(X)$.

Exercise 14. Draw the graph of a function with a minimum at X_0, and below that graph draw the graph of its derivative. What do you see?

Exercise 15. How are the two propositions A.13 and A.15 different?

Exercise 16. For each of the following functions, find the points where the first derivative is zero and use the second derivative to determine which are minima and which are maxima.

a. $f(X) = (1/3)X^3 - 5X^2 + 16X - 7$.
b. $f(X) = (1/3)X^3 - 10X^2 + 96X + 42$.
c. $f(X) = (1/3)X^3 - X^2 + X + 4$.

Recall from an earlier section that we pointed out that "=" can mean two different things. First, $Y = f(X)$, and that holds for all X. In this case, when we find dY/dX, we are finding $f'(X)$. But if we have $D(P) = S(P)$, we cannot say that $dD(P)/dP = dS(P)/dP$. That is, the slope of demand is not equal to the slope of supply even if quantity demanded equals the quantity supplied. So in the first case, the derivative of one side is the derivative of the other side; whereas in the second case, the derivative of one side is not the derivative of the other side. When we use "=" as an equilibrium condition (as we do in the case of supply and demand), the derivative of one side is not the derivative of the other. We cannot differentiate across the equality in that case.

Section Summary:
In this section, we have looked at what we mean by a maximum and related the maximum to the derivative. We have also seen how we can use the second derivative to determine which points are maxima and which are minima.

A.5 Convexity

In this section, we will look at an important concept that we will use quite a bit — the idea of a convex set. We start with the definition.

Definition A.16: *We say a set is **convex** if the straight-line segment connecting any two points in the set stays within the set, possibly on the boundary.*

Perhaps the easiest way to understand the concept is to draw some pictures. In Figure A.6, we show a set that is convex, while Figure A.7 shows a set that is not convex.

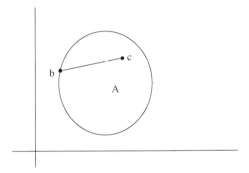

Figure A.6 The set of points inside and on the circle labeled A is a convex set. No matter which two points we pick in the set, the straight-line segment connecting them is in the set. The straight line connecting the points b and c is clearly in the set.

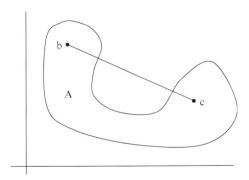

Figure A.7 Here the line connecting the two points b and c in the set A goes outside the set. Hence, this set is not convex. Note that there are points in the set where a straight line connecting the points would be in the set. But what matters is if there is even one line connecting two points in the set that goes outside the set, then the set is not convex.

There is another convexity idea of which we will have need. We define it next.

Definition A.17: *A set is **strictly convex** if the straight-line segment connecting any two points stays strictly inside the set except possibly at the end points.*

When we say "strictly inside the set," we mean that the line cannot be on the boundary or edge of the set (except possibly the end points of the line). By the edge or boundary, we mean the line defining the set.

Again, let us look at some examples. First, the set in Figure A.6 is strictly convex. No matter which two points we pick, the straight-line segment joining them will always be inside the set. Even if both points are on the edge of the circle, the rest of the points on the straight line will be strictly inside the set. For a set that is convex but not strictly convex, consider Figure A.8. We can argue that the set is convex; but for the points b and c on the edge, the line segment joining them is also on the edge, which violates the definition of strict convexity.

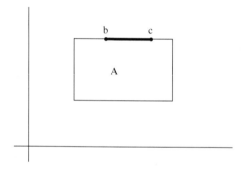

Figure A.8   The set A is the inside of the rectangle and includes the edges. Suppose that we look at the two points b and c, which are on the upper edge of the rectangle. The straight line connecting these two points coincides with the edge, which is part of the set. Hence, this line segment satisfies the convexity definition. You can check other points to see that this set is convex. But the set is not strictly convex; the line segment connecting b and c lies on the edge, which is not allowed for strict convexity.

We have drawn examples of sets that are closed figures, figures whose boundary is one line that goes all the way around the set, but the concepts also apply to sets that are not closed figures.

Exercise 17. Consider the following set. Suppose that the curve in the graph below extends forever as shown. The set A is the set of points on or above the curve. Is A convex? Strictly convex?

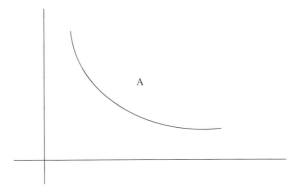

Exercise 18. Draw a set that is not a closed curve (so that the edge of the curve does not connect with itself, as in Exercise 17) such that the set is not convex.

Exercise 19. Draw an example of each of the following kinds of sets:

    a. A set that is convex and has a differentiable edge.

    b. A set that is strictly convex and has a differentiable edge.

    c. A set that is convex and whose edge is not differentiable.

    d. A set that is strictly convex and whose edge is not differentiable.

Section Summary:
In this section, we have defined the idea of both convex set and strictly convex set. We will use these concepts in upcoming chapters.

A.6   Contrapositive and Converse

In this section, we introduce a logical device that will be of substantial use to us — the contrapositive. Much of what we do in the rest of this text depends on understanding the rather intricate relationship between a statement and its contrapositive. We also introduce the idea of converse, as it is also something that we will use.

Definition A.18: *A **logical statement** (or a **statement**, or a **proposition**) means a statement that starts with "If…" and has a following "then … ."*

The structure of the statement indicates that there is a logical process going on. The statement (or proposition, as we will call it) starts with some assumed conditions, the conditions that follow the "If." Once the "If" statements are given, then there is a conclusion, the "then" statement. The "then" statement follows as a logical consequence of the "If." Hence, there is some logic that connects the "then" to the "If." So "If" some assumptions hold, "then" some conclusion follows logically from those assumptions. One aspect of what we want to do is to provide the logical link between the "If" and the "then," that is, the proof of the proposition. Thus, the proof is the logic that requires the "then" to follow from the "If." How will we proceed to do this?

Of course, the best way is to proceed directly. Start with the "If" and whatever else we know (from definitions or previously proved propositions), and move to the conclusion, the "then." But sometimes this is a hard thing to do. What alternative strategy might we pursue?

One way to attempt to move forward is to realize that there is one other way to state the proposition that has the same essential content as our "If… then …" statement — the contrapositive. What is the contrapositive?

Definition A.19: *Suppose that we have a logical statement "If A, then B." The **contrapositive** of this statement is a logical statement "If not B, then not A."*

Obviously, it is important to keep track of which is the "If" and which is the "then." To form the contrapositive, we take not the conclusion, and it implies not the "If."

We assert that the contrapositive is true if and only if the original statement is true. That is, either the statement and its contrapositive are true or the statement and its contrapositive are false. We cannot have the statement be true and the contrapositive false, or the statement false and the contrapositive true. Let us see if we can understand why one implies the other.

Suppose that we have a statement "If A, then B." That means that every time A occurs, B follows. If B does not occur, then A could not have occurred — because if A had occurred, B would follow. Hence, "If not B, then not A."

This suggests a strategy for proof. Suppose that we wish to prove that B follows from A. Suppose that for whatever reason, there is no obvious direct way to proceed. Well, if we could prove the contrapositive is true, then we would know that the original statement is also true. Hence, we can try to prove the contrapositive instead.

An example would probably be helpful. Suppose that the following proposition is true: If profit is maximum at an output X_0, then at X_0 marginal revenue equals marginal cost. What is the contrapositive of this statement? Compare to "If A, then B." What is playing the role of A? In this case, A is "profit is maximum at X_0." What about B? Here, B is "marginal revenue equals marginal cost at X_0." The contrapositive, "If not B, then not A," would be:

If marginal revenue is not equal to marginal cost at X_0, then profit is not maximum at X_0.

Again, if the original statement — "If profit is maximum, MR = MC" — is true, then the contrapositive — "If MR $\neq$ MC, the profit is not maximum" — must also be true. Hence, if we were to prove the contrapositive, we would also know that the original statement is true.

There is one other statement related to the original statement. This one is called the converse. We define it next.

Definition A.20: *Suppose that we have a logical statement "If A, then B." The* **converse** *of this statement is a logical statement "If B, then A."*

Again, it should be clear that we need to keep track of which is A and which is B. In this case, we are reversing the roles of A and B in the original statement to obtain the converse. **The bad news is that a statement can be true, yet the converse can be either true or false.** There is no reason why the converse must necessarily be true just because the original statement is true.

The examples we have looked at so far are pretty simple. What happens when things get more complicated, as they almost surely will? Suppose that we have a compound A statement. Now what?

So we have "If A1 and A2, then B." So both A1 and A2 must be true before we can expect that B will logically follow. If either A1 or A2 is missing, then there is no reason to think that B must follow. What is the contrapositive of this statement? Again, the contrapositive is "If not B, then not A." So we would have "If not B, then not A1 or not A2." Note again, if either A1 or A2 is missing, there is no logical reason to think that B will be forthcoming. So if we were to use this statement for a proof, how do we proceed? We start with not B and we need to show that either not A1 happens or not A2 happens. Suppose we wish to show that not A1 happens (exactly how we made this decision is not clear at this point — maybe trial and error). So we have to show "If not B, then not A1." But what about A2? It is not irrelevant to the process! What we will do is to assume that A2 is true, along with B. Thus, our contrapositive would be "If A2 and not B, then not A1." We could do the same with A2 to obtain "If A1 and not B, then not A2."

What if B is the compound? Now we have "If A, then B1 and B2." In this case, A implies both B1 and B2. We can treat this as two separate propositions, and we are back where we started. So we would have two propositions, not one. We would have "If A, then B1" and "If A, then B2." We would obtain the contrapositive of each statement separately and prove them one at a time.

The converse of the compound assumption statement is as follows. We start with the statement "If A1 and A2, then B." The converse would be "If B, then A1 and A2."

Exercise 20. For each of the following statements, state the contrapositive and the converse (observe that we have no reason to think that these are actually logical propositions — that is, that there is a reason why the conclusion actually follows for logical reasons from the assumptions!):

   a. If I washed the car, then it rains.
   b. If I went fishing, then I always catch fish.
   c. If I went fishing and it rains, then I catch fish.
   d. If I dance, then I sprain my ankle.

Exercise 21. State the contrapositive and converse of proposition A.13.

Section Summary:
In this section, we have examined what we mean by a proposition, the contrapositive of the proposition, and the converse of the proposition. We have also examined how they are related with regard to the truth content, i.e., if the statement is true, then the contrapositive must also be true.

A.7 Summary

In this chapter, we have introduced the primary tools we will need for this course. The tools are both mathematical and logical. They will be put to use over and over in the rest of these notes. Careful attention to them now will pay dividends later.

Terms Defined:

- Union of sets
- Intersection of sets
- Function

- Slope of a straight line
- Tangent
- Slope of a curve
- Differentiable function
- Tangency of two curves
- Derivative
- Continuous function
- Maximum of a function
- Minimum of a function
- Second derivative
- Convex set
- Strictly convex set
- Logical statement
- Contrapositive
- Converse

Chapter 1

Review of Supply and Demand

In this chapter, we will review some of the economic concepts that you studied in your principles course. Our objective is to provide a broad overview of the essential ideas in economics. Much of what we will do later builds the basis for the tools you see here.

1.1 Introduction

A typical definition of economics is:

> Economics is a social science studying the allocation of scarce resources among alternative uses.

The implication of scarcity is that choices must be made. On a macro level, a society has to decide how many (and which) resources to devote to Head Start programs and how much to devote to road and bridge repair. In a micro framework, we may view the consumer as a choice maker who must decide how to allocate his or her income among alternative choices. In other words, the consumer will choose how much of each commodity to buy, given the prices of the goods and income. The firm must decide (choose) how much output to produce and how many of each input to purchase. Clearly, this idea of scarcity and therefore choice is important in economics.

There are two elements in a choice process: the set of alternatives from which we choose (the choice set), and a criterion for choosing among those alternatives (an objective function). In our study of economics, we will try to carefully set out both of these elements. Once we have a set of alternatives and a criterion, we can apply the criterion to the set of alternatives and see what choice results. We will be looking for the general characteristics of the element chosen. We will also want to know how the choice would change if we allowed something in the problem to change.

Before going further, we should try to fit what we have said above into the idea of a model. To generate the set of alternatives, we will have to make some assumptions and define terms. To generate the criterion, we will define more terms and may have to do some construction. Once we have the criterion and the set of alternatives, we will have a proposition concerning the element chosen. We intend to then use that proposition to derive a useful economic tool, such as demand or supply. To find demand or supply will require repeated use of the proposition when some factor in the choice problem changes.

It is useful to distinguish variables, which the actor can choose, from parameters, which could change but which the actor cannot change. For example, for a competitive firm, the firm does not choose the selling price, but does choose the quantity of output. In this setting, the quantity of output is a variable and the price is a parameter. For the consumer, we assume that the consumer cannot change the price but does choose the quantity to purchase. The quantity to purchase is a variable and the price is a parameter. Our focus will be on the individual actors in a microeconomic setting. To that end, we now turn to markets and how prices are determined. After all, in the competitive case, prices are not determined by either the individual producer or individual consumer. How are they determined? As you know, in competition, prices are determined in markets.

By a market, we mean an institution where buyers and sellers meet to trade. Note that when we say "an institution," we do not necessarily mean a physical space. We mean that somehow buyers and sellers, each having information from several on the opposite side of the market, make choices about the quantity of a good they want to trade. Often the trade is for money, and the price of the good is the amount of money a person has to give up to get one more unit of the good. **The price is always for one unit of the good.** As the economist sees it, then, it is the combined efforts of all buyers and sellers together that determine the price. In the language of economics, the market supply and market demand come together and the price and quantity traded are determined. We will return to the ideas of supply and demand later in this chapter, but before we do, we will examine the role that price plays in our economic society.

Price plays at least two roles, that of a rationing device and that of directing the flow of resources. We start with the role of rationing a given supply of goods. The idea is that not every one can have the good. Only those with enough income and the desire for the good will get it. Those who get the commodity are willing to give up the satisfaction that the money spent on the good represents. So if the price of a yo-yo is $2, then only those with enough money and the desire to get the yo-yo will have it. Some people will have enough money but not want the good. Others may want the good, but do not have the money to buy it. Furthermore, those who do buy a yo-yo for $2 will give up the satisfaction of what could have been purchased with the $2 if the yo-yo was not purchased. Suppose that all the yo-yos are sold and consumers still want more. The price would not have adequately rationed the good. The value of the last yo-yo sold would be greater than the value of the $2 spent in some other way. The price would rise as a result. The price would rise to the point where the number of units sold is exactly equal to the number of units produced. What about the other side of the market?

In order to attract resources to the production of yo-yos, the resources, when used to produce yo-yos, must bring in a return at least as great as another use of the resources. Thus, if we are using labor, machines, and wood to make yo-yos, we would need to make as much money from that use as we would if we used that same labor, machines, and wood to make model airplanes. If the price of yo-yos is too low, then not enough resources will be drawn to the production of yo-yos, and people will not get the quantity of yo-yos they want at that price. Hence, the price will have to rise.

In short, the price reflects opportunity cost. For the consumer, the price paid reflects the value of what the consumer could have purchased instead. For the producer, the price reflects the value of another product the producer could have produced. And the price acts to ration the goods among the consumers and the resources among the firms.

The other role that price plays is to direct the flow of resources. Suppose that as a result of the World Yo-Yo Championship appearing on YouTube, there is an increase in the demand for yo-yos. In that case, we know that the price will rise. That means that yo-yo producers are suddenly making more profit than they had made before. Before the increase in demand, the amount of profit they made was enough to keep the resources flowing to the firm. Now with the greater profit, the firm commands more resources and resources flow into the yo-yo industry, exactly as consumers want. When the yo-yo craze cools off and sales of yo-yos fall, the price falls and the resources are drawn into another industry where the profits are higher. Thus, a change in the price, which will change profit, will cause resources to move into the profitable industries and out of less profitable ones.

Note that all of this happens without planning or without explicit government direction. Individuals following their own self-interest end up allocating resources. Goods are produced in quantities that people want at prices people are willing to pay. This is a truly astounding outcome and system. We will have much to say about this system, both in terms of how the elements of the system are developed and about how the system actually operates. So how does this process of price determination occur, at least as the economist sees it? We turn to that question now.

> **Section Summary:**
> In this section, we have introduced the market system that we are about to study. We have also examined the role that prices play. An understanding of how prices are determined is crucial to understanding this system.

1.2   Demand and Supply

In this section, we will examine the basic demand and supply model that you learned in principles. We will start with some definitions.

Definition 1.1: *Demand is a relationship between price and quantity, and shows the number of units of a good an individual would choose at each price with all else not changing.*

You will see that the structure of this definition will appear frequently in what follows. The structure is this (pay attention to the underlined words, as they are the common elements in the structure we are discussing):

Definition: XXX is a relationship between W and Z showing blah blah with some stuff fixed.

The structure is designed to help us understand some important facts about the concept. First, when we say that something is a relationship, you should ask: What is being related? Usually, because we want to draw a graph, the things that are being related are the variables that go on the axes. In the general definition, W and Z are the things that go on the axes. In the case of demand, we know then, by the definition, that price goes on one axis and quantity on the other. Now note that there are lots of possible relationships between price and quantity that we could draw. So what does this relationship tell us that no other relationship would tell? The showing phrase of the definition ("blah blah" in the general definition) gives us the special feature of this relationship. For demand, the showing phrase is "the number of units of a good an individual would choose at each price." Note that this concept is defined for one individual. Third, there are, apparently, a number of things held fixed in this relationship, but the list is not specified in the definition. The list of items that are fixed, not changing, are often called the ***determinants*** of the curve. In the case of demand, we would have other prices, income, tastes, and expectations about the price of the good included in the list of determinants. Earlier we discussed what we mean by a parameter. In the case of demand, all the items on the determinant list are parameters to the individual. The individual can choose quantity at each price, but not income, tastes (at least in this formulation), or other prices. The price of the good is a parameter as well. It is a parameter because the individual consumer cannot determine the price of the good. Finally, note that in our definition of demand, we have that the price is the independent variable and quantity is the dependent variable. The definition says that given the price, the individual chooses the quantity; quantity depends on price. This part of the definition tells us the axis on which we put price and the axis for quantity. The only trouble is that in economics, we put price — the independent variable — on the vertical axis and quantity — the dependent variable — on the horizontal axis. This is backwards from standard practice.

We know that the demand by the individual does not determine price, but given what we said in the previous section, we would expect all buyers together to have a say about price. Hence, we need the demand for all consumers together.

Definition 1.2: *Market demand is the sum of the quantities demanded by all consumers at each price, with all else not changing.*

In this definition, we are given instructions about how to obtain the demand by all consumers at the same time. At each price, we simply take the quantities that each individual would demand at that price and add them up. Note what we are assuming here, that each consumer will pay the same price for the good. Hence, we pick a price and, at that price, add the quantities of the good that each consumer would demand to get the total quantity demanded at that price. We would then move on to the next price. Note that the list of determinants of demand includes all those that we had before plus one more — the number of consumers in the market.

Before going on to the supply side, one more concept will be useful. It is important to know when we are moving along a curve and when the curve shifts. We need some language to signal when each of these occurs.

Definition 1.3: *The* **quantity demanded** *is the quantity all consumers together would choose at a specific price given all determinants.*

We now have the language that we need. When the price of the good changes, we have a change in the quantity demanded. When some determinant changes, we have a change in demand. Thus, changes in price move us along the curve; changes in determinants make the whole curve move. Demand refers to the whole curve, not just a specific quantity. So when we say "demand," we mean the whole curve; and when we say "demand changes," we mean the whole curve shifts. If we mean that we move along the demand, which can only be caused by a change in price, we say "the quantity demanded changes."

Definition 1.4: *Supply is a relationship between price and quantity showing the number of units of a good a firm would supply at each price with all else not changing.*

The same general ideas as before apply here. What variables go on the axes? How do you know? What items go on the list of fixed items, the parameters? The technology, the price of other goods for both inputs and possible outputs the firm could produce, expectations about the price of the output, taxes, nature, and possibly some government regulations. You should see that these fixed elements are the determinants of supply. Again, we need a market version of this same idea.

Definition 1.5: *Market supply is a relationship between price and quantity, and shows the number of units of a good all firms would produce at each price with all else fixed.*

Again, note the tacit assumption behind this definition. We are assuming that each firm charges the same price. So at each price, we find the quantity that each firm would produce at that price and add up those quantities. In addition, there is an added assumption that the firms are all producing the same good — otherwise, we would be trying to add apples and oranges. Again, we have a number of items fixed, not changing. One more item is now fixed: the number of firms in the market.

Definition 1.6: *The **quantity supplied** is the quantity all firms together would produce at a specific price given all determinants.*

Again, when we say that there is a change in supply, we mean that the whole curve shifts or moves. If we mean a movement along the supply curve, which can only be accomplished by a change in the price of the good, we say that there is a change in the quantity supplied.

You already know what the curves look like, and we will draw them now. Just to be clear, we generally expect that as price falls, consumers will buy more. They will find the lower price an inducement to substitute this good for other now more expensive goods. And the supply will have a positive slope. It is hard to give a short reason, but increasing output in the presence of a fixed factor reduces labor productivity and causes costs at the margin to rise, requiring a higher price. In any case, we have the graph shown in Figure 1.1.

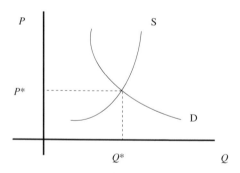

Figure 1.1   This graph shows the market demand and market supply for a good. We have price on the vertical axis and quantity on the horizontal axis.

You can see that in Figure 1.1, one particular price, P^*, and one particular quantity, Q^*, have been identified. They are the equilibrium price and quantity. To be complete, we will define the idea of equilibrium now and apply that definition to the case of a market.

Definition 1.7: *By an **equilibrium**, we mean a value of a variable at which there is no force acting on the variable to cause it to change.*

In the case of price, an equilibrium price is a price where there is no force acting on the price that would cause the price to change. A similar statement would be true for the equilibrium quantity. So how can we be sure that when we get to P^* and Q^*, there are no forces acting on either price or quantity? What we need to try to do is to identify the forces that would act on the price. What forces are there? Usually, consumers would like the price to fall. They will try to act in a way that will cause the price to go down. Most often, businesses want the price to rise, and will act to make the price go up. However, no one firm will want to raise the individual price above what others are charging, but they will want for the price that all receive to go up so that they can obtain more profit. What we need to do now is to use this definition of equilibrium and these forces to see if the intersection of supply and demand is an equilibrium. What happens if the price is above the intersection of supply and demand as shown in Figure 1.2?

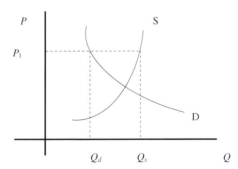

Figure 1.2 In this graph, we have a price above the intersection of demand and supply. The quantity demanded is Q_d and the quantity supplied is Q_s. More is provided in the market than consumers want. There is a surplus, and firms' inventories rise. Firms now see the advantage of lowering price, and consumers do not object.

At price P_1 above the intersection of supply and demand, we see that the quantity supplied, Q_s, is more than the quantity demanded, Q_d. There is a surplus. Hence, firms find their inventories rising. To encourage consumers to buy more of the good, firms now have an incentive to lower price. Note that the consumer wants the price to go down, so the combined efforts of firms and consumers lead to a lower price.

You can work out what happens when the price is below the intersection of supply and demand.

Exercise 1. Suppose that the price is below the intersection of supply and demand. What forces cause the price to rise? Fully explain. You should have some reference to a shortage in your answer!

When we get to the intersection of supply and demand, P^* and Q^*, observe that we have neither a surplus nor a shortage. Without a surplus, there is no incentive for the firm to lower price (with the consumer applauding); and without a shortage, there is no incentive for the consumer to bid up the price (with the firm leading the cheers). Hence, the forces that combined to move price in either the case of shortage or surplus are no longer active, and we are back to simply having consumers wanting a lower price and firms wanting a higher price. No motion results, and we have equilibrium.

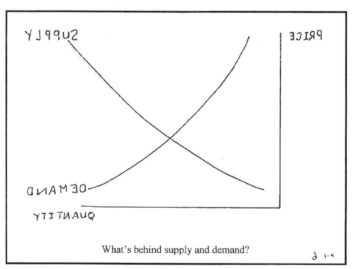

What's behind supply and demand?

> **Section Summary:**
> In this section, we have provided definitions of demand, market demand, supply, market supply, and equilibrium. We have also seen how equilibrium is obtained in the market.

1.3   Using Demand and Supply

For economists, the tool of supply and demand, the market, is a very powerful device. When an economic question arises, our first instinct is to think about how supply and demand could be used to understand what is going on. We should point out that even though this is the first tool economists draw on, it is not always the tool that should be applied. Note the assumptions we have made to use supply and demand. We have assumed that many firms are producing the exact same good and that many consumers buy that good. We have assumed that all consumers pay the same price and that all firms receive the same price. We have also assumed that neither the individual consumer nor the individual producer can determine or affect the market price. You can see that in the market for automobiles, these assumptions are not likely to be true. In fact, except possibly for agricultural commodities, it is hard to think of many goods where these requirements are met.

So why do economists rely so heavily on this tool? There are a couple of reasons. First, supply and demand are relatively simple and they can be a starting point for a more complicated analysis. Second, even if the actual market we observe does not satisfy the assumptions of the model, we often see that the model works well. We might expect that if the model does not reflect reality well, as supply and demand do not reflect the market for automobiles well, the analysis of the model would be badly flawed. But the fact is that we can glean some understanding of the world even when the model is not a very accurate reflection of reality. So how do we use supply and demand?

The primary way we use supply and demand is to try to understand what makes a price change and the direction of change. So we start with supply and demand, and find the equilibrium price and quantity. We then bring in a change — some determinant of either supply or demand (or possibly a determinant of both) changes. We then move either the supply or demand (depending on which determinant changed), and we find the new equilibrium price and quantity. We can then compare the starting equilibrium price and quantity with the ending equilibrium price and quantity. This process is called comparative statics. It is statics rather than dynamics because all we know is the starting point and the ending point. We do not know how we got from the start to the end; we do not know whether the price moved past the new equilibrium and then came back or whether the price went straight to the new price. If we knew the path that price took, we would be interested in a dynamic question. The word "comparative" suggests that we are comparing equilibria. How does this actually work?

Suppose that we start at the equilibrium shown in Figure 1.3, where the price is P_1 and the quantity is Q_1. Now suppose that there is an increase in income for consumers. We know that income is a determinant of demand. If the good is normal, that is, if having more income means that we buy more of the good, then demand would shift right to D'. Therefore, the new equilibrium would occur at price P_2 and the quantity will be Q_2. Both price and quantity rise.

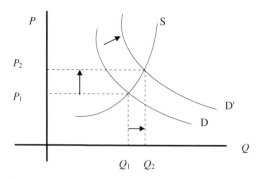

Figure 1.3   In this graph, we show the effect on the equilibrium price and quantity of an increase in income. Both price and quantity rise.

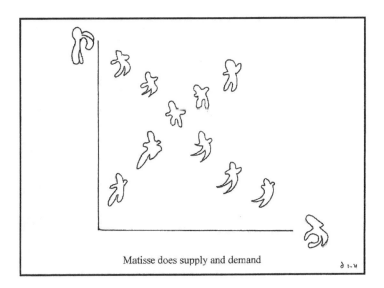

Matisse does supply and demand

Here are some exercises for you to work on.

Exercise 2. For each of the following, draw a graph with supply and demand for the good spaghetti (the dry noodles). Properly label the axes and the curves. Find the equilibrium, and label the equilibrium price P_1 and the equilibrium quantity Q_1. Then, given the information in each part of the question, shift the relevant curve, find the new equilibrium, and determine what happens to both price and quantity.

a. There is a study released that indicates that eating pasta is not healthy.
b. The price of tomato sauce rises.
c. There is a freeze in Florida causing the tomato crop to fail.
d. The price of wheat, an essential ingredient to pasta, rises.
e. The price of linguini, an alternative pasta, rises as linguini becomes the pasta of the day.

Exercise 3. Suppose that we have the market for homes that first-time home buyers are likely to consider. Suppose that an equilibrium is established in this market. Suppose that the government offers an $8,000 cash award for first-time home buyers. What impact will this reward have on the demand for homes by first-time buyers? What will happen to the equilibrium price and quantity of homes for first-time buyers? Does the first-time buyer actually save $8,000 on the house? That is, will the price be $8,000 less than the initial equilibrium price? Explain.

Section Summary:
In this section, we have looked at how economists use supply and demand, the method of comparative statics.

1.4   Summary

In this chapter, we have reviewed the most fundamental and useful tool in economics — supply and demand. We know that this is a powerful (but also a restrictive) way to look at the world. To better understand this tool, it is important to understand the basis for the individual curves, the individual demand and individual supply. This will lead to a better understanding of when to use the tool and when the tool will likely lead us astray.

Terms Defined:

- Demand
- Market demand
- Supply
- Market supply
- Quantity demanded
- Quantity supplied
- Equilibrium

Chapter 2

Preferences, Utility, Demand

Key Concepts:

- Budget set
- Preferences
- Indifference curves
- Utility maximization
- Demand

Goals:

- Determine the alternatives available to the consumer.
- Develop a way to represent the consumer's preferences.
- Combine preferences with the alternatives to find what the consumer chooses.
- Use the choice process to derive the consumer's demand curve.

In this chapter, we will examine the underpinnings of demand. The root of this theory goes back to the "Marginal Revolution." Perhaps the individual who did the most to lay the foundation of much of what we do here is Alfred Marshall (1842–1924), who pushed the idea of the consumer as a utility maximizer given the budget to its conclusion with demand. While much of the development he followed will not be pursued here, it does provide the basis of what we do, which dates from the middle of the 20th century. Considerable work has been done beyond what is presented here.

41

This study will probably be a bit foreign to you as it is axiomatic in nature. This is done for a couple of reasons. First, the theory should be carefully presented in the context of the assumptions upon which it rests. To do otherwise is to pretend that the theory explains more than it actually does. Second, regardless of your major, careful reasoning from assumption and definition is a critical skill and one that can be developed here. Finally, you will learn something about microeconomics as we do this. The argument is structured so that the essential elements of the theory are here and if you were to go on, you would find the elements again in a more technical form. So onward!

You are a consumer! You probably shop nearly every week, at least at the grocery store. As you step into the store, you have a series of choices before you. Have you already decided how much to spend, or do you buy what you need? Do you have a list of items to buy? How closely do you adhere to that list? Do you have coupons to use? Are there certain brands you prefer? Do you carry a calculator to keep track of what you have spent?

Many of these questions you have probably answered, at least to some extent, before you even enter the store. But the store owner wants you to buy even more than you intended, and offers temptations at various places in the aisles. How will you respond? Much of what we are talking about in this chapter aims to address questions like these.

2.1   Introduction

This chapter is devoted to examining how the consumer chooses. When trying to develop an understanding of choice, it is useful to realize that there are two important pieces in the choice process. First, there are some items that could be chosen — what we will call the choice set or set of alternatives. Second, there is a criterion or objective or goal. When the objective is applied to the choice set, we expect that a winner will be produced; the winner is the choice of the chooser. To pursue this point of view, we will need to identify the choice set for the consumer and then the objective the consumer pursues. Following the tradition in economics, we will suppose that the consumer acts to maximize utility given the budget. We will have much more to say about each of these, but for the moment, we should think of utility as being some kind of satisfaction or happiness. The budget, as we are all aware, constrains what we may choose. The idea is that the consumer chooses to provide himself or herself with the greatest possible happiness given his or her budget. Once we have obtained a characterization of that choice, we will then find a way to derive demand. At this point, we will also provide an approach to the problem using calculus. This is a long chapter and, because it is the first with new economics content, it is probably the hardest as you will need to become accustomed to the approach.

2.2 Getting Started

In this section, the basic assumptions and notation for the consumer's problem will be introduced. This section is fundamental for the analysis that is presented in this chapter and the next.

We need to introduce one primary actor, the consumer. In this setting, the consumer chooses a combination of goods, X and Y, to purchase and presumably consume. The consumer has an income (exactly where it comes from is not clear), which we will denote M, and faces prices for both goods. The price of X is P_x and the price of Y is P_y. We will shortly translate these considerations into a budget constraint, but first, let us list some assumptions we will use in the development of demand. In addition to listing the assumptions, we will also say something about how one might go about changing some of them and what impact they have on the analysis.

Assumptions 2.1:
a. *There are two goods, X and Y, with $X \geq 0$ and $Y \geq 0$.*
b. *Both goods can be infinitely divided.*
c. *The consumer knows his or her income and the price of each good.*
d. *No consumer can affect his or her income or the price of any good.*
e. *Both prices (and income) are strictly positive.*
f. *The consumer's choices do not depend on what others choose.*

Assumptions narrow the focus of the analysis and restrict how the analysis can be reasonably applied. What restrictions do these assumptions generate and how can the restrictions be relaxed? Let us focus on assumption a first. Well, surely there are more than two goods in the world. Even at the level of food and clothing, there is always shelter and entertainment. Isn't this an important restriction — only allowing two goods? In fact, it is possible to include as many goods as we like, but then mathematics becomes the language of the discourse, which limits the audience. In addition, it turns out that we do not lose much generality by assuming only two goods, but gain a good deal of opportunity for graphical analysis which extends our understanding.

What about the second assumption, that all goods can be divided infinitely? That means that we can take any good, a Ferrari for example, and divide it into smaller pieces. What sense does it make to say that someone consumed a tenth of a Ferrari? They consumed the left front fender? Probably not! But if we think about the service that a Ferrari provides, transportation (in a certain style), we can easily divide that up. Think of the Ferrari as being a stock of services which can be used a little at a time. We could use ten minutes of Ferrari time. That divides the good, Ferrari time, or use of the Ferrari, into pieces as small as we want. This is the sense of assumption b. But you might argue that there is a problem. If someone buys the Ferrari, then they have paid a lot of money for this ten minutes of use. The counterargument would be that we need to put the price in terms of the good we are buying. We are buying Ferrari minutes. We need the price of a Ferrari minute. One way to think about this is as if we were to rent the Ferrari rather than buy it outright. An alternative way to think about this would be if there were well-functioning resale markets, we could buy the Ferrari, use it for ten minutes, and then resell it in the resale market. Of course this does not work as the resale markets are not that available, although, with eBay, they are becoming more available and more competitive.

The third assumption is that the consumer knows the price of each good and income. Of course we do! As the model is currently set up, the consumer apparently works some and generates some fixed amount of income in exchange. Presumably, the consumer knows how much that income is. And of course we all know the prices of all goods! But in truth, it would not be hard for us to find the price of some good that you do not know. How can we justify this assumption? The primary strategy is to assume that the cost of acquiring information about the price is just a phone call away. And with access to the Web, we can probably find the price of just about any commodity quickly, so the cost of acquiring information is very small. There is another way to think about this assumption. Suppose that one good is tomatoes next year and the other is tomatoes now. We know the price of tomatoes now, but we cannot know the price of tomatoes next year. Hence, if we assume that we know the price of both goods, we are essentially ruling out the possibility that there is any uncertainty. If we wish to alter this assumption, there are two ways we can do so. The first is to explicitly include the cost of acquiring information about prices in our budget. In that case, we would have some search cost that we would have to account for. The second is to explicitly allow uncertainty. This latter task is difficult, and one that we will have a bit to say about in Chapter 13. For now, we will maintain the assumption that the consumer knows all prices and income.

Assumption d says that the consumer cannot affect any price. At one level, this seems perfectly accurate. Imagine going to the grocery store. I get to the checkout counter with my box of cereal. The cashier swipes the box over the scanner and the computer pulls up the price, $3.78. At what point do I get to object? At what point do I get to say that the maximum I am willing to pay is $2.50? You can imagine how the cashier would react if I said that — her response would be, "Either pay up or get out." I have nothing to say about the price. Yet for some goods, like a car, I have something to say about what I will pay; a certain amount of bargaining goes on. What is the upshot? For most goods that we encounter, we pay the price that we are told to pay. Hence, I will maintain that assumption here. But if we want to look at the world of goods where the price is to be bargained over, then we would have to generate models where bargaining occurs. There are such models, but they are more complicated than we can easily manage. On simplicity grounds, I will keep this assumption.

Assumption e says that all prices and income are positive. Specifically, the prices and income must be strictly positive. If either a price or income is zero, the economics of this consumer's choice becomes uninteresting. In addition, it is very rare that we see zero prices or zero income.

The final assumption says that one consumer's choices do not affect what another consumer chooses. Of course we are all independent consumers! We are not affected by what our friends buy. Not at all! Ok, well, maybe just a little! The fact is that in this case the assumption is pretty much off the mark. To correct it would require considerably more of a theory than we can easily manage. The odd thing is that apparently, for most consumption cases, the fact that this assumption is not true does not seem to reduce the ability of the theory to predict what will happen. So on the grounds of simplicity, we will stick with this assumption.

Section Summary:

In this section, we have listed the basic assumptions for our theory of consumer choice. We have also looked at the restrictions placed on the theory as a result, and some ways to possibly restructure the assumptions. We now turn to the consumer's problem, starting with the derivation of the set of alternatives the consumer faces.

2.3   The Budget Constraint

In this section, we lay out the alternatives the consumer could choose. The alternatives are determined by the consumer's income and the prices of the goods.

What can we say about the set of alternatives the consumer faces? Suppose that the consumer buys X units of the good X.[1] How much does the consumer spend on X? Well, the price (remember price is

---

[1]It is common in economics to use a symbol like X to stand for both the good and a variable indicating some unknown quantity of the good. As you go through this material, the practice will become less confusing.

always per unit) is P_x, so the expenditure would be $P_x \times X$ (we will write this as $P_x X$). What about Y? By the same reasoning, the consumer spends $P_y Y$ on Y. As there are only two goods, the total amount spent will be $P_x X + P_y Y$. The requirement for the consumer is that he or she cannot spend more than he or she has, which is the income, M. Thus, we require $M \geq P_x X + P_y Y$. We can graph this equation on an axis system with Y on the vertical axis and X on the horizontal axis.

The way to proceed is to turn the inequality into an equality (hold the inequality for a moment), and then solve the equation for the variable on the vertical axis, Y in this case. We obtain the following expression:

$$Y = (M/P_y) - (P_x/P_y)X.$$

Because to the consumer, M, P_x, and P_y are all positive constants (assumptions d and e of 2.1), this is an equation of a straight line. The Y-intercept is (M/P_y), and the X-intercept is (M/P_x). We have the graph shown in Figure 2.1.

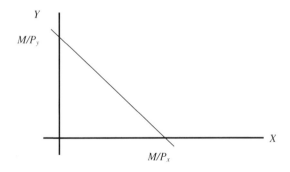

Figure 2.1 In this graph, we have the budget constraint.

Exercise 1. Show that the X-intercept is M/P_x.
Exercise 2. Now go back and bring in the inequality. What does the inequality tell us?

Recall from assumptions 2.1 that $X \geq 0$ and $Y \geq 0$. Hence, when we bring all of these factors together, we see the budget set as shown in Figure 2.2.

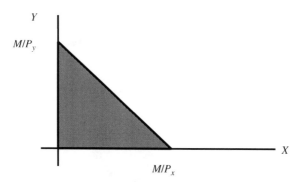

Figure 2.2   The interior and edge of the dark triangle is the consumer's budget set, that is, the combinations of X and Y the consumer can afford.

Exercise 3. What happens to the budget line when the price of X rises? Explain how you know.

Exercise 4. What happens to the budget line when income rises? Explain how you know.

Exercise 5. What happens to the budget line when income and both prices are multiplied by the same positive constant, k? Explain how you know.

Exercise 6. What is the slope of the budget line? In what units is the slope measured? If the slope is $-P_x/P_y$, how can the units be Y/X?

Definition 2.2: *The **budget set** (or choice set) is the set of alternatives that the consumer can afford, the set bounded by the budget line and the two axes.*

> **Section Summary:**
> In this section, we have developed the consumer's budget constraint and the set of alternatives the consumer can afford to choose, the budget set. We have also seen what makes the budget line move. What we need now is some criteria or objective to finish the choice process. That criteria will be preferences, which we discuss next.

2.4   Preferences

In this section, we wish to find a way to represent a consumer's preferences. By preferences, we mean the ability to compare (and decide which, if either, is the better of) two commodity bundles. Thus, preferences are the ability to compare combinations of goods. We will start by defining some useful concepts.

Definition 2.3: *A **commodity bundle** is an amount of X and an amount of Y, written as (X, Y). A commodity bundle is an ordered pair.*

In the definition of preferences, which is next, we will say that R is a relationship between two commodity bundles. What we mean is that given two commodity bundles, W and V, R tells us which of the two bundles, W or V, is the more preferred. Suppose $W = (X_1, Y_1)$ and $V = (X_2, Y_2)$. If (X_2, Y_2) is the more preferred bundle, we would write $V R W$. The idea is to compare bundles of goods, not the goods themselves.

Definition 2.4: *Let W, V, and S be commodity bundles. Let R be a relationship between two commodity bundles. R is read as "is at least as preferred as." If R satisfies the following three properties, we say R is a **preference relation**:*

a. *Completeness — For any two bundles, W and V, either $W R V$ or $V R W$ or both.*

b. *Transitivity* — *For any three bundles, W, V, and S, if W R V and V R S, then W R S.*

c. *Reflexivity* — *For each bundle W, W R W must hold.*

The first of these properties is called completeness. It says that the consumer can rank any two bundles. This seems like a natural requirement, and one that consumers can easily satisfy, but a problem arises when there is a good in the bundle about which the consumer knows little. I have not ever had any hot chili peppers. Any bundle including hot chili peppers would not be a bundle I would be able to rank, because I do not know how well I like (or dislike) hot chili peppers.

The second requirement, transitivity, is a consistency requirement. It says that if I like bundle W better than V and V better than S, then I surely would like W better than S. When we look at how consumers actually choose, this axiom is regularly violated. Why? Well, the process of making consistent choices is very hard! There are some arguments that suggest that consumers should want to be consistent, but in truth, we are a pretty inconsistent lot. There is a remarkable body of work launched by Sonnenschein's article on non-transitive choice, indicating that transitivity is not required for the generation of demand.[2] However, we would need substantially more mathematics to reach that conclusion. So while the assumption is not an accurate reflection of reality (is any assumption reflective of reality?), its lack of veracity does not implode the value of what we are about to do.

The final requirement is essentially a definition of a weak (rather than a strong) ranking. That is, it is a "greater than or equal to" rather than a "strictly greater than." We will examine the strict idea later (see definition 2.9).

Before going on, note again that the consumer is comparing one combination of goods with another combination of goods. Commodity bundles are being compared. That is, we are not asking

---

[2] Sonnenschein, Hugo, "Demand Theory Without Transitive Preferences, with Applications to the Theory of Competitive Equilibrium," in *Preferences, Utility, and Demand*, edited by Chipman, Hurwicz, Richter, and Sonnenschein, Harcourt Brace Jovanovich, Inc., New York, 1971, pp. 215–223.

if the consumer prefers apples to oranges, but whether 6 apples and 4 oranges is preferred to 3 apples and 5 oranges. Consider this example. We know that we are supposed to eat more fruit and vegetables and that we do not care what combination we consume, only that more total is desired. Suppose that we are told what constitutes a serving of each. The total servings of fruit and vegetables is the focus. In this example, we would prefer 4 fruit and 3 vegetables to 1 fruit and 4 vegetables because the total servings is larger in the first bundle. On the other hand, as long as the total number of servings stays the same, we do not care which bundle we get. So 3 fruit and 4 vegetables seems the same to us as 4 fruit and 3 vegetables.

The definition of preferences may seem confusing. What is going on here? One way to think about the idea of preferences is that preferences are a lot like "greater than or equal to" when applied to numbers. For any two numbers W and V, either $W \geq V$ or $V \geq W$ or both. "Greater than or equal to" is complete. And clearly "greater than or equal to" is transitive. If $W \geq V$ and $V \geq S$, then $W \geq S$ must hold. And for any number W, $W \geq W$. So why are we going to all this trouble to define preferences when we already have a perfectly good concept, "greater than or equal to"? The problem is that "greater than or equal to" applies only to numbers, not to pairs of numbers. What does it mean to say that $(5, 7) \geq (7, 5)$? The problem is that among pairs of numbers (or triples or longer strings of commodities), we have no natural way to define "greater than or equal to." Preferences are essentially "greater than or equal to" for commodity bundles. We define the concept of preferences by the properties they possess. In part this is a good thing! If there were a definition of "greater than or equal to" that applied to pairs of goods, what room would there be for individual differences? After all, we do not all like the same combination of goods the same!

A useful way to think more deeply about the idea of preferences is to ask what we mean if we say that W is not as preferred as V. What does this mean? It does not mean that there is no relationship between W and V, but it means that W is not the chosen bundle between W and V. We are assuming that the consumer has preferences, but that W is not the winner when V is available. The definition of preferences says that either $W R V$ or $V R W$ (or both); this is completeness. So if W is not as preferred as V (that is, $W R V$ is not true), then it must be that $V R W$ is true. Thus, one of the two bundles has to be at least as preferred as the other (or both). The one thing we do not allow the consumer to say is "I cannot rank these two bundles."

Section Summary:
So far we have a definition of preferences, which is an important part of the consumer's problem. But how can we use this concept? One way would be to find some kind of graphical representation of preferences. The question is: how can we find a way to graphically represent preferences? We will be developing the idea of indifference curves next.

2.5   Indifference Curves

In this section, we will develop a geometrical representation of a consumer's preferences — indifference curves. There are several steps in that process, and we start with defining the idea of indifference.

Definition 2.5: *Let W and V be commodity bundles. We say that a consumer is **indifferent** between W and V if $V R W$ and $W R V$, and we write $W I V$ (or $V I W$).*

Exercise 7. Show that indifference is transitive (i.e., if $W I V$ and $V I S$, then $W I S$).

Again, it is useful to think about what we mean when we say that the consumer is not indifferent between W and V. Indifference requires that both $W R V$ and $V R W$. So if we have W not indifferent to V, we must have at least one of $W R V$ or $V R W$ not true. We have these cases:

a. $W R V$ and not $V R W$.
b. Not $W R V$, but $V R W$.
c. Neither $W R V$ nor $V R W$ holds.

Now the last is impossible, as the definition of R says that at least one of $W R V$ or $V R W$ holds. Thus, having neither $W R V$ nor $V R W$ is impossible. So if W is not indifferent to V, we must have $W R V$ and not $V R W$ or $V R W$ and not $W R V$. We will come to a definition of this concept later (see definition 2.9).

Definition 2.6: *The set of all commodity bundles the consumer finds indifferent to W is called the* **indifference curve** *through W.*

Note that the name of this concept (indifference CURVE) seems to assume that this set will in fact be a curve, something we do not yet know to be true. Second, while we have defined the indifference curve through W, we would get the same indifference curve if we took any other bundle in that indifference curve and used it to generate the indifference curve. The question is: how can we find an indifference curve? One way would be to take the intersection of the bundles at least as preferred as W with the set of bundles that W is at least as preferred as. We develop the mechanics of this process now.

Definition 2.7: *The set of all commodity bundles V so that V R W is called the* **better than W** *set and is noted* BT_W.

Note that BT_W is not really strictly "better than." It is strictly "better than **and** as preferred as."

Definition 2.8: *The set of all commodity bundles that W is at least as good as (all V so that W R V) is called the* **worse than W** *set and is noted* WT_W.

A similar comment applies to "worse than" as applies to "better than."

It should be clear that given a bundle W, any other bundle V must be in either BT_W or WT_W or possibly both (why?). Furthermore, the indifference curve is the intersection of BT_W and WT_W. This intersection contains all the bundles V that satisfy both $V R W$ and $W R V$, the bundles indifferent to W.

Exercise 8. Suppose that V is in both BT_W and WT_W. Show that
$V\,I\,W$ holds.

Definition 2.9: *We say that W is **strictly preferred** to V if W R V and not V R W. We write W P V.*

Exercise 9. Look back at our discussion of what it means to say
that W is not indifferent to V (directly following
Exercise 7). How can we restate this in terms of
"strictly preferred"?

The key to understanding what we mean by P is to figure out what
we mean by **not** $W\,P\,V$. What does this mean? Let us look more carefully
at the definition of P.

$W\,P\,V$ requires that two things be true, $W\,R\,V$ and not $V\,R\,W$. So
not $W\,P\,V$ means that at least one of the two conditions is false. So for
not $W\,P\,V$, we would have either:

a. $W\,R\,V$ and $V\,R\,W$; or
b. not $W\,R\,V$ and not $V\,R\,W$; or
c. not $W\,R\,V$ and $V\,R\,W$.

For a, we would have $W\,I\,V$ by definition. For b, if we have neither
$W\,R\,V$ nor $V\,R\,W$, then R is not complete. We know that at least one
of $W\,R\,V$ or $V\,R\,W$ must hold by completeness. So this alternative is
not possible. For c, if we have not $W\,R\,V$ and $V\,R\,W$, then we have
$V\,P\,W$. So not $W\,P\,V$ means either $W\,I\,V$ or $V\,P\,W$.

Exercise 10. Show that if $W\,P\,V$, then it cannot be true that
$W\,I\,V$.
Exercise 11. Show that for all bundles V so that $V\,R\,W$, exactly
one of $V\,P\,W$ or $V\,I\,W$ holds.
Exercise 12. Show that if $V\,R\,S$ and $S\,I\,W$, then $V\,R\,W$ also holds.

Exercise 13. Show that P is transitive. That is, if $W P V$ and $V P S$, then $W P S$.

HINT: To show that $W P S$, you need to show that $W R S$ and not $S R W$. You should be able to easily show that $W R S$. The problem is to show that if not $V R W$ and not $S R V$, then not $S R W$. One way would be to show the contrapositive. One form would be: If not $V R W$ and $S R W$, then $S R V$. What does it mean to say not $V R W$? You should be on your way!

The above is pretty abstract. It would be good to do a relatively simple example. The example has the advantage of providing an additional insight to the idea of indifference curves. Now be warned that this example is a bit of a pathological case; I do not expect many consumers to actually have preferences like these.

Definition 2.10: *Let* $W = (X_1, Y_1)$ *and* $V = (X_2, Y_2)$. *We say that* W *is **lexicographically preferred** to V if $X_1 > X_2$ and we write $W L V$. We say that V is lexicographically preferred to W if $X_2 > X_1$ and we write $V L W$. If $X_1 = X_2$, we say that W is lexicographically preferred to V if $Y_1 > Y_2$ ($W L V$) or V is lexicographically preferred to W if $X_1 = X_2$ and $Y_2 > Y_1$ ($V L W$).*

First, is this a preference relation like R or like P? Second, the definition asserts that this ranking device is a preference relation. Is it?

Exercise 14. Show that lexicographic preferences are complete and transitive. Are they reflexive?

You should conclude that L is like "strictly preferred" and satisfies both completeness and transitivity.

We can now find the indifference curves for lexicographic preferences. We will do this by starting with a bundle W and finding BT_W and WT_W, and then finding the intersection of these two sets. The bundle $W = (X_0, Y_0)$ is shown in Figure 2.3.

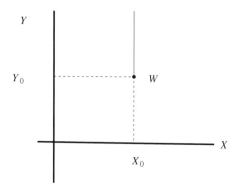

Figure 2.3   In this figure, we find BT_W to be the set of points to the right of the vertical line through X_0 including the solid line vertically above W, but not the dashed line below W.

The bundles better than W are those with more X than W, to the right of W, and those with as much X as W and more Y, those directly above W on the solid line. So BT_W is the set to the right of W (not including the dotted vertical line below W but including the solid vertical line above W).

Exercise 15.   Find WT_W for the W shown in Figure 2.3 and using the lexicographic preferences.

Exercise 16.   Find the intersection of BT_W and WT_W for the lexicographic preferences. What do you find?

The outcome is that the indifference curve through W consists of only one point, W. This is not a curve in the sense that we usually use the term. What have we learned? The lesson is that we can have preferences, but not have continuous indifference curves.

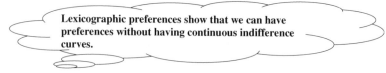

Lexicographic preferences show that we can have preferences without having continuous indifference curves.

What has to happen to get continuous indifference curves? The following proposition, due to Debreu, fills the gap.[3] We shall, in what follows, assume that this condition is satisfied — unless specifically warned that it may not hold.

Proposition 2.11: *If the consumer has preferences, R, and if both BT_W and WT_W contain their boundary, then continuous indifference curves exist.*

The proof of this proposition requires substantially more mathematics than we can muster, so we will accept it as true. What we will need to do next is see what properties indifference curves have.

Exercise 17. Suppose that for lexicographic preferences, the above condition had held, that is, both BT_W and WT_W included their entire edge. What would the indifference curves look like for this consumer?

We are now ready to find some properties of indifference curves. To do so, we need to add a condition.

Definition 2.12: *Let W and V be two commodity bundles. We say W is* **more than** *V if W has at least as much of every good as V and more of some good.*

Definition 2.13: *Let W and V be two commodity bundles. We say V is* **less than** *W if V has no more of any good than W and less of some good.*

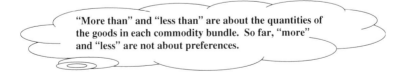

"More than" and "less than" are about the quantities of the goods in each commodity bundle. So far, "more" and "less" are not about preferences.

---

[3]Debreu, G., *Theory of Value*, Cowles Foundation, John Wiley & Sons, New York, 1959.

Exercise 18. Draw an axis system with X on the horizontal axis and Y on the vertical axis. Draw in a commodity bundle W and find all the bundles more than W. Now find all the commodity bundles less than W.

Exercise 19. Suppose that W is not more than V. Must W be less than V? Explain!

Exercise 20. Are "more than" and "less than" a preference relation? Are "more" and "less" together complete, transitive, and reflexive? To be complete, for any two bundles, W and V, it must be true that either W is more than V or W is less than V or V is more than W or V is less than W. Does this happen? For transitivity, take three bundles W, V, and S, and assume W is more than V and V is more than S. Is W also more than S? What if W is less than V and V is less than S, is W also less than S?

Definition 2.14: *When we say that **more is preferred to less**, we mean that for any bundle W that is more than a bundle V, W is strictly preferred to V.*

This definition connects "more" and "less" to preferences.

Exercise 21. Suppose that a consumer has lexicographic preferences. Is more preferred to less? Explain how you know.

Proposition 2.15: *If R is a preference relation with continuous indifference curves and more is preferred to less, then indifference curves have a negative slope.*

We wish to prove this proposition. How should we proceed? One way would be to start with the idea of continuous indifference curves and more preferred to less, and then derive the slope of indifference. We could probably do this. But to become accustomed to the style of proof we will encounter later, it may be useful to try a proof by contrapositive. The contrapositive of the above statement would be: If R is a preference relation and the indifference curve has a positive slope, then more is not preferred to less. We will try to prove this statement.

Proof 2.16: We will prove the contrapositive. Suppose that we have continuous indifference curves and they have a positive slope. Then we would have two bundles on the same indifference curve with one bundle more than the other. But that means that more is not preferred to less, as the consumer is indifferent between them.   □

Exercise 22.   Draw the graph that goes with the proof of proposition 2.15.

Proposition 2.17: *If R is a preference relation and more is preferred to less, then indifference curves cannot cross.*

Exercise 23.   State the contrapositive of proposition 2.17.

Proof 2.18: We will do the contrapositive. The contrapositive says that if indifference curves cross and R is a preference relation, then more is not preferred to less. Consider the graph in Figure 2.4.

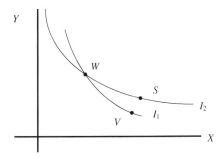

Figure 2.4   Here we show that indifference curves cannot cross if more is preferred to less. The consumer must be indifferent between W and S, and indifferent between W and V, and therefore indifferent between V and S (why?). But S is more than V, so more cannot be preferred to less.

The bundle S is indifferent to the bundle W because both are on I_2. The bundle W is indifferent to the bundle V because both are on I_1. Hence, the bundle S is indifferent to the bundle V. But S is more than V, so more is not preferred to less.   □

In summary, every commodity bundle is on one and only one indifference curve. A bundle is on one because of the completeness of preferences. A bundle is on only one because indifference curves cannot cross. There are, evidently, an infinite number of indifference curves even if only a few are drawn.

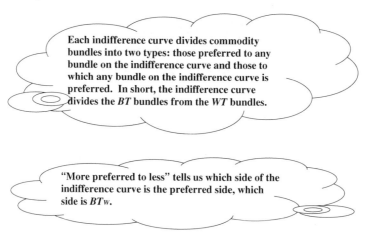

Each indifference curve divides commodity bundles into two types: those preferred to any bundle on the indifference curve and those to which any bundle on the indifference curve is preferred. In short, the indifference curve divides the *BT* bundles from the *WT* bundles.

"More preferred to less" tells us which side of the indifference curve is the preferred side, which side is *BTw*.

Exercise 24. Draw an axis with X and Y, and choose a commodity bundle W with positive amounts of both X and Y. Assume more is preferred to less. Draw an indifference curve through W. Carefully find the bundles more than W. Also find the bundles BT_W. How are these two sets different?

Exercise 25. Suppose for any bundle $W = (X, Y)$ where $X = Y$, BT_W and the "more than W" set are exactly the same, and the WT_W are all points not more than W. What will the indifference curves look like in this case?

> **Section Summary:**
> In this section, we started with the idea of preferences and then developed indifference curves. In addition, we discovered that indifference curves cannot cross, and that they will be negatively sloped if more is preferred to less. This representation of preferences is all we need to move to demand. However, there is an additional concept that is a useful way to represent the consumer's preferences based on indifference curves: utility. In the next section, we will see how to generate utility from preferences.

2.6   Utility

So far we have preferences, which we can represent by indifference curves. In this section, we will start with indifference curves and develop the concept of utility. Utility is an important idea because economists often say that a consumer acts to maximize utility subject to the budget. This consumer behavior is the basis for demand.

Definition 2.19: *Utility is the assignment of real numbers, U, to commodity bundles so that the following rules are satisfied*:

a. $U(W) \geq U(V)$ *if $W \, R \, V$.*
b. $U(W) = U(V)$ *if $W \, I \, V$.*

We can generate utility numbers based on preferences by using indifference curves. Consider the following procedure (and Figure 2.5!).

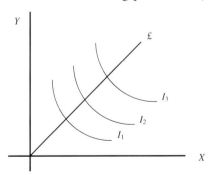

Figure 2.5   In this graph, we find utility by numbering the indifference curves by measuring along a ray from the origin. This numbering satisfies the definition of utility.

Suppose, then, that we have some indifference curves as shown in Figure 2.5. Then we draw a straight line out from the origin through the indifference curves, labeled £. Now we number the indifference curves by the distance from the origin along the line £. If we assign every bundle on I_1 the distance from the origin to I_1 along £, and then every bundle on I_2 the distance from the origin to I_2 along £, we would have an assignment of numbers that satisfies the requirements of utility.

Note that we have not specified the units of measurement. Thus, we could use inches, angstroms, light years, meters, or any suitable measure we want. Furthermore, we need not start our measurement at zero. We could start the measurements at 5 or −700. All that matters is that the numbers get larger as we hit higher indifference curves and that each bundle on the same indifference curve gets the same number. This kind of utility number is called ordinal. That is, only the order of the numbers matters, not the relative magnitude. So a bundle with a utility number of 4 need not be twice as preferred as a bundle with the utility number of 2. Note as well that we could have chosen a different straight line from the origin, and the numbers assigned to the indifference curves would have changed, but the new assignment would still satisfy the requirements for utility. The bottom line is this: We pick some arbitrary measure and stick with it, but it does not matter which one we choose as long as we satisfy the utility requirements. The outcome of the analysis of utility maximization will not depend on the particular utility index chosen.

What we have done is to establish a utility function, $U(X, Y)$. That is, we have assigned a utility number to each commodity bundle, and that assignment satisfies the requirements that U rises as we come to more preferred bundles and U stays the same along indifference curves.

We may now define an important concept that is much used in economics: marginal utility. You will find the adjective "marginal" attached to a variety of nouns. Marginal means the added, the extra, the change in.

Definition 2.20: *The **marginal utility** relates the consumption of a good, X, and utility, and shows the change in utility when X changes,* *with the consumption of all other goods held constant. We denote marginal utility by MU_x, where the subscript X is the good whose consumption is changing, or by $\frac{\Delta U}{\Delta X}$.*

Exercise 26. Suppose that we are at a commodity bundle and at that point, MU_x is 5. Suppose that X increases by 0.3 units. How much will utility rise as a result? What if we increase X by ΔX? What will the increase in utility be then?

We may use this definition to find the slope of the indifference curve.

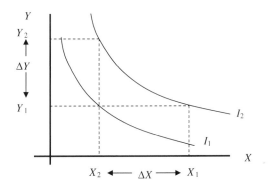

Figure 2.6   In this figure, we look at how to find the slope of the indifference curve.

We see from Figure 2.6 that the slope is $\Delta Y/\Delta X$. We need an expression for this slope in terms of utility. When X falls from X_1 to X_2 (X falls by ΔX), utility falls by $MU_x \times \Delta X$. When we go back to the original indifference curve, utility returns to its original value. To get back to the original indifference curve, we increase Y by ΔY. Utility will rise by $MU_y \times \Delta Y$. Because we start and stop at the same level of utility, we must have

$$MU_x \times \Delta X + MU_y \times \Delta Y = 0.$$

If we solve this for $\Delta Y / \Delta X$, the slope of indifference, we find

$$\frac{\Delta Y}{\Delta X} = \frac{-MU_x}{MU_y}.$$

The slope of the indifference curve is the negative of the ratio of marginal utilities. This term will be useful in our following discussion of utility maximization.

Exercise 27. In what units is the slope of the indifference curve measured? How do you know?

Exercise 28. Suppose that we have differentiable indifference curves and BT_W is strictly convex for each W. Does the slope of indifference rise or fall as X increases? Explain how you know.

Exercise 29. Draw some standard indifference curves and explain how you would find marginal utility from the indifference curves.

Exercise 30. Suppose that we define the marginal rate of substitution as the negative of the slope of the indifference curve. If we assume that we have a diminishing marginal rate of substitution, what must the indifference curve look like (assume the indifference has a negative slope)? What other assumption is diminishing marginal rate of substitution equivalent to?

Section Summary:

In this section, we have introduced the idea of utility and found how to build utility from indifference curves. We have also found utility and marginal utility. We can put utility together with the budget set to find the bundle the consumer would choose. Once we have done this, we can find demand. We turn to these issues now.

2.7   Utility Maximization Given the Budget

In this section, we will state and prove the utility maximization proposition. Once this is done, we can then use the proposition to derive the consumer's demand for the good X (done in Section 2.8). This is an important exercise as it yields one of the two basic curves in economics — demand. This exercise builds on all that we have developed so far in this chapter and material from the "Some Building Blocks" chapter.

Consider the definition of a maximum (see definition A.12). Here are some important facts we see from the definition. We start with $Y = f(X)$, and we determine whether a particular value of X provides a maximum for the function by the associated value of Y. If Y can get larger for some other X, we do not have the value of X that provides a maximum. Second, as we have defined the maximum, X_0, it is a local maximum, i.e., a maximum only for values near X_0, not for all possible values of X. Finally, observe that the maximum need not be unique — that is, there could be many values of X giving the same value of Y which is the largest possible value of Y. With these thoughts in mind, we can now turn to the consumer's problem.

The primary behavioral assumption we make is that the consumer maximizes utility given the budget. This means that the consumer chooses a commodity bundle so that there is no other bundle available that could yield higher utility. Put in slightly different words, the consumer chooses a commodity bundle from the budget set that provides the greatest possible utility. What would it mean to say that utility is not maximum? If utility is not maximum, there is some other combination of X and Y that yields greater utility than the one we have chosen. In short, if we are not at the maximum, there is a way to make utility rise.

What we want to know is what bundle that will be. Let us start by looking at the graph in Figure 2.7. Suppose that we start with a budget line and choose some bundle on the budget line, W. Now we know that through every commodity bundle there is an indifference curve, so there is an indifference curve through W. What we want to know is whether W is the utility maximum given the budget. If it is not, we want to know where the utility maximum will be.

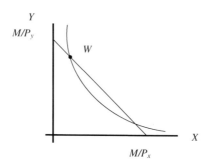

Figure 2.7   Suppose that the consumer chooses the bundle W on the budget line. We know there is an indifference curve through W. Suppose the indifference curve looks as shown. Is W a utility maximum? How do we know?

In Figure 2.7, we see that W cannot be the utility maximum. The indifference curve divides all bundles into two sides — and because one side is the BT_W side, there are bundles the consumer prefers to W in the budget set. So if W is not utility maximum, which bundle is? The following proposition provides the answer.

Proposition 2.21: Utility Maximization Given the Budget
If   a.   *assumptions 2.1 hold,*
     b.   *the consumer has differentiable indifference curves,*
     c. BT_W *is strictly convex for each* W,
     d.   *more is preferred to less,*
     e.   *at* (X_0, Y_0) *utility is maximum given the budget,* $X_0 > 0$,
        $Y_0 > 0$,
Then   f.   *at* (X_0, Y_0) *all income is spent,*
     g.   *at* (X_0, Y_0) *an indifference curve is tangent to the budget line.*

We shall shortly prove this proposition. But before we do, we will say a bit about what the assumptions rule out. First, because indifference curves are differentiable, they cannot have corners. BT_W is strictly convex, so the curves cannot bend back on themselves. This assumption also rules out thick indifference curves or zones of indifference. "More is preferred to less" tells us which side of the indifference curve is the preferred side. The requirement that $X_0 > 0$ and $Y_0 > 0$ means that we do not have a utility maximum on either axis. The consumer buys positive amounts of both goods.

Before we prove this proposition, we need to consider how we might proceed. First, there are two conclusions. In fact, then, there are really two propositions. The first only has one conclusion, f.

If   a.   assumptions 2.1 hold,
           b.   the consumer has differentiable indifference curves,
           c. BT_W is strictly convex for each W,
           d.   more is preferred to less,
           e.   at (X_0, Y_0) utility is maximum given the budget, $X_0 > 0$, $Y_0 > 0$,
Then   f.   at (X_0, Y_0) all income is spent.

The second only has one conclusion, g.

If   a.   assumptions 2.1 hold,
           b.   the consumer has differentiable indifference curves,
           c. BT_W is strictly convex for each W,
           d.   more is preferred to less,
           e.   at (X_0, Y_0) utility is maximum given the budget, $X_0 > 0$, $Y_0 > 0$,
Then   g.   at (X_0, Y_0) an indifference curve is tangent to the budget line.

We will prove these one at a time. How can we proceed with the first? Given that income does not directly show up in our assumptions (except that the consumer knows M and $M > 0$), it is not obvious how we might do the proof directly. Perhaps a proof by contrapositive would be appropriate. How would we state the contrapositive of this proposition? We need to start with not f and then show that one of a, b, c, d, or e is not true. Which one should we choose? There is an art to the choice here, but the assumption that makes most sense to pursue is e. Why e? First, e is always assumed. We can imagine that there are preferences that do not satisfy one of the conditions b, c, or d. But we will always assume e. Second, e is relatively easy to work with. That is, the condition not e is easy to identify. But to have to try to show not b, for example, could be very hard. So we will use e as the starting point for our contrapositive.

Roughly, the contrapositive we will work on is: If not f, then not e. But what do we do with a, b, c, and d? We may use them as part of the "if." Thus, the statement we wish to prove is:

If a, b, c, d, and not f, then not e.

If we can prove this, we will know that the original statement is true.

Proof 2.22: If all income is not spent at (X_0, Y_0), then we wish to show that utility is not maximum at (X_0, Y_0) given the budget. Suppose that all income is not spent. Then there is leftover income, and we can buy more of both goods. Because more is preferred to less (assumption d), utility will rise and hence could not have been maximum at (X_0, Y_0). $\square$

FROM THE LITERATURE

One use of utility maximization that might not be expected is in biology, where selection of a mate is sometimes seen in terms of a person searching for a job. The question is, what search strategy does a cricket, say, use to search for a mate? Is the better strategy one where the female sets a threshold (in terms of the song, or some other feature of the male) and accepts the first male that exceeds the threshold? An alternative is to search over a given number and accept the highest ranked male in that set. In the latter case, what number of males should the female include in the search pool? These strategies can be seen as utility maximization processes. See Robert Gibson and Tom Langen, "How Do Animals Choose Their Mates?," *TREE*, Vol. 11, No. 11, November, 1996, pp. 468–470.

Exercise 31. Before going on to prove g, think about what we have done. In what way have we used the assumptions b and c in this proof? Do we need them at all to prove f?

Turn now to g. Here is the proposition we wish to prove.

If   a.   assumptions 2.1 hold,
      b.   the consumer has differentiable indifference curves,
      c. BT_W is strictly convex for each W,
      d.   more is preferred to less,
      e.   at (X_0, Y_0) utility is maximum given the budget, $X_0 > 0$, $Y_0 > 0$,

Then   g.   at (X_0, Y_0) an indifference curve is tangent to the budget line.

Again, we will use the contrapositive.

Exercise 32. State the contrapositive for if a, b, c, d, and e, then g.

Proof 2.23: Assume that an indifference curve is not tangent to the budget line at (X_0, Y_0) as shown in Figure 2.8. We wish to show that utility is not maximum given the budget. By f, we must be on the budget line (because of the previous proof and the assumption d). Hence, (X_0, Y_0) is on the budget line, but an indifference curve is not tangent to the budget line at (X_0, Y_0). Therefore, an indifference curve must cut (by assumption b) the budget line at (X_0, Y_0). Both sides of the indifference curve will be below the budget line. On one side of the indifference curve, we have bundles preferred to any point on the indifference curve, and therefore preferred to (X_0, Y_0). Thus, (X_0, Y_0) is not the most preferred bundle in the budget set, and (X_0, Y_0) cannot be utility maximum given the budget.   □

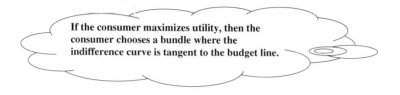

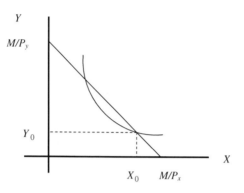

Figure 2.8   In this graph, the point (X_0, Y_0) is on the budget line but does not maximize utility given the budget. There are bundles preferred to (X_0, Y_0) in the budget set.

Exercise 33. In Figure 2.8, given more preferred to less, shade in the bundles preferred to (X_0, Y_0); these are the bundles better than (X_0, Y_0). Now identify those bundles that are preferred to (X_0, Y_0) and also that are affordable by the consumer.

Exercise 34. In Figure 2.8, find the bundles more than (X_0, Y_0).

Exercise 35. Where did we use the assumptions b, c, and d in the above argument to prove g?

What is the conclusion? For the consumer who maximizes utility, and we assume that all consumers do this, then they will choose a bundle on their budget line, and, given differentiable indifference curves, the chosen bundle will be at the tangency of the budget line and the indifference curve. This is shown in Figure 2.9.

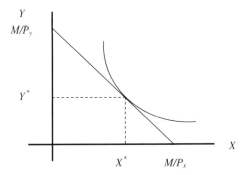

Figure 2.9 In this graph, the point (X^*, Y^*) is the utility maximum given the budget.

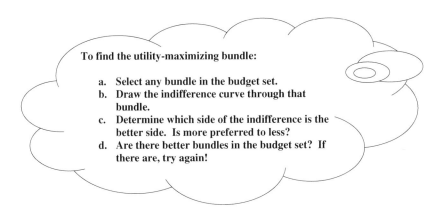

To find the utility-maximizing bundle:

a. Select any bundle in the budget set.
b. Draw the indifference curve through that bundle.
c. Determine which side of the indifference is the better side. Is more preferred to less?
d. Are there better bundles in the budget set? If there are, try again!

Exercise 36. State the converse of the utility maximization proposition. Do you expect the converse to be true? Is the converse true in this case? Can you prove it?

FROM THE LITERATURE

Are there limits to utility maximization? The answer is, obviously, yes, there are limits! While there are models of rational addiction, most people would argue that addiction cannot be a utility-maximizing strategy (see http://www.stat.columbia.edu/~cook/movabletype/archives/2010/12/rational_addict.html for an argument against the rational addiction model, or http://www.slate.com/id/2171373 for a counterpoint). And there is a "literature" on the economics of sleeping, where economists have traded barbs over how much sleep is optimal, how much time in bed is optimal, and why the two might be different. You can find these items as follows. Gary Becker and Kevin Murphy, "A Theory of Rational Addiction," *Journal of Political Economy*, Vol. 96, No. 4, August, 1988, pp. 675–700. A counterpoint can be found in Jon Elster, "Emotion and Economic Theory," *Journal of Economic Literature*, Vol. 36, No. 1, March, 1998, pp. 47–74. Elster's work is aimed at a larger target than Becker and Murphy's paper, and so offers a broader view of decision making. The literature on sleeping is a bit hard to locate, but see Emily Hoffman, "The Deeper Economics of Sleeping: Important Clues Toward the Discovery of Activity X," *Journal of Political Economy*, Vol. 85, No. 3, June, 1977, pp. 647–650.

We can build on what we already know and restate the utility maximization condition. We know from the above that if utility is maximum given the budget, then the consumer chooses a bundle so that an indifference curve is tangent to the budget line. That means that at the utility maximum, the slope of the budget line has to be equal to the slope of the indifference curve. We know that the slope of the budget line is $-P_x/P_y$. We also know that the slope of the indifference curve, from Section 2.6, is $-MU_x/MU_y$. Hence, if utility is maximum given the budget, we must have the following condition:

$$\frac{MU_x}{MU_y} = \frac{P_x}{P_y}.$$

Alternatively, we may write this condition as follows:

$$\frac{MU_x}{P_x} = \frac{MU_y}{P_y}.$$

Because $1/P_x$ is the number of units of X we can purchase with a dollar, the ratio MU_x/P_x is the change in utility when expenditure on X is changed by a dollar. At the utility maximum, the extra utility per extra dollar spent must be the same on each good.

There is another way to think about utility maximization. If the consumer maximizes utility, the consumer chooses the goods X and Y so that the slope of the budget equals the slope of the indifference curve. The slope of the budget is the negative of the ratio of prices. The ratio of prices measures how many units of Y trade for one unit of X in the market. The slope of the indifference tells the number of units of Y the consumer must obtain for one unit of X to stay indifferent. Thus, the rate at which Y trades for X in the market must be equal to the rate at which Y trades for X for the individual if utility is maximum given the budget. Because all consumers face the same prices, at the utility maximum, they must all be willing to trade the same number of units of Y for a unit of X as dictated by the market.

> Exercise 37. Suppose that the ratio of prices indicates that 4 Y trade for 1 X. Draw a graph showing what must be true if a consumer, when spending all income at (X_0, Y_0), says that they prefer to trade 3 Y for 1 X.

Before going on, we should address a rather obvious question. Do consumers actually behave this way, maximize utility given the budget? Think about your own behavior — you are a consumer! When you go to the grocery store, do you actually see if there is some other combination of goods you could put in your grocery cart that would make you happier? Most of us are not so calculating! So if this hypothesis does not describe how consumers behave, of what use is this theory? There are two factors that lead economists to continue to use this assumption. First, there is no other assumption we could make that yields the results that this assumption yields. We find demand and, furthermore, this demand seems to help explain what happens in the world with some efficiency. Second, it is hard to imagine that consumers want to do positive harm to themselves. We may not get right to the maximum, but we are probably in the neighborhood! Thus, we use this assumption because it works.

My bike helmet? No, it's my utilityometer! I'm going shopping!

Section Summary:
In this section, we have stated and proved the utility maximization proposition. The primary tool was the contrapositive. Our statement was: If utility is maximum given the budget, then at the utility-maximizing bundle, an indifference curve must be tangent to the budget line. It is the main workhorse of the next section: finding demand.

2.8   Finding Demand

In this section, we will use the tool developed in the previous section to find the consumer's demand for the good X. To start, please review the definition of demand in definition 1.1. What did you learn? You should see the definition of demand as a set of instructions for the derivation of the demand curve from utility maximization. How? Well, demand tells the amount of a good, say X, the consumer chooses at each price with other factors held constant. So we need a mechanism to determine what the consumer chooses, which is utility maximization given the budget, and then we need to hold other factors constant. So we should hold M, P_y, and the consumer's indifference curves constant. The indifference curves represent tastes, and tastes are not changing. How then do we get demand as a result? Follow these steps and consult Figure 2.10. Note that we have drawn two graphs, one to depict utility maximization given the budget (on top) and one for demand (below). Note the differences in how the two axis systems are labeled.

To find demand:

1. Given M, P_x, and P_y, draw the consumer's budget line on the axis system with X on the horizontal axis and Y on the vertical axis. Mark P_x on the vertical axis of the demand graph (below).
2. Draw in some indifference curves in the utility maximization graph (top) and use the utility maximization proposition (2.21) to find the bundle the consumer chooses, (X_0, Y_0). Bring the X_0 value into the demand graph (below). This gives us one point on the demand curve.
3. Now change the price of X to P_x'. Suppose that $P_x' < P_x$. Using the same M and P_y as in step 1, draw the new budget line (top). Mark P_x' on the demand graph (below).
4. Using indifference curves from the same family as in step 2 and the utility maximization proposition (2.21), find the bundle the consumer chooses (top), (X_0', Y_0'). Bring the X_0' value into the demand graph (below). This gives us another point on the demand curve.
5. Continue this process for all possible prices of X to obtain the consumer's demand for X.

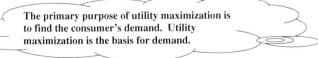

The primary purpose of utility maximization is to find the consumer's demand. Utility maximization is the basis for demand.

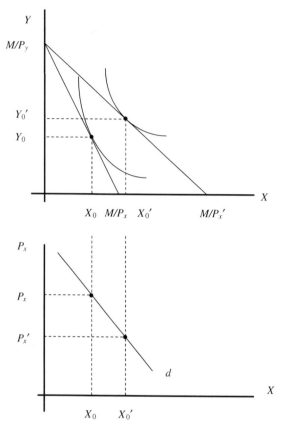

Figure 2.10   These two graphs illustrate how demand is derived for the good X.

You may have some questions about what we have done. First, when we assume a price of X, price of Y, and income, how do we know exactly where the budget line will go? Well, given that we do not have numbers and we do not have marks on the axes, we do not know. But it does not matter. What matters is that the budget line has a negative slope and that the intercepts are M/P_x and M/P_y. What about where to put P_x on the vertical axis for demand? Where does it go? Again, we cannot know for sure, but we know it is some point on the vertical axis. Choose one.

What matters now is what happens when the new price, P'_x, is introduced. In this case, we have that $P'_x < P_x$. Hence, the budget line has to swing out to the right (why?), and the new price is below the original price in the demand graph. How much does the budget line swing out? We do not know for sure. How far below the original price of X will the new price be? We cannot tell. All we can discern is that the demand has a negative slope; we cannot tell how negative it is. There is one other question you might have: How do we know where the tangency of the indifference curve and the budget line is? In truth, we do not know. So put the first tangency in where it looks nice. Given that indifference curves cannot cross, the next tangency is somewhat restricted in where it can be.

Exercise 38. Suppose that we allow the price of X to rise rather than fall. What difference would that make in the derivation of demand?

Exercise 39. Suppose that after we have derived the demand, the income rises to a new level M' and stays there. Derive demand again. Use the same prices that you used the first time. What can you say about what happened to the demand curve?

Exercise 40. Suppose that we derive demand for X once (use two prices). Now suppose that we lower the price of Y to P'_y, where the price of Y now stays. Derive demand for X again using the same prices for X as for the first derivation. What happens to the demand for X as a result of this decrease in the price of Y?

Exercise 41. Suppose that we multiply both prices and income by the same positive constant, k. What happens to the utility-maximizing choice? How do you know? What does this tell us about demand? Suppose we have $X = X(P_x, P_y, M)$ for a demand curve. What must be true when we multiply all prices and income by the same positive constant, k? What happens to $X = X(kP_x, kP_y, kM)$?

Exercise 42. Suppose we have the following information: Income $= 16$, $P_x = 1$, $P_y = 1$. In the graph below, draw the budget line we would get using this information. Now suppose that the price of X rises to 2. What budget line would we have then? Use the budget lines you just graphed and utility maximization to find demand. Plot the demand on a graph with P_x on the vertical axis and X on the horizontal axis. A ruler will be a big help!

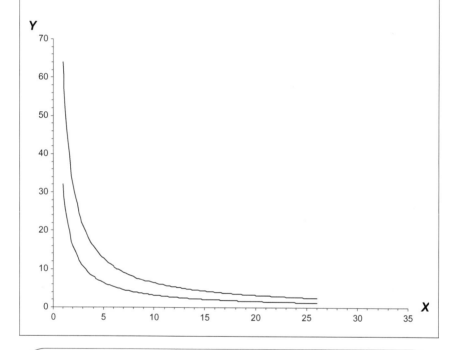

Section Summary:

In this section, we have found the demand curve by repeated application of the utility maximization given the budget proposition. This activity is the culmination of our efforts to find demand, one of the two important concepts for price determination in a market. In the next section, we take up how to find demand using calculus.

2.9 Finding Utility Maximum and Demand with Calculus

We wish to now use the more elegant calculus methods for finding the utility maximum and then the demand. To do this, we will need a utility function and the budget constraint. We already know the budget constraint, so our immediate focus will be on what we can use for the utility function. The problem is that the consumer could have any one of a large variety of utility functions, so we have to pick one, and we are looking for an easy one to use. Suppose that we use $U = XY$. What would the indifference curves look like? Well, to be indifferent means to keep utility the same, so we would want the combinations of X and Y so that $X \times Y$ is constant. Suppose we hold utility constant at U^*. If we solve for Y, we would get $Y = U^*/X$. You can see that as X rises, the value of Y must fall. The indifference curves for this utility function would become asymptotic to the X-axis and the Y-axis, and look as we have shown. This utility function will do.

The consumer's problem is to maximize $U(X, Y) = XY$ for given values of M, P_x, and P_y. Suppose for the moment we assume that $M = 200$, $P_x = 2$, and $P_y = 5$. How do we solve this problem? First, write the budget constraint: $200 = 2 \times X + 5 \times Y$. This equation tells the combinations of X and Y that cost exactly \$200. We know that the consumer will choose some combination of X and Y on this line. Now solve the budget equation for Y to get $Y = (200/5) - (2/5)X$. We may plug this equation into the utility function. If we maximize the resulting expression, we will find the utility-maximizing quantity of X. We can then find the corresponding value of Y by plugging back into the budget. Let us carry out these steps. First, plug our expression for Y into the utility function to get

$$U = X \times ((200/5) - (2/5)X).$$

We can now maximize this function to find the optimal value of X. How do we find the maximum? We know (see proposition A.13) that if a function has a maximum, then the derivative of the function must be zero at the maximum. We will find the derivative of our U, set it to zero, and solve for the optimal X. Let us proceed with the derivative of U:

$$U' = 1 \times ((200/5) - (2/5)X) + X(-2/5).$$

We now set this expression to zero and solve for X:

$$(200/5) - (2/5)X - (2/5)X = 0$$
$$200/5 - (4/5)X = 0$$
$$200/5 = 4X/5$$
$$200 = 4X$$
$$X = 50.$$

We can now find the optimal value of Y by plugging into the budget expression:

$$2X + 5Y = 200$$
$$2(50) + 5Y = 200$$
$$100 + 5Y = 200$$
$$5Y = 100$$
$$Y = 20.$$

We now know that our utility-maximizing choice is $(50, 20)$, 50 units of X and 20 units of Y.

To be sure this choice is a utility maximum, we need to check the second derivative (see proposition A.15). From above,

$$U' = 1 \times ((200/5) - (2/5)X) + X(-2/5).$$

Therefore, $U'' = -(4/5) < 0$, so we have a maximum!

How can we find demand? Realize that demand tells the amount of X for each P_x. So now we need for P_x to be a variable. Thus, our budget becomes

$$P_x X + 5Y = 200.$$

If we solve for Y, we get $Y = 40 - (P_x/5)X$. Plug into the utility function to get

$$U = X \times (40 - (P_x/5)X).$$

To find the utility-maximizing choice, find the derivative of U and set it to zero. First, the derivative:

$$U' = 1 \times (40 - (P_x/5)X) + X(-P_x/5)$$
$$= 40 - (2P_x/5)X.$$

Before we find demand, we need to be sure we have a maximum. We do that by finding the second derivative and seeing if the second derivative is negative. If the second derivative is negative, we have a maximum. What is the second derivative of our function?

$$U'' = -(2P_x/5) < 0.$$

We have a maximum! Now we can find our demand. Go back to U', set this expression to zero, and solve for X:

$$40 - (2P_x/5)X = 0$$
$$40 = (2P_x/5)X$$
$$X = 5 \times 40/(2P_x) = 200/(2P_x) = 100/P_x.$$

This, then, is the consumer's demand curve when $M = 200$ and $P_y = 5$.

But what if we did not know the specific values of M or P_y? Could we find the demand then? Follow the same procedure. Here is the budget constraint:

$$M = P_x X + P_y Y.$$

Solve the budget constraint for Y:

$$Y = (M/P_y) - (P_x/P_y)X.$$

Plug into the utility function:

$$U = X \times ((M/P_y) - (P_x/P_y)X).$$

Find the maximum by finding the derivative of U and setting it to zero:

$$U' = 1 \times ((M/P_y) - (P_x/P_y)X) + X \times (-(P_x/P_y)) = 0.$$

Before solving for X, check the second derivative of U:

$$U'' = -2(P_x/P_y) < 0.$$

So we have a maximum! Now solve $U' = 0$ for X:

$$(M/P_y) - 2(P_x/P_y)X = 0$$

$$(2P_x/P_y)X = M/P_y$$

$$2P_x X = M$$

$$X = M/(2P_x).$$

Here is our demand! Note that something rather odd happens here; P_y does not enter the demand for X. This is not what we would usually expect to happen, and this result occurs because of the special nature of the utility function we have here. Also note that this consumer spends half of the income on X. How do we know that? Well, expenditure on X is $P_x X$. From demand, if we multiply through by P_x, we get $P_x X = M/2$. Hence, half of M is spent on X. Both of these outcomes are not what we would generally expect. If we had a different utility function, we would likely get a different outcome.

What if we do not know the income, prices, or even the utility function?[4] Now the objective is to maximize utility, $U(X, Y)$, subject to $M = P_x X + P_y Y$. How to proceed? Exactly as before! Solve the budget for Y and plug into the utility:

$$U(X, \{(M/P_y) - (P_x/P_y)X\}).$$

To maximize, we need to distinguish the derivative of U as only X changes, the partial derivative of U with respect to X, denoted $\frac{\partial U}{\partial X}$, from the derivative of U as only Y changes, the partial derivative of U with respect to Y, denoted $\frac{\partial U}{\partial Y}$. You should recognize these as MU_x and

---

[4]The remainder of this section has partial notation.

MU_y, respectively. We may proceed as usual and find the derivative of this U with respect to X — remembering that Y depends on X, and, at a maximum, this derivative must be zero. So U changes as X changes because U depends directly on X; this is the $\frac{\partial U}{\partial X}$ term. But then when X changes, Y also changes because of the budget. This change is captured by $\left(\frac{-P_x}{P_y}\right)$. And as Y changes, U also changes, which is the term $\frac{\partial U}{\partial Y}$. So the total change in U due to a change in X is as follows:

$$U'(X, Y) = \frac{\partial U}{\partial X} + \frac{\partial U}{\partial Y}\left(\frac{-P_x}{P_y}\right).$$

If we have a maximum, this term must be zero. That means that, upon rearrangement, we have the following:

$$\left(\frac{\frac{\partial U}{\partial X}}{\frac{\partial U}{\partial Y}}\right) = \left(\frac{P_x}{P_y}\right).$$

We recognize this equation! The left-hand side is the (negative of the) slope of the indifference curve and the right-hand side is the (negative of the) slope of the budget constraint! This is exactly the condition we got in definition 2.20.

Here are some utility functions for you to practice with.

Exercise 43. Suppose that we have the standard budget constraint, $M = P_x X + P_y Y$. Find the demand for the following utility functions. As always, be sure to check the second derivative.

a. $U = X^{1/2} + Y^{1/2}$.
b. $U = X^{1/2} Y^{1/2}$.
c. $U = X^2 + Y^2$.

Exercise 44. Based on Exercise 41, could the following be demand equations obtained from utility maximization given the budget? Explain how you know!

a. $X = M - P_x X + P_y Y$.
b. $X = (M/P_x) - (P_y/P_x^2)$.

> **Section Summary:**
> In this section, we have used calculus to find the consumer's utility-maximizing choice and also the consumer's demand curve. We had to assume that we knew the utility function to obtain the actual demand curve.

2.10 Summary

In this chapter, we have done several things:

A. Developed the consumer's budget constraint.
B. Found a way to represent preferences by indifference curves.
C. Connected indifference to utility.
D. Stated and proved the utility maximization subject to the budget proposition.
E. Used the proposition to derive the consumer's demand.

There are two big lessons you should take from this chapter:

A. Consumers act to maximize utility subject to a budget.
B. The utility-maximizing consumer generally will choose a bundle so that an indifference curve is tangent to the budget line.

We now have the consumer's demand on a firm footing. Demand is one of the two big concepts in price determination in markets; the other is supply. Before we get to supply, we need to clean up a few details with regard to demand, including the factors that determine its slope, and something about elasticity.

Terms Defined:

- Budget set
- Commodity bundle
- Preference relation
- Indifferent
- Indifference curve
- Better than, worse than

- Strictly preferred
- Lexicographically preferred
- More than, less than
- More preferred to less
- Utility
- Marginal utility
- Utility maximization

Chapter 3

Income and Substitution Effects and Elasticity

Key Concepts:

- Income effect
- Substitution effect
- Slope of demand
- Giffen good
- Inferior good
- Elasticity

Goals:

- Isolate the income and substitution effects.
- Relate the slope of demand to the income and substitution effects.
- Examine the elasticity of demand.
- See how elasticity relates to the expenditure on the good.

The previous chapter tells us how to derive demand. We have the expectation that demand will have a negative slope, but we do not know how steep or flat the demand will be. In this chapter, we will approach the question from a theoretical point of view and add an empirical measurement, elasticity, before we end.

3.1   Introduction

The exact slope of the demand curve clearly depends on the consumer's preferences. But what are the elements of the preferences that determine the slope? In this chapter, we will look at the forces determining the slope of demand: substitution and the impact of real income. In addition, we will look at a way to measure responsiveness of the quantity demanded to changes in price: the price elasticity of demand.

One application of elasticity is in the field of taxation. If the government wants to raise revenue, they want to impose a tax on a good that consumers will continue to buy even after the tax has been imposed. Thus, for raising tax revenue, the government wants a good with a demand curve that is more vertical. How can we tell which demand is more vertical? Can't we just look at the curve and tell? How can we measure the "verticality" of demand in a way that allows comparison across goods? Why isn't the slope the answer to this question? This chapter will help address these issues!

3.2   Income and Substitution Effects

In the previous chapter, we derived the demand curve using utility maximization. While we used calculus as one way to do this, we also carried out the derivation geometrically. We will pursue the geometrical process here to have a closer look at the slope of demand. In particular, we want to know how the slope of demand is related to the changes in real income and relative prices that occur when the price of the good changes. These are the income and substitution effects. We will find these effects and relate them to the slope of demand.

Recall the process for deriving demand that we used in the last chapter. To find demand:

1. Given values for M, P_x, and P_y, draw the consumer's budget line on the axis system with X on the horizontal axis and Y on the vertical axis — the utility maximization graph. Draw a new axis system, demand, with P_x on the vertical axis and X on the horizontal axis. Mark the value of P_x we started with on the vertical axis of the demand graph.

2. Draw in some indifference curves in the utility maximization graph and use the utility maximization proposition (2.21) to find the bundle the consumer chooses, (X_0, Y_0). Bring the X_0 value into the demand graph. This gives us one point on the demand curve.

3. Now change the price of X to P'_x. Suppose that $P'_x < P_x$. Using the same M and P_y as in step 1, draw the new budget line. Mark P'_x on the demand graph.

4. Using indifference curves from the same family as in step 2 and the utility maximization proposition (2.21), find the bundle the consumer chooses, (X'_0, Y'_0). Bring the X'_0 value into the demand graph. This gives us another point on the demand curve.

5. Continue this process for all possible prices of X to obtain the consumer's demand for X.

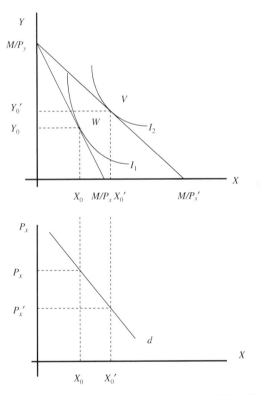

Figure 3.1 We show the derivation of demand for the good X utilizing utility maximization given the budget with these graphs.

Observe that to find demand we change the price of X, P_x. When we change the price of X, two things happen to the budget. First, if P_x falls, the budget line swings out, and the consumer has command over more commodity bundles than before. That is, the consumer seems richer! That apparent increase in income means that usually the consumer would buy more of the good. Hence, we have one reason for the consumer to buy more as the price falls. But there is a second reason. If P_x falls, then X becomes relatively less expensive than other goods, and the consumer has a reason to substitute X for other goods — again, a reason for the demand to be downward-sloping. We have two reasons, then, for the demand to slope down, one having to do with apparent income (not actual income, M, because M is fixed along demand), and one having to do with substitution of X for other goods. We wish to sort these out and see if there are other reasons for the downward slope of demand. Furthermore, could there be any reason why demand might slope up? We will start with some (guess what?) definitions. One symbol that will frequently appear is Δ, which is shorthand for the phrase "the change in."

Definition 3.1: *The **slope of demand** is the amount that the quantity demanded changes when there is a change in the price of the good. We denote the slope as $\frac{\Delta X}{\Delta P_x}$.*

Before we go on, there is one little puzzle we should clear up. When you look at a graph of the demand curve, you see P_x on the vertical axis and X on the horizontal axis. That would lead you to believe that the slope should be in terms of change in price over change in quantity, or price over quantity. Price is a function of quantity. In other words, we would expect the demand curve to be written as $P_x = f(X)$. However, from the definition of demand, we see that $X = f(P_x)$, that is, the quantity demanded is a function of the price. From this, we would expect X to be on the vertical axis, not P_x. What happened? For whatever reason, the convention of price on the vertical axis was established, and we will continue the tradition.[1] So when we think

---

about the slope of demand, it will be in terms of the change in X divided by the change in price.

Note that because we have defined the slope in terms of the quantity demanded, we know that we are moving along demand and that all other prices, income, and the consumer's tastes are not changing.

What we want to do is to somehow separate the two forces that are causing demand to have a negative slope. One of the reasons has to do with income apparently changing. We might say that real income changed even though money income did not. What we need is a definition of real income that will allow us to know when it is changing and when it is not. On the one hand, we could use some kind of price index as we do in macro. But a more fruitful way to proceed is to think that as long as the well-being of the consumer does not change, the consumer's real income has not changed. We measure well-being by utility, so if utility does not change, real income does not change.

Definition 3.2: *We say that two bundles represent the **same real income** if they are on the same indifference curve, have the same utility.*

Substitution occurs when the price of one good changes relative to the price of another good. Hence, the impulse to substitute must be related to how expensive one good is compared to another.

Definition 3.3: *We say that the **ratio of relative prices** (the relative price ratio or relative prices) is the ratio of the price of X to the price of Y, P_x/P_y.*

Exercise 1. Where do you see the relative price ratio in the consumer's problem? Be specific!

We can now state the definitions of the two effects we described above.

---

he had the second highest score on the annual mathematics exam among the students graduating in mathematics at the University of Cambridge. He clearly knew what he was doing! He was also one of John Maynard Keynes' professors.

Definition 3.4: *The **income effect** is that part of the movement along demand due to a change in real income with relative prices held fixed. We denote the income effect as* $\frac{\Delta X}{\Delta I}|_{relative\ prices\ fixed}$.

Note that in the denominator of the income effect, we have ΔI, not ΔM. ΔI represents a change in real income, the indifference curve, not a change in money income, M.

We are now ready for the remaining effect, the one due to substitution.

Definition 3.5: *The **substitution effect** is that part of the movement along demand due to a change in relative prices with real income held fixed. We denote the substitution effect as* $\frac{\Delta X}{\Delta P_x}|_{real\ income\ fixed}$.

The question is, how can we find these effects? Let us go back to the original derivation of demand. Look again at Figure 3.1. The initial utility maximization point is at W when the price of X is P_x. When the price of X falls to P'_x, the new utility maximization point is at V. How are the real income and relative prices different at V compared to W?

At W, the relative prices are P_x/P_y. At V, the relative prices are P'_x/P_y. What about the real income? We are using the indifference curve to measure real income, so the real income at W is I_1, and at V real income is I_2.

	Relative Prices	Real Income
W	P_x/P_y	I_1
V	P'_x/P_y	I_2

We see that both the real income and relative prices have changed as P_x changed. To find the substitution effect, we must hold real income fixed. To find the income effect, we must hold relative prices fixed. That means we need to find a new bundle, let's call it T, so that T has the same real income as W and the same relative prices as V. Furthermore, T must be a bundle that satisfies the utility maximization requirement that the indifference curve and budget line are tangent.

Where is T? T has to be on I_1 to have the same real income as W. But it must be tangent (for utility maximization reasons) to a budget line with slope $-P'_x/P_y$ so that the relative prices are the same as at V. Note that the bundles we will observe are W and V. We will not usually ever see T. But to get to the effects underlying the choice process, we need to construct T. We show that construction next!

To find T, we need to find a point on the indifference curve I_1 where the consumer would choose (therefore we need a tangency between an indifference curve and a budget line) if relative prices were P'_x/P_y. Those relative prices are the slope of the budget line at V. So we need a budget line with the same slope as V's budget line, keeping relative prices as they are at V, tangent to the I_1 indifference curve so that real income is the same as at W. This is shown in Figure 3.2.

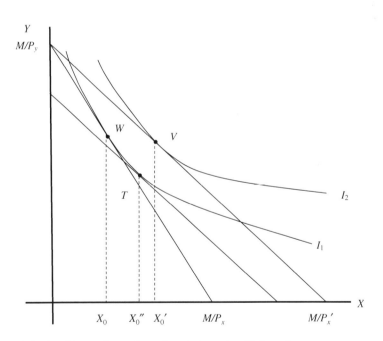

Figure 3.2 In this graph, we have found the point T that allows us to separate the income and substitution effects. T is on I_1 (so real income is the same as at W) where I_1 is tangent to a budget line parallel to the budget line used to find V, so relative prices are P'_x/P_y.

We now have the following elements:

	Relative Prices	Real Income
W	P_x/P_y	I_1
V	P_x'/P_y	I_2
T	P_x'/P_y	I_1

As we go from W to T, we see that only the relative prices have changed, not real income, so we have the substitution effect. As we move from T to V, we see that only the real income has changed, not relative prices, so we have the income effect. We can now say something about the sign of these effects.

Recall that the substitution effect is $\frac{\Delta X}{\Delta P_x}|_{real\ income\ fixed}$. To find this effect, start at W and move to T. In this case, we can see from Figure 3.2 that X increased, so the change in X, ΔX, is positive. Furthermore, we know that to get the new budget line, we allowed price to fall, so the change in price, ΔP_x, is negative. Thus, we have the following outcome:

$$\frac{\Delta X}{\Delta P_x}\bigg|_{real\ income\ fixed} = \frac{+}{-} < 0.$$

Exercise 2. What would we get if we went from T to W rather than from W to T? What would happen to X if we go from T to W? What would happen to the price of X if we go from T to W? Does it matter which direction we go to find the substitution effect?

Proposition 3.6: *For a consumer satisfying the utility maximization proposition where both X and Y are goods, then the substitution effect is strictly negative.*

We will not prove this proposition. In part an adequate proof requires some mathematics. The key idea, though, arises from the negative slope of the indifference curve and the strict convexity of BT_W.

As we decrease price, the budget line has to flatten, and if we are to stay on the same indifference curve, the amount of X rises as price falls. The strict convexity means that we cannot stay at the same point on the indifference curve so that the substitution effect cannot be zero.

What about the income effect? Recall that the income effect is $\frac{\Delta X}{\Delta I}|_{relative\ prices\ fixed}$. In this case, what can we say about the income effect? We need to know about how X and real income, I, change as we move from T to V. In Figure 3.2, we can see that as we go from T to V, X increases, so $\Delta X > 0$, and so does the value of I, so $\Delta I > 0$. Hence, we would have the following:

$$\frac{\Delta X}{\Delta I}\bigg|_{relative\ prices\ fixed} = \frac{+}{+} > 0.$$

Is there a similar proposition for the income effect? Sadly, there is not. We will examine what happens when the income effect goes the "wrong" way in a moment. But first we should see how these effects are related to the slope of demand.

Recall that demand is $X = f(P_x, P_y, M,$ and some other factors). To find the slope, we ask: what happens to X if we change P_x by a little? We would denote the slope of demand as $\frac{\Delta X}{\Delta P_x}$. We can see by the equation that if P_x changes, then X must change because X depends on P_x while holding all other variables constant. This change would be exactly the substitution effect, $\frac{\Delta X}{\Delta P_x}|_{real\ income\ fixed}$. We know that there is also an impact on real income (not on money income). As P_x changes, the real income changes; this change would be $\frac{\Delta I}{\Delta P_x}$. The change in real income will also affect X, all else not changing, which would be the income effect, $\frac{\Delta X}{\Delta I}|_{relative\ prices\ fixed}$. These two combined are the entire cause of the change in X, the slope of demand. Hence, we would have the following equation:

$$\frac{\Delta X}{\Delta P_x} = \frac{\Delta X}{\Delta P_x}\bigg|_{real\ income\ fixed} + \frac{\Delta X}{\Delta I}\bigg|_{relative\ prices\ fixed} \times \frac{\Delta I}{\Delta P_x}.$$

In this equation, we have that the slope of demand is the substitution effect plus the income effect times the change in real income due to a change in the price. We will call this equation Slutsky's equation. In the geometry, it is hard to see how large the term $\frac{\Delta I}{\Delta P_x}$ is (measuring how much real income changes when price changes). However, this term is negative (if price rises, real income falls). We will take $\frac{\Delta I}{\Delta P_x}$ to be -1 and put the magnitude of the term in with the income effect. Hence, we would have the following restatement of Slutsky's equation:

Slope of demand = substitution effect − income effect.

The minus sign before the income effect comes because a change in P_x has the opposite effect on real income. In the analysis above, Figure 3.2, we see that the substitution effect was negative and the income effect was positive. We would thus have

$$\underset{(-)}{\text{Slope of demand}} = \underset{(-)}{\text{substitution effect}} - \underset{(+)}{\text{income effect}} \qquad < 0.$$

So the slope of demand should be negative, and it is! In this case, both the income effect and the substitution effect work to make the slope negative. Can we get any other result? The next section will address this question!

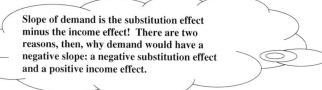

Slope of demand is the substitution effect minus the income effect! There are two reasons, then, why demand would have a negative slope: a negative substitution effect and a positive income effect.

Section Summary:
In this section, we have introduced the construction of the income and substitution effects. We have tied these effects to the slope of demand. We now have an explanation for the negative slope of demand.

3.3   Giffen Goods

One particular case where income and substitution effects can shed some light is the case of the Giffen good. We examine it now.

In Figure 3.3, we have shown the case of a Giffen good. Again, we start with P_x, P_y, and M, draw the budget line, and then have the consumer show their indifference curves representing their preferences and determine the utility-maximizing choice given the budget. At the price P_x, this consumer chooses the bundle W including X_0 units of the good X, which gives us one point on demand. We now allow the price of X to fall to P_x', and the budget line swings out. A new utility maximum is found on the new line, at V, yielding X_0' units of X. Here X_0' is less than X_0, so as the price falls, the consumer chooses less of the good X, yielding an upward-sloping demand! How does this happen?

First note that we have not violated any of the assumptions we have so far made. The BT_W sets are strictly convex and more is preferred to less for all bundles. Thus, the preferences are allowed under our assumptions. To see what happens, again construct the income and substitution effects. Construct the bundle T on I_1 to keep real income the same as at W, and so that T is the tangency (satisfies the utility maximization condition) with a budget line with slope P_x'/P_y so that relative prices are the same as at V. Such a T is shown in Figure 3.3.

The substitution effect is the movement from W to T. Here X increases as P_x falls, holding real income constant, so the substitution effect is negative as before. No surprise there, as proposition 3.6 suggested that this would happen. Now for the income effect, we move from T to V. Here we see that X falls yet real income rises. Therefore, the income effect is negative. Furthermore, the size of the income effect (essentially the distance from X_0'' to X_0') is greater than the substitution effect (essentially the distance from X_0 to X_0''), so the negative income effect outweighs the negative substitution effect, and demand has a positive slope as shown. Check Slutsky's equation:

$$\text{Slope of demand} = \underset{(-)}{\text{substitution effect}} - \underset{(-)}{\text{income effect}} > 0.$$

Definition 3.7: *A good is **inferior** if the income effect is negative.*

Definition 3.8: *A good is **Giffen** if the demand for the good is positively sloped.*

Thus, a Giffen good is a strongly inferior good. You should be aware that no economist is going to base much policy on the possibility of an upward-sloping demand. Yet the theory we have worked so hard to develop does not rule out this possibility. Are there examples of this odd situation?

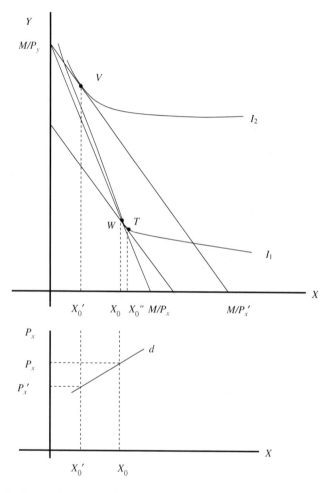

Figure 3.3   In this figure, we show the very odd case of a Giffen good in which the demand slopes upward. Why does this happen? If we examine the income effect, we see that it is negative and larger in magnitude than the substitution effect. Thus, demand has a positive slope in this case. No economist believes that this happens very much, but it is a possibility that the theory does not rule out.

Consider this possibility. Suppose there is a blight on an agricultural good that is the staple of a local diet, say potatoes. The price of potatoes skyrockets as a result. The people of this country, say an island, usually eat a stew of a small piece of meat and a large number of potatoes. When the price of potatoes rises, what do they do? Normally we would think they would buy fewer potatoes and more meat. If they buy more meat, the stew will be smaller, as they will have to give up a lot of potatoes because meat is much more expensive than even the now-higher-priced potatoes. They go to bed hungry! What to do? As an alternative, they buy a little less meat, and add some potatoes to the stew, and go to bed fuller. So the price of potatoes rises, and they eat more potatoes.

Exercise 3. It is possible to have a good that is inferior, but not Giffen. Draw the indifference curves for this case, and isolate the income and substitution effects.

Exercise 4. Write the budget constraint equation ($M = \ldots$). Now find the derivative of the budget constraint with respect to P_x. What did you get? If we think of this as the size of the change in real income when P_x changes, then how could we rewrite the Slutsky equation?

Exercise 5. From about 1955 through 2005, the price of houses rose every year, and yet more houses were purchased than the previous year. Is this evidence that housing is a Giffen good? Does the demand for housing slope upward?

Section Summary:

In this section, we have looked at the case of an upward-sloping demand curve, and the income and substitution effects that go with this case. This is not a case we expect to often find in reality, but does show an alternative not ruled out by theory.

3.4   Elasticity

Generally speaking, we know that the demand curve will have a negative slope. Yet what the theory does not tell us is how negative the slope will be. Sometimes knowing how responsive quantity demanded is to a change in price has important policy implications. For example, suppose that a government wishes to raise revenue by taxing some good. What good should they tax? I am convinced that they should tax zucchini and asparagus (two well-known poisons). Will this allow the government to raise much money? Well, even for consumers who like these goods, if the price rises much, they will simply switch to other vegetables, such as broccoli or peas, and the tax revenues will not rise much. The slope of the demand for zucchini or asparagus is very flat. The government's efforts to raise revenue by taxing asparagus or zucchini will not work. On the other hand, if they tax a good like chocolate, which has few substitutes and whose demand is steeper, they will not reduce the quantity demanded much, and they will gain tax revenue. Clearly the government has an interest in the slope of demand and which goods have a steeper demand. This suggests that the slope of demand is the best choice for answering the question of responsiveness. This section is devoted to finding ways to measure the responsiveness of the quantity demanded to a change in price. Isn't slope of demand exactly the right concept?

If we use the slope of demand to measure responsiveness, then we need to be able to compare the slope of demand for various goods. The question we are asking is, in what units is the slope of demand measured? If the units are the same for all goods, we can compare across goods. If not, we will need another measure of the responsiveness of quantity demanded to a change in price. The slope of demand is the change in the quantity demanded divided by the change in the price. The units will be quantity of the good divided by the price. For gasoline, that would be gallons divided by dollars per gallon. The slope would have units of gallons/($/gallon), which is gallons^2/$. What about zucchini? Zucchini is sold by the pound, so the slope of demand would be pounds/($/pound) or pounds^2/$. Can we compare slope of demand across goods? The answer is pretty clear that we cannot! So what can we do? We turn to a new concept — elasticity.

Definition 3.9: *The **price elasticity of demand** is the percentage change in quantity demanded divided by the percentage change in price; we will use ε to stand for elasticity.*

Note that in the definition, we are moving along demand because the definition says to use the quantity demanded. For a formula, we compute elasticity as follows:

$$\varepsilon = \frac{\frac{\Delta X}{X}}{\frac{\Delta P_x}{P_x}}.$$

Because demand has a negative slope, the change in X is the opposite sign from the change in P_x, so elasticity will be negative. Because the comparison of negative numbers is sometimes confusing, we drop the negative sign or take the absolute value.

Before going on, we need to check to see what units elasticity is in. Will we run into the same problem we had with slope, that we cannot compare the elasticity across goods?

In the numerator, we have the change in X over X. For gasoline, the change in X would be gallons and X would be gallons. The ratio of gallons to gallons is a unit-less number, a pure number. We have the same situation in the denominator, so elasticity is the ratio of a unit-less number to another unit-less number. The result is that elasticity does not have units! Thus, we can compare across goods.

On the other hand, we really want a measure of responsiveness that reflects the slope of demand because we know that the slope is the right measure of responsiveness. How is elasticity related to slope of demand?

$$\varepsilon = \frac{\frac{\Delta X}{X}}{\frac{\Delta P_x}{P_x}} = \frac{\Delta X}{X} \frac{P_x}{\Delta P_x} = \frac{P_x}{X} \frac{\Delta X}{\Delta P_x} = \frac{P_x}{X} \times slope\ of\ demand.$$

Thus, the elasticity is proportional to the slope of demand. This is good, as we know that the slope of demand is what we should use to measure how responsive quantity demanded is to a change in price.

FROM THE LITERATURE

In an urban area, it is often the case that there are several different grocery stores, each with a variety of locations. One question
that would be of interest to these firms is whether the elasticity
of demand varies by store. What implications would that have for
the owner of several stores in a variety of areas? Grocery stores
can keep track of sales by Universal Product Code (UPC) and
thus have sufficient information for researchers to estimate the
elasticity of demand for broad categories of goods. One study
based on such data reports that the elasticity of demand for some
broadly defined goods (bath tissue, canned seafood, bottled juice,
etc.) does depend on the location of the store, reflecting a variety of variables reflecting the makeup of the consumers around
the store location. You can find more details in Stephen Hoch,
Byung-Do Kim, Alan Montgomery, and Peter Rossi, "Determinants of Store-Level Elasticity," *Journal of Marketing Research*,
Vol. 32, No. 1, February, 1995, pp. 17–29.

Proposition 3.10: *If demand is a negatively sloped straight line, then the elasticity falls as quantity rises.*

Proof 3.11: Suppose we have a negatively sloped straight line for demand. Now compute the elasticity at two different points. Because the slope is the same at both points, the elasticity will be determined by the point on the demand where we are. As we move down demand, P_x falls and X rises, so the ratio P_x/X will get smaller (the numerator is getting smaller while the denominator is getting larger, so both act to make the ratio smaller). Hence, elasticity must fall as well.   □

The importance of this proposition is that we now know that the elasticity is likely to change as we move along demand. That is, elasticity is a property of a point on demand, not a property of the demand itself.

> Exercise 6. Suppose that we have a linear demand. Is there a point where the elasticity is exactly one?
>
> Exercise 7. Suppose that we have two linear demands that cross at the point (X^*, P^*). Which of the two demands is more elastic at that point? How do you know?

Now that we have the idea of elasticity, it makes some sense for us to consider what one might make of the idea of a large value for elasticity or a small value. We use the following definition to sort out these ideas.

Definition 3.12: *We say that demand is* **elastic** *if* $\varepsilon > 1$. *We say that demand is* **inelastic** *if* $\varepsilon < 1$. *We say that demand is of* **unitary elasticity** *if* $\varepsilon = 1$.

It looks like the number 1 plays a big role here. What does it mean to say that demand has an elasticity of 1? Because elasticity is the percent change in X divided by the percent change in price, if this ratio is 1, that means the percent change in quantity demanded equals the percent change in price. If elasticity is greater than 1, we know that the percent change in quantity is larger than the percent change in price. Think about this last statement. Quantity demanded changes more than price changes in percentage terms. This suggests that the consumer is responsive to the change in price. If the percent change in quantity were less than the percent change in price, then we would think that the consumer is not very responsive. Can we tell much about what the demand curves might look like in these cases? The answer is no, except in the limiting case, when ε is 0 or infinite. We consider these cases next.

Definition 3.13: *We say that demand is* **infinitely elastic** *if* ε *is infinite.*

In this case, we will have a demand curve that is horizontal. Here price does not change, so the percentage change in price is zero. We have a zero in the denominator, which we will take to give an infinite value for elasticity. We show this case in Figure 3.4.

Definition 3.14: *We say that demand is* **infinitely inelastic** *if* ε *is zero.*

In this case, the percent change in X must be zero. Hence, X cannot change. This makes the demand vertical, as shown in Figure 3.5.

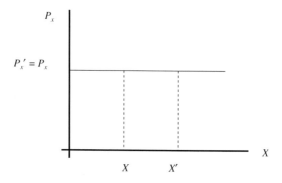

Figure 3.4   Here demand is horizontal so that the price does not change, making the percent change in price equal to zero. Hence, the elasticity will be infinite.

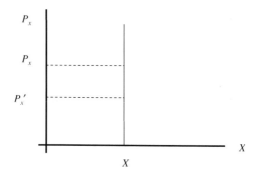

Figure 3.5   Here demand is vertical so that the quantity does not change as price changes, making the percent change in quantity equal to zero. Hence, the elasticity will be zero.

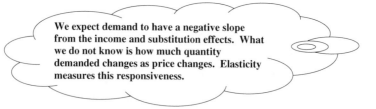

We expect demand to have a negative slope from the income and substitution effects. What we do not know is how much quantity demanded changes as price changes. Elasticity measures this responsiveness.

There is one more characterization of elasticity that will be useful, that is, how expenditure changes as we move along demand. We turn to this proposition now.

Proposition 3.15: *If, as we move down demand, the expenditure on X rises, then demand is elastic.*

Proof 3.16: Let us start by drawing a graph (Figure 3.6) representing the situation, and then re-writing the proposition.

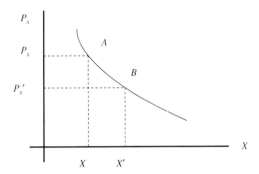

Figure 3.6 We move from *A* to *B* on the demand, and we assume the expenditure rises. That means that the percentage change in *X* is larger than the percentage change in P_X, so demand is elastic.

Expenditure is price times quantity. The proposition we are trying to prove is:

$$\text{If } P'_x X' > P_x X, \quad \text{then } \varepsilon > 1.$$

The elasticity involves percent changes, so we need to identify changes that are occurring in the graph. Let

$$\Delta X = X' - X$$
$$\Delta P_x = P_x - P'_x.$$

Note that we have defined these Δ's so that they are both positive. We can now rewrite these expressions as:

$$P_x = P'_x + \Delta P_x$$
$$X' = X + \Delta X.$$

Now because we have assumed

$$P'_x X' > P_x X,$$

the following must be true:

$$P'_x(X + \Delta X) > (P'_x + \Delta P_x)X.$$

If we multiply these out, we obtain the following:

$$P'_x X + P'_x \Delta X > P'_x X + X \Delta P_x.$$

Cancel the common term to obtain

$$P'_x \Delta X > X \Delta P_x.$$

If we now divide by $P'_x X$, we obtain the following:

$$\frac{\Delta X}{X} > \frac{\Delta P_x}{P'_x}.$$

This expression says that the percentage change in X is greater than the percentage change in price, so $\varepsilon > 1$ must hold, and we are done!   □

"Ok. So you wrote this song and no one will touch it?"
"Yep."
"They'll be sorry!"

Let us look again at the graph associated with this proposition (see Figure 3.7).

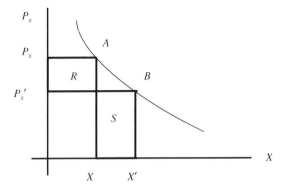

Figure 3.7 The area of R is $X \Delta P_x$ and the area of S is $P'_x \Delta X$. If area S is greater than area R due to the greater expenditure on X, then we see that demand must be elastic. The consumer is more responsive to the change in price.

Because expenditure rises as we move down demand, the area S must be larger than the area R. That means that area $S, P'_x \Delta X$, is greater than area $R, X \Delta P_x$, so the percent change in X must be larger than the percent change in P_x and demand is elastic.

Notice that this characterization is essentially the same as the definition of elasticity. That is, no matter how we turn this proposition around, it will be true. What would have happened if we had moved up demand rather than down? What if expenditure at B had been less than A? In each case, we can deduce something about the elasticity as a result. Furthermore, if we start with an assumption that demand is elastic, we can deduce something about the expenditure as we move along demand. So the proposition goes both ways.

Exercise 8. Suppose that $P_x X$ does not change as we move along demand. What can we say about the elasticity of this demand curve?

Exercise 9. Suppose that the consumer always spends half of their income on X. Write an equation reflecting this fact. Now solve the equation for X to obtain the demand curve. Now what can you say about the elasticity of this demand?

Exercise 10. Suppose that the demand for X is unitarily elastic. Is there any conclusion we can draw about the elasticity of demand for Y?

Exercise 11. Suppose that, as we move up demand, the expenditure on X rises. What can we say about the elasticity of demand?

Exercise 12. Suppose that demand is linear. Will the expenditure on X rise or fall as we move down demand? How do you know?

Section Summary:
We have looked at how elasticity is defined, and how it is related to expenditure on a good.

3.5   Summary

In this chapter, we have looked at topics related to the slope of demand. The important points you should take from this chapter are as follows:

A. We isolated the income and substitution effects.

B. The slope of demand is the substitution effect minus the income effect, which is Slutsky's equation.

C. Price elasticity of demand measures the responsiveness of the quantity demanded to changes in the price.

D. Price elasticity is related to how expenditure on a good changes as we move along demand.

In the next chapter, we turn to the firm and focus on the firm's costs.

Terms Defined:

- Slope of demand
- Same real income
- Ratio of relative prices
- Income effect
- Substitution effect
- Inferior good
- Giffen good
- Price elasticity of demand
- Elastic, inelastic, unitary elasticity
- Infinitely elastic
- Infinitely inelastic

Chapter 4

Moving Toward Profit:
The Firm's Costs

Key Concepts:

- Technology, production function
- Diminishing returns
- Isoquants
- Isocost
- Cost minimization, least cost combination
- Total variable cost
- Total cost
- Average cost
- Marginal cost

Goals:

- Develop ways to represent the technological choices the firm faces.
- Develop the total variable cost curve.
- Find the marginal cost and average total cost.
- Find the relationship between the marginal, average, and total costs.

The previous chapters have been devoted to the consumer's problem and the finding of the individual's demand. It is time to turn to the other side of the market, and look at how firms make decisions and how the supply can be determined. We will start with an overview of the firm's problem and then move on to the determination of the firm's costs.

4.1   Introduction

Suppose that you have a basket-making business which you operate from your garage. In your garage, you have a substantial workspace and the equipment needed to put together baskets. One question you want to answer is: how many baskets do I need to make? As basket making is your livelihood, you want to make as much money as you can. The amount you get to keep is the revenue you bring in above the cost of production. An important part of the determination of your profit as a basket maker (your income) is the cost of production. What determines your cost? What if you add workers? What will happen? We know that the number of baskets produced will rise, but so will the expenses. Will your profit rise as a result? A lot depends on how much costs rise relative to the revenue. A clear understanding of the cost will be important to you, and it is the subject of this chapter.

A firm has the primary objective of making choices that will result in the most profit. Profit is the revenue taken in minus the cost of production. Thus, we will have to talk about the factors that determine the firm's revenue and the factors that determine the firm's cost. We will start by looking at each of these activities to motivate why we examine costs first.

Let us start by looking at the money the firm makes by selling output. We will assume that the firm only produces one output so that the computation of revenue is easy to do; it is just the price of the output times the quantity of output sold. For the moment, imagine that the firm sells each unit for the same price so that each buyer pays the same as any other buyer. The firm's revenue would then be $P \times X$, where P is the price and X is the quantity sold.

Let us consider some different kinds of firms so that we can see what complications can arise. We will consider a firm in each of three different industries: a corn farmer, the local electric company, and a maker of liquid soap. We will start with the corn farmer.

What can the corn farmer control? While the following description of what the farmer does is not accurate, it does give a feel for the decisions the farmer must make. In the spring, the farmer decides how much corn to plant as well as the amount of other crops. When the farmer harvests the crops in the fall, the farmer then sells the corn for whatever the market will bear. Note that the farmer does not have a say in what the price will be. Even if the farmer won a prize at the county fair for his corn, he cannot charge a higher price for it than the market offers. No one, faced with a taste test, could distinguish one farmer's corn from another. There is no basis for a higher price for one corn than another.[1] Thus, the farmer has some control over the amount of corn produced (though nature obviously plays a role here), but not over the price. This means that the amount of revenue that the farmer generates is simply the market price times the quantity produced. If the farmer increases or decreases the amount of corn produced, his revenue will rise or fall, but the revenue of no other farmer will change. If this farmer could somehow affect the price of corn by the amount of corn he grew, then it would be different; changes in this farmer's output (and therefore revenue) would have an impact on the revenue that other farmers generate. But as it stands, if no one farmer can affect the price, the revenue of one farmer is independent of the amount of revenue other farmers make. This is an important point because it allows us to then consider each farmer independently, an easier task.

What happens in the case of the local electric company? Let us suppose, for the sake of argument, that there is only one local electric company and that the consumer buying electricity can only go to that one source. In this case, the firm chooses the price and the consumer chooses the quantity to purchase. Note how much different this case is from the case of the corn farmer. Here the electric company chooses the price, not the quantity — exactly the opposite of the farmer. Now because there is no other firm in the market, this firm stands alone and need not consider how other firms will behave. Again, the total revenue

---

[1] It is clear that if a farmer produces organic products, he may be able to charge more for the organic product. But the farmer still has to accept the market price for the organic product, and cannot charge more than the organic market price.

is the price times the quantity of electricity sold. One firm's revenue does not depend on what other firms do, as there are no other firms. Again, we can consider this firm by itself without worrying about other firms.

Consider now the firm making liquid soap. There are lots of firms making liquid soap. What distinguishes my liquid soap from yours? As a manufacturer of liquid soap, I will try to find a way to distinguish my soap from others by the scent that I offer, the purity of my product, the skin softeners, the price, and by other means. I want you to think that my product is superior in some way so that you will buy it. And of course I have to worry about the price that other firms will charge. If some other firm puts its product on sale, I know that it will affect their revenue, but it will also affect my revenue as some of my less-than-loyal customers will switch to the other brand. Thus, my revenue will fall. In this case, what other firms do will affect their revenue, but more importantly my revenue too. So we cannot ignore how the firms interact. If the other firm puts its product on sale, I can respond by putting my product on sale or I can offer combinations of my soap together with a toothpaste I also produce. This will affect my revenue and also the revenue of the other firm. Our revenues are interrelated, and in our efforts to determine the quantity the firm will produce at each price, we need to take into consideration how the firms interact. This makes the problem a whole lot more complicated!

This latter case makes the general computation of a firm's revenue messy. It may make sense to look at cost and see how much different the cost computation is for these firms. Maybe it will make sense to develop a theory of cost first.

For the corn farmer, once the farmer knows the number of acres of corn to plant, the costs are pretty clear. The cost includes seed, fertilizer, herbicide, insecticide, land rent, capital cost, fuel for the tractor and harvester, possibly some cost to dry the grain, insurance, implicit cost of labor, and probably a few other items. For the electric company, there is the cost of fuel to produce electricity, capital cost, labor cost, insurance, land rent, and a variety of other expenses. Similarly, for the liquid soap firm, the costs consist of the cost of raw materials, labor, capital, land, insurance, utilities, advertising, and some other costs. Note that neither the corn farmer nor the electric company has advertising costs.

In any case, the process of finding the cost seems to be remarkably similar for all of these firms. Hence, we will first examine how to find the cost for the firm. We will assume that the process of finding cost is the same for all firms. Once we understand cost, then we will turn our attention to revenue and deal with the three different firms one at a time.

Section Summary:
In this section, we have looked at three different firms. We concluded that for two of the firms, the corn farmer and the electric company, the revenue of one firm is related to the revenue of no other firm. The revenue of these firms is independent of the revenue of other firms. For the liquid soap maker, the revenue of one firm is related to the revenue of other liquid soap makers. These firms are interdependent. In the case of the corn farmer or the electric company, we can treat each firm separately, at least on the revenue side. But for the liquid soap maker, we cannot consider one firm without seeing how the other firm interacts. These firms must be considered at the same time. On the cost side, we argued that the firms are remarkably similar in their cost computations, and so we could have one model for cost that would serve all of the firms. Thus, we will start by looking at the firm's cost as it will be the same regardless of whether we have firms like corn farmers or electric companies, or liquid soap makers.

4.2   Assumptions for the Firm

As in the case of the consumer, there are some blanket assumptions that will be applied to our consideration of all firms. It would be good to have a look at these assumptions, and talk a bit about what restrictions they impose and how the assumptions could be changed to be more realistic.

Assumptions 4.1:
a. *The firm produces one output, $X \geq 0$.*
b. *The firm uses two variable inputs, labor, $L \geq 0$, and capital, $K \geq 0$.*
c. *There is a fixed factor (this is a short-run analysis).*

d. *The inputs and output are infinitely divisible.*
e. *The firm is given the input prices, w (wage) for labor, w > 0, and r (rental rate) for capital, r > 0. The firm cannot affect the input prices by its own effort.*
f. *The technology for producing the output is known and does not change.*
g. *There are no externalities.*

Let us look at these assumptions to see what is ruled out. Surely there are very few firms that produce only one good. In fact we can build models where the firm produces more than one good, but again, more mathematics will be needed. While this assumption is somewhat restrictive, the main results we will obtain will apply to a large extent to firms producing more than one output. Similarly, the assumption of two variable inputs is overly restrictive, but we lose little from this assumption and gain some geometrical opportunities.

We now turn to assumption c. The short run implies that there is a fixed factor, some factor that cannot change over some period of time. The factor takes time to change. To be concrete, we will assume that the fixed factor is the physical size of the building in which the production occurs. We will call this the scale of plant, and we will assume that it does not change in the short run. We will examine the long run, when all factors are variable, in Chapter 9.

In assumption d, we are assuming that inputs and output are infinitely divisible. We have seen a similar assumption in the case of the consumer, and we will make the same argument here. For a machine, where the problem most obviously arises, we will think of the machine as having a stream of services that we can purchase in units as small as we like either by renting the machine or by buying the machine and then selling it in the used machine market when we are done. While neither of these is perfectly true, this will allow us to work with the model in some semblance of reality.

Assumption e says that the firm is given input prices and cannot change them. There are several aspects of this assumption that are important. The first is that the firm knows the prices of inputs. That is, there is no need to search for the information or to have to pay to acquire the prices of inputs. Second, there is a certainty here in that the firm is not uncertain about what the prices of inputs might be.

Thus, if we were to extend this model to production today and tomorrow, the firm would know its input prices with certainty in the future. If wages are bargained, then the firm may know labor prices in the future, but capital prices or the prices of raw materials would likely be unknown. Of course, for raw materials, firms could buy them in futures markets to overcome some of the price uncertainty. Still, when dealing with the future, uncertainty is likely to occur. Finally, this assumption says that the firm cannot affect the input prices. This last statement is a bit of a concern. Generally, we would think that the firm does have something to say about the prices of inputs, especially labor. At the very least, we expect that there is some negotiation that goes on over wages and working conditions. There are models that include such features, but they are more complicated than this one, and are built on the model we present here. Therefore, we will maintain this assumption even though we know it does not adequately reflect reality.

Assumption f is about what the firm knows in terms of production processes. Suppose we think of the technology as being a set of recipes for making the good. In almost every case, there is more than one way to produce a good. If we are making cement, we can do it in small batches where each worker makes some cement in a wheelbarrow, or in large batches where we use a cement mixer and one worker. The first way is a labor-intensive way and the second is a capital-intensive way. But no matter the good, we assume that the firm knows all of the possible recipes and that no new recipes are added to the file during the production period. The technology does not change.

Finally, we assume that there are no externalities. In this case, we mean that the costs of one firm are not affected by the production of another firm. Suppose, for example, that in the production of bottled water, the bottled water plant is downstream from a brand new purple dye manufacturer. Some of the purple is a waste product dumped into the stream where the bottled water plant gets its water. The cost of production for the bottled water firm is affected by the production of the dye. This kind of situation we wish to rule out for now. There is a substantial literature on what happens in the presence of externalities, so this assumption has been relaxed and the analysis extended in that direction.

> **Section Summary:**
> So far we have examined the assumptions we will employ for the analysis of the firm. It is time for us to begin to develop our model of costs. We start with the technology.

4.3   Representing the Firm's Technology — Isoquants

In this chapter, we will develop the firm's short-run cost curves. These curves will apply to all of the firms we will study, regardless of whether the firm is like the corn farmer, the electric company, or the liquid soap producer. The problem the firm faces is to find the cost of production at each output. There are two main elements of cost. One is the cost of the inputs needed to produce the good, and the other is the technology for producing the good. Once we have these elements, we can generate the firm's costs. We will start by looking at the technology. Suppose that we start by choosing a level of output to produce. The problem is that once we have a quantity of output to produce, there are a variety of ways, different recipes, that the firm could use to generate that output. Thus, the firm must choose which recipe, which combination of labor and capital, to use to produce the output. We assume that the choice will be so that at each output, the expenditure on variable inputs will be as small as possible. That is where the input prices come in. To begin the process, we need to develop a way to represent the recipes, the technology, that the firm has. That is the focus of this section. We start (as always) with some definitions.

Definition 4.2: *An **input combination** is a quantity of labor and a quantity of capital. We denote the input combination as an ordered pair,* (L, K).

This is a concept similar to a commodity bundle and will play the same role for the firm.

Definition 4.3: *The **production function** tells the maximum output that can be produced at each input combination.*

The production function, then, represents the technology. At each input combination, the firm knows how much output can be produced by each possible recipe. If there are two different recipes using the same combination of inputs but producing two different levels of output, only one of the recipes will be included in our information (at that input combination): the recipe producing the greater output. Thus, for each combination of labor and capital, we have a corresponding quantity of output. We can write the production function as $X = f(L, K)$. We have the expectation that as we increase the amounts of the variable inputs, output will also increase at least up to the point of the capacity of the firm. We can draw the graph of the technology, the production function, as shown in Figure 4.1. The graph has three dimensions. One axis, the vertical axis, is for output, X or $f(L, K)$. The other two axes, which form the floor of the graph, are for labor, L, and capital, K.

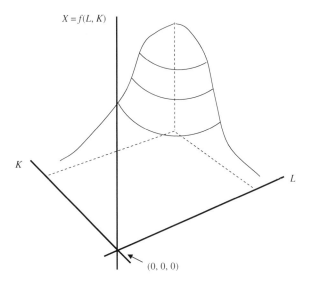

Figure 4.1 In this graph, we have a three-dimensional picture with L and K in the base of the graph and output, $X = f(L, K)$, on the vertical axis. The production function is shown as a mountain that rises up from the origin.

We would like to be able to find a way to represent the technology without having to draw a three-dimensional graph. How can we do this? We shall proceed as follows.

Definition 4.4: *The X_0 isoquant is all combinations of L and K that produce X_0 units of output.*

The word "isoquant" is not one you will find in the dictionary. It is made up by using a Greek prefix, *iso-*, meaning "equal," with the suffix, *-quant*, meaning "quantity." Thus, isoquant means same quantity — exactly what it is! We will set out to find an isoquant. Then observe that we can find an isoquant for each possible quantity of output, and we will have a two-dimensional representation of the technology. How can we find an isoquant?

First, we choose a level of output, X_0. We then measure up the vertical axis X_0 units. We then construct a plane parallel to the floor exactly X_0 units off the floor. This plane will slice the mountain along a curve. We then project the curve into the floor, the (L, K) plane. The projection will be the isoquant corresponding to X_0 level of output, the X_0 output isoquant. Have a look at Figure 4.2.

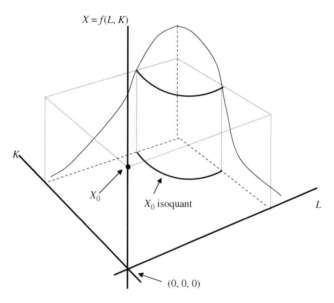

Figure 4.2   In this graph, we build on Figure 4.1 and slice the production function X_0 units from the floor. We hold output constant and then find the combinations of L and K that produce that output, the X_0 isoquant, which is found in the (L, K) plane.

So now if we draw the two-dimensional version of this graph on the (L, K) axis system, we would get the graph as shown in Figure 4.3.

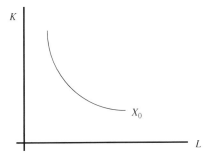

Figure 4.3   In this graph, we show the X_0 isoquant in the plane with L on the horizontal axis and K on the vertical axis. This isoquant represents all combinations of L and K that produce exactly X_0 units of output.

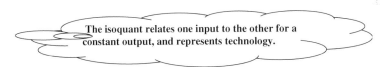

The isoquant relates one input to the other for a constant output, and represents technology.

Now as the output changes, we will generate more and more iso-quants. Note that every input combination will end up on some iso-quant. After all, each input combination will produce some amount of output. Notice too that as we increase both inputs, we will increase out-put.[2] Furthermore, isoquants cannot cross. If they did cross, it would suggest that one input combination could produce two different levels of output. But one of the two levels would be larger, and the smaller one would not be a usable recipe. As long as more of both inputs means more output, we cannot have isoquants cross. You can prove this by contrapositive.

> Exercise 1. Prove that if more inputs produce more output, then isoquants cannot cross.

---

[2] Of course, if there is a capacity constraint, then at some point, we will not be able to increase output regardless of how many more inputs we add.

Definition 4.5: *We say a firm is* **technologically efficient** *if they are producing on their production function.*

What we have in mind with this definition is that a firm does not use an input combination to produce output, and then somehow throw away some of that output. Thus, if the firm chooses an input combination on a given isoquant and produces that output, it is technologically efficient.

Section Summary:
We now have a two-dimensional representation of the technology: the family of isoquants. Each isoquant shows the combinations of inputs that produce the same level of output. There is a curve for each level of output, and every input combination is on some isoquant. We will use isoquants in our derivation of the total variable cost for the firm. There is another two-dimensional representation of technology, total product, and we explore this next.

4.4   Representing the Firm's Technology — Total Product

There is another way for us to generate a two-dimensional representation of technology. We can slice the production function parallel to either the L- or K-axis. We provide the definitions and construction for these curves now, even though we will not be using these concepts until Chapter 10.

Definition 4.6: *Total product is a relationship between a variable input and output, and shows the output that can be produced at each quantity of the variable input with the other variable input held fixed. We denote total product of the variable input L when K is held fixed at K_0 as* $TP_L(K = K_0)$.

We carry out this construction now. So suppose we hold $K = K_0$ and slice the production function along that line (parallel to the

(L, X) wall). That slice is the total product of labor when $K = K_0$ (see Figure 4.4).

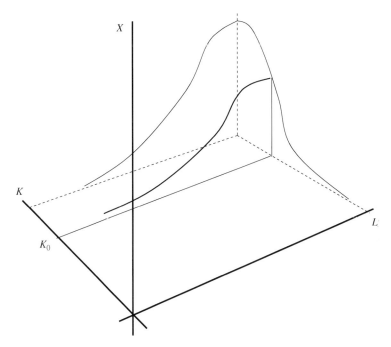

Figure 4.4   In this graph, we slice the production function parallel to the (L, X) plane exactly K_0 units from the L-axis. That slice is the total product of labor when $K = K_0$.

Exercise 2. Derive the total product of capital by choosing a level of labor, L_0, and hold L at that level to find the total product of capital, $TP_K(L = L_0)$.

We can draw the two-dimensional graph showing the total product (see Figure 4.5). Note that we will get a total product of labor for each quantity of capital, so that the total product curves are also a representation of the production function and tell us the technology.

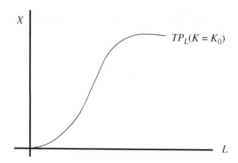

Figure 4.5   In this graph, we show the total product of labor when $K = K_0$. The subscript on TP tells us the input that varies, and $K = K_0$ tells us that capital is constant at K_0.

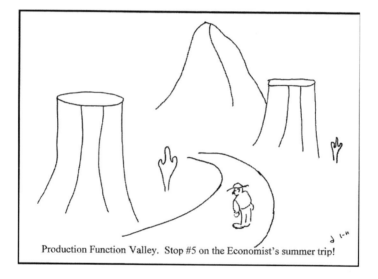

Production Function Valley. Stop #5 on the Economist's summer trip!

There is one more concept we can provide for which we will have a use, the marginal product. Here is the definition.

Definition 4.7: *The **marginal product** of a variable input is a relationship between a variable input and output showing the change in output due to a change in the variable input with all other inputs held fixed. We denote the marginal product by MP_L when L is the variable input.*

We can use the following formula to help us see what the marginal product is.

$$MP_L = \frac{\Delta X}{\Delta L}.$$

It is also true that MP_L is the slope of the production function when we hold K constant. What shape do we expect the marginal product to have?

Definition 4.8: *The* **Law of Diminishing Returns** *states that the marginal product may at first rise, but it must eventually fall.*

Note that the law is about the marginal product. Therefore, all inputs except one are held fixed. It is the fixed factor that causes the law to be true. In short, with only one variable factor, say labor, but fixed capital, as we increase labor, we are spreading the capital over more and more units of labor so that the impact is to reduce the productivity of the labor. This law seems to be empirically driven, and is widely assumed.

We can also use the marginal product to find the slope of the isoquant. Suppose that we start at a point on a specific isoquant, say the isoquant representing ten units of output. So we are using (L_1, K_1) to produce 10 units of output. Now decrease the capital by ΔK units. Output falls by $MP_K \times \Delta K$. Why is this? Capital changes by ΔK. Each unit of capital changes output by MP_K. Hence, $MP_K \times \Delta K$ is the change in output due to a change in K of ΔK.

$$\Delta Q = -MP_K \times \Delta K.$$

The negative in the above equation is due to output falling. Now we need to change L by enough to make output rise by exactly enough to get back to 10 units of output. Thus, we need $\Delta Q = MP_L \times \Delta L$. The two ΔQ's must be the same, so we have the following:

$$MP_L \times \Delta L = -MP_K \times \Delta K.$$

If we solve for $\Delta K/\Delta L$, we would have the slope of the isoquant (think of ΔK being the rise and ΔL being the run). Here is what we get for the slope:

$$\frac{\Delta K}{\Delta L} = \frac{-MP_L}{MP_K}.$$

This is a useful fact we will have use for later.

Section Summary:
We now have a second graphical representation of the technology: total product. We then found the marginal product and found that the shape of the marginal product is determined by diminishing returns. We also found that the slope of the isoquant is the (negative of the) ratio of marginal products. We will use these concepts in Chapter 10 when we come to demand for inputs. We return to finding cost; we need one more concept, some way to determine the input combination the firm would choose at any given output, and the associated variable cost.

FROM THE LITERATURE

There is a market for organic milk, which is produced by a technology that is similar to the technology for standard milk. Is there any difference between the two technologies and, if so, what does that tell us about the cost of production for these dairies? One might also wonder if there is any difference in efficiency between the two kinds of dairies. Here, efficiency means that the firm is operating at the least cost to produce output. It turns out that according to one study, there is a difference in the technologies, and the conventional dairy farms are more efficient, but within organic farms there is little difference in efficiency. You can find this article at: Carlos Mayén, Joseph Balagtas, and Corinne Alexander, "Technological Adoption and Technical Efficiency: Organic and Conventional Dairy Farms in the United States," *American Journal of Agricultural Economics*, Vol. 92, No. 1, 2009, pp. 181–195.

4.5   The Least Cost Combination Proposition

In this section, we will state and prove the primary proposition needed to find the firm's costs. To start the process, we will need to define the concept for which we are looking: total variable cost. Once we have that, and the proposition we state and prove in this section, we can then look at how to find total variable cost in the next section.

Definition 4.9: *The **total variable cost** (TVC) is a relationship between output and dollars showing the minimum expenditure on variable inputs for each level of output with input prices and technology not changing.*

What we need to find for each output is the input combination that will cost the least. How do we find the expenditure on an input combination? Well, we know the input prices, so we can find how much each bundle costs. For the moment, let E stand for the expenditure on the variable inputs:

$$E = wL + rK.$$

The firm spends wL on labor (the wage of w for each of L units of labor) and rK on capital (the rental rate of r for each of K units of capital). Based on this computation, we have the following definition.

Definition 4.10: *The **isocost** is all combinations of L and K that cost exactly E dollars.*

This concept is similar to the budget line. Again, the prefix *iso-* means "equal" and the suffix *-cost* means, well, cost! So the isocost is the combinations of inputs that have the same cost. For given values of E, we can easily compute the L- and K-intercepts. Because the wage and rental rate are constant to the firm, and E is taken as a constant, the isocost will be a straight line with a negative slope. We show this in Figure 4.6.

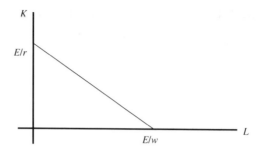

Figure 4.6 This graph shows the isocost line, all combinations of L and K that cost exactly E dollars.

Exercise 3. How do we know that the isocost is a straight line? Check to see that the intercepts given in Figure 4.6 are correct. Now, what would happen to the isocost if w were to fall? What if E were to get larger?

We can now combine the technology, the isoquants, with the isocost to determine the combination of L and K that the firm would choose to produce a given level of output. Suppose that we start with a level of output X_0. We know there is an isoquant representing that level of output. Now suppose that the firm has E dollars to spend on variable inputs. Draw in the associated isocost. Suppose that the outcome is as shown in Figure 4.7.

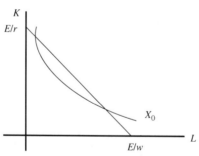

Figure 4.7 In this figure, we have the X_0 isoquant and the E isocost. Is E the smallest amount of money the firm can spend to produce X_0?

Can the firm produce X_0 with fewer than E dollars spent on variable inputs? How do we know? Well, if we pull the isocost in parallel to itself, the value of E, expenditure on variable inputs, will be smaller. Hence, we can reduce expenditure on variable inputs. Where will the minimum expenditure isocost be for the X_0 isoquant? The following proposition provides the answer.

Proposition 4.11: Least Cost Combination

If   a.   *assumptions* 4.1 *hold,*

  b.   *the firm has isoquants that are differentiable,*

  c.   *the set of bundles producing at least X units of output is strictly convex for each X,*

  d.   *the expenditure on variable inputs to produce X_0 units of output is minimum at (L_0, K_0) with $L_0 > 0$ and $K_0 > 0$,*

Then   e.   *at (L_0, K_0) there is an isocost tangent to the X_0 isoquant.*

Before proving this proposition, let us have a look at it. It should remind you of the utility maximization proposition 2.21. The two are very similar, but with some important differences. First, for utility maximization, we have a maximum problem; for least cost, we have a minimum problem. Second, in utility maximization, we have an added conclusion that we are on the budget line. Here we seem to get that part of the conclusion free (as you will see, we construct the isocost through the chosen point). But the same differentiability and convexity requirements hold for both propositions. Let us look a bit more closely at the first difference — the maximum vs. the minimum.

In utility maximum, the objective is utility, the curved lines in the graph. The constraint is the budget, which we hold fixed. In the case of least cost, the isocost, a sort of budget, is the objective, while the curved line, the output or isoquant, is held fixed. Hence, we have reversed the roles of the objective and constraint in the two problems. This suggests that we could probably do the least cost problem as a maximum problem. How can we state it?

If we see the least cost as saying roughly "if expenditure on variable inputs to produce X_0 is minimum, then the isocost and isoquant are tangent," then we would restate it as a maximum as "if output is maximum given a level of expenditure on variable inputs, then the isoquant and isocost must be tangent." In the language of mathematics, these problems are dual problems. To solve one essentially solves the other. Why did we state the cost problem as a minimum while utility was a maximum?

There is a natural reason for the cost proposition to be a minimum; we will use the proposition to find total variable cost, which is defined (see definition 4.9) as the <u>least</u> expenditure on variable inputs at each output. So we need a <u>minimum</u> cost proposition to find TVC. For demand, the primary point of utility maximization — to assume that the consumer maximizes satisfaction given the budget — seems a bit more natural than to assume that the consumer minimizes expenditure to achieve a given level of satisfaction. So we have before us a proposition about minimizing expenditure on variable inputs. How do we prove it?

You can anticipate the response! We will use the contrapositive. Basically, the contrapositive will say that if the isocost is not tangent to the isoquant and if statements a, b, and c in proposition 4.11 are true, then the expenditure on variable inputs is not minimum. Here we go!

Proof 4.12: Look at Figure 4.8. Choose a point on the X_0 isoquant, (L_0, K_0). Now construct the isocost through (L_0, K_0) and assume, for the contrapositive, that the isocost is not tangent to the isoquant at that point. Then there are combinations of L and K that cost less than (L_0, K_0) and still produce X_0. Hence, the expenditure on variable inputs is not minimum at (L_0, K_0). □

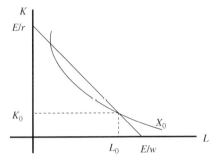

Figure 4.8   In this figure, we have the X_0 isoquant and the E isocost. We have constructed the isocost through (L_0, K_0) and it is not tangent to the X_0 isoquant. Is expenditure on variable inputs minimum at (L_0, K_0)?

Exercise 4.   In Figure 4.8, identify the input combinations that cost less than (L_0, K_0) and yet still produce X_0 output.

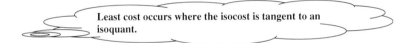

Least cost occurs where the isocost is tangent to an isoquant.

It should be clear to you that a firm that minimizes cost will end up on its production function and will therefore be technologically efficient. Because we assume cost minimization for all firms, all firms satisfy this condition.

We are now ready to find the total variable cost.

Section Summary:
In this section, we have stated and proved the least cost combination proposition. This will be the main workhorse for our development of the TVC, which we do in the next section.

4.6   Finding Total Variable Cost and Total Cost

In this section, we will use the least cost combination proposition to find total variable cost. Once we have TVC, we can then find total cost. We start with the steps we need to use to find TVC. You will want to refer to Figure 4.9 as we go through the steps, where you will also see the step numbers in square boxes.

To find total variable cost:

1	Choose a level of output, X_1, and draw the X_1 isoquant in the upper graph of Figure 4.9. Also mark X_1 on the horizontal axis of the TVC graph, the lower graph in Figure 4.9.
2	Given w and r, and using the least cost combination proposition 4.11, find the combination of L and K that provides the minimum expenditure on variable inputs. Call that input combination (L_1, K_1).
3	Compute the expenditure, E_1, on variable inputs for that output, namely $E_1 = wL_1 + rK_1$. Mark that expenditure on the vertical axis of the TVC graph.
4	Choose a new, higher level of output, X_2. Draw the X_2 isoquant in the upper graph of Figure 4.9.
5	Given the same w and r, and using proposition 4.11, find the input combination that minimizes expenditure on variable inputs, (L_2, K_2).
6	Compute the expenditure $E_2 = wL_2 + rK_2$, and mark that expenditure on the vertical axis of the TVC graph.
7	Continue this process for all possible outputs to obtain the total variable cost curve.

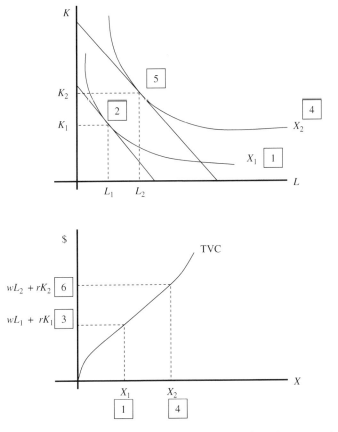

Figure 4.9 Here we find the cost-minimizing input combinations at each output (in the top graph), and transfer the output and the corresponding minimum cost for variable inputs to the bottom graph to obtain TVC.

You no doubt have some questions. For example, you might wonder how we know where X_1 goes on the horizontal axis of the TVC graph. Well, we cannot know exactly where it goes. What matters is that we know $X_2 > X_1$, so X_2 should be to the right of X_1 on the axis. We do not know how far apart they are. Similarly, we do not know exactly where to put $wL_1 + rK_1$ or the second expenditure on the vertical axis of the TVC graph. We know that the second expenditure is greater than the first, but we do not know how much more. Finally, note that the TVC goes through the origin. That is because if we produce zero output, we need no variable inputs.

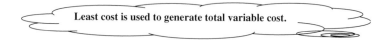

Least cost is used to generate total variable cost.

Exercise 5. Consider the graph given below. How do we know that $wL_2 + rK_2$ is less than $wL_1 + rK_1$? Observe that $L_2 > L_1$ while $K_2 < K_1$. How can we know for sure which input combination costs more?

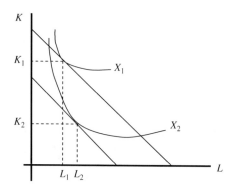

You might wonder why the TVC has the shape that it does. Suppose that we start at a given combination of variable inputs, which generates a level of output, X_0, and some amount of cost. This gives us one point on TVC. Now double the inputs. The cost will double. But what happens to the output? If output more than doubles, we can see that the TVC curve will rise, but not as fast as in the case where output exactly doubles. Once we are past the point where this large increase in output plays a role, the TVC will start to grow faster as a doubling of the variable inputs, and therefore double cost, will not increase output as fast as in the double-output case.

As you might suspect, the variable costs are not all the costs the firm faces. As we pointed out in assumptions 4.1, we are in the short run; there is a fixed factor. That fixed factor is not free. So there are some costs associated with that fixed factor: the fixed costs.

Exercise 6. Suppose that $w = 2$ and $r = 1$. Draw an isocost in the graph below (HINT: choose some level of cost and then graph the isocost for that level of cost). Now find the least cost combination for each of the levels of output shown, and draw the TVC on a graph with X on the horizontal axis and $ on the vertical axis.

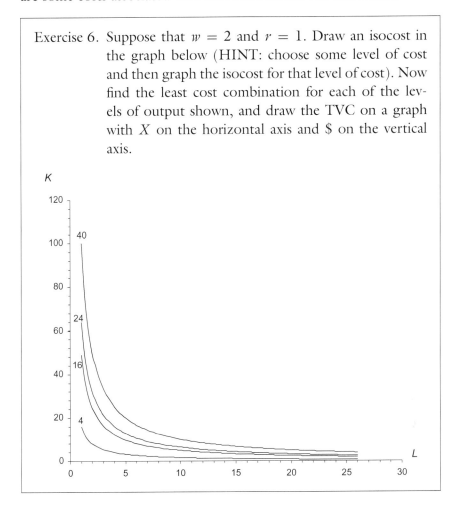

Definition 4.13: *Total fixed cost* (TFC *or* FC) *is a relationship between output and dollars showing the cost of the fixed factors at each output.*

Because the factors are fixed, that is, they do not change as the amount of output changes, the total fixed cost will also be constant as shown in Figure 4.10.

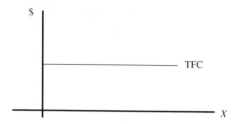

Figure 4.10   In this graph, we show the total fixed cost (TFC). These are costs that do not change as output changes.

We can now move on to find the total cost, whose definition is given next.

Definition 4.14: *Total cost* (TC) *is a relationship between output and dollars showing the sum of total fixed cost and total variable cost at each output.*

This definition provides explicit instructions for finding TC. We simply add the TFC to the TVC at each output. The details are shown in Figure 4.11.

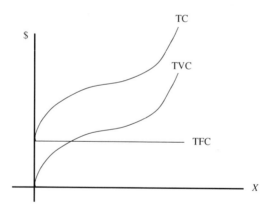

Figure 4.11   At each output, we add the TFC to the TVC to get TC. Thus, TC is parallel to TVC and is exactly TFC units higher than TVC.

Before going on, we should point out one component of total cost that we have so far ignored: a normal amount of profit. In some way, when the firm owner comes to work, the firm owner brings with him or her some capital, both physical capital as well as human capital. These might be inputs that seem to be free to the firm. But the firm has to pay for them or the owner will move them to another, more fruitful line of work. Thus, we include the cost of the owner-owned resources and include a normal profit or return in the cost of the firm. When our graphs show a zero profit, the firm is still making a normal return, the return equal to the return it could make in its best alternative.

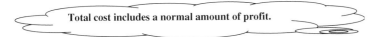

Total cost includes a normal amount of profit.

> **Section Summary:**
> In this section, we have used the least cost combination proposition (4.11) to derive the total variable cost (4.9). By adding the total fixed cost, which is given to us, we find the total cost. These are important concepts for profit. But there are some other forms of these costs that will be useful. We turn to them now.

4.7   Average and Marginal Cost

In this section, we will discover geometrical ways to find the average and marginal costs from the total cost. The methods can be used more generally to find average and marginal from a total. We start with some definitions.

Definition 4.15: *The **average total cost** (ATC) is a relationship between output and dollars per unit of output showing the total cost per unit of output at each output.*

This definition tells us to put output on the horizontal axis and dollars per unit of output on the vertical axis. Then at each output, we find the total cost and divide it by that output to get the ATC. We can represent this computation[3] as

$$ATC(X_1) = TC(X_1)/X_1.$$

---

[3]We will start using functional notation more regularly. When you see $ATC(X)$, you will know that ATC is a function of X. When you see $ATC(X_1)$, we mean the value of ATC when $X = X_1$, the value of the function when $X = X_1$.

How can we do this geometrically? Consider the graph in Figure 4.12. Choose an output, X_1, and find, in the upper graph, TC at X_1 or $TC(X_1)$. Now draw a straight line from the origin to the point $(X_1, TC(X_1))$. What is the slope of that straight line? The slope is rise over run. The rise is exactly $TC(X_1)$. The run is exactly X_1. The slope is the ratio of those two numbers, which is ATC at X_1.

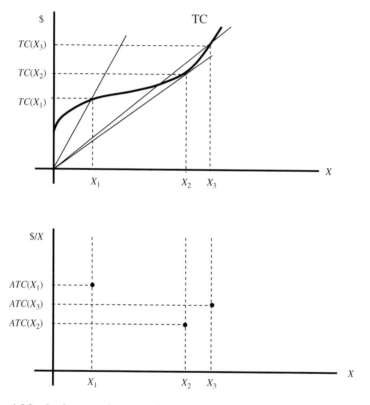

Figure 4.12   In these graphs, we see how to derive the average from the total. We take a straight line from the origin to the curve, and the slope of that line is the average at the corresponding X value.

At this moment, we do not know the magnitude of ATC at X_1. We will simply mark that point on the vertical axis of the lower graph to provide one point on the graph of ATC. How do we get another point? We repeat the process! Pick another output, find the TC at that output, draw a straight line from the origin to that point on the TC curve, and the slope of that straight line is the ATC at that output. We show the outcome with two other outputs (X_2 and X_3) in Figure 4.12.

What we see from Figure 4.12 is that $ATC(X_2)$ is lower than $ATC(X_1)$, and that $ATC(X_3)$ is above $ATC(X_2)$ but below $ATC(X_1)$. Thus, the ATC will be U-shaped.

Obviously, the shape of the ATC will depend on the shape of the TC. A differently shaped TC will yield a differently shaped ATC. But if the TC has the general shape we show above, then the ATC will have the general shape we have derived here. Does it matter where we put the first point for ATC? Given that we primarily care about the relative position of the points on ATC, the exact placement of the first point is not of very much importance. What about that other curve, the marginal cost?

Definition 4.16: *The **marginal cost** (MC) is a relationship between output and dollars per unit of output showing the change in total cost due to a change in output at each level of output.*

There are several ways of thinking about MC that may be useful to us at various points in time. If we think about discrete changes in output, then we might think of MC as

$$MC = \frac{\Delta TC}{\Delta X}.$$

An alternative way to proceed is to think of MC as the slope (or derivative) of TC. This is the point of view we will take now. Consider the graph in Figure 4.13.

Again, in the top graph, we have the total cost and we have identified three different levels of output, X_1, X_2, and X_3. We will find the MC at each output and mark that MC on the graph below. To find the MC, we need to find the slope. To do that, we will take the straight line tangent to the curve at each of the identified outputs. What do we find? In our graph, it appears that the marginal is positively sloped, but this may be due to not finding the marginal at enough points. In any case, we now need to ask how the average and marginal are related. Again we turn to a graph (Figure 4.14)!

In this graph, start at X_1. We find the average as the slope of the line from the origin, labeled A_1. To find the marginal at X_1, we find the slope of the TC curve at X_1, which is the slope of the line M_1. We see that A_1 is steeper than M_1, so the average is larger than the marginal at X_1. We show this on the bottom graph of Figure 4.14. Again, we cannot know how much more the average is than the marginal.

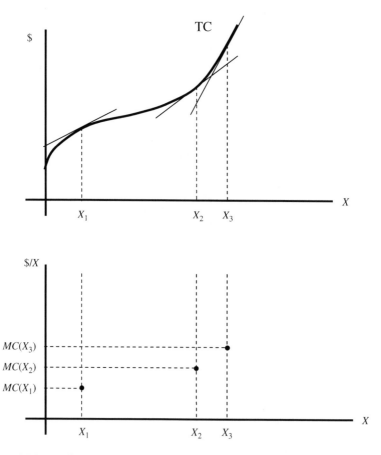

Figure 4.13   In these graphs, we see how to derive the marginal from the total. We take the slope of total at each output, and the slope is the marginal at that X value.

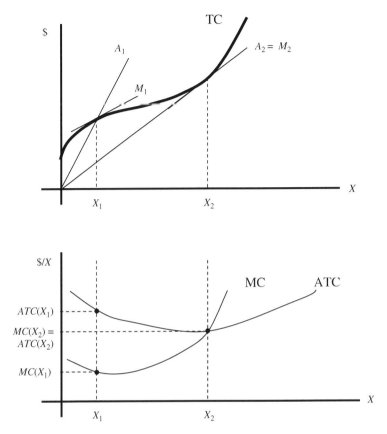

Figure 4.14 In these graphs, we combine the derivation of the marginal with the derivation of the average. We are able to see the relationship between the two in the lower graph.

Now at X_2, we do the same. What do we find? At X_2, the slope of the line from the origin, A_2, is the same as the slope of the curve, the slope of M_2. Hence, the average and the marginal are the same at X_2. We also see that the average at X_2 is less than the average at X_1 (A_1 is steeper than A_2). And the marginal at X_2 is greater than the marginal at X_1 (M_2 is steeper than M_1). What happens as output goes up from X_2? You should see that both the average and the marginal are getting bigger. But you should also see that the slope of the curve, the marginal, becomes larger than the slope of the line from the origin, the average, so the marginal will lie above the average once X is larger than X_2.

Two ways of thinking about MC:
1.   slope of TC (or TVC); and
2.   change in TC when output changes by one unit.

Frankly, the spaghetti reminds me of cost curves from my econ class.

Exercise 7. Go back to the total product curve in Figure 4.5 and find MP from TP using the geometrical tools developed for MC. Suppose MP falls. Must TP also fall? How do you know?

Exercise 8. Suppose that we know that the MC falls as X rises. What does the falling MC tell us about the TC?

Exercise 9. Suppose that the MC is constant and the TFC is zero. What will TC look like then? What if the TFC is positive? What will the ATC be in each case?

This process will generally work to find the average and the marginal from the total. Furthermore, we will be able to correctly place the marginal relative to the average as well. There are a couple of useful propositions that come from this geometrical device.

Proposition 4.17: *If the* ATC *has a minimum at* X_0, *then the line from the origin to the* TC *must be tangent to the* TC *at* X_0 (*see Figure* 4.14).

Exercise 10. What is the contrapositive of this statement?

Exercise 11. Prove proposition 4.17 using the contrapositive style of proof.

Proposition 4.18: *If the* ATC *has a minimum at* X_0 *and* TC *is differentiable, then at* X_0 *the* MC *must equal the* ATC.

Exercise 12. Prove proposition 4.18. Do you need the contrapositive here?

Exercise 13. Mimic the definition of average total cost (definition 4.15), and define the average variable cost (AVC) and average fixed cost (AFC).

Exercise 14. Use the methods developed above to find the average variable cost from the total variable cost, and the average fixed cost from the total fixed cost.

Exercise 15. We know that the TC and TVC are parallel. Does that mean that the ATC and AVC are also parallel? Explain!

Exercise 16. When we defined MC in definition 4.16, we based the definition on the total cost. Perhaps we should have called it the marginal total cost. We did not define the marginal variable cost or the marginal fixed cost. Use definition 4.16 as a model, and define the marginal variable cost and the marginal fixed cost. How are the marginal cost, the marginal variable cost, and the marginal fixed cost related?

There is one more matter we should take up in this section: finding total cost from average total cost. A similar argument would apply to the other average costs. From the definition of ATC, we have that $ATC = TC/X$. Hence, it must be true (multiplying both sides by X) that $ATC \times X = TC$. Therefore, at any given output, given the ATC, we can find the TC. Examine Figure 4.15.

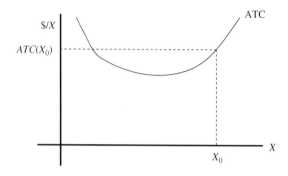

Figure 4.15   In this graph, we see that $TC(X_0)$ is $ATC(X_0) \times X_0$, which is exactly the area of the rectangle from the origin to X_0 to the ATC to the vertical axis at $ATC(X_0)$ and back to the origin.

We start by choosing an output, X_0. Then find the ATC at that output, $ATC(X_0)$. We multiply them together. Note that X_0 is the length of the horizontal side of the rectangle formed by X_0 and $ATC(X_0)$, and $ATC(X_0)$ is the length of the vertical side. Thus, $ATC(X_0) \times X_0$ is exactly the area of that rectangle. Note that while we can do this at each output, we are not able to say much about the shape of the resulting TC curve. So at any output we can find the TC from the ATC, but we cannot see what the general shape of the TC curve will look like from this information.

Exercise 17. Start with an AFC. Find the TFC at each output. What has to be true of these areas?

Proposition 4.18 says that the marginal must cut the average at the minimum of the average. This turns out to be true as a general statement. But there is another fact that is also useful, the average marginal fact. We will examine this idea in a very general setting as it is true for all averages and marginals. We will not restrict our attention to cost as the relationship is true for product, revenue, or utility. In fact, it is true for any marginal and average.

Proposition 4.19: The Average Marginal Fact

If the total and the average curves are differentiable, then for $X > 0$, the average curve falls if and only if the marginal curve is below the average curve.

Proof 4.20: Notice that this proposition is an "if and only if" proposition. This terminology means that we have two propositions, a statement and its converse, and both are true. So one proposition says that if the total and average are differentiable, if the average falls, and $X > 0$, then the marginal is below the average. The converse says that if the marginal is below the average, $X > 0$, and the total and average are differentiable, then the average is downward-sloping.

We will prove this proposition essentially by computation. We are in an unusual position in that we can see the truth of both the statement and its converse by looking at the outcome of the computation.

We know the average, $A(X)$, is defined as the total, $T(X)$, divided by X. Hence, the total is the average times X:

$$T(X) = A(X) \times X.$$

Because this equation is an identity, that is, it is true for all values of X, the derivative of each side must be equal. We will need the product rule for the right-hand side, and remember that the marginal, $M(X)$, is the derivative of the total:

$$M(X) = A'(X) \times X + A(X).$$

Now the difference between $M(X)$, the marginal, and the average, $A(X)$, is $A'(X) \times X$. If X is positive, as we assume, then $M(X) > A(X)$ if and only if $A'(X) > 0$. Furthermore, if $M(X) < A(X)$, then $A'(X) \times X < 0$ must hold, and for $X > 0$, $A'(X) < 0$ must be true. $\square$

Exercise 18. Use the idea of the average marginal relation to say what happens if $M(X) < A(X)$.

Exercise 19. Suppose that $A(X)$ has a minimum at X_0. What must be true of $A'(X_0)$? Use the average marginal fact to find the relationship between $A(X_0)$ and $M(X_0)$.

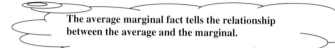

The average marginal fact tells the relationship between the average and the marginal.

Section Summary:
In this section, we started with the TC and found ways to obtain the ATC and MC from the total cost. Starting with the ATC, we also found the individual TC values. One other question remains: How is the marginal related to the total?

4.8   The Fundamental Theorem

In this section, we will examine a very special and useful theorem. It is a result we will use repeatedly in upcoming chapters. The theorem is motivated by the desire to start with marginal cost and somehow recover the total cost. Can we do this? If not, why not?

Proposition 4.21: The Fundamental Theorem
Given outputs X_1 and X_2 with $X_1 < X_2$, the area under the marginal cost between X_1 and X_2 is $TC(X_2) - TC(X_1)$.

Before proving this, there are a couple of points we should make. First, this is a theorem. Thus, we would expect there to be an "if" and a "then" part to this statement. Yet these are not clearly present. What are we to make of this? The approach we will take is that the proposition is true for almost all possible "if" statements, and is thus only a conclusion. As long as we have an MC curve derived from a TC curve, we can expect this statement to be true. Second, though we have stated it for the case of costs, it is true for all marginals and their totals. So the theorem applies to marginal product and total product, to marginal revenue and total revenue, and to marginal utility and total utility. It is a very important and useful theorem. How can we prove it? What we will do is to draw an MC, choose two levels of output, and approximate the area under the MC and see what we get. To ease the computation, we will select two outputs that are a specified distance apart, but the theorem is true for any two levels of output. The outputs we will choose are X_1 and $X_1 + 3$. Let us proceed with the proof.

Proof 4.22: Our job is to find the area under the MC between X_1 and X_2. We start with two levels of output, X_1 and $X_1 + 3$. Now we divide the interval between X_1 and $X_1 + 3$ into three parts. Figure 4.16 shows the details.

We can approximate the area under MC as the area of rectangle A plus the area of rectangle B plus the area of rectangle C, as shown in Figure 4.16. Area A is the rectangle from X_1 to $X_1 + 1$ and then up to $MC(X_1 + 1)$ and back to the left to just above X_1 and then back to the X-axis at X_1. Areas B and C are found in the same way.

$$\text{Area under MC between } X_1 \text{ and } X_1 + 3 = \text{ Area A} + \\ \text{Area B} + \\ \text{Area C.}$$

Area A is $(X_1 + 1 - X_1)$ wide (Why is this?). We will use the height on the right-hand side for the vertical distance. Thus,

$$\text{Area A} = MC(X_1 + 1) \times (X_1 + 1 - X_1) = MC(X_1 + 1).$$

Similar computations can be made for areas B and C:

$$\text{Area B} = MC(X_1 + 2) \times (X_1 + 2 - (X_1 + 1)) = MC(X_1 + 2).$$
$$\text{Area C} = MC(X_1 + 3) \times (X_1 + 3 - (X_1 + 2)) = MC(X_1 + 3).$$

Therefore,

Area under MC between X_1 and $X_1 + 3$
$$= MC(X_1 + 1) + MC(X_1 + 2) + MC(X_1 + 3).$$

Call this equation *.

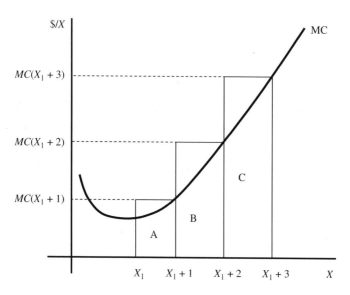

Figure 4.16   In this figure, we start with the MC curve. Then pick outputs $X_1, X_1 + 1, X_1 + 2, X_1 + 3$ and find the MC at $X_1 + 1, X_1 + 2, X_1 + 3$. We can then find the area of the rectangles A, B, and C, which approximates the area under the MC between X_1 and $X_1 + 3$.

Equation * is not what we want. We want the area under MC between X_1 and $X_1 + 3$ to be the difference of two total costs, not the sum of three marginal costs. What to do? About the only tool we have is the definition of MC. We use it now:

$$MC(X_1 + 1) = \frac{TC(X_1 + 1) - TC(X_1)}{X_1 + 1 - X_1}$$

$$= TC(X_1 + 1) - TC(X_1).$$

$$MC(X_1 + 2) = \frac{TC(X_1 + 2) - TC(X_1 + 1)}{X_1 + 2 - (X_1 + 1)}$$

$$= TC(X_1 + 2) - TC(X_1 + 1).$$

$$MC(X_1 + 3) = \frac{TC(X_1 + 3) - TC(X_1 + 2)}{X_1 + 3 - (X_1 + 2)}$$

$$= TC(X_1 + 3) - TC(X_1 + 2).$$

We plug these into the equation * above:

Area under MC between X_1 and $X_1 + 3$

$$= TC(X_1 + 1) - TC(X_1)$$
$$+ TC(X_1 + 2) - TC(X_1 + 1)$$
$$+ TC(X_1 + 3) - TC(X_1 + 2).$$

But some terms cancel! We are left with:

Area under MC between X_1 and $X_1 + 3 = TC(X_1 + 3) - TC(X_1)$,

which is what we are looking for. We are done! □

Look at Figure 4.16. We have approximated the areas under MC, yet clearly our approximations are larger than the actual area. How can we get the result with an approximation? The answer is a bit hard to provide, but technically given the way we have computed the MC, the MC curve should be a stair step rather than a continuous curve. However, even given the curve, the proof can be refined. Suppose that instead of taking one-unit changes in X, we take a half-unit change in X. Now the approximation is better! What happens if we keep making the change in X smaller and smaller? The approximation becomes better and better, and as the change in X approaches zero, then we get the actual area under the curve. The important observation is that we keep getting this canceling that goes on in the last step of the proof so that we are only left with the point $TC(X_2) - TC(X_1)$.

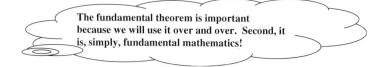

The fundamental theorem is important because we will use it over and over. Second, it is, simply, fundamental mathematics!

Exercise 20. What if we went from X_1 to $X_1 + 4$? What difference would it make in the proof? What if we start with X_1 and go to $X_1 + 3.5$? How might we proceed then? Finally, we approximated the area under the MC; why does this computation come out exactly as we said it would? Why doesn't the approximation cause our answer to be off by a little?

So why is this the fundamental theorem? Well, first of all, it is fundamental for what we want to do. Second, it is the (famous) First Fundamental Theorem of Calculus! Just for the record, you have just seen the proof of that theorem! What the theorem says is that if f is the derivative of F, then the area under f between a and b ($b > a$) is $F(b) - F(a)$. The area under f is sometimes called the integral of f.

Again, what does the theorem say? It says that the area under the marginal is the **CHANGE** in the total. Is the area under the marginal the total? No, the area under the marginal is the **CHANGE** in the total; the area under the marginal is not the total (at least not in general).

Section Summary:
In this section, we have stated and proved the fundamental theorem. We will have use for this theorem in later chapters. But now we can do the problem of least cost and also of finding the total variable cost using calculus!

4.9 Using Calculus to Find the TVC

In this section, we will find the TVC using calculus. We will start with the production function, find the cost-minimizing choice of labor and capital, and then find the total variable cost. To start, we will need a production function. What can we use? There is a pretty standard production function that economists use: the Cobb–Douglas function.[4] We will use this function with $a = b = 1/3$. The least cost problem for the firm is to choose L and K so that $wL + rK$ is minimum and so that X is some fixed value, X^*, so $X^* = L^{1/3}K^{1/3}$. We will solve the production function for K and substitute into the isocost, and then minimize the isocost with respect to the only remaining variable, L. From the production function, we have

$$K^{1/3} = L^{-1/3}X^*$$

$$K = L^{-1}X^{*3}.$$

Now substitute into the isocost:

$$E = wL + rX^{*3}L^{-1}.$$

To minimize, we use the theorem that says if $f(L)$ has a minimum, then the first derivative with respect to L is zero. So we find the derivative of E where L is the variable:

$$E' = w - rX^{*3}L^{-2} = 0.$$

Before going on, we should check to see if we have a minimum, which we can do by finding the second derivative of E. If the second derivative is positive, we have a minimum. Here is the second derivative of E:

$$E'' = -rX^{*3}(-2)L^{-3} = r2X^{*3}L^{-3},$$

which is positive for $L > 0$. We have a minimum.

---

[4]The function takes a general form of $X = L^a K^b$, where a and b are constants. If $a + b = 1$, then we say the function exhibits constant returns to scale; a doubling of inputs exactly doubles output. If $a + b < 1$, then we have decreasing returns to scale; a doubling of inputs less than doubles output.

We now solve our E' expression for L to find the L that minimizes cost:

$$w - rX^{*3}L^{-2} = 0$$
$$wL^2 = rX^{*3}$$
$$L^2 = (r/w)X^{*3}$$
$$L = (r/w)^{1/2}X^{*3/2}.$$

This is the value of L that provides the minimum cost for the level of output X^*.

We also need the cost-minimizing value of K. To obtain this, we use the expression from the production function:

$$K = L^{-1}X^{*3}.$$

Replace L with $L = (r/w)^{1/2}X^{*3/2}$ to obtain

$$K = (r/w)^{-1/2}X^{*-3/2}X^{*3}$$
$$= (w/r)^{1/2}X^{*3/2}.$$

We may now put the optimal values of L and K into the isocost to get the TVC:

$$E = w(r/w)^{1/2}X^{*3/2} + r(w/r)^{1/2}X^{*3/2}$$
$$= 2(rw)^{1/2}X^{*3/2}.$$

Because E is the expenditure on variable inputs, it is TVC and here we have the expression that is TVC for this production function:

$$TVC = 2(rw)^{1/2}X^{*3/2}.$$

Exercise 21. Suppose that $TVC = 2(rw)^{1/2}X^{*3/2}$, $r = 81$, and $w = 16$. Also assume that TFC is 100. Write the TC function. Also find MC, ATC, and AVC.

Exercise 22. Suppose that the production function were $X = L^{1/4}K^{1/4}$. Use the wage of w and the rental rate of r. By cost minimization, find the TVC curve.

Exercise 23. Suppose that the production function were $X = L^{1/2}K^{1/2}$. Use the wage of w and the rental rate of r. By cost minimization, find the TVC curve.

Exercise 24. Suppose that we have the following equation for TVC and that $TFC = 50$:

$$TVC = X^3 - 48X^2 + 798.$$

a. Find TC, MC, ATC, and AVC.
b. Graph MC and AVC.
c. Find ATC and AFC. Show that ATC = AVC + AFC.

Section Summary:
In this section, we have applied the techniques of calculus to the problem of cost minimization and to find the TVC. We have also found the ATC, AVC, and MC.

4.10 Summary

In this chapter, we have achieved the following important outcomes:

A. Represented technology by isoquants and total product curves.
B. Developed the isocost.
C. Stated and proved the least cost combination proposition.
D. Used the least cost combination proposition to derive TVC.
E. Found both the MC and ATC, and their relationship to each other.
F. Found the relationship between the MC and TC.

There are three major conclusions you should take with you from this chapter:

A. The firm's costs are derived from the least cost process, that is, firms generally try to minimize the cost of production at each output.
B. Generally, least cost occurs where an isoquant is tangent to the isocost.
C. The area under the marginal is the change in the total.

These costs will be essential to the computation of profits for the firm. Also note that we will use these cost curves regardless of the kind of firm we encounter, be it a corn farmer, an electric company, or a liquid soap maker. We need to turn now to the other half of profit — revenue. Once we have the general revenue concepts, we will first apply them to the case of the corn farmer, the competitive firm.

Terms Defined:

- Input combination
- Production function
- Law of Diminishing Returns
- Isocost
- Isoquant
- Technologically efficient
- Total product
- Marginal product
- Total variable cost
- Total fixed cost
- Total cost
- Average total cost
- Marginal cost
- Average marginal fact
- Fundamental theorem

Chapter 5

Profit Maximization: The Case of Competition

Key Concepts:

- Profit maximization
- Shutdown condition
- Supply for the competitive firm

Goals:

- Develop the profit maximization proposition for competitive firms.
- Develop the shutdown condition for competitive firms.
- Derive the competitive firm's supply curve.

In Chapter 2, we derived one of the two big concepts in economics — demand. In this chapter, our interest will be on the other side of the market — supply. Primarily at this point, we will think about the firm as the supplier. Hence, we will need to understand how firms make decisions and how these decisions are used to find the supply curve for the firm. This is our goal for this chapter.

5.1   Introduction

Suppose that you are in the business as a producer of chocolate-covered graham crackers. There is nothing to distinguish your chocolate-covered grahams from another's. You are trying to decide how many boxes of these to produce. How do you decide? On the one hand, you have computed costs using the methods of the previous chapter. You know what the price of chocolate-covered grahams is. How do you integrate these pieces of information to inform your decision? This chapter will help you figure out the answer!

So far we have looked at the firm's costs, but costs are only half of the information that firms need to make decisions. Firms also need to know revenue. The revenue and cost together determine profit which, in our model, is the focus of the firm's attention. We will assume that firms act to maximize profit. Is this an accurate description of how firms behave?

At one level, it is clearly not a very descriptive assumption. We know firms that do things that raise their cost without discernable impacts on their revenue. You must have seen firms supporting charities and other worthwhile projects. These clearly cost something without discernable revenues attached. One could argue that these activities enhance the firm's reputation, but reputation is not revenue. So why do economists stick with this assumption? While not a perfect reflection of reality, the assumption does seem to reflect quite a bit about how businesses make decisions. We have seen news stories of firms that break laws in the pursuit of profit. Tales of Wall Street greed abound. These are, to a large extent, behaviors that start with profit maximization. For the economist, the assumption of profit maximization is the simplest assumption we can make that captures a sizable part of the behavior of firms. While not perfect, it is also not a bad assumption.

To make progress toward understanding how this assumption yields results, we need to move forward with our discussion of the general revenue concepts. We will then develop the revenue concepts for competitive firms, which we will then combine with the cost concepts of the previous chapter to obtain profit. Once we have profit, we can move to profit maximization, the shutdown condition, and the firm's supply curve. Here we go!

5.2 Revenue Concepts

In this section, we will develop the revenue concepts that will be used for all firms. When we are done with the general concepts, we will turn to the particular case of the competitive firm and see what the revenue curves look like in this case. We begin with definitions.

Definition 5.1: *Total revenue* (TR) *is a relationship between output and dollars showing price, P, times quantity sold, X.*

We can use a formula to find total revenue: $TR(X) = P \times X$.

Definition 5.2: *Marginal revenue* (MR) *is a relationship between output and dollars per unit of output showing the change in total revenue due to a change in output at each level of output.*

We can think of MR in a variety of ways. We can find the MR by using the following formula: $MR = \frac{\Delta TR}{\Delta X}$. Alternatively, MR is the slope or derivative of TR. You should realize that we can use the fundamental theorem here.

Exercise 1. State the fundamental theorem using MR and TR.

Definition 5.3: *Average revenue* (AR) *is a relationship between output and dollars per unit of output showing total revenue per unit of output.*

Again, we can use a formula to compute the average revenue: $AR = \frac{TR}{X}$. But there is one more concept we need, and we define it now, even though it is not a revenue concept.

Definition 5.4: *Profit* (π) *is a relationship between output and dollars showing the total revenue minus the total cost at each output.*

You can see that profit is a total relationship, as it involves output and dollars, not an average or marginal relationship that involves output and dollars per unit of output. You should also see that the profit could be negative; there is nothing in the definition that guarantees profit is positive. We use the word "profit" for both the case where the profit is positive and the profit is negative. You will also note that we have not defined marginal or average profit. We leave that to you now.

Exercise 2. Use the definitions of marginal revenue and average revenue as models, and define the marginal profit and the average profit.

Section Summary:
In this section, we have defined the terms we will need to complete the problem for the firm: total revenue, marginal revenue, average revenue, and profit. We will now explore the case where the firm is competitive. This is the case that was represented by the corn farmer.

5.3   Revenue for Competitive Firms

Economists are very precise about what the word "competitive" means.

Definition 5.5: *By competitive, we mean that the chooser, whether buyer or seller, cannot affect the price.*

So far we have twice used this definition without saying the word "competitive." We used this concept when talking about consumers, and we assumed that they could not affect the prices of the goods they purchase. In other words, the consumer was acting competitively. Similarly, we assumed that the firm was competitive in the purchase of inputs. The firm cannot affect the price of labor or capital. This is not an assumption that is new to us, but it is about the first time that we have used the name "competitive" in this way.

Note what the idea of competition means. It means that no firm producing this good can affect the price of its output. Our example in the previous chapter of the corn farmer fits this definition rather well.[1]

---

[1] There are some issues here. Farmers are often the recipient of subsidies from the government. In addition, the buyer of the corn is likely to be a large food processing firm, not a competitive buyer. Furthermore, farmers rarely grow corn for sale at the time the corn is harvested; rather, they sell the largest share of their corn with a futures contract, essentially agreeing to the price before they even sow the seed. These elements

A part of the assumption of competition is that the firm can sell all it wants at the going price. There is no incentive for the firm to lower price in this environment.

Note what the assumption rules out. Firms like automobile manufacturers are not competitive as we have used the term. They are fierce rivals, but they are not competitive. Thus, the auto industry is not competitive. We would not see competitive firms advertising their good. The reason to advertise is to somehow improve one's market position. But given that competitive firms cannot affect the price, advertising will not allow them to raise their price; and given that they can sell all they can produce at the given price, the advertisement will not increase the volume of sales. Advertising is just a cost, and has no benefit to competitive firms. These competitive firms do not advertise.

In short, the price is a parameter to the firm. It is constant as far as the firm is concerned, but of course it could change due to forces beyond the firm's control.

Recall our conversation about the corn farmer. One advantage of looking at firms like a corn farmer is that its revenue is independent of the revenue of other firms. This is the competitive assumption at work. Because the farmers are competitive, they cannot affect price, and the revenue of a farmer depends only on the decisions he makes about the quantity of corn to produce (with the help of nature). Thus, we can look at the decision making of each farmer separately. Hence, we will be looking at the revenue for a firm, not at the industry or how the farmers interact.

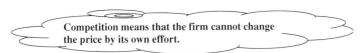

Competition means that the firm cannot change the price by its own effort.

Because total revenue is price times quantity, and price is constant, the total revenue will be linear and passes through the origin as shown in Figure 5.1.

---

make the corn farmer a bit less like the competitive case than we have portrayed. But we will maintain the corn farmer as our example of a competitive firm.

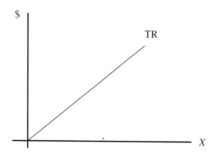

Figure 5.1   Total revenue is price (a constant in competition) times quantity, which yields a straight line through the origin.

Exercise 3. How do we know that TR is a straight line? Put the equation into slope-intercept form; does it satisfy the requirements for a straight line? What is its slope?

Exercise 4. Use the geometric methods we developed in Chapter 4 to find the AR and the MR from the TR in Figure 5.1.

Because the slope of the TR is the MR, you should find that the MR is the same as the price of the good; and also by computation, AR is also equal to the price. The case of competition is the only time you will have the situation where $MR = AR = P$. We have graphed the results in Figure 5.2.

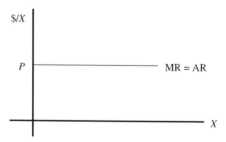

Figure 5.2   In this graph, we show the MR and AR for the competitive firm. Both are equal to the price of the good.

5.4   Profit Maximization for Competitive Firms

Before going to the proposition, it would make sense to understand the basis of the argument. Here is how the discussion will proceed. Suppose we start with the firm producing some level of output; call it X_1. The firm is making some amount of profit at that point. The question we want to address is whether the firm would want to increase output or not. We assume that the criterion that the firm uses is profit. The set of alternatives the firm could choose would be all possible positive quantities of output, including zero output. If profit would increase by the increase in output, then the firm would want to do this. On the other hand, if the firm would make profit smaller by increasing output, they would not want to do this. Consider the case when output rises. If the firm increases output, two things happen. First, by selling more output, they increase revenue. The increase in revenue by itself is good for profit. However, the firm also has to produce the added output, so they face added cost. By itself, the added cost is bad for profit. We have two things happening due to the increase in output: revenue rises and so does cost. If the increase in revenue is larger than the increase in cost, then profit will rise. But if the increase in revenue is less than the increase in cost, then profit will fall. Rather obviously, we need to know the amount of increase in revenue compared to the increase in cost. Where do we find this information? It should be apparent to you that the MR and MC will somehow be involved here, as they tell the change in revenue and the change in cost. But we will also use the fundamental theorem to complete the computation. The details are in the proof! Here is the proposition.

Proposition 5.6: Profit Maximization for the Competitive Firm

If   a.   *the assumptions of least cost hold,*

        b.   *the* MC *and* MR *are continuous,*

        c.   *at* X_0, $0 < X_0 < \infty$, *profit is maximum for the competitive firm,*

Then d.   *at* X_0, MR $=$ MC.

You know we are going to prove this proposition. How will we do that? Of course, we will use the contrapositive. How can we state the contrapositive?

If   a.   the assumptions of least cost hold,

      b.   the MC and MR are continuous,

      c.   at X_0, MR $\neq$ MC,

Then d.   profit is not maximum at X_0.

This is the proposition we will prove. Once we are done with this, we will know the output the firm will produce.

What do we have to show to say that profit is not maximum? For profit to not be at a maximum requires that there is some output where profit is higher than it is where we are. That means that we need to see what happens to profit as we change output. Can we see profit in Figure 5.3? Because we do not see total revenue or total cost, we cannot see profit in this graph. But we can tell if profit rises or falls from the current output. The details of how we can do this will come out in the proof, but the essential thing is that we need to show that by changing output, we can somehow make profit rise. If profit can rise, profit cannot be maximum. If the only thing profit can do is fall, then profit is maximum.

Also note that the only thing the competitive firm can change is the output. The firm cannot change price because competitive firms have no control over price. So the only thing the firm can do is to increase or decrease output.

Proof 5.7: We wish to show that if MR is not equal to MC, then profit is not maximum. That means that if MR is not equal to MC, there is an output where profit would be higher. There are two cases: if MR $>$ MC, then profit is not maximum; and if MR $<$ MC, then profit is not maximum. We start with the first case and leave the second to the reader.

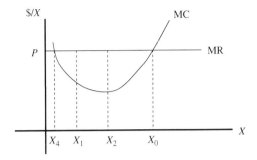

Figure 5.3   In this figure, we see the firm increase output from X_1 to X_2. Because total revenue increases by more than total cost, profit rises and is not maximum at X_1.

Suppose that $MR > MC$. Then we must be at an output such as at X_1 in Figure 5.3 (how do we know this?). Suppose we increase output to X_2. We know that TR rises by the area under MR between X_1 and X_2 (according to the fundamental theorem). TC rises by the area under MC between X_1 and X_2 (according to the fundamental theorem). Because $MR > MC$, by hypothesis, the increase in total revenue is greater than the increase in total cost. Hence, profit rises and is not maximum at X_1.   □

Exercise 5. Do the other half of the proposition; if $MR < MC$, then profit cannot be maximum.

Exercise 6. Suppose that X_0 is the output where $MR = MC$. Why can't we argue that we increase X toward X_0 because profit is maximum at X_0?

Exercise 7. Why is it important to say (as X rises from X_1 to X_2) that total revenue rises by more than total cost, rather than that total revenue is greater than total cost?

Exercise 8. Why is it important that we increase (rather than decrease) X in the above proof?

HINT: We are asserting that profit is largest at the output where $MR = MC$. If profit rises as we move away from that X, then profit would not be maximum there.

Exercise 9. State the converse of the profit maximization proposition. Use Figure 5.3. Is the converse true in this case? You can check by starting at X_4 and seeing what happens to profit as we change output from X_4. Is it ever possible to increase profit from X_0?

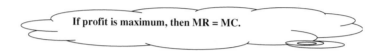

If profit is maximum, then MR = MC.

The profit maximization proposition 5.6 is an important proposition. It will be the basis of our efforts to find the supply curve for the competitive firm. Before we get there, there is one more matter we must consider. The proposition seems to apply to cases where X_0 is not zero (and not infinity). Are there ever times when the firm will want to produce zero output, to shut down? We address this question next!

"Yeah, I hired this econ major to scoop ice cream. All he does is mutter about marginal revenue and marginal cost."

> **Section Summary:**
> In this section, we have stated and proved the profit maximization proposition for the competitive firm. This is an important and useful proposition that will be valuable in our search for the competitive firm's supply curve. This proposition is at the heart of the economist's view of the firm. When you think about how a firm makes decisions, as a student of economics, you should start with the assumption that the firm maximizes profit. This basic behavioral assumption also leads to the derivation of the firm's supply curve. Before we look for supply, there is one more matter we need to discuss: the case where the firm decides to produce zero output.

5.5 The Shutdown Condition

The profit maximization proposition holds for values of X between zero and infinity that maximize profit. Could it ever be that the firm wishes to produce zero output? Could zero be a profit-maximizing choice for the firm? Let us consider that possibility now.

Suppose that the firm was losing money at its profit-maximizing output. The owner thinks for a while and wonders: if they shut down, that is, if they produced zero to the end of the short run before re-evaluating their options, would they be better off? If the firm produces zero output, what profit will they earn? If they sell zero, they will have zero revenue. If they produce zero, their variable cost will be zero as they will not need any of the variable inputs to produce output, but their fixed cost will still have to be paid until the end of the short run. So the firm would have a cost equal to their fixed cost. Hence, profit would be equal to the negative of the total fixed cost.

What are the alternatives the firm faces? If the firm produces zero, they lose their fixed cost. If they produce at the profit maximum, they gain whatever profit (could be negative) there is. The firm wishes to do whichever will lead to the larger profit. We need to know the profit at X_0. Can we tell how much that profit is?

Suppose we look at the graph of the firm that we have so far examined. Can we determine the amount of profit from the information we have so far used?

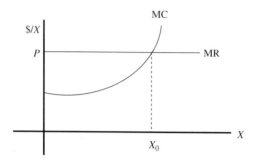

Figure 5.4   We wish to find the profit at X_0. We can easily see the total revenue at X_0, but not the total cost. Hence, we cannot determine the profit from only the marginal curves.

In Figure 5.4, we have shown the MR, the MC, and the profit-maximizing output, X_0. We want to know the profit at X_0. Profit is total revenue minus total cost. We need to find the total revenue and the total cost; the difference is profit. The total revenue is easy because total revenue is price times quantity, and the price is P and the quantity is X_0. Hence, the total revenue is the area of the rectangle from the origin up to the MR line and then over to X_0. Now what about the total cost? Well, one way to proceed would be to do the same kind of thing, that is, to multiply the quantity times $MC(X_0)$. But this will not give us the total cost as MC times X is not total cost; we need the ATC to do this. What about the fundamental theorem? We know from the fundamental theorem that the area under the MC is the change in total cost. Why not use this theorem and look at the area under MC between zero and X_0? Here is what we get:

Area under MC between 0 and X_0 = $TC(X_0) - TC(0)$.

So if $TC(0)$ is 0, then we have the total cost. Is $TC(0) = 0$? The answer is, sadly, no. $TC(0) = $ TFC. But maybe all is not lost. Can we see the total fixed cost in Figure 5.4? The obvious choice would be where the MC crosses the vertical axis. But this point is measured in $/X$, and TFC is measured in $, so this cannot be right.[2] In fact, there is no way to find the TFC from Figure 5.4 and hence no way to determine the level of profit. To find profit, we will need to add some information to our graph. What information should we add? If we had ATC, we could find TC; and then with the TR we already found, we could find profit. Let us have a look! Check out Figure 5.5.

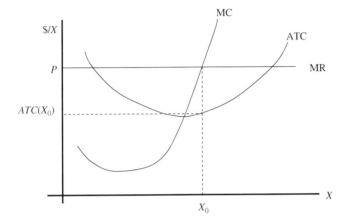

Figure 5.5 In this graph, we find $TR(X_0)$, the area of the rectangle from the origin to P to X_0. We also find $TC(X_0) = ATC(X_0) \times X_0 = $ the area of the rectangle from the origin to $ATC(X_0)$ to X_0. In this case, the firm is making a positive profit.

Now that we have the ATC, we can find the total cost. Recall the definition of ATC, which is that $ATC(X_0) = TC(X_0)/X_0$. If we multiply both sides by X_0, we get $TC(X_0) = ATC(X_0) \times X_0$ (recall the parentheses indicate that we have a function, and in this case the function is evaluated at X_0). We can find $ATC(X_0)$ by going up the X_0 line until we run into the ATC curve. The vertical distance (shown on the $/X$ axis) marked $ATC(X_0)$ is this number. Now if we multiply it by X_0, we get the area of the rectangle from the origin to the $ATC(X_0)$

---

[2]If this argument does not convince you, think about what happens to MC if total fixed cost changes. Then note that if this point were TFC, the MC would have to change as TFC changes.

line to X_0, $TC(X_0)$. We already know $TR(X_0)$. In this case, we see that the profit is positive.

Let us now consider the problem the firm faces when trying to decide whether to produce or shut down. If the firm produces zero, their profit would be minus total fixed cost. Under what conditions would the firm want to continue production? If the firm could produce X_0 with a profit larger than minus the total fixed cost, they would stay in business to the end of the short run. If, at X_0, profit is less than minus the total fixed cost, the firm would want to shut down and produce zero. In either case, at the end of the short run, the firm might want to consider what to do. Should they do something to reduce their costs (new plant and equipment) or should they go out of business permanently? The following proposition addresses this question.

Proposition 5.8: Shutdown Condition

If the competitive firm has a price above the AVC at profit maximum, then the firm will stay in business to at least the end of the short run. If the competitive firm's price is below the AVC at profit maximum, then the firm will shut down and produce zero in the short run.

Proof 5.9: We know that the firm has to choose between producing at the profit-maximizing output or zero. The firm will choose the more profitable of the two. Thus, we would have these conditions:

$$\text{If profit at } X_0 > -TFC, \quad \text{then stay in business.}$$
$$\text{If profit at } X_0 < -TFC, \quad \text{then shut down.}$$

We can write an expression for profit at X_0:

$$\text{Profit at } X_0 = \pi(X_0) = P \times X_0 - TC(X_0) = P \times X_0 - TVC(X_0) - TFC.$$

We are comparing, then, $P \times X_0 - TVC(X_0) - TFC$ with $-TFC$:

$$\text{If } P \times X_0 - TVC(X_0) - TFC > -TFC, \quad \text{then stay in business.}$$
$$\text{If } P \times X_0 - TVC(X_0) - TFC < -TFC, \quad \text{then shut down.}$$

We can rewrite the above as follows:

$$\text{If } P \times X_0 - TVC(X_0) > 0, \quad \text{then stay in business.}$$
$$\text{If } P \times X_0 - TVC(X_0) < 0, \quad \text{then shut down.}$$

Alternatively, we can write the following:

$$\text{If } P \times X_0 > TVC(X_0), \quad \text{then stay in business.}$$
$$\text{If } P \times X_0 < TVC(X_0), \quad \text{then shut down.}$$

If we divide both sides by X_0, we would get these expressions:

$$\text{If } P > TVC(X_0)/X_0, \quad \text{then stay in business.}$$
$$\text{If } P < TVC(X_0)/X_0, \quad \text{then shut down.}$$

Of course, the expressions on the right-hand side of the inequality are the AVC:

$$\text{If } P > AVC(X_0), \quad \text{then stay in business.}$$
$$\text{If } P < AVC(X_0), \quad \text{then shut down.} \qquad \square$$

It would make sense for us to illustrate the case where the firm decides to produce zero and shut down. Observe that to do this, we need the AVC, not the ATC. In Figure 5.6, we show this development. Figure 5.6 shows the case where the price is above the average variable cost, so that the firm more than covers its variable costs. In this case, its loss at the profit-maximizing output is less than the fixed cost, and they should stay in business.

Figure 5.7 shows the case where the price is below the AVC, and the firm now cannot cover its variable cost from its revenue. Hence, the firm loses both the fixed cost and part of the variable cost. Clearly, the firm would be better off to produce zero and only lose its total fixed cost.

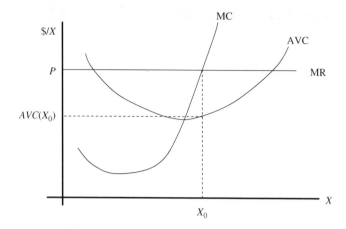

Figure 5.6   Here P is above $AVC(X_0)$, and the firm covers all of its variable cost and part of its fixed cost. Clearly, the firm is better off producing X_0 than zero, where the firm would lose all of its TFC.

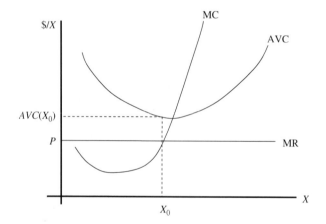

Figure 5.7   In this graph, P is below $AVC(X_0)$, so if the firm produces X_0, they lose all of their fixed cost and part of their variable cost. They would be better off producing zero and only losing their TFC.

If $P > AVC$, then the firm should continue to produce even if profit is negative. If $P < AVC$, then the firm should shut down.

We now have the second big piece needed for the derivation of supply. We turn to this process next.

Exercise 10. The shutdown condition is stated in terms of the AVC, not the ATC. Why is the AVC the right choice and not the ATC?

Exercise 11. Go back to Figure 5.4 and see if you can tell if the firm should shut down or not from the information given.

FROM THE LITERATURE

Do firms maximize profits? What alternative is there? One possibility is that firms attempt to minimize cost (which would be implied by profit maximization). So the firm might be more concerned about the costs, and let the revenue take care of itself. Does this happen? One study of dairy farmers in New York suggests that dairy farmers were more closely aligned with cost minimization than with profit maximization. What difference would there be between firms acting to minimize cost compared to maximizing profit? Firms should try to minimize cost regardless of the output produced. Profit maximization is a strategy to choose the level of output to produce. Here is the citation for this study: Loren Tauer, "Do New York Dairy Farmers Maximize Profits or Minimize Costs?," *American Journal of Agricultural Economics*, Vol. 77, No. 2, May, 1995, pp. 421–429.

Section Summary:
In this section, we have seen that from the marginal curves alone, we cannot determine the amount of profit the firm makes. To find profit, we need some added curves: the average curves. In addition, we have developed the shutdown condition, and illustrated it as well. In the next section, we will combine the profit maximization proposition and the shutdown condition to find the firm's supply curve.

5.6   The Competitive Firm's Supply

In this section, we combine the profit maximization proposition and the shutdown condition to obtain the competitive firm's supply curve. This will provide the construction of the second big concept in economics: supply. We start with a definition of the concept we are seeking.

Definition 5.10:   *The firm's **supply curve** is a relationship between output and dollars per unit of output showing the number of units a firm would choose to produce and sell at each price with input prices and technology not changing.*

The definition is about the choices that the firm makes. We know that the firm acts to maximize profit. Hence, we can now look at quantities the firm would choose to produce at each price. Of course we know that at some prices the firm will decide to shut down, so we will have to take that into consideration as well. Consider Figure 5.8.

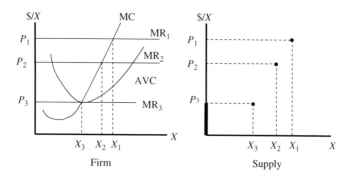

Figure 5.8   In the left graph, we have the firm choosing the profit-maximizing output at a variety of prices. We bring the prices and the associated quantities to the graph on the right to find supply. Observe that when the price falls below the AVC, then the firm produces zero output according to the shutdown condition.

In the left graph, we have the competitive firm with the AVC and MC curves. We draw in a price, P_1. We know that for a competitive firm, the price and MR are the same. By the profit maximization proposition 5.6, we know that if there is a profit maximum, then MR = MC, so the firm chooses X_1. Because $P_1 > AVC$ at this output, by the shut-down proposition 5.8, the firm would supply X_1 units at a price of P_1. We show that combination in the right graph. This is one point on the firm's supply curve. What about a second point?

If the price should fall to P_2, the MR becomes MR_2 and now the firm would choose X_2 output. Again, $P_2 > AVC$ at X_2, so the firm will supply X_2 at this price. Again, we show the combination of quantity supplied of X_2 when the price is P_2 in the right graph. This is another point on the supply curve. When the price (and MR) falls to P_3, now the $MR = MC$ at X_3 just so that $P_3 = AVC$ at that X. We do not quite know what the firm will do; assume for the moment that they produce X_3. But at any price below P_3, the firm will shut down as $P < AVC$ at those outputs. Thus, in the right graph, we would have zero produced at prices below P_3. This is shown as a dark line on the vertical axis in the right graph. Now the question is, what is the graph on the right?

It is supply, by construction. But observe that because the axis system is the same for both graphs, we could overlay the right graph on the left. What would we find? The points that we have so far identified as being points on the supply curve would all lie on the MC curve. They have to by the profit-maximizing proposition. In addition, we produce zero at any price below P_3 according to the shutdown condition.

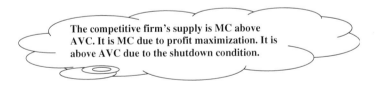

The competitive firm's supply is MC above AVC. It is MC due to profit maximization. It is above AVC due to the shutdown condition.

Exercise 12. Look back at Figure 5.8. It is easy to see that the points we have identified in the right-hand graph are on the MC curve. How do you know that the points on the supply between the prices we have used are also on the MC curve?

Section Summary:
In this section, we have applied the profit maximization proposition and the shutdown condition to obtain the competitive firm's supply curve. We have found that the supply is the firm's MC above the AVC curve. We have now found the second big piece needed for price determination in a competitive market. We can now see what makes the firm's supply curve shift.

5.7 What Makes the Competitive Firm's Supply Curve Shift?

In this section, we will examine what makes the competitive firm's supply curve shift. At one level, the answer is pretty easy. Because supply is part of the MC, whatever makes the MC shift makes the supply shift! But that only moves the question one level back. What makes the MC shift?

The MC is the slope of TC, so to make the MC shift, the slope of TC would have to change. We know that TC is the sum of TVC and TFC. Changes in TFC move the TC up and down in a parallel fashion, so changes in TFC will not affect the slope of TC. Therefore, the only way for the slope of TC, and hence MC, to shift is for there to be a change in the TVC curve. Where did we get TVC?

Look back to Chapter 4, where we derived the TVC from the isoquants and isocost. In the construction of the TVC, we held the input prices and the technology fixed. So if there is a change in any input price or in the technology, then the TVC will shift. Note that the TVC cannot shift parallel to itself as it must always pass through the origin. Hence, changes in the input prices or the technology will cause the TVC to shift, which causes a change in the slope of TC, which causes MC to shift, which is a shift in the firm's supply.

Exercise 13. Does a change in the TFC cause the firm's supply to shift?

Exercise 14. Go back to the derivation of the TVC curve in Chapter 4. For given technology, price of labor, and price of capital, find the TVC and the MC. Now allow the price of labor to fall. Derive the TVC again, and the new MC. What happens to the supply curve?

Section Summary:
In this section, we found what makes the firm's supply curve shift by connecting with work we did earlier. We discovered that a change in input prices or technology will cause the firm's supply curve to shift. We turn now to a discussion of profit maximization using calculus.

5.8 Profit Maximization with Calculus

In this section, we will again extend the analysis done before by bringing in some mathematics. As before, we know that if there is a maximum for the profit function, then the derivative of the profit function must be zero. Suppose that we are given the following MC and MR. Find the profit-maximizing output.

$$MC(X) = (X - 4)^2 + 10$$
$$MR = 110.$$

We know, from the profit maximization proposition, that if profit is maximum, then MR = MC must hold. So set these equal and solve for the value of X:

$$110 = (X - 4)^2 + 10$$
$$100 = (X - 4)^2$$
$$\pm 10 = X - 4$$
$$X = 14 \quad \text{or} \quad -6.$$

While it is tempting to reject $X = -6$ as a maximum, we should check the second derivative of profit to be sure. The second derivative of profit is $MR' - MC'$:

$$\pi'' = 0 - 2(X - 4) = -2(X - 4) = -2X + 8.$$

Evaluate π'' at 14 to get $\pi''(14) = -20$. Thus, our profit maximum is at $X = 14$.

What if we are not given $MC(X)$, but $TC(X)$ along with MR? Then what? We would find $TR(X)$ and form the profit function, and then maximize that function. Suppose we have the following information:

$$TC(X) = (1/3)X^3 - 6X^2 + 36X + 40$$
$$P = 400.$$

We can find total revenue:

$$TR(X) = P \times X = 400X.$$

Profit is:

$$TR(X) - TC(X) = 400X - ((1/3)X^3 - 6X^2 + 36X + 40)$$
$$\pi(X) = -(1/3)X^3 + 6X^2 + 364X - 40.$$

To find a maximum, we find the first derivative and set it to zero:

$$\pi'(X) = -X^2 + 12X + 364 = 0$$
$$= X^2 - 12X - 364 = 0$$
$$= X^2 - 12X + 36 - 400 = 0$$
$$= (X - 6)^2 - 400 = 0$$
$$(X - 6)^2 = 400$$
$$X - 6 = \pm 20$$
$$X = 26 \quad \text{or} \quad -14.$$

Before going on, we should compute the second derivative of profit to see which output is the maximum:

$$\pi''(X) = -2X + 12.$$

When $X = 26$, $\pi''(X) = -40 < 0$, so $X = 26$ is a maximum.

We can easily compute the profit the firm earns in this case:

$$\pi(X) = -(1/3)X^3 + 6X^2 + 364X - 40$$
$$= -(1/3) \times (26)^3 + 6 \times (26)^2 + 364 \times 26 - 40$$
$$= -(17576/3) + 4056 + 9464 - 40$$
$$= 7621.333.$$

Note that because $\pi > 0$, $P > \text{ATC} > \text{AVC}$. Hence, this firm would not shut down. On top of this, we can also find the ATC curve for this firm:

$$ATC(X) = TC(X)/X = [(1/3)X^3 - 6X^2 + 36X + 40]/X$$
$$= (1/3)X^2 - 6X + 36 + 40/X.$$

Note that $TVC(X) = (1/3)X^3 - 6X^2 + 36X$, and TFC $= 40$. Thus, from the above, we know that $AVC(X) = (1/3)X^2 - 6X + 36$ and $AFC(X) = 40/X$. We can graph these separately and then add them. With some effort (by completing the square), we find that AVC is a parabola of the form $(Y - k) = a(X - h)^2$ where, in this case, $a = (1/3)$, $h = 9$, and $k = 9$. Here, Y stands for AVC and X is output. So the parabola is U-shaped with the lowest point at the point $(9, 9)$. The average fixed cost is a constantly declining function that becomes asymptotic to the X-axis. When we add $AVC(X)$ and $AFC(X)$ to get $ATC(X)$, we see that $ATC(X)$ will be substantially above $AVC(X)$ for small values of X and then $ATC(X)$ and $AVC(X)$ will get closer and closer as X rises. Now it is your turn. Try these exercises!

Exercise 15. Suppose that $P = 79$ and $MC(X) = X^2 - 50X + 655$. Find the profit-maximizing output. In this case, do you get two positive outputs? How can you tell which output provides the maximum profit? Which of the two outputs is the profit maximum? Use the second derivative to find out!

Exercise 16. Suppose that $P = 141$ and $TC(X) = (1/3)X^3 - 30X^2 + 920X + 50$. Find the profit-maximizing output for this firm. Does this firm make a positive profit at the maximum? Also find the AVC and the AFC. Write the equation of supply curve (i.e., find MC).

Exercise 17. Suppose that $P = 4$ and $TC(X) = (1/3)X^3 - 10X^2 + 95X + 100$. Find the profit-maximizing output for this firm. Does this firm make a positive profit at the maximum? Find the AVC at the profit maximum. What should this firm do?

Section Summary:
In this section, we have applied calculus to the problem of finding the profit maximum. We have also found a way, based on the second derivative of profit, to distinguish a maximum from a minimum.

5.9   Summary

In this chapter, we have achieved the following:

A. Found the profit maximum for the firm.
B. Developed the shutdown rule.
C. Derived the competitive firm's supply curve.

The following are important lessons to take from this chapter:

A. If profit is maximum, then $MR = MC$.
B. If $P < AVC$, then the firm will shut down in the short run.
C. The competitive firm's supply is the MC above the AVC.
D. We also examined the reasons for the supply curve to shift. The supply shifts if there is a change in the input prices or in the technology.

In the next chapter, we will take up the case of an industry where there is a single firm, like the electric company.

Terms Defined:

- Total revenue
- Average revenue
- Marginal revenue
- Profit
- Competition
- Supply curve

Chapter 6

Monopoly

Key Concepts:

- Demand and average revenue
- Marginal revenue lies below demand
- Profit maximization
- Supply for the monopoly
- Comparison of monopoly and competition

Goals:

- Relate average revenue and demand.
- Find MR when demand slopes downward.
- Find the profit-maximizing output and price.
- Compare the outcome of monopoly to competition.

So far we have looked at the case of supply for the competitive firm. But we know that there are a lot of firms that are not competitive. So what alternatives are there? One alternative is the monopoly, the case where one firm is the market. The example we used of a monopoly firm in Chapter 4 was the electric company. Keep that idea in mind as we begin this investigation!

6.1   Introduction

In some sense, we all know what monopoly firms are, and we do not like them. We believe that they waste resources and generally keep their prices high. In this chapter, we will start by taking the general revenue concepts and developing the revenue curves for the case when the firm is a monopoly. Once we have revenue, we can combine it with the standard cost curves and find profit. This will be followed by profit maximization, the standard assumption for firm behavior. Unlike the case of competition, we will find both the profit-maximizing quantity and the price. Once we have looked carefully at the monopoly, we will compare this outcome with the competitive case. Is the monopoly price high? Do they misallocate resources? Time to find out!

6.2   Revenue for a Monopoly

In this chapter, we will examine the profit maximization problem faced by the monopoly. The word "monopoly" has a prefix, *mono-*, meaning "single," and a suffix, *-poly*, meaning "seller." So the monopoly is the case of a market or industry where there is a single seller. In our earlier discussion about firms, we used the electric company as an example of a monopoly. Because there is only one firm in the industry, the firm is the market. Consequently, the firm faces the market demand. This will have impacts on the firm's revenue, and we turn to that matter now.

In the previous chapter, we developed the ideas of total revenue, average revenue, marginal revenue, and profit. We will use those ideas here — they are defined in the same general way. However, we now wish to apply these to the case of the monopoly.

We will start by thinking about total revenue. To find TR, we need both price and quantity sold. Generally speaking, when dealing with any firm, but especially a monopoly, the consumer expects to have the firm determine the price and the consumer decides the quantity to purchase. The firm does not choose the quantity. Second, the firm chooses one of the two, either price or quantity, but not both. So it seems that we should have the firm choose the price, and then from demand we would get the quantity consumers purchase. If this story is accurate, the firm would then be choosing the profit-maximizing price rather than the profit-maximizing quantity. However, in an effort to use what we have already done, we will see the firm as choosing the quantity, not the price. We will then use demand to determine price.

Note again that the firm can choose one of the two, either price or quantity; they cannot choose both price and quantity. You see the role played by demand. If the firm chooses price, then the quantity is obtained from the demand curve. If the firm chooses quantity, the price is obtained from the demand curve. Let us explore the role played by demand a bit further. What follows should remind you of our discussion following the slope of demand in Chapter 3.

We know from the definition of demand that the demand is written so that the quantity demanded is a function of the price, $X = X(P)$. This poses a bit of a problem (also discussed in Chapter 3, immediately following definition 3.1). To find total revenue, we multiply price times quantity. Hence, we would have $TR = P \times X = P \times X(P)$. In this equation, total revenue is a function of price. However, we have defined total revenue as a function of quantity. To leave the quantity a function of price will not allow us to find TR as the definition requires. If we could take demand and rewrite it so that price is a function of quantity, we would be fine. In that case, $TR = P \times X = P(X) \times X$ and total revenue would depend on X, not P. Thus, we will have to re-write the demand curve to make the price a function of quantity.

Suppose for the moment that the market demand for a good is $X = 5000 - 10P$. This says that the quantity demanded, X, is a function of price. What if we now want the price to be a function of quantity? We simply solve the above function for P. Here is what we get:

$$10P = 5000 - X$$
$$P = 500 - (1/10)X.$$

We would now use this function, average revenue, to find total revenue. We would have the following:

$$TR(X) = P \times X = (500 - (1/10)X) \times X = 500X - 0.1X^2.$$

You can see what would have happened if we had not made this change. We would have had $X = 5000 - 10P$. If we put that in the formula for

TR, we would have had $TR(X) = (5000 - 10P) \times P$. There is no X in this equation, which does not satisfy the definition of total revenue, so it is not a usable way to proceed.

Exercise 1. Graph the TR we have just found.

Thus, we have found the total revenue. However, in general, we do not know much about its shape. But, based on the demand, we can find the average revenue and the marginal revenue for the monopoly. We start with the average revenue.

Proposition 6.1: *If we solve the monopolist's demand for P, then the resulting equation is* AR.

Proof 6.2: We will proceed directly. Suppose we have solved the firm's demand for P, so we have $P = P(X)$. By definition, average revenue is total revenue divided by output:

$$AR(X) = \frac{TR(X)}{X} = \frac{P(X) \times X}{X} = P(X).$$

Hence, $AR(X) = P(X)$, which is the demand curve solved for P. The technical language is that $AR(X)$ and the demand are inverse functions. □

If we have $X = X(P)$, then we have demand. If we have $P = P(X)$, then we have AR. We will need both these concepts in what follows, and will refer to the AR form to mean $P = P(X)$. If we talk about demand, we mean $X = X(P)$. In any case, the AR and the demand look like the same function to us.

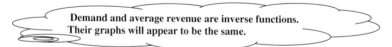

Demand and average revenue are inverse functions. Their graphs will appear to be the same.

We may now turn to the marginal revenue. Look back at proposition 4.19, the average marginal fact. It says that if the average is falling (that is, if the average has a negative slope), then the marginal must lie below the average. Hence, we know from that proposition that the MR must lie below the AR. We show this in Figure 6.1.

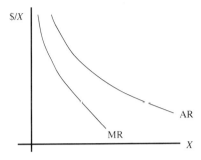

Figure 6.1 In this graph, we show the AR for the monopoly along with the MR, which lies below the AR. You should also know that the AR and demand are essentially the same curve.

There is an alternative way to find the MR and see its relationship to AR, which we will pursue now. One assumption was made in what we just did that may not be apparent, and we will highlight it now. In finding MR, the one important and basic assumption is that all consumers pay the same price. It is not the case in a monopoly that some consumers pay one price and other consumers pay another. Suppose the firm contemplates a reduction in price; that means that every consumer will pay the lower price, not just the new consumers in the market.

We will find MR by starting at some level of output and increasing output by one unit. We will then find what happens to the price and the revenue, and try to place the MR relative to the AR.

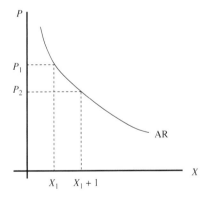

Figure 6.2 MR is the change in TR when output changes. Here we change output by one unit, and find the change in TR that results.

Proposition 6.3: *If the average revenue slopes down, then the marginal revenue will lie below the average revenue.*

Proof 6.4: Look at Figure 6.2. Here we show the downward-sloping average revenue (demand) curve. Suppose that the firm is producing X_1 units of output. The firm generates some amount of total revenue, $P_1 \times X_1$. Now suppose that we increase output to $X_1 + 1$, one unit more than X_1. The new total revenue will be $P_2 \times (X_1 + 1)$. We can now find the marginal revenue of the new unit, $MR(X_1 + 1)$:

$$MR(X_1 + 1) = \frac{\Delta TR}{\Delta X} = \frac{TR(X_1 + 1) - TR(X_1)}{X_1 + 1 - X_1}$$

$$= \frac{P_2 \times (X_1 + 1) - P_1 \times X_1}{X_1 + 1 - X_1}.$$

Now multiply the numerator out and note that the denominator is exactly 1, because that is how much X changed, by one. We obtain the following:

$$MR(X_1 + 1) = P_2 \times X_1 + P_2 - P_1 \times X_1$$

$$= P_2 + X_1 \times (P_2 - P_1).$$

Note that $X_1 \times (P_2 - P_1) < 0$ because $P_2 < P_1$. Hence, $MR(X_1 + 1) < P_2 = AR(X_1 + 1)$. This argument holds for all X, so MR lies below AR.   □

A key fact is that the price falls as X rises, that is, the AR has a negative slope. Because of that, as X rises, the price falls from P_1 to P_2. Note now the assumption we have made. The consumers that were once paying a higher price are now paying a lower price, and that reduction in revenue offsets some of the increase in revenue from selling another unit, the price of that unit, P_2. Thus, the marginal revenue is the gain in revenue from the sale of another unit, P_2, minus the revenue given up because to sell that unit, the price had to fall.

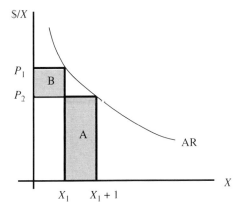

Figure 6.3   MR is area A minus area B. Area A is the revenue gained from selling one more unit at price P_2. Area B is the revenue given up due to having to lower the price to get someone to buy the extra unit.

In Figure 6.3, you can see the gain in revenue from selling one more unit, the price of that unit, P_2. Area A is exactly P_2. But the firm has to give up area B because to get someone to buy the extra unit, they had to lower the price for all buyers! The amount they give up is the difference in price $(P_1 - P_2)$ times the number of units they were selling at the higher price, X_1. The MR is area A minus area B, just as the computation in proof 6.4 says. The conclusion is that MR is less than the price which is AR, so MR lies below the AR.

Another alternative way to derive the expression for MR is to take the derivative of the total revenue. We know that TR $= X \times P(X)$. Thus,

$$MR(X) = TR'(X) = P(X) + X \times P'(X).$$

This expression agrees with our computation above,

$$MR(X_1 + 1) = P_2 + X_1 \times (P_2 - P_1).$$

You can see that $P(X)$ and P_2 are the same, and $X_1 \times (P_2 - P_1) = X \times P'(X)$. The latter equality results because in our initial computation, we have $dX = 1$, and $(P_2 - P_1)$ is dP, so $dP/dX = (P_2 - P_1)/1$.

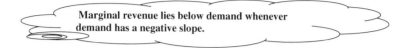

Marginal revenue lies below demand whenever demand has a negative slope.

We are now ready to bring the cost curves into the computation, and look for the profit maximum. Do you see what will happen as a result?

Exercise 2. Suppose that the firm can charge a different price for each unit of the good. Thus, the consumer pays P_1 for the first unit, P_2 for the second, P_3 for the third, and so on, where P_1 is the price on the demand for the first unit, P_2 is the price on demand for the second unit, and so on. What would MR be then?

Exercise 3. Suppose that $P = 100 - 5X$ is average revenue. Find TR and MR. Graph both average revenue and MR. At each X, how is MR related to price?

Exercise 4. Recall the definition of price elasticity of demand from Chapter 3. Following the definition of price elasticity, we found that expenditure on a good is related to price elasticity. Suppose demand is inelastic. What happens to expenditure on a good as the price falls? Suppose that the firm is a monopoly. How is consumer expenditure on the good related to the firm's total revenue? What conclusion can you draw concerning what happens to total revenue as price falls (and quantity rises)? What can you say about marginal revenue when demand is inelastic? Explain how you know!

> **Section Summary:**
> In this section, we have developed the revenue curves for the monopoly. These curves are different than for the competitive case, as the MR slopes down for monopoly but is horizontal for the competitive case. Now that we have the revenue for the monopoly understood, we can bring in the cost curves to complete the picture. The cost curves will be the same as in the competitive case. The process of finding the profit maximum will be next!

6.3   Profit Maximization for a Monopoly

In this section, we will work on finding the profit-maximizing choice for the monopoly firm. We have developed the revenue concepts in the previous section, and we have the cost curves from Chapter 4, so we are ready to go. We start with the profit maximization proposition, which will be familiar to you. Then we find the price the firm charges, and examine the shutdown condition. We will find the firm's supply in the following section.

Proposition 6.5: Profit Maximization for Monopoly

If   a.   *the assumptions of least cost hold,*

       b.   *the* MC *and* MR *are continuous,*

       c.   *at* $X_0, 0 < X_0 < \infty$, *profit is maximum for the monopoly firm,*

Then   d.   *at* X_0, MR = MC.

Proof 6.6: By contrapositive. We wish to show that if MR is not equal to MC, then profit is not maximum. That means that if MR is not equal to MC, there is an output where profit would be higher. There are two cases: if MR > MC, then profit is not maximum; and if MR < MC, then profit is not maximum. We start with the first case and leave the second to the reader.

Suppose that MR > MC. Then we must be at an output such as at X_1 (how do we know this?) in Figure 6.4.

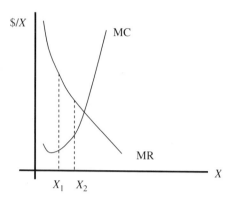

Figure 6.4   In this graph, we see that as we increase output from X_1 to X_2, the increase in total revenue is greater than the increase in total cost, so profit rises. Hence, profit cannot be maximum at an output like X_1.

Suppose we increase output to X_2. We know that TR rises by the area under MR (how do we know this?). TC rises by the area under MC (how do we know this?). Because MR > MC, by hypothesis, the increase in total revenue is greater than the increase in total cost. Hence, profit rises and is not maximum at X_1.   □

Exercise 5. The proof of the second case is left to the student. Now is a good time to try this!

Exercise 6. How is the statement and proof of this proposition different from the competitive case?

Exercise 7. In Exercise 4, we discussed what happens to marginal revenue when demand is inelastic. Can a monopoly ever find a profit maximum on the inelastic portion of its demand? How do you know?

Exercise 8. Use the result of Exercise 2 and find the profit-maximizing output for the firm that can charge a different price for each unit.

Exercise 9.   In the proof, we said that as X rises from X_1 to X_2, total revenue rises. How do we know TR rises and does not fall? After all, MR is falling.

FROM THE LITERATURE

We have examined firms as if they choose output, yet most firms that are not competitive choose the price. Does the choice of price reflect profit maximization? Again, in the context of sports, one might ask how firms set prices. In part, the price will depend on alternatives that the fan might have for their entertainment dollar. In a given location, there may not be more than one team from a given sport available for the fan to see. So if someone in Chicago wants to see hockey, they only have the Blackhawks to watch. However, there is hockey at the collegiate level and basketball, so the pricing decision does not just depend on what hockey prices might be. One study suggests that the pricing of NHL hockey tickets is strongly related to the profit maximization hypothesis. You can find details at D. Ferguson, K. Stewart, J. Jones, and Andre Le Dressay, "The Pricing of Sports Events: Do Teams Maximize Profits?," *Journal of Industrial Economics*, Vol. 39, No. 3, March, 1991, pp. 297–310.

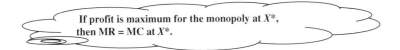

If profit is maximum for the monopoly at X^*, then MR = MC at X^*.

Now that we have found the output the monopolist produces, we need to see what price the monopolist charges. Note again that the monopolist chooses either the quantity to produce or the price to charge, not both. So what price will the monopolist charge?

The binding restriction on the monopoly is the demand. Hence, we can use the demand to determine the price to charge. Consider Figure 6.5.

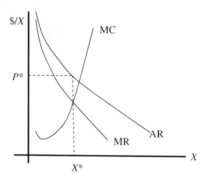

Figure 6.5   In this graph, the profit-maximizing output is X^*. The corresponding price is P^*.

In this graph, we see that when the profit-maximizing output is X^*, the corresponding price is P^*. But why cannot the price be higher than P^*? Suppose it was. Look at what happens as a result; the outcome is in Figure 6.6.

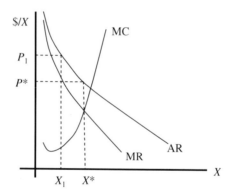

Figure 6.6   At a price higher than P^*, such as P_1, the firm would only sell X_1 according to the demand. But we already know that X_1 is not the profit-maximizing choice for the firm.

When the price is above P^*, then the firm will only sell X_1 units of the good. This is less than the profit-maximizing quantity, which occurs at X^*, the output where MR and MC intersect. Hence, the firm would not choose a price of P_1, or any price above P^*, because the firm would sell too little output at that price to maximize profit.

It is clear that the firm would not charge a lower price, because to do so would increase the number of units sold beyond the profit-maximizing output. Hence, when the quantity is X^*, the corresponding price must be the price on the demand curve, P^*.

One might now ask about whether the firm would ever want to produce zero output. Will there be a shutdown condition for the monopoly? In fact, there is. It is the very same condition as we had for the competitive firm, and the analysis leading to this conclusion is exactly the same as before. You should go through the process to check your understanding.

Exercise 10. What is the shutdown condition for the monopoly? Why is this condition the correct condition?

Section Summary:
In this section, we have developed the profit-maximizing proposition for the monopoly. In addition, we found the price the monopolist will charge and looked at the shutdown condition. We are now ready to examine the monopolist's supply.

6.4 Supply for a Monopoly

In this section, we will look for the supply for the monopoly. We will base this search on the profit-maximizing hypothesis, and the information we have developed above.

Consider Figure 6.7. Here we have the demand for the firm's output (market demand and essentially the AR), the firm's associated MR, and the MC curve. From these we determine the profit-maximizing output and price, labeled X^* and P^*, in the graph. If this point is above the AVC, then this is the only point on the supply as the firm will not produce any other quantity and therefore will set no other price. Hence, there is no other point on the monopolist's supply.

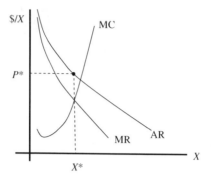

Figure 6.7   In this graph, the profit-maximizing output is X^*. The corresponding price is P^*. If the price is above the firm's AVC at X^*, then this point is the only point on the monopolist's supply.

You might wonder exactly how this can be. After all, in the case of the competitive firm we found the supply by varying the price the firm faces, finding the profit-maximizing output, and utilizing the shutdown condition.

To find the competitive firm's supply, we need the price to change. The only way the price could change in this exercise is if the competitive market demand changes. So why can't we change demand here and see what happens? The problem is that in the competitive case, we do not care how the demand changes; all that matters is the price that is generated in the market. But in monopoly, the way demand shifts will matter. We could have demand shift in two different ways and yet their respective MR curves could cross the MC at the same output, but the prices would be different. This causes a good deal of ambiguity for the concept of supply. Rather than allow this ambiguity, we simply refuse to allow the demand to shift at all.

Exercise 11. Return to Exercises 2 and 8. What is the lowest price the monopolist would charge at profit maximization in the case that the firm could charge a different price for each unit (each consumer pays a different price)?

> **Section Summary:**
> In this section, we developed the supply for the monopoly firm. The supply turned out to be a point, not a curve. You should remember how the competitive firm looked and how the results of monopoly are different from the results of the competitive firm. We will begin the comparison in the next section.

6.5   How Is a Monopoly Different from a Competitive Firm?

As citizens, we know that it is widely thought that monopoly is a bad thing and that competition is a good thing. Yet when we look at the profit-maximizing propositions, we can hardly tell them apart, suggesting that monopoly is not that much different from the competitive model. How much different are they? In this section, we will begin to examine this issue. It will come up for discussion again in the next chapter.

One difference we can easily see is that the competitive firm's supply is the same as its marginal cost above the AVC curve. The monopoly firm's supply is simply a point at the profit-maximizing output and the associated price from the demand curve. It is often argued that monopoly will charge a higher price than will occur in a competitive market. We will look at this issue in a moment, but we need to start with a look at some graphical analysis.

"Being a monopolist is not all it's cracked up to be. Some people go without rather than pay our exorbitant prices."

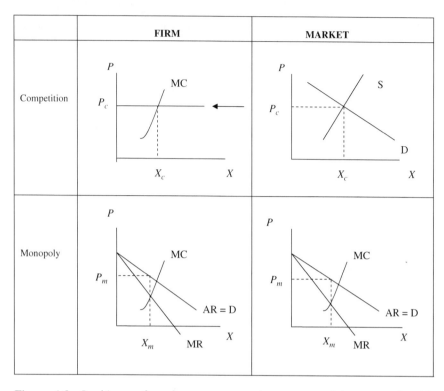

Figure 6.8   In this set of graphs, we compare the outcome of the monopoly with competition. In the upper right, we have the competitive market; it is the standard supply and demand where price is determined. In the upper left is the competitive firm taking the price from the market and maximizing profit where MR = MC. The two lower graphs are the monopoly firm and market. But because the market and the firm are the same, we have the same graph for both the market and the firm. Again, we have profit maximization and MR = MC for the monopoly.

In Figure 6.8, we have four graphs, one each for the competitive market and firm and one each for the monopoly market and firm. The upper right is the competitive market, where the price is determined. It is the familiar supply and demand graph. The firm, shown in the upper left, takes the price from the market and maximizes profit. In the lower two graphs, we have the monopoly where the firm is also the market. First, observe that when we draw supply and demand, we are assuming that the market is competitive. Second, the **competitive firm's supply** is its MC above the AVC. The **market supply for competition** is the horizontal sum of the individual firms' supply, their MC curves (above AVC).

We can now compare the outcome at the market level if we make some assumptions. Suppose we consider two different scenarios. In one scenario, the market is competitive. In the second scenario, the market is monopoly. Suppose that the market demand is the same whether the firm is competitive or monopoly. Now bring in the cost curves and suppose that the MC for the monopoly is the same as the sum of the MC curves for the competitive firms. We would then have this proposition.

Proposition 6.7: *If the demand under competition would be the same as the demand under monopoly, and if the MC for the monopoly would be the same as the sum of the individual competitive firms' MC curves, then the profit-maximizing monopoly produces less output and charges a higher price than would occur under competition.*

Proof 6.8: We start with the graph in Figure 6.9. Here we show the monopoly with demand D and MR and the monopoly marginal cost, MC_m. We find profit maximization for the monopoly as usual, and the firm chooses X_m which requires a price of P_m. Under competition, we look for supply and demand to determine price and quantity. In this case, we have assumed that the sum of the individual competitive firms' MC is the same as the MC for the monopoly, and because MC is supply, the market supply under competition would be the sum of the individual firms' supply or MC_m. So under competition, we would have a price of P_c and a quantity of X_c. We see that the competitive quantity is larger than the monopoly's and the competitive price is lower than the monopoly price. □

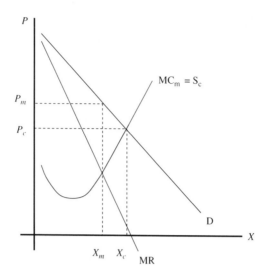

Figure 6.9   In this graph, we see that the monopoly would maximize profit at X_m (use MC_m and MR to find monopoly profit maximization), whereas the competitive market would end up where supply (equal to MC_m by assumption) and D intersect, at X_c and P_c. We get a greater output and lower price under competition compared to monopoly.

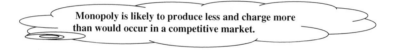

Monopoly is likely to produce less and charge more than would occur in a competitive market.

> Exercise 12. Return to Exercises 2, 8, and 11. How does the monopoly which charges a different price for each unit (to each consumer) compare to the competitive case? Focus on the price of the last unit the monopoly sells.

This outcome is one of the reasons why economists like the competitive model so much. It yields better results than we find under monopoly. But you should be a bit suspicious of this result. One of the assumptions we made to generate this result was that the MC for the monopoly is equal to the sum of the individual competitive firms' MC curves. But this suggests that there is no cost advantage to a firm from being large. Surely one of the reasons why monopoly happens is that there are some economies of scale and the firm finds a way to lower the cost by getting larger. This thought would suggest that the MC for the monopoly would be lower than the sum of the individual competitive firms' MC curves. So the above result might not hold. Still, economists prefer competition to monopoly, and in the next chapter we will come back to this issue with a better approach.

Section Summary:
In this section, we have compared the monopoly firm to the situation under competition. We have discovered that when we draw supply and demand, we are assuming that the market is made up of competitive firms. In addition, we have argued that if the MC for the monopoly is the same as the sum of the individual competitive firms' MC, then the monopoly will charge more and produce less than would occur under competition. This suggests that there is something undesirable about monopoly.

6.6 Monopoly Profit Maximization Using Calculus

In this section, we will use calculus to find the profit-maximizing output and price. We assume that we are given the demand, and from that we find the revenue concepts. The cost concepts are then introduced, and profit is found, followed by the maximization process.

Suppose that we have a market demand $X = 48 - 0.5P$. Recall that total revenue is price times quantity. If we use the demand to get price times quantity, we would have the total revenue in terms of P, while our cost would be in terms of X. So we need to rewrite the demand as average revenue. If we do this, we would get $P = 96 - 2X$. Then total revenue, $P \times X$, would be:

$$\text{TR} = (96 - 2X)X.$$

Exercise 13. Explain how we got $P = 96 - 2X$ from $X = 48 - 0.5P$.

Suppose that we are given the total cost as $(1/3)X^3 - 3X^2 + 16X + 10$. We can now write profit as TR – TC:

$$\pi = (96 - 2X)X - (1/3)X^3 + 3X^2 - 16X - 10.$$

Simplify this equation to obtain the following:

$$\pi = 96X - 2X^2 - (1/3)X^3 + 3X^2 - 16X - 10$$
$$= -(1/3)X^3 + X^2 + 80X - 10.$$

The first derivative of profit is

$$\pi' = -X^2 + 2X + 80.$$

We will set this to zero and solve for X to find the profit-maximizing choice:

$$-X^2 + 2X + 80 = 0.$$

The expression factors are as shown:

$$(-X + 10)(X + 8) = 0.$$

So $X = 10$ or $X = -8$ are the possible profit maxima.

Only one of these solutions makes sense — probably producing negative amounts of output will not work. But there is a more compelling reason. Only one of the two provides a maximum. The other is a minimum. How do we know? We use the second derivative test, proposition A.15. We go back to the first derivative and find the second derivative. Here is what we get:

$$\pi''(X) = -2X + 2.$$

Now evaluate at the two points where the first derivative is zero:

$$\pi''(10) = -2 \times 10 + 2 = -20 + 2 = -18.$$
$$\pi''(-8) = (-2) \times (-8) + 2 = 16 + 2 = 18.$$

We can see that because $\pi''(10) < 0$, we have a maximum at $X = 10$. Because $\pi''(-8) > 0$, we know we have a minimum at $X = -8$.

We now need to find the equilibrium price. This is pretty easy to do. We simply put the profit-maximizing quantity back into the average revenue and solve for P:

$$P = 96 - 2X = 96 - 2 \times 10 = 96 - 20 = 76.$$

We can also find the amount of profit the firm makes. Plug the profit-maximizing output into the profit function and evaluate. Our profit function (from above) is:

$$\pi = -(1/3)X^3 + X^2 + 80X - 10.$$

When $X = 10$, $\pi = -(1/3)10^3 + 10^2 + 80 \times 10 - 10 = -1000/3 + 100 + 800 - 10 = 1670/3$.

Exercise 14. Find the profit maximum for the following demand and total cost curves:

    a. $X = (135/3)-(1/3)P$, $TC = (1/3)X^3-10X^2+175X + 50$.

    b. $X=(273/4) - P/4$, $TC=(1/3)X^3-(53/2)X^2+623X + 25$.

    c. $X = 125 - 0.2P$, $TC = (1/3)X^3 - (15/2)X^2 + 601X + 30$.

Exercise 15. For problem c in Exercise 14, assume that the monopolist's MC is the supply that would exist if the market were competitive. Find the MC. Now find the price that would hold if the market were competitive by finding the intersection of the MC and the AR. Find the corresponding quantity. Compare your results with the price and quantity the monopoly would produce. What do you find?

Exercise 16. In this section, we have assumed that the firm chooses the quantity of output to produce. We also pointed out that this seems to be out of step with what we would expect. Why does the firm not choose the price and allow the market to determine the quantity sold? Suppose $X = 48 - 0.5P$ and TC $= (1/3)X^3 - 3X^2 + 16X + 10$. This is the same data we used in our example above. Find TR by multiplying X by P. What do you get? Now replace X in TC with $48 - 0.5P$. What do you get? Write an expression for profit using the TR and TC you have just found. What do you get? Find the value of P that maximizes profit. What do you get? How does this result relate to what we found earlier?

Section Summary:
In this section, we have used calculus to find the profit-maximizing output the monopoly firm will produce and the price the firm will charge.

6.7   Summary

In this chapter, we have examined the monopoly and the following results are important lessons from this chapter:

A. For monopoly, average revenue is the inverse of demand.

B. MR lies below the demand (or average revenue).

C. If profit is maximum, then MR $=$ MC.

D. The monopoly seems to produce less and charge a higher price than we would obtain under competition.

The comparison of monopoly and competition will arise again in the next chapter, where we will also ask what kind of regulation we might consider for a monopoly.

Terms Defined:

- Demand
- Average revenue
- Marginal revenue

Chapter 7

More Monopoly

Key Concepts:

- To properly allocate resources, we need for the ratio of marginal social benefit to marginal social cost to be the same for all goods
- When price measures marginal social benefit and marginal cost measures marginal social cost, then competitive markets properly allocate resources
- Regulation of monopoly to properly allocate resources can be achieved with a price ceiling
- Regulation of monopoly requires the cooperation of the monopoly and is difficult to achieve

Goals:

- Establish a criterion for proper allocation of resources.
- Apply the criterion to worlds with monopoly.
- Examine ways to regulate the monopoly to achieve competitive outcomes.
- Examine the case of natural monopoly.

In the previous chapter, we determined that under some conditions, monopoly does charge a price higher than would occur under competition. We knew monopoly was bad! Is this the end of the story? Are there other ways to demonstrate the badness of monopoly? We will try to develop the argument in this chapter.

7.1   Introduction

So far our understanding of the imperfection of monopoly is due to the higher price charged by monopoly. We can see the impact of monopoly in other ways. In this chapter, we will develop the ideas of consumer surplus, producer surplus, and dead weight loss. We follow this with a discussion of a criterion for efficient allocation of resources, and apply the criterion to the case of monopoly. If monopoly is all that bad, what can be done about it? What forms of regulation are there? Do they work? Regulation of monopoly by using a price ceiling will be discussed, and the possible failure of regulation in the presence of natural monopoly will also be considered.

7.2   Consumer and Producer Surplus

The point of economic activity is to make people better off. We would like to find a way to spend our scarce resources to make the total satisfaction of the society as high as possible. The problem is that we have many people with many different wants and needs, and we have a variety of ways we could spend our resources. Which allocation would be the one that provides the greatest satisfaction to the society?

We start by looking at a measure of satisfaction from the consumption of a good.

One way to think about market demand is as the highest price that some consumer is willing to pay at each quantity. As the quantity increases, the highest price consumers are willing to pay falls. We call this price the marginal willingness to pay or the demand price.

Definition 7.1: *The **marginal willingness to pay** or **demand price** of quantity X_1 is the price on the demand curve at quantity X_1.*

In Figure 7.1, we see for the first unit that the consumer is willing to pay up to P_1. That makes P_1 the marginal willingness to pay or demand price.

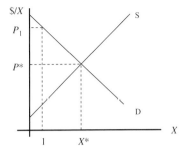

Figure 7.1   The consumer buying the first unit of the good would be willing to pay a price of P_1, the marginal willingness to pay or demand price.

Definition 7.2: *The **total willingness to pay** for units up to X_1 is the area under the demand between the origin and X_1.*

> Exercise 1. You should be thinking that the marginal willingness to pay is the change in the total willingness to pay as quantity changes by 1. Is this the standard marginal–total relationship? Explain how you know. Is the marginal the slope of the total in this case?

In Figure 7.2, we show the total willingness to pay for the quantity X^*, the total amount of value that consumers get from the consumption of the good up to X^* output.

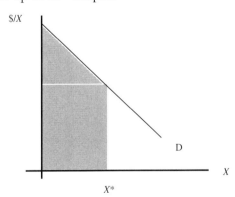

Figure 7.2   The total willingness to pay for X^* units is the area under demand up to X^*, the shaded area.

In our world, all consumers pay the same price for all units of the good. This means that consumers are getting more value than they paid for. Suppose we have a market that has an equilibrium at the quantity X^* and the corresponding price is P^*, as shown in Figure 7.3. Think about the consumer of the first unit of the good. That consumer would be willing to pay up to price P_1 for the good, the demand price, a measure of the value of the first unit to the consumer. Yet the consumer only has to pay P^*. That means that the consumer got a surplus value of $P_1 - P^*$ by consuming that unit of the good. As we work our way toward X^*, each added unit has a smaller surplus value than the previous unit. When we get to X^*, that unit has no surplus value, and the price paid is exactly what the good is worth. The total of all this surplus value is the consumer surplus, as shown in Figure 7.3.

Definition 7.3: *Consumer surplus is the value the consumer places on the good, the demand price, minus the price the consumer pays for the good for all units consumed.*

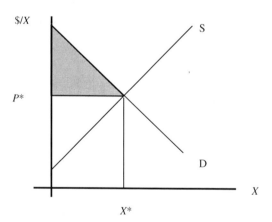

Figure 7.3   The consumer surplus is the amount of value the consumer obtains above what he or she pays for the good, the area under demand above P^*, as shown in the shaded area.

Exercise 2. Suppose that we have a market and the consumer is forced to buy more than X^* at the price P^*. What will the consumer surplus be then?

Exercise 3. Suppose that we have a market and the consumer buys X^*, but pays a price higher than P^*. What will the consumer surplus be then?

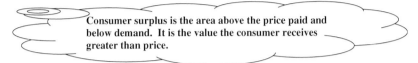

Consumer surplus is the area above the price paid and below demand. It is the value the consumer receives greater than price.

We need to be a bit careful. The problem is that it may happen that there is some externality that occurs during the consumption of the good. So suppose that you buy a good, say a pogo stick, and people come from miles around to see you do tricks on the pogo stick. They get a positive externality out of your consumption of the pogo stick. In that case, the sale of the pogo stick would be worth to society more than the price paid; there would be value to those watching you do pogo stick tricks! In that case, we will need a concept called the marginal social willingness to pay.

Definition 7.4: *The **marginal social willingness to pay** of a given quantity is the sum of the willingness to pay for that quantity plus the value of the externality of that quantity.*

In our above discussion, the marginal willingness to pay and the price are the same. But in the presence of externalities, the marginal social willingness to pay and the price will be different. In what follows, we will, for the most part, assume away the externalities in consumption. It is not that we believe that there are none or that they have a small impact, but that the assumption leads us to a useful conclusion.

Suppose we now turn to cost. We already know that the cost to the firm to produce another unit is the marginal cost. We also know that under competitive conditions, the marginal cost is the firm's supply. If we look at supply as we just looked at demand, we would see that at the first unit, the smallest price that would induce a firm to produce that unit is the price on the supply curve, P_1, the supply price. For the second unit, the firm would require a higher price, say P_2. We also know that the firm sells all units for the same price, P^*. So for the first unit, the firm gets $P^* - P_1$ surplus value. For the second unit, the surplus value is $P^* - P_2$. If we continue up to the equilibrium output, we obtain a surplus.

Definition 7.5: *Producer surplus is the price the producer receives for the good minus the value the firm places on the good for all units sold.*

You can predict that the producer surplus is the area above the supply and below the price line. This is shown in Figure 7.4.

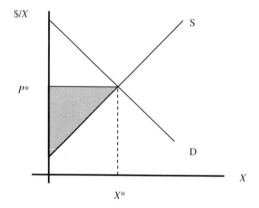

Figure 7.4   The producer surplus is the area above the supply and below the market price, as shown in the shaded area.

Exercise 4. Suppose that we have a market and the firm is forced to produce more than X^* at the price P^*. What will the producer surplus be then?

Exercise 5. Suppose that we have a market and the producer produces X^*, but receives a price higher than P^*. What will the producer surplus be then?

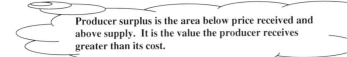

Producer surplus is the area below price received and above supply. It is the value the producer receives greater than its cost.

As is true in the case of the consumer, there are externalities to consider. The cost to the firm is not necessarily the cost to society of that extra unit. What if there is an externality in production? Suppose that a steel mill produces both steel and air pollution. Now the cost to society of a ton of steel is both the cost of the resources needed to produce the steel as well as the cost to society of the air pollution, the increased cost of health care and the like. Obviously, we need a concept of marginal social cost.

Definition 7.6: *Marginal social cost* (MSC) *is the cost to society of producing an added unit of output.*

Section Summary:
In this section, we have developed the ideas of consumer and producer surplus as well as the idea that price is a measure of the value of a good to the consumer and that marginal cost measures the value of the resources that go into the production of the good. Based on these definitions, we will develop a criterion for how resources should be allocated. That is the next task.

7.3 How Should Resources Be Allocated?

In this section, we will look at an idea for how to evaluate an allocation of resources. We will do this based on the definitions and concepts we have just developed, but we will need to do so within the confines of a model. Hence, we start with some assumptions.

Assumptions 7.7:
a. *There are two goods, X and Y.*
b. *We know the price of each of the goods, P_x and P_y, respectively.*

c. *We know the* MSC *of each good,* MSC_x *and* MSC_y.
d. *There is a limited amount of resources to spend on the production of X and Y.*
e. *There are no unemployed resources.*
f. *Inputs and outputs are infinitely divisible.*
g. *Either there are no externalities in consumption or production or the externalities are properly paid for.*

The question is whether we should take resources out of the production of one good and place them into the production of the other good. Suppose we have two goods, spaghetti and linguini (only talking about the noodles). If the amount of resources needed to produce one pound of spaghetti is the same as the amount of resources needed to produce one pound of linguini, then we could reduce spaghetti production by a pound and lose the value to society measured by the price of spaghetti. We could then take the freed-up resources from the spaghetti and use them to make linguini. The society gains a value equal to the price of linguini. If the price of linguini is greater than the price of spaghetti, then we gain more than we gave up, and the society is better off. But what if the quantity of resources needed to produce one unit of a good is not the same as the quantity of resources needed to produce one unit of the other good? What do we do then?

There are a couple of options. Suppose we are producing Jaguars and yo-yos. One approach is to produce one fewer of the Jaguars so the society loses value equal to the value of the Jaguar. We take the resources from that one Jaguar and produce as many yo-yos as possible, and then the value we gain is the price of yo-yos times the number of additional yo-yos produced. A second way is to take a dollar's worth of resources from the production of the Jaguar and we would lose some small amount of value from the tiny portion of the Jaguar that was not produced, but we would take the resources and produce as many more yo-yos as possible. The society would gain the price of the yo-yos times the number of added yo-yos produced. While the two approaches are very similar, they differ in how the quantity of resources we trade is determined. We will follow the second method.

Suppose, then, that we take a dollar's worth of resources away from the production of a good. How many units of the good do we give up? We are reducing cost by one dollar, and we want to know the change in quantity of output produced. This should suggest to you that a marginal cost concept could be useful here. We are looking for the change in quantity if cost changes by one dollar — exactly the reciprocal of the marginal cost. In our case, because we want to include all the costs of the good that fall on society, we would use the MSC. So if we change the amount of resources needed to produce a good by one dollar, then the change in output of that good will be 1/MSC. What is the value of that change in output to society? The society values each unit by its price, so we multiply this change in quantity by the price of the good. We have the following outcome.

Definition 7.8: *Price/MSC is the change in value to society due to changing the spending by one dollar on the resources devoted to the production of the good. We will call this the change in social satisfaction.*

We are now ready to state the proposition we are looking for. It should not be a surprise to you.

Proposition 7.9: *If assumptions 7.7 hold and the satisfaction to society is maximum, then for each pair of goods X and Y, we must have $\frac{P_x}{MSC_x} = \frac{P_y}{MSC_y}$.*

Proof 7.10: We will prove the proposition by using the method of contrapositive. The contrapositive says if $\frac{P_x}{MSC_x} \neq \frac{P_y}{MSC_y}$, then social satisfaction is not maximum. There are two possible cases. Case 1 is if $\frac{P_x}{MSC_x} > \frac{P_y}{MSC_y}$, then social satisfaction is not maximum; and Case 2 says if $\frac{P_x}{MSC_x} < \frac{P_y}{MSC_y}$, then social satisfaction is not maximum. We will do Case 1 and leave Case 2 to the student.

For Case 1, we have $\frac{P_x}{MSC_x} > \frac{P_y}{MSC_y}$. We need to propose a new allocation of resources that leaves the society better off. Suppose we reduce the amount of resources used to produce good Y by one dollar. The quantity of good Y produced will fall by $1/MSC_y$. That output has a price of P_y. Thus, by reducing the resources to good Y by a dollar, the society loses P_y/MSC_y. If we now take the dollar's worth of resources we have freed up and put them in the production of X, we will gain $1/MSC_x$ more units of X and each unit of X has a price of P_x. By putting more resources into the production of X, we have gained P_x/MSC_x of value. Note that we have again reached full employment; there are no resources left over to use. But we gained P_x/MSC_x value and gave up P_y/MSC_y. Because $P_x/MSC_x > P_y/MSC_y$, there is a net gain in value and the society is better off. Hence, social satisfaction cannot be maximum. □

> Exercise 6. Prove Case 2.

We now have a criterion for deciding if we have a good resource allocation. Observe that we have not assumed any particular method of allocating resources. We have not assumed that we have competitive or monopoly markets. Before using the criterion, we should point out that this criterion has another name.

Definition 7.11: *Allocative efficiency* *occurs when* $\frac{P_x}{MSC_x} = \frac{P_y}{MSC_y}$.

We will see this condition arise again in Chapter 11. But now we can apply this criterion.

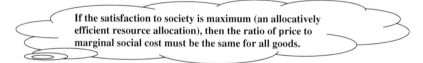

If the satisfaction to society is maximum (an allocatively efficient resource allocation), then the ratio of price to marginal social cost must be the same for all goods.

Section Summary:
In this section, we have stated and proved the primary proposition that we will use (in this chapter) to decide if resources are allocated as they should be. The proposition says that if we have an allocation that maximizes the social satisfaction, then the ratio of price to marginal social cost must be the same for all goods.

7.4   Do Monopolies Lead to a Misallocation of Resources?

In this section, we will apply the criterion that we developed in the previous section to a world including both competitive and monopoly firms. We will discover that when monopoly is present, there is a problem, but we cannot (yet) argue that monopoly is necessarily the culprit.

Suppose that there are two goods, X and Y. Suppose that X is produced under competitive conditions and Y is produced by a monopoly. How can we apply the proposition we previously developed? Look at the proposition. It says that if we start with a maximum of social satisfaction, then the ratio of price to marginal social cost for each good must be the same across goods. But we are looking to see if we have maximum social satisfaction; we do not yet know that this is true. On the other hand, we do know (by the contrapositive) that if the ratio of price to marginal social cost for each good is not the same across goods, then the total satisfaction of the society is not maximum. Hence, we will look to see if the ratio of price to marginal social cost is the same for all goods in this setting. A graph will help, as shown in Figure 7.5.

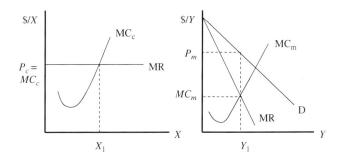

Figure 7.5   On the left, we have the competitive firm where at profit maximum, $P_c = MC_c$. On the right, we have the monopoly firm where at profit maximum, $P_m > MC_m$.

Here we have two graphs side by side. On the left, we have the competitive firm; and on the right, we have the monopoly. We also show the marginal cost for each firm. Two points need to be made.

First, the two marginal costs are the marginal social costs. This assumes that somehow we have managed to internalize all of the externalities so that the firm's marginal cost is marginal social cost. Second, there is no reason to think that the marginal cost of the monopoly will be the same as the marginal cost of the competitive firm or even that the marginal cost of the monopoly is the sum of the individual competitive firms' marginal costs.

Now suppose that both firms act to maximize profit. We know that they will each produce so that $MR = MC$. In the case of the competitive firm, $MR = P$, so at the profit maximum, we have P_c, the competitive price, equal to MC_c, the competitive marginal social cost. For the monopoly, by profit maximization, the firm produces so that $MR = MC$, but because of the monopoly condition, P_m, the monopoly's price, is greater than MR. So we have $P_m > MC_m$, the monopoly's marginal social cost. The conclusion is that we have $P_c/MC_c < P_m/MC_m$. Thus, by proposition 7.9, we now know that a world that includes both monopoly firms and competitive firms will not allocate resources to maximize social satisfaction. Is this misallocation due to the monopoly?

If we have only competitive firms, then we know that P/MC will be equal to one at profit maximum for all firms. But having P/MC the same for all firms does not guarantee that social satisfaction is maximum. Look again at proposition 7.9; it says that IF social satisfaction is maximum, THEN the ratio of price to marginal cost is the same for all goods. It does not say that IF the ratio of price to marginal cost is the same for all goods, THEN social satisfaction is maximum. We need the converse of the proposition we proved to establish whether monopoly is bad!

Exercise 7. State the converse of proposition 7.9.

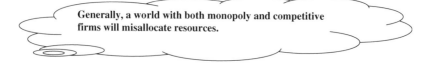

Generally, a world with both monopoly and competitive firms will misallocate resources.

Section Summary:
In this section, we have shown that a world with some monopoly and some competitive firms will not allocate resources so that the satisfaction of the society is maximum. However, we cannot lay the blame for the misallocation at the feet of the monopoly. For that, we need to examine the converse of proposition 7.9. We will take up this matter in the next section.

7.5 Under What Conditions Will Competition Allocate Resources Optimally?

In this section, we will examine the converse of proposition 7.9. If we can find a reason to believe that the converse is true, then we could conclude that competition does yield a socially desirable outcome for the society. Of course there may be other resource allocation mechanisms that also satisfy the requirements, but at least we would know that monopoly is a problem.

What are we looking for? Roughly speaking, the converse of proposition 7.9 says that if the ratio of price to marginal cost is the same for all firms, then social satisfaction is maximum. If we were to try to prove this proposition, we would need to start where the ratio of price to marginal cost is the same for all goods and then look at reallocations of resources to see what happens. We would need social satisfaction to fall no matter how we reallocated resources to be sure that we are at a maximum of social satisfaction. The reallocation would be by taking a dollar's worth of resources from the production of one good and using those resources in the production of the other. Let us examine what happens when we do this.

Suppose for a moment that small changes in the amount of output will not change the price of the good. If we take resources away from the production of one good and place them in the other, the crucial issue is what happens to the marginal social cost of each good. Let us suppose that the MSC has a positive slope for all goods. Now suppose that we are at a point where $P_x/MSC_x = P_y/MSC_y$. What if we take a dollar's worth of resources from the production of X? What happens?

Less X is produced. Because the MSC has a positive slope, MSC_x falls. Given no change in P_x, the fall in MSC_x makes P_x/MSC_x rise. If we now take the resources and put them in the production of Y, the amount of Y increases and, due to the positive slope of MSC, we have a higher MSC_y. For a constant P_y, the ratio P_y/MSC_y will fall. We are left with $P_x/MSC_x > P_y/MSC_y$, and we know that social satisfaction is not maximum at the new allocation of resources. Moreover, we know that the initial allocation is better than the new one. You should see that a similar argument works if we had started with $P_x/MSC_x = P_y/MSC_y$ and then reduced the production of Y and increased the production of X. This leads us to the converse of proposition 7.9.

Exercise 8. In the above paragraph, there is a statement: "Moreover, we know that the initial allocation is better than the new one." How do we know this?

Exercise 9. Start with $P_x/MSC_x = P_y/MSC_y$, and assume that the MSC has a positive slope for both goods. Now reduce the amount of resources used to produce Y by one dollar, and take those resources to produce X. Show that the society is worse off at the new allocation of resources.

Exercise 10. We have assumed that the price does not change as we make these adjustments. Assume that demand is negatively sloped and provide an argument showing that even if price changes, the society is worse off moving away from an allocation where $P_x/MSC_x = P_y/MSC_y$.

Proposition 7.12: (Converse of proposition 7.9) *Assume that assumptions 7.7 hold, that the* MSC *is positively sloped for all goods, and that* $P_x/MSC_x = P_y/MSC_y$. *Then, resources are allocated to maximize social satisfaction.*

We have essentially proved the proposition in our above efforts. You should be able to write out the formal proof.

> Exercise 11. Prove proposition 7.12.

We can now say that if we have all firms competitive in all industries, then with positively sloped MSC curves, the resulting allocation of resources will maximize social satisfaction. This provides a very strong case for competitive markets and for the regulation of monopoly. Again, we assumed no externalities in consumption so that price equals marginal social benefit. If price does not equal marginal social benefit, then we cannot be sure we will get an optimal allocation of resources under competition.

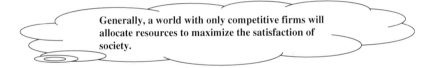

Generally, a world with only competitive firms will allocate resources to maximize the satisfaction of society.

Section Summary:
In this section, we have examined the converse of proposition 7.9. This converse provides us with a basis for saying that competition is a desirable way to allocate resources. In the next section, we will use consumer and producer surplus to find that competition is good.

7.6   Using Consumer and Producer Surplus

In this section, we will put to use some ideas we developed earlier in this chapter: consumer and producer surplus. Our objective is to see that competition is a desirable way to allocate resources.

Earlier we discussed consumer and producer surplus. Suppose that we have a competitive market. We know how to find the consumer and producer surplus. In this case, we know that the total surplus — the sum of consumer and producer surplus — is maximum. That is, there is no other amount of output and price that will make the total surplus larger. This is evidence that we have a desirable outcome from the competitive process. What if we have a monopoly firm? Assume, as we did in Chapter 6, that the monopoly's MC would be the same as the sum of the competitive firms' MC if the market were converted to competition. In that case, we can see that the total surplus would be less than under competition, and therefore monopoly does not properly allocate resources. The amount by which monopoly's surplus is less than the surplus that would occur in competition is called the dead weight loss. These concepts are illustrated in Figure 7.6.

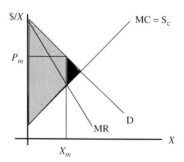

Figure 7.6   The total surplus for monopoly is shown with the lighter shading. The dead weight loss is shown with the darker shading. The two shaded areas together are the total surplus under competition.

> Exercise 12. Explain why the light shaded area in Figure 7.6 is the sum of the consumer and producer surpluses for monopoly.

In this case, you can see that the monopoly provides less surplus than would occur under competition, again assuming that the competitive supply is the same as the MC for the monopoly. Hence, monopoly misallocates resources.

Section Summary:
In this section, we have examined the resource allocation issue again, this time using the concepts of producer and consumer surplus. In the next section, we take up regulating the monopoly.

7.7 Regulating the Monopoly

In the previous section, we learned that competitive firms allocate resources to maximize the satisfaction of society. We also know that in a world of firms where there is one monopoly and one competitive firm, resources are misallocated. Hence, we know that the problem in the latter case is the monopoly. We should be looking for ways to regulate the monopoly so that results similar to competition can be obtained. When we say we want competitive-like results, what do we mean? We mean that we want the firm to choose to produce so that price equals marginal cost. How can we achieve this?

One obvious way to alter the behavior of the monopoly is to impose a tax on the monopoly. What kind of a tax should we impose? Suppose that we observe the monopoly before we impose the tax and could identify the amount of profit the monopoly earns. What if we then impose a tax equal to the amount of monopoly profit? This tax does not alter the behavior of the firm. The tax is like a fixed cost to the firm, which does not affect the marginal cost. Thus, the amount of output produced, the marginal cost, and the price do not change when we have a tax equal to the profit.

> Exercise 13. Show that marginal cost is not affected by a tax equal to the amount of monopoly profit. Treat the tax as if it were a fixed amount like a total fixed cost. How does a change in total fixed cost affect MC? Explain!

"So I put a video on YouTube, 'Regulation of Monopoly!'"
"Oh, I bet that got lots of hits!"

What if we put a tax on the monopoly for each unit of output produced? What happens then? In this case, we add to the cost of production by the amount of the tax. If we think about the amount needed to produce another unit, the firm now pays the marginal cost to cover the added resources plus the amount of the tax per unit. Thus, the marginal cost rises vertically by the amount of tax per unit. This will reduce the profit-maximizing output and raise the price. Figure 7.7 tells the story.

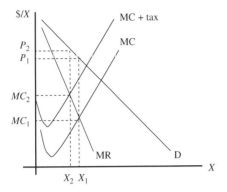

Figure 7.7 MC is the marginal cost before the tax, and MC + tax is the marginal cost after the tax. The profit-maximizing output falls and price rises due to the tax.

We can see that the tax, which causes the MC to rise vertically by the tax per unit, makes the profit-maximizing output fall and the associated price rise. And at the same time, MC also rises. After the tax, $P > MC$ holds, so the tax has not accomplished its goal of making $P = MC$. Still, P is closer to MC, so maybe we just need to raise the tax higher. But here is the problem. In monopoly, $P = AR > MR$ for all $X > 0$. Because at profit maximization, we have $MR = MC$, we have, for all $X > 0$, $P = AR > MR = MC$. So $P = MC$ can never hold in this world. Thus, a tax does not achieve our goal, unless we end up at zero output, which is probably not what we want. Note too that the tax causes the monopoly to reduce output, and we want the monopoly to increase output (recall the monopolist produces less and charges more than under competition).

What other techniques can we use? One alternative is to use a price ceiling. How do price ceilings work? A price ceiling means that the firm cannot charge a price higher than the price ceiling, but can charge a price equal to or less than the price ceiling. We need to examine how this affects the revenue of the monopoly. We start with the demand. Suppose that we impose a price ceiling of P_c. What impact will this have on the demand? Figure 7.8 illustrates the case.

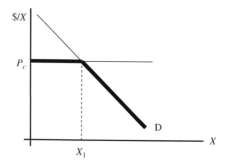

Figure 7.8 Suppose we have a price ceiling of P_c. Then, the firm cannot charge more than P_c and the top section of the demand is not possible; only the part of D below P_c is.

Here the firm cannot charge a price higher than P_c, the price ceiling, so the firm cannot get on the part of the demand above P_c. For levels of output smaller than X_1, the firm cannot charge a price on the demand curve but can only charge P_c. For levels of output greater than X_1, the firm will charge the price on the demand curve.

> Exercise 14. We wish to find total revenue when there is a price ceiling. Start by looking at what happens when there is a price ceiling. For $X < X_1$ (Figure 7.8), what will TR be? Remember that for these outputs, the price is a constant, P_c. Draw a graph of this TR. We can now find the TR for the monopoly with a price ceiling. Draw the TR for the monopoly without the price ceiling (see Chapter 6, Exercise 1). Now introduce the TR that would hold for the price ceiling. Combine the two TRs to find the TR for the monopoly given the price ceiling.

Next we turn to MR. We know that in Figure 7.8, the demand is horizontal up to the output X_1. Hence, the price is constant up to X_1. Given our experience with a competitive firm whose price is constant, we know that MR must also be constant and equal to the price up to output X_1. Once we get to X_1, we are on the downward-sloping demand for the monopoly. In this setting, we know that the MR will fall below the demand. Because we are some distance down demand, we know that by X_1 the MR will be below demand, and thus there will be a gap in the MR. We show this in Figure 7.9.

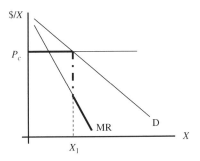

Figure 7.9   Given the price ceiling P_c, the MR is horizontal as long as we are on P_c and then falls down to the original MR at X_1, leaving a gap.

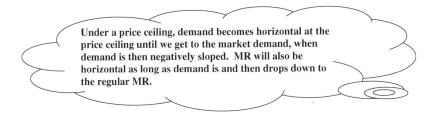

Under a price ceiling, demand becomes horizontal at the price ceiling until we get to the market demand, when demand is then negatively sloped. MR will also be horizontal as long as demand is and then drops down to the regular MR.

Exercise 15. Use the TR you found in Exercise 14 and find the MR using the slope of TR. What do you find?

Section Summary:
In this section, we have examined the impact of a tax on the monopoly and found that a tax would not generate competitive results. We have also looked at how a price ceiling affects demand and marginal revenue for the monopoly. The question remains: Where do we set the price ceiling?

7.8   Where Do We Set the Price Ceiling?

We now have sufficient information to figure out where to place the price ceiling for the monopoly. First, it is clear that we need to set the price ceiling below the price the monopoly would charge if there were no restriction. After all, the monopoly charges a price that is too high, and we want to make the monopoly reduce the price they charge and make price equal to MC. So suppose we put the price ceiling, P_{c1}, a bit below the monopoly price, P_m, as shown in Figure 7.10.

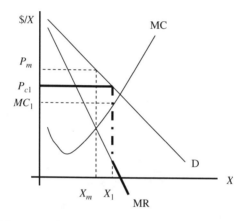

Figure 7.10   Without restriction, the monopoly would produce X_m and charge a price of P_m. With the price ceiling P_{c1}, the MC now cuts MR in the gap in MR at X_1 and the monopoly charges the price ceiling price, P_{c1}.

In Figure 7.10, the monopoly would produce X_m and charge P_m if there were no restriction. With the price ceiling, the MR given the price ceiling is flat along P_{c1} until we hit demand and then drops down to the original MR. The MC cuts through the gap in the new MR at X_1. Thus, X_1 is now the profit-maximizing output given the price ceiling. The monopoly would produce X_1 and charge P_{c1}. However, we are still left with $P_{c1} > MC_1$, the MC at X_1. Hence, this price ceiling does not achieve our goal. What should we do? What if we lower the price ceiling? Consider Figure 7.11, where we show this outcome.

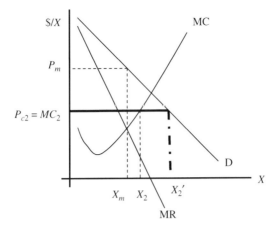

Figure 7.11   Without restriction, the monopoly would produce X_m and charge a price of P_m. With the price ceiling P_{c2}, the MR now cuts MC at X_2 and the monopoly charges the price ceiling price, $P_{c2} = MC_2$. But quantity demanded, X_2', is greater than quantity supplied, X_2.

In Figure 7.11, the monopoly would produce X_m and charge price P_m if there were no restriction. With the price ceiling, P_{c2}, we have a horizontal MR until we hit demand at X_2'. The MR drops down to the original MR, which is now negative. The firm produces X_2 given the price ceiling, and the price charged is P_{c2} which is equal to the MC, MC_2. We have now achieved our goal of getting price equal to marginal cost. However, there is another problem.

In Figure 7.11, at P_{c2}, consumers want to consume X_2', which is more than is being produced. We know that if the price is held down so that the quantity demanded, X_2', is greater than the quantity supplied, X_2, consumers will act to bid up the price. In this case, they cannot, but they will try to do so in an illegal fashion. In short, a black market will arise. We now have a choice to either spend resources to enforce the price ceiling, detracting from its value, or we can find a new price ceiling. We opt for the latter. Where else can we set the price ceiling? Somewhere between the two we have already looked at. But there is some evidence we can consider to guide us further.

In the previous chapter, we saw that the monopoly might produce less and charge more than would occur in a competitive market. The competitive market was represented as the point where the demand and the MC cross. If this is the competitive outcome, why not look there? Consider Figure 7.12. Here the price ceiling, P_{c3}, crosses the demand where MC crosses demand, at X_3. The MR then drops down to the original MR and we have profit maximization at X_3. The firm charges the price ceiling price, P_{c3}, which is equal to the MC at that output, MC_3. Thus, price equals marginal cost, which is our goal. Furthermore, the quantity demanded is X_3, precisely the quantity being produced. This will work! If we want to properly regulate a monopoly, we should set a price ceiling equal to the price where MC and demand cross. How easy is this to do?

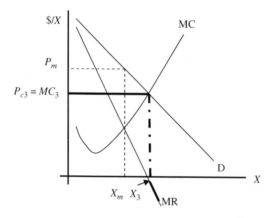

Figure 7.12   Without restriction, the monopoly would produce X_m and charge a price of P_m. With the price ceiling P_{c3}, the MR now cuts MC at X_3 and the monopoly charges the price ceiling price, P_{c3}.

First, if we are a regulator, we have to rely on the firm we are regulating to obtain information about the MC and the demand. This information will not be independently verifiable. Needless to say, the firm has an incentive to not tell the whole truth because their profit is likely to be less than when they are not regulated. But even if we have the data, it is often the case that the MC is difficult to find. Imagine trying to find the MC of producing a car. Exactly how do we do this? At the very least, doesn't the answer depend on which accessories are included? So what do we mean by "the MC?" Often it is a lot easier to find the average cost. Thus, to implement the rule we have outlined above — find where MC crosses demand — may be very hard to do. It would be easier to find where ATC crosses demand. Will this work?

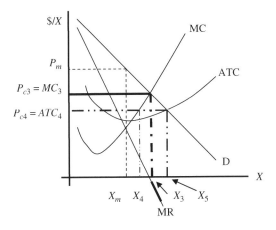

Figure 7.13 Without restriction, the monopoly would produce X_m and charge a price of P_m. With the price ceiling P_{c3}, the firm produces X_3 and charges P_{c3}. If we set the price ceiling where ATC cuts demand, at P_{c4}, the firm produces X_4 and charges P_{c4}, but there is a shortage at this price, and a black market will arise.

Suppose we set the price ceiling using the ATC rather than the MC. Figure 7.13 shows what would happen. Here the price ceiling is at P_{c4}, where the ATC cuts the demand. The MR will be horizontal to the demand and then fall to the original MR. The MR intersects MC at X_4, but the quantity demanded will be more, X_5. As we discussed before, a black market will arise, and the price ceiling will lose its value. The point is that to use ATC rather than MC to set the price ceiling will lead to failure.

FROM THE LITERATURE

We think of a monopoly as being a single firm out for everything it can get. But could a monopoly be a not-for-profit firm? One case is where there is a ferry to an island off the coast that is owned by the islanders and run as a not-for-profit firm. The firm has to set aside money to replace and repair boats as needed, but in every other way acts as a monopoly as they are the only ferry service to that island. This is not the only structure for such firms, and the question of how to regulate them is of interest especially to those who use the ferry regularly. You can find details of the variety of structures for ferry services to islands off the coast of the Netherlands (and some for Germany too) and some proposed regulatory structures in: Broos Baanders and Gordon de Munck, "Towards Regulation of Historically Grown Monopolies: Market Models for the Dutch West Frisian Island Ferries," Paper presented at the 2006 European Transport Conference, available at http://www.etcproceedings.org/paper/towards-regulation-of-historically-grown-monopolies-market-models-for-the-dutc/. They also examine models of regulation for this industry.

Section Summary:

In this section, we have applied our criterion for resource allocation to the problem of finding a way to regulate monopoly. We have discovered that there is a way to impose a price ceiling on the monopoly to achieve the desired outcome, namely $P = MC$. However, this outcome depends on the regulator knowing the firm's MC, which may be difficult even if the regulator has full cooperation of the firm. Reliance on the ATC rather than the MC leads to sub-optimal results. In the next section, we take up this question again, with the case of natural monopoly.

7.9 Natural Monopoly

In this section, we will examine the case of the natural monopoly and see what problems arise when we try to regulate this form of monopoly. This happens when the marginal cost of production is falling, and competition will not work.

Exercise 16. Show that if the MC curve falls as output rises, a competitive firm will not have a profit maximum at a finite output.

However, if the MC falls, the monopoly can exist. Figure 7.14 shows this case.

Exercise 17. What will the total cost have to look like if the MC falls as output rises starting from zero? What will the ATC look like and how will it be positioned relative to the MC?

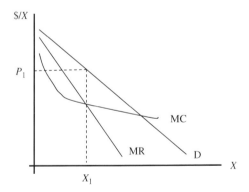

Figure 7.14 The natural monopoly faces a downward-sloping MC curve. You can see that X_1 is the profit-maximizing choice and the price is P_1.

In this case, you can see that the profit-maximizing output is X_1 and that the firm will charge a price of P_1.

Exercise 18. Use the standard profit-maximizing argument to establish that X_1 is the profit-maximizing choice in Figure 7.14.

Suppose that we want to regulate this firm. We know that a price ceiling is a good way to proceed and that we should put the price ceiling where the MC crosses the demand. Suppose that we do this. What will the outcome be? Figure 7.15 shows what happens. Here we have also added the ATC curve. You can see that if we use this price ceiling, the firm will face negative profits.

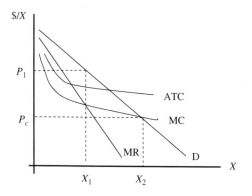

Figure 7.15   The natural monopoly faces a downward-sloping MC curve. With regulation, you can see that X_2 is the profit-maximizing choice and the price is P_c. The price ceiling causes profit to be negative.

Exercise 19. Where is the profit in Figure 7.15? How do you know profit is negative?

This case suggests that if we have a natural monopoly, where the MC falls, regulation will eventually drive the firm from business. The only way out is to decide if a subsidy sufficient for the firm to make some profit is acceptable. If the value to society of having the monopoly is greater than the subsidy, the subsidy would be the preferred solution.

Regulation of a natural monopoly to make price equal to MC will lead to negative profits.

Section Summary:
In this section, we have looked at the case of the natural monopoly. Here we have found that a price ceiling will leave the firm with a negative profit, which will eventually drive the firm from business. In the next section, we will approach the problems we have been examining with mathematics.

7.10 Some Computations

In this section, we will look at the problem of setting a price ceiling using mathematics. We start with the standard monopoly problem.

Suppose that a monopoly has the demand and total cost as follows:

$$P = 176 - 5X$$

$$\text{TC} = (1/3)X^3 - 5X^2 + 140X + 100.$$

Exercise 20. Write the profit function for the monopoly, and find the profit-maximizing output and price.

Exercise 21. Find the marginal cost for this firm. Find the output and price where $P = MC$.

Exercise 22. Graph the demand, MR, and MC of this firm. Show the outcomes of the two previous exercises in your graph.

Exercise 23. Suppose that the firm had faced a price ceiling of 136. Find the level of output where the price ceiling intersects demand. What would the MR look like now? What output would the firm produce? What price would the firm charge? What would the MC be at this output? Would $P = MC$ at this output?

Exercise 24. Suppose that a firm has a marginal cost as given below along with the demand curve:

$$MC = 180/X$$
$$P = 200 - 10X.$$

   a. Find the total revenue and marginal revenue for this firm.

   b. Find the output so that $MR = MC$. What price will the firm charge?

   c. Suppose that we try to set a price ceiling at the point where MC and demand cross. What price should we choose? At what output will this occur?

Exercise 25. Suppose that a competitive firm has the total cost curve given below. Assume the price is $10.

$$TC = 100X^{0.5} + 100.$$

   a. Find total revenue, and write the profit function.

   b. Find the output where the derivative of profit is zero.

   c. Is this a profit maximum? Check the second derivative of profit.

   d. Find the total cost at the output you found in part b, and also the total revenue. What can you say about profit in this case?

Section Summary:
In this section, we examined the outcome of natural monopoly with computations.

7.11   Summary

In this chapter, we have done four things:

A. First, we established a rule for the efficient allocation of resources. In the absence of consumption externalities, and with a positively sloped marginal cost, the ratio of price to marginal social cost should be the same for all producers of all goods.

B. We applied this criterion to the case of monopoly and found that the existence of monopoly leads to a misallocation of resources.

C. We examined ways to regulate a monopoly and found that a price ceiling will force the monopoly to satisfy the ratio of price to marginal cost to be everywhere the same, but that the regulator may have trouble getting satisfactory information from the monopoly. So this may not be a feasible solution.

D. We also examined the case of the natural monopoly and found that an added problem arises in this case. That is, at the desired price ceiling, the firm will face negative profit.

Neither the competitive case nor the monopoly case is particularly realistic. However, the competitive case provides a model of how resources should be allocated. The monopoly provides a powerful counterpoint. But most firms are neither competitive nor monopoly. In the next chapter, we examine the case of oligopoly, where the firms have interrelated revenues.

Terms Defined:

- Marginal willingness to pay, demand price
- Total willingness to pay
- Consumer surplus
- Marginal social willingness to pay
- Producer surplus
- Marginal social cost
- Price/marginal social cost
- Allocative efficiency
- Dead weight loss

Chapter 8

Oligopoly

Key Concepts:

- Interrelated revenues
- Cournot duopoly
- Cartels
- Stackelberg duopoly

Goals:

- Establish models where revenues are interrelated:
  - o Cournot.
  - o Cournot with collusion.
  - o Stackelberg.
- Examine the behavior of firms with interrelated revenues.

One might argue that most of the firms we see in the world are neither competitive nor monopoly. In this case, the analysis of the previous three chapters is not applicable. Is there any work on firms that is a bit more realistic?

8.1   Introduction

In this chapter, we will examine the situation where firms are neither competitive nor monopoly — the case of oligopoly. As you know, the case of oligopoly, that of the liquid soap maker, is more complicated as now the revenues of the firms are interrelated, and we will have to account for the relationship. The problem we face is that there are a large number of ways that firms could have interrelated revenues. Here is the problem. If I, as one liquid soap producer, decide to lower price, I will have an impact on my revenue. I hope it goes up as the lower price attracts customers from other brands of liquid soap. So much for customer loyalty! But the problem is that I also affect the revenue of the other firm — they lose customers and hence have smaller revenues. I can be sure that the other firm will not stand for that! They will do something to regain those wayward customers. And whatever they do will have impacts on me. This interaction now makes the problem of finding the profit maximum a bit more complicated! However, there are some general models that will be helpful in developing our understanding of this most common of worlds. We will examine several models of how firms might be related, including the models of Cournot, a cartel, and Stackelberg, while using concepts from game theory in this discussion. All of these models will include only two firms. You can be sure that more intricate models have been developed, and that this is a rich area of research. We start with Cournot.

8.2   Cournot

We will now examine a world of two firms, where the firms produce the same good and face a market demand which they split in a manner yet to be determined. Because they produce the same good, the consumer will not pay more for the good from one producer than the other; hence, both charge the same price. Each firm is assumed to choose a level of output to produce. The problem is that neither firm knows what the other will do, but realizes that what the other firm does will affect them. We will temporarily assume that the two firms choose simultaneously, though this assumption will be relaxed later in this section. For ease of exposition, we will assume that the demand is linear. Thus, we would have the AR form of demand:

$$P = A - B(X_1 + X_2),$$

where X_1 is the amount firm 1 produces and X_2 is the amount firm 2 produces. Both A and B are positive constants, and P is the price.

Firm 1 computes its revenue as $P \times X_1 = (A - B(X_1 + X_2)) \times X_1$. Firm 2 does a similar computation. Note that the amount of output firm 2 produces affects the revenue of firm 1. So somehow, firm 1 has to take this into consideration when deciding how much to produce.

Exercise 1. Write an equation for the total revenue of firm 2.

Exercise 2. Find the marginal revenue for firm 1, MR_1. Graph this equation on an axis system with X_1 on the horizontal axis and $\$/X_1$ on the vertical axis. What happens to MR_1 when X_2 increases? Does the slope of MR_1 change when X_2 changes? How do you know?

Suppose that each firm has a constant marginal cost, C_1 for firm 1 and C_2 for firm 2. We also assume that fixed costs are zero. We can now write the profit for each firm. We would have the following expression for firm 1:

$$\pi_1 = (A - B(X_1 + X_2)) \times X_1 - C_1 X_1.$$

Exercise 3. Write an equation for the profit of firm 2.

How to proceed? Consider firm 1. If we do what we normally do, that is, take the derivative of profit with respect to X_1 and solve for X_1, the result will depend on X_2. What we need is some kind of equilibrium concept that involves both firms. Each firm wants to do the best it can given what the other firm does, so it makes sense for each firm to maximize profit given the output of the other firm. But how do we determine how much each firm will produce? If we have an equation telling what each firm will do given what the other does, we can solve them simultaneously to get the solution. That is what we will do, and the outcome would be equilibrium. We will define the equilibrium concept we are looking for first.

Definition 8.1: *A **Nash equilibrium** is a combination of outputs, one for each firm, so that once we have the Nash equilibrium, neither firm has an incentive to change output. That is, each firm is maximizing profit given the output of the other firm.*

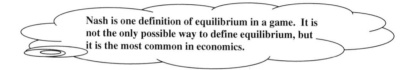

Nash is one definition of equilibrium in a game. It is not the only possible way to define equilibrium, but it is the most common in economics.

In the Cournot case, a Nash equilibrium will occur when the derivative of the profit equation for firm 1 (equal to zero) and the derivative of the profit equation for firm 2 (equal to zero) are both satisfied. Before we carry out this process, we need one more definition.

Definition 8.2: *The **best reply function** (BRF) (sometimes called a reaction function or best response) tells the optimal (profit-maximizing) output to produce for a firm, given the output of the other firm.*

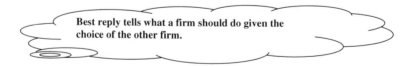

Best reply tells what a firm should do given the choice of the other firm.

How can we find the best reply function? What we need to do is to find the profit-maximizing choice for each firm given the output of the other firm. That suggests that we find the derivative of the firm's profit function. If we can solve that function for the firm's output in terms of the amount the other firm produces, we have the best reply function. Before turning to the algebraic derivation of the best reply, let us have a look at a graphical representation of the process in Figure 8.1.

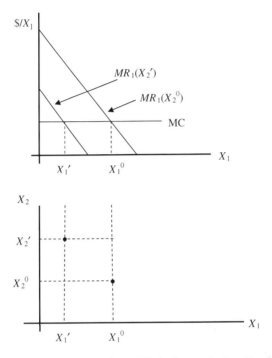

Figure 8.1 In the top graph, we show MR before and after X_2 changes together with MC. We find the profit-maximizing output X_1 for each X_2. Now, in the lower graph, plot the profit-maximizing choice of X_1 for each value of X_2. This is the best reply function.

In Figure 8.1, we show how to find the best reply function graphically. In Exercise 2, you found the MR for firm 1, MR_1. To graph this, we need a value for X_2. Choose some value for X_2, say X_2^0, and draw the MR_1 for that value of X_2. Call that $MR_1(X_2^0)$. Now mark the value of X_2^0 on the vertical axis of the lower graph. Using that MR and MC equal to a constant, we find the profit-maximizing choice for firm 1, X_1^0. This gives us one point on the best reply function. Suppose that X_2 rises to X_2'. Then the MR will shift down to $MR_1(X_2')$ parallel to $MR_1(X_2^0)$, and the new profit maximum point for firm 1 will be smaller, X_1'. This gives us a second point on the best reply function. But we need not depend on the geometry to allow us to find the best reply. We can do the job using algebra, and we do that next.

Exercise 4. In Figure 8.1, when X_2 rises, how do we know that the new MR_1 is parallel to the old (given the straight line MR)? If X_2 rises by ΔX_2, how much does the MR_1 shift down?

Exercise 5. In Figure 8.1, how do we know where the profit-maximizing output is? What rule do we follow?

Section Summary:
In this section, we introduced the Cournot model, the idea of the Nash equilibrium, and best reply functions. We have suggested a way to find the Nash equilibrium, and we do that next.

8.3   Finding a Nash Equilibrium in Cournot

We can now approach the problem with mathematics. There is a best reply function for each firm. For firm 1, we would find the best reply by maximizing firm 1's profit given a value of X_2:

$$\frac{d\pi_1}{dX_1} = A - 2BX_1 - BX_2 - C_1 = 0.$$

We have a similar computation for firm 2 assuming that X_1 is given:

$$\frac{d\pi_2}{dX_2} = A - 2BX_2 - BX_1 - C_2 = 0.$$

We can rewrite these equations to provide more insight. Solve the first for X_1, yielding this best reply for firm 1:

$$X_1 = \frac{A - C_1 - BX_2}{2B}.$$

Now solve the second for X_2 to obtain firm 2's best reply:

$$X_2 = \frac{A - C_2 - BX_1}{2B}.$$

What these equations tell us is, for firm 1, what output, X_1, to choose to maximize profit given that firm 2 has chosen X_2 amount of output to produce. For firm 2, the equation tells us the amount of output firm 2 should produce (X_2) to maximize profit given that firm 1 has decided to produce X_1. These are the BRFs for firm 1 and firm 2. Now we turn to the task of finding the Nash equilibrium.

Proposition 8.3: *If (X_1^0, X_2^0) is a Nash equilibrium, then (X_1^0, X_2^0) is the solution to the best reply functions for firm 1 and firm 2.*

Proof 8.4: We will use the contrapositive. Suppose that (X_1^0, X_2^0) is not a solution to the two best reply functions. Then either (X_1^0, X_2^0) is not on firm 1's best reply or it is not on firm 2's best reply (or both). If (X_1^0, X_2^0) is not on firm 1's best reply, then there is some value of X_1 that will increase firm 1's profits given X_2^0. That means that we cannot be at the Nash equilibrium. If (X_1^0, X_2^0) is not on firm 2's best reply, then there is a value of X_2 that will increase firm 2's profits given X_1^0. Hence, firm 2's profit would increase and (X_1^0, X_2^0) cannot be a Nash equilibrium because at Nash, neither firm can increase profit given the choice of the other firm. □

Proposition 8.5: *If (X_1^0, X_2^0) satisfies both firms' best reply functions, then (X_1^0, X_2^0) is a Nash equilibrium.*

Proof 8.6: Again, use the contrapositive. Suppose that (X_1^0, X_2^0) is not a Nash equilibrium. Then there is a value for X_1 that would yield greater profit given X_2^0 than X_1^0. But then X_1^0 would not be on the BRF for firm 1. Similarly, if there is a value of X_2 that provides greater profit for firm 2 than X_2^0 given X_1^0, then X_2^0 cannot be on firm 2's BRF as the best reply provides the greatest profit given the output of the other firm. Thus, (X_1^0, X_2^0) cannot be on both BRFs.   □

Therefore, to find Nash, we require both BRFs to hold at the same time. If both equations are true at the same time, then firm 1 has chosen an output to produce consistent with firm 2's choice and vice versa. Here is what we would get.

Plug firm 2's outcome into firm 1's equation:

$$
\begin{aligned}
X_1 &= \frac{A - C_1}{2B} - \frac{1}{2}X_2 = \frac{A - C_1}{2B} - \left[\frac{A - C_2 - BX_1}{4B}\right] \\
&= \frac{2A - 2C_1 - A + C_2}{4B} + \frac{BX_1}{4B} \\
\frac{3X_1}{4} &= \frac{A - 2C_1 + C_2}{4B} \\
X_1 &= \frac{A - 2C_1 + C_2}{3B}.
\end{aligned}
$$

By similar computations, we get the following for X_2:

$$
X_2 = \frac{A - 2C_2 + C_1}{3B}.
$$

Exercise 6. Complete the algebra to show that our expression for X_2 is correct.

These are the Nash equilibrium values. Note that if $A + C_1 < 2C_2$, then firm 2 will produce zero output. There is a similar condition for firm 1.

We can also find the price that will prevail in the market:

$$P = A - B(X_1 + X_2) = A - B\left[\frac{2A - C_1 - C_2}{3B}\right]$$

$$= A - \left[\frac{2A - C_1 - C_2}{3}\right] = \frac{A + C_1 + C_2}{3}.$$

Note that both firms charge the same price.

We can also compute the profit that each firm generates:

$$\pi_1 = P \times X_1 - C_1 X_1 = \{P - C_1\} \times X_1$$

$$= \left\{\left[\frac{A + C_1 + C_2}{3}\right] - \frac{3C_1}{3}\right\} \times \left(\frac{A - 2C_1 + C_2}{3B}\right)$$

$$= \frac{(A - 2C_1 + C_2)^2}{9B}.$$

By similar computations, we obtain the following expression for profit for firm 2:

$$\pi_2 = \frac{(A - 2C_2 + C_1)^2}{9B}.$$

Exercise 7. Do the algebra necessary to obtain the profit expression for firm 2.

One way to think about the Nash values is that they simultaneously satisfy the best reply functions. It will be helpful to graph these functions. The outcome is shown in Figure 8.2. The Nash equilibrium is at the intersection of these two best reply functions.

Exercise 8. Do the algebra necessary to graph the best reply for firm 2. How do we know that these functions are straight lines?

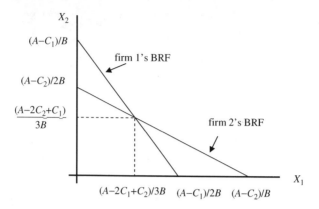

Figure 8.2   In this graph, we have the best reply functions for firm 1 and firm 2. The intersection is the Nash equilibrium.

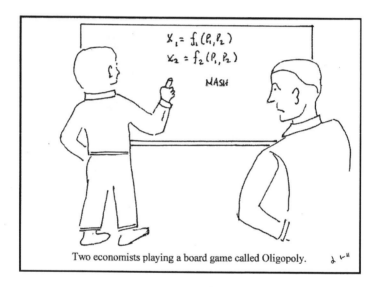

Two economists playing a board game called Oligopoly.

Exercise 9.   Suppose that the total cost for firm 1 is $C_1 X_1^2$. What will the best reply function be now? What if the total cost for firm 2 is $C_2 X_2^2$? What will we get for firm 2's best reply? What is the Nash equilibrium in this case?

Exercise 10. Suppose that the demand curve is $P = 180 - 2(X_1 + X_2)$, $C_1 = 40$, and $C_2 = 50$. Write the profit function and find the best reply functions for both firms. Compute the Nash equilibrium in this case. What price will be charged for this good? How much profit does each firm make?

Section Summary:

In summary, we have the following Nash equilibrium outcomes for the Cournot model:

$$X_1 = (A - 2C_1 + C_2)/3B$$

$$X_2 = (A - 2C_2 + C_1)/3B$$

$$P = (A + C_1 + C_2)/3$$

$$\pi_1 = \frac{(A - 2C_1 + C_2)^2}{9B}$$

$$\pi_2 = \frac{(A - 2C_2 + C_1)^2}{9B}.$$

8.4   Are Nash Equilibriums Stable?

There is one other matter that we need to address. If we were to get away from the Nash equilibrium, would the firms react in such a way that we would move back to the Nash equilibrium? Is the Nash equilibrium stable? Under what circumstances will the equilibrium be stable?

Consider the best reply for firm 1 alone. What does it tell us? For any given value of X_2, the best reply for firm 1 tells the output firm 1 should produce. It is firm 1's best reply to firm 2's choice. If, for a given X_2, firm 1 were at an X_1 not on the best reply, the firm would know what to do; it should move toward the best reply. Because firm 1 can only adjust X_1, we only see the point A moving left or right, not up or down. We show this in Figure 8.3.

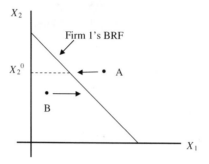

Figure 8.3   If firm 1 were at A (firm 2 chooses X_2^0), firm 1 would want to choose a smaller output, so X_1 would decrease. If firm 1 were at B, it would want to increase output.

Exercise 11. Suppose that firm 1 chooses X_1^0 below, and firm 2 is at A. Given firm 2's BRF shown below, what output adjustment would firm 2 want to make? If firm 2 were at B, what adjustment would it want to make to output? Draw in an arrow showing which way we would move. Explain.

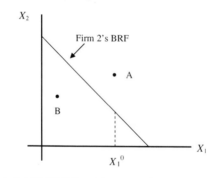

If we combine these graphs, we would get the following situation as shown in Figure 8.4. In Figure 8.4, we have the forces on firm 1 as shown in Figure 8.3, and the forces on firm 2 as discovered in Exercise 11. At A, firm 1 wants to decrease output (so the arrow to the left), and firm 2 wants to decrease output (so the arrow down). Hence, we will move to the southwest of A. Exactly what the motion will be we cannot tell from the information given; we would need to know how much change each firm would want to make. But we do know that we will move toward the Nash equilibrium!

In Figure 8.4, we see that no matter where we start, we are pushed to the Nash equilibrium. Because the forces automatically push us to the Nash point, we say that the Nash equilibrium is stable. But not all Nash equilibriums are stable.

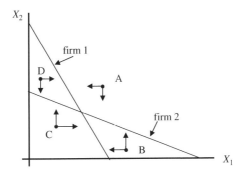

Figure 8.4   At a point like A, firm 1 wants to decrease X_1 and firm 2 wants to decrease X_2. This combination will move us to the Nash equilibrium. A check of points B, C, and D indicates that we will end up at Nash. Nash is a stable equilibrium in this case.

The key issue for stability is the slope of the best reply functions. If firm 1's best reply is steeper (has a more negative slope) than firm 2's, then the Nash equilibrium is stable. Suppose that we have best reply functions as shown in Figure 8.5. You can see that in this case, Nash may not be stable.

Exercise 12. Explain why the arrows in Figure 8.5 are correct.

Suppose we start at either B or D. In this case, we will move away from the Nash equilibrium. If we start at either A or C, we could move to the Nash, or we could be pushed into the unstable areas like B or D. There is no guarantee that if we get away from the Nash equilibrium, we will automatically come back to it. This situation is an unstable Nash equilibrium.

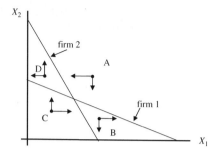

Figure 8.5 At B, firm 1 wants to increase output and firm 2 wants to decrease output. Hence, we move away from the Nash equilibrium. If we start at A or C, we could move directly to Nash, or be pushed to a point like B or D and then never get to Nash.

We can use the above to address a question that should have perplexed you. Exactly how do firms get to the Nash equilibrium? Of course, one could imagine that each firm could compute the BRF for the other and then find the Nash. But that means each firm would have to know the other firm's cost, an unlikely fact. So how might we proceed? One possible scenario is for the firms to move sequentially. So firm 1 makes a choice, followed by firm 2, and so on. Suppose we try this. Firm 1 moves first, and assumes that firm 2 will produce zero. Figure 8.6 shows the situation.

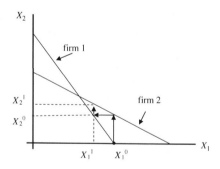

Figure 8.6 If we start with firm 1 producing X_1^0, and firm 2 producing 0, firm 2 will adjust output to its BRF. Firm 1 will then be off its BRF and will reduce output to X_1^1. The process will continue until we end at the Nash equilibrium.

Firm 1 believes firm 2 will produce 0, so firm 1's best reply is shown at X_1^0 in Figure 8.6. Given that firm 1 produces X_1^0, firm 2's BRF says that firm 2 should produce X_2^0. But if firm 2 produces X_2^0, then firm 1's

BRF says that firm 1 should produce X_1^1. And if firm 1 produces X_1^1, then firm 2 should produce X_2^1. The process will continue until the Nash equilibrium is reached. You should convince yourself that if firm 2 had moved first, the same outcome would have occurred.

Exercise 13. Suppose that firm 2 had moved first and assumed that firm 1 would produce zero output. What sequence of moves would follow? Would we end up at the Nash equilibrium?

Exercise 14. Suppose that we have the best replies shown in Figure 8.5. Suppose we see what happens when the firms play in order starting with firm 1. Will we move to the Nash equilibrium in this case? Explain how you know!

FROM THE LITERATURE

Here is another look at whether firms maximize profits or not. This time the setting is a sports league, in this case soccer. The particular question here is whether firms act to maximize profit or maximize the number of wins. Because the teams are members of a league, the revenues of the individual teams are interrelated, and game theory applies. One aspect of the profit maximization choice is how firms respond to variations in spending on talent by other teams. One study estimates best reply functions under the assumption of profit maximization and then under the win maximization hypothesis. While both models predict the relative rankings of the teams, the win maximization model provides a better estimate of the actual outcome. While the analysis seems to favor win maximization, one might wonder whether win maximization is essentially profit maximization in disguise if we think about how actions today may affect profit in the next year or two. For complete details, see Pedro Garcia-del-Barrio and Stefan Szymanski, "Goal! Profit Versus Win Maximization in Soccer," *Review of Industrial Organization*, Vol. 34, No. 1, February, 2009, pp. 45–68.

Section Summary:
If firm 1's best reply is steeper (has a more negative slope) than firm 2's, then the Nash equilibrium is stable. We can also see how firms interact so that they end up at the Nash equilibrium. One question arises. The Cournot model assumes that the firms act independently of each other. What if they were to collude? What would happen then? We take up this issue in the next section.

8.5   Collusion in Cournot

Suppose that rather than act as rivals, the two firms decided to collude. What would happen then? Collusion means that the two firms agree to act together, as one. To simplify the matter, we will assume that the two firms have identical costs; $C_1 = C_2 = C$. Because the two firms are acting as one, they become a monopoly, and the monopoly solution will occur. Suppose that the market demand is $P = A - BX$. The cost of production is CX. Hence, profit will be

$$\pi = (A - BX)X - CX.$$

The profit-maximizing output will be $X = (A - C)/2B$, and the price will be $P = (A + C)/2$.

Exercise 15. Maximize the above profit function and find the profit-maximizing output, price, and profit.

The total profit will be $[(A - C)^2]/4B$, which will be split between the two firms. Suppose that the firms split the profit equally so that each firm gets $[(A - C)^2]/8B$ in profit. Note that if the firms had gone with the Cournot solution (and with each firm having the same costs), they would have had a profit of $[(A - C)^2]/9B$, which is less. So both firms are better off by colluding than by pursuing the Cournot solution.

Still, one wonders: If the firms collude, is there an incentive to cheat? Would one firm want to reduce the price it offers and undercut the other firm? Is the collusive agreement stable?

One way to proceed is to assume that the two firms have split the output equally so that each firm would sell $(A - C)/4B$ output. If firm 1 assumes that firm 2 will produce $(A - C)/4B$ and charge a price of $(A + C)/2$, then firm 1 will want to increase the amount it produces and charge less. This action will result in greater profit. How can we determine this?

We know the output that firm 2 is producing. If we use firm 1's best reply function, we can determine the best output firm 1 should produce — the output that would maximize firm 1's profits given the output of firm 2. If we do this, what do we get? Firm 1's best reply function is

$$X_1 = \frac{A - C}{2B} - \frac{1}{2}X_2.$$

Given that firm 2 will produce $(A - C)/4B$, we can compute the profit-maximizing quantity for firm 1:

$$X_1 = \frac{A - C}{2B} - \frac{1}{2}\frac{(A - C)}{4B} = \frac{3(A - C)}{8B}.$$

Firm 1's profit would be found using the profit function:

$$\pi_1 = (A - BX_1 - BX_2)X_1 - CX_1 = (A - C - BX_1 - BX_2)X_1$$
$$= \left[(A - C) - \frac{3(A - C)}{8} - \frac{(A - C)}{4}\right]\frac{3(A - C)}{8B}$$
$$= \frac{1}{B}\left[\frac{3(A - C)}{8}\right]^2.$$

If firm 1 stays in the cartel, they earn a profit of $[(A - C)^2]/8B$. You can see that the profit firm 1 would generate by cheating would increase compared to what it could earn if it stayed in the cartel. The result is that firm 1 will want to cheat. Of course, what works for firm 1 will also be true for firm 2. Hence, there is serious pressure to move away from the cartel solution. We know that in this case, there is pressure to move to the Nash equilibrium.

> One of the problems that cartels face is that there is an incentive to cheat on the cartel agreement, which effectively ends the cartel.

Section Summary:
In this section, we have examined what happens if the firms in a Cournot world try to collude. The outcome is that the firms want to cheat on the cartel agreement, and this pressure will make it hard for the cartel to be kept together.

Are there other ways the two firms might interact? On the one hand, it seems clear that a firm knows that what it does depends on what the other firm does. Would it make sense for a firm to take into consideration how the other firm will respond? We examine this model in the next section.

8.6   Stackelberg's Model

In the Cournot model, the two firms see each other as equals in the market; neither firm has more market power than the other. It could be that one firm is the stronger or leading firm, and acts to set the price which the other then takes. Stackelberg's model takes the Cournot model and imposes this added condition: that one firm is the price leader, and sets the price for the market. Thus, firm 1 acts first, and firm 2 simply reacts to what firm 1 does. How might we build on Cournot to obtain a price leadership model?

Suppose that we have the same setup as before — two firms producing an identical good, facing a market demand, and each firm has different costs. Assume now that firm 1, when deciding how much to produce, realizes that firm 2 has a best reply function just as firm 1. Suppose that firm 1 computes firm 2's best reply and uses it in computing firm 1's profit. Here is what we would have.

We know firm 2's best reply is

$$X_2 = \frac{A - C_2 - BX_1}{2B}.$$

We replace X_2 in firm 1's profit with firm 2's BRF so that firm 1's profit becomes

$$\pi_1 = (A - B[X_1 + [(A - C_2)/2B] - (X_1/2)]) \times X_1 - C_1 X_1$$
$$= (A - BX_1 - ((A - C_2)/2) + (BX_1/2)) \times X_1 - C_1 X_1$$
$$= \{(A - BX_1 + C_2)/2\} \times X_1 - C_1 X_1.$$

We maximize this function with respect to X_1 to find firm 1's profit-maximizing output. The derivative is as follows:

$$\frac{d\pi_1}{dX_1} = \{(A - BX_1 + C_2)/2\} - (BX_1/2) - C_1 = 0$$
$$= (A + C_2)/2 - BX_1 - C_1 = 0$$
$$X_1 = \{A + C_2 - 2C_1\}/2B.$$

We may now compute X_2 by plugging back into the reaction function:

$$X_2 = \{(A - C_2)/2B\} - (1/2)X_1$$
$$= \{(A - C_2)/2B\} - (1/2)\{A + C_2 - 2C_1\}/2B$$
$$= (A - 3C_2 + 2C_1)/4B.$$

What price will prevail in the market?

$$P = A - B(X_1 + X_2)$$
$$= A - B(A + C_2 - 2C_1)/2B - B(A - 3C_2 + 2C_1)/4B$$
$$= A - A/2 - C_2/2 + 2C_1/2 - A/4 + 3C_2/4 - 2C_1/4$$
$$= A/4 + C_2/4 + 2C_1/4 = (A + C_2 + 2C_1)/4.$$

The total amount sold will be $X_1 + X_2$:

$$X_1 + X_2 = (3A - C_2 - 2C_1)/4B.$$

Exercise 16. Suppose that firm 2, but not firm 1, sees itself as the price leader. Compute X_2, X_1, and price under this assumption.

Exercise 17. Could both firm 1 and firm 2 see themselves as price leader? Do you get the same market price and division of output between the two firms?

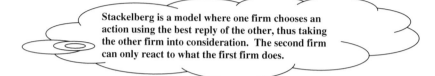

Stackelberg is a model where one firm chooses an action using the best reply of the other, thus taking the other firm into consideration. The second firm can only react to what the first firm does.

Section Summary:
In summary, the equilibrium for the Stackelberg game yields the following results:

$$X_1 = (A + C_2 - 2C_1)/2B$$
$$X_2 = (A - 3C_2 + 2C_1)/4B$$
$$P = (A + C_2 + 2C_1)/4$$
$$\pi_1 = \frac{(A + C_2 - 2C_1)^2}{8B}$$
$$\pi_2 = \frac{(A - 3C_2 + 2C_1)^2}{16B}.$$

You can see that the results are different from the Cournot case. Firm 1 produces more in Stackelberg than in Cournot. We cannot tell if firm 2 produces more or less with Stackelberg. And we cannot tell which price is higher. But firm 1 has more profit under Stackelberg than Cournot. In the next section, we compare the outcomes of the two models we have developed above.

8.7   Comparing Cournot and Stackelberg

In this section, we will examine how the solutions to the Cournot model and the Stackelberg model are different. We start with a table showing the key outcomes.

	Cournot	Stackelberg
X_1	$\dfrac{A - 2C_1 + C_2}{3B}$	$\dfrac{A - 2C_1 + C_2}{2B}$
X_2	$\dfrac{A - 2C_2 + C_1}{3B}$	$\dfrac{A - 3C_2 + 2C_1}{4B}$
P	$\dfrac{A + C_1 + C_2}{3}$	$\dfrac{A + C_2 + 2C_1}{4}$
π_1	$\dfrac{(A - 2C_1 + C_2)^2}{9B}$	$\dfrac{(A - 2C_1 + C_2)^2}{8B}$
π_2	$\dfrac{(A - 2C_2 + C_1)^2}{9B}$	$\dfrac{(A - 3C_2 + 2C_1)^2}{16B}$

Exercise 18. For which model is X_1 larger? X_2? Under which model does firm 1 have the larger profit? Firm 2?

Exercise 19. Suppose that both firms have the same cost so $C_1 = C_2 = C$. What can you say about the relative sizes of the outputs and profits under the two models?

Exercise 20. Suppose that both firms have the same cost so $C_1 = C_2 = C$. Suppose that the two firms together acted as a monopoly. What output would be produced? What price would be charged? Is it true that in Stackelberg, the first firm effectively acts as a monopoly? How do you know?

Suppose that in the Stackelberg model, we take the Stackelberg output for firm 2 and use that in firm 1's profit function rather than firm 2's BRF. What will firm 1's profit-maximizing output be then? It seems likely that we should get firm 1's Stackelberg output:

$$\pi_1 = \left(A - BX_1 - B\left[\frac{A - 3C_2 + 2C_1}{4B} \right] \right) X_1 - C_1 X_1$$

$$= \left(\frac{3A + 3C_2 - 2C_1}{4} - BX_1 \right) X_1 - C_1 X_1.$$

We find the profit maximum by taking the derivative of profit, setting it equal to zero, and solving for X_1:

$$\frac{d\pi_1}{dX_1} = \frac{3A + 3C_2 - 6C_1}{4} - 2BX_1 = 0$$

$$X_1 = \frac{3}{8}\left(\frac{A + C_2 - 2C_1}{B}\right).$$

This is not firm 1's Stackelberg output. What conclusion can we draw from this? What we have computed is firm 1's profit maximum given firm 2's Stackelberg output. Hence, we have that, given firm 2's output, firm 1 chooses an output that is not on firm 1's BRF. What this means is that firm 1 could generate more profit by producing the quantity we just computed as long as firm 2 did not adjust its output. Stackelberg allows firm 1 to decide on an output given how firm 2 responds. But once firm 1 has decided how much to produce, there is no choice left for firm 2. So Stackelberg for firm 1 assumes that firm 2 cannot avoid the outcome of firm 1, and firm 2 cannot adjust output once firm 1 has decided what to do. This allows firm 1 higher levels of profit than would occur under Cournot. Thus, firm 1 will stay at its Stackelberg output because it gets a larger profit than it would under Cournot.

Exercise 21. Use firm 2's Stackelberg output and the output we just computed for firm 1 into firm 1's profit function. What do you get? Does firm 1 make more profit using the Stackelberg output or the output we just computed?

We can also see, then, that the Stackelberg output is not a Nash equilibrium; Cournot is the Nash equilibrium. The graphs in Figure 8.7 tell the tale.

The upper graph of Figure 8.7 shows profit maximization for firm 1 given firm 2's BRF. In other words, we have put firm 2's BRF into firm 1's demand, which is the demand that firm 1 faces given the Stackelberg model. We compute total revenue and marginal revenue, and have graphed MR as well. The MC is horizontal at C_1. We find the profit-maximizing output for firm 1, which is the Stackelberg output. We trace that output into the lower graph, which shows the reaction function that we developed in the Cournot case. The equilibrium is on firm 2's best reply, but not on firm 1's best reply. Firm 1's best reply assumes the Cournot rules for how the firms interact; but firm 1 sets the price in this case, and the Cournot rules do not apply to firm 1. But they do apply to firm 2, which means that firm 2's best reply is the appropriate relation for firm 2.

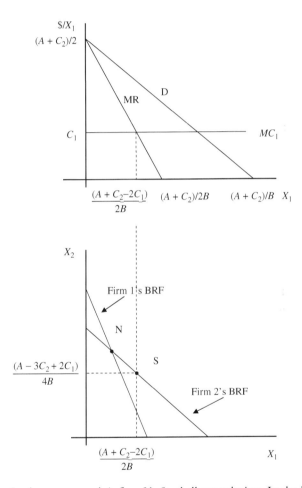

Figure 8.7   In the upper graph is firm 1's Stackelberg solution. In the lower graph, we show the Nash equilibrium, N, and the Stackelberg solution, S. We see that under Stackelberg, firm 1 produces more and firm 2 produces less than under Nash.

The Stackelberg solution is shown in the lower graph for both firms and is noted with an S. The Nash equilibrium, which is the Cournot solution, is noted with an N. We know that under Stackelberg, firm 1 produces more than it would under Cournot. We also know that firm 1 is not on its BRF, but firm 2 is on its BRF. Hence, we have the solution shown.

> **Section Summary:**
> In this section, we have compared the Cournot solution to the Stackelberg solution. We found that under Cournot, firm 1 produces less than under Stackelberg, but firm 1 makes more profit under Stackelberg than under Cournot. Still, given firm 2's output, firm 1 could make even more profit than the Stackelberg solution, but then firm 2 would alter its output, and we would return to the Nash equilibrium.

8.8   Summary

In this chapter, we have examined several models where the revenues of the firms are interrelated:

A. Cournot duopoly.
B. Cournot duopoly with collusion.
C. Stackelberg's model of price leadership.

These models are more complicated than either monopoly or competition, but are clearly more realistic than either of those. Still, one might argue that even these models are not very well attuned to the world. You should also note that the idea of supply as we have traditionally thought about it has not appeared in our discussion. You should also see that the firm's demand, even in these simple models, depends on what the other firm does.

The models presented here are straightforward alterations in the standard monopoly model. As you study more economics, you will find a rich variety of models of the ways that firms can interact. We have barely touched the surface.

Where do we go from here? Up to now, we have focused on the short run and how firms behave in that setting. In the next chapter, we will examine a model of the long run. Our primary focus will be on competitive firms. In the long run, all factors are variable, and we will need a way to find the costs when all factors can change. Once we have the costs, we can go on to revenue and profit maximization.

Terms Defined:

- Nash equilibrium
- Best reply function
- Cournot
- Stackelberg

Chapter 9

The Long-Run Competitive Model

Key Concepts:

- Finding long-run average total cost from short-run average total cost
- Finding long-run marginal cost
- Developing the long-run adjustment mechanism in the competitive case

Goals:

- Develop the long-run cost curves.
- Develop the long-run revenue concepts for competitive firms.
- Examine how price and quantity adjust in the short and long run.
- Examine the efficiency of the long-run outcome.

In this chapter, we completely shift gears and consider models that consider the future explicitly — long-run models. We move to an examination of the long run, and our focus will be on how the firm behaves in the long run.

9.1   Introduction

Suppose you start a basket-making business in your garage. You have work space there to weave the baskets. Your baskets are sturdy and useful; they become more popular, and you have to add some employees. At the same time, the garage gets a bit more crowded. You begin looking for a new place to make baskets. Up to this point in our study, we have only answered the question of how many baskets you should make to maximize profit. We have not considered questions such as what size of manufacturing space you need, or what capacity for producing baskets would be best. We turn to those questions now.

Here, our focus is on how the firm behaves in the long run. Up to this time, there has always been some factor (or factors) that was fixed and thus gave rise to fixed costs. The long run is a period of time in which some factors, the factors that were fixed in the short run, can now vary. Hence, in the long run, all factors are variable. In particular, we will assume that the capacity of the manufacturing facility will be a variable to be determined. We will start by looking at the cost structure in the long run and then bring in the revenue side. Profit maximization will be assumed. Finally, some important variations in the cost structure, constant costs and decreasing costs, will be considered.

9.2 Long-Run Costs

As you recall, in the short run, there is some fixed factor: the capacity of the firm. We are aware that the firm can push production past the capacity to some extent, but we would expect that the cost of production would rise quickly once capacity is reached. Another way to consider the capacity is as the capacity that the factory is designed to produce. Of course the actual usage may well differ from the designed capacity, and could be larger or smaller. In either case, the capacity will be chosen in the long run and will be fixed in the short run. Still, we need to know where we will see the capacity of the firm's production operation. We assume that the design capacity will occur at the output where short-run average total cost has its minimum. If the firm changes the capacity, the short-run average total cost (SRATC) will move, and so will the short-run marginal cost (SRMC). We will label the SRATC by the output where its minimum occurs. Thus, when SRATC has a minimum at X_1, that SRATC would be $SRATC_1$. The associated SRMC would be $SRMC_1$. The SRMC cuts the SRATC at the capacity. Hence, each SRATC represents a different capacity. We show this in Figure 9.1.

Definition 9.1: *The **scale of plant** for a firm is the choice of a particular short-run capacity for production, X_c, which is the output where the SRATC has its minimum*

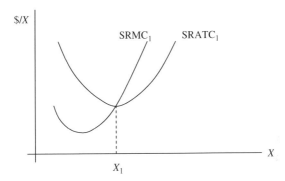

Figure 9.1   In this graph, we show the SRMC and the SRATC. The scale of plant is the output where the SRATC has its minimum, X_1. Thus, these curves are labeled SRATC$_1$ and SRMC$_1$.

The question we need to ask, then, is how we get the long-run costs. We will start by defining the concepts we need, and then will pursue the derivation of the relevant cost curves showing their relation to the short-run curves.

Definition 9.2: *At each output, the **long-run average total cost** (LRATC) is the minimum, for all possible scales of plant, of the short-run average total costs.*

This definition is a bit tricky. Here is what we are doing. Choose a level of output. At that output, find the lowest possible short-run average total cost for all scales of plant. We are holding output constant and allowing the scale of plant to change. If we do this at each output, the resulting curve is the long-run average total cost. This process is sometimes called finding the (lower) envelope curve.

Second, observe that at each output, the LRATC is equal to some short-run average total cost. That is, at each output, there is a short-run average total cost that coincides with the long-run average total cost.

It is important to see what we are not doing. What we are not doing is connecting the minimum points on each of the short-run average total costs. In Figure 9.2, we can see that the minimum points of the short-run average total costs need not be on the long-run average total cost.

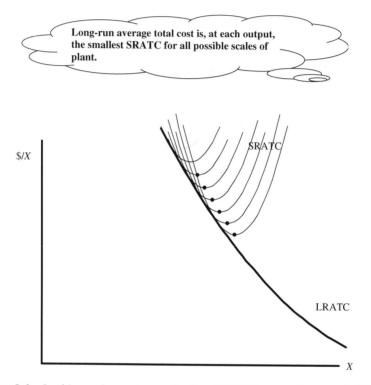

Figure 9.2   In this graph, we show a family of SRATC curves for several different scales of plant. The minimum point on each curve is shown with a dot. We have also shown the LRATC, which is the lower envelope. You can see that the minimum points on each SRATC are not on the LRATC.

You may wonder about the marginal cost. In order to define the long-run marginal cost, we will need the long-run total cost. We provide that definition next, followed by the long-run marginal cost.

Definition 9.3: *The **long-run total cost** (LRTC) relates output and dollars, and shows long-run average total cost times output at each output.*

Exercise 1. Suppose we are given the SRATC at some output, X_1. How do we find the SRTC at that output?

Exercise 2. Show that if, at X_1, the SRTC for some scale of plant is above LRTC, then the SRATC for that scale of plant must be above the LRATC at X_1.

Exercise 3. Show that if, at X_1, the SRTC for some scale of plant cuts the LRTC, then the SRATC for that scale of plant must also cut the LRATC.

There are two ways to find the LRTC. The first is to follow the definition; simply multiply LRATC by output at each output. A second way is to find the SRTC for each scale of plant and then find the lower envelope curve for that family of SRTCs. Either way will yield the LRTC. Proposition 9.4 provides the justification for the lower envelope approach to LRTC.

Proposition 9.4: *If the SRTC and LRTC are differentiable and at X_0 we are on the LRTC, then at X_0 there is a SRTC for some scale of plant tangent to the LRTC.*

Proof 9.5: We proceed by contrapositive, which says that if at X_0, for all scales of plant, no SRTC is tangent to LRTC, then we are not on LRTC. At X_0, take the SRATC that is equal to LRATC at that X_0. Now SRTC for that scale of plant equals LRTC at X_0. If this SRTC is not tangent to LRTC at X_0, then the SRTC must cut the LRTC. But then the SRTC is below the LRTC for some X. Hence, SRATC must be below LRATC, which means that at X_0, we cannot be on LRATC and thus not on LRTC. □

Exercise 4. Draw a graph showing the LRATC with an SRATC cutting LRATC at some X. Directly below, draw a graph showing the associated SRTC and LRTC. Explain how the SRATC cutting the LRATC violates the definition of LRATC.

Proposition 9.4 is very useful as it not only tells us that at each X, there is an SRTC tangent to LRTC, but it also identifies which SRTC will be the right one (which scale of plant is the right one) — the SRTC associated with the SRATC tangent to LRATC at that output.

What about the LRMC? This is a bit more interesting!

Definition 9.6: *The **long-run marginal cost** (LRMC) relates output and dollars per unit of output, and shows the change in LRTC due to a change in output at each output.*

Note that the LRMC is related to LRTC, just as the marginal cost in the short run is related to the total cost. In short, the LRMC is the slope of the LRTC.

We wish now to find points on the LRMC. We know one point on the LRMC because we know that the LRMC must cut the LRATC at the minimum of the LRATC (this is proposition 4.18). But we can get even more points on LRMC by realizing that the marginal cost is the slope of total cost and that at some outputs, SRTC is tangent to LRTC, so at those outputs, the short-run marginal must also be equal to the long-run marginal. Proposition 9.7 provides the details.

Proposition 9.7: *If both $SRTC_1$ and LRTC are differentiable, and if $SRATC_1$ is tangent to LRATC at X_0, then LRMC must equal the $SRMC_1$ at X_0.*

Proof 9.8: If the $SRATC_1$ is tangent to LRATC at X_0, then $SRATC_1 = LRATC$ at X_0. If we multiply both sides by X_0, we get $X_0 \times SRATC_1 = X_0 \times LRATC$, so the $SRTC_1 = LRTC$ at X_0. Because $SRTC_1$ and LRTC are differentiable, $SRTC_1$ must be tangent to LRTC at X_0. Again, no SRTC can cut the LRTC at any output, so if they are equal, they must be tangent (given that both curves are differentiable). If $SRTC_1$ is tangent to LRTC at X_0, then the slope of $SRTC_1 =$ the slope of LRTC. The slope of $SRTC_1$ is $SRMC_1$ and the slope of LRTC is LRMC, so at X_0, $SRMC_1 = LRMC$ must hold.   □

Exercise 5. In the statement "so the $SRTC_1 = LRTC$ at X_0. Because $SRTC_1$ and $LRTC$ are differentiable, $SRTC_1$ must be tangent to $LRTC$ at X_0," explain why the underlined portion is true.

Consider the graph in Figure 9.3. Here we have the $SRATC_1$ and the $SRMC_1$. Note that the $SRMC_1$ cuts through the minimum point on the $SRATC_1$. We also know that because the $SRATC_1$ is tangent to the $LRATC$ at X_0, the $LRMC$ must also equal the $SRMC_1$ at that output. Hence, we have one point on the $LRMC$. We can get other points by taking other outputs and finding the points on the $LRMC$ in the same fashion.

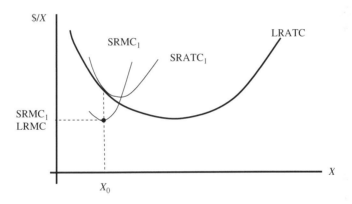

Figure 9.3 $SRATC_1$ is tangent to the $LRATC$ at X_0. Therefore, $SRTC_1$ is tangent to $LRTC$ at X_0, which makes $LRMC = SRMC_1$ at X_0.

Exercise 6. In Figure 9.3, what output would X_1 be?

In Figure 9.4, we have added $SRATC_3$ tangent to $LRATC$ at X_4. Because $SRATC_3$ equals $LRATC$ at X_4, the $LRMC$ must be equal to $SRMC_3$ at X_4. At X_2, $SRATC_2$ is tangent to the $LRATC$. In this case, the $SRMC_2$ cuts the $SRATC_2$ at X_2, so the $LRMC$ is equal to the

SRMC$_2$ at X_2. Note that X_2 is the minimum of the LRATC, so the LRMC should cut the LRATC at that output (and it does!).

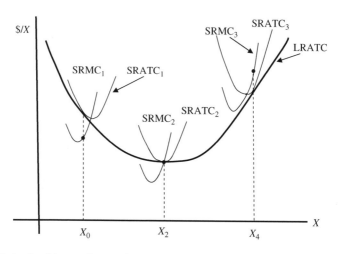

Figure 9.4   In this graph, we show three outputs and the SRATC tangent to the LRATC at each of those outputs. We also show the SRMC for each of the scales of plant, and identify, with a large dot, the point on the SRMC that is also on the LRMC.

Now we have all of the long-run cost curves.

> **Section Summary:**
> In this section, we have developed the long-run cost concepts needed for profit maximization. We found LRATC from the family of SRATCs. We then found LRTC and LRMC. We examined the relationship between the SRMC and LRMC as part of the process for finding LRMC. To complete the profit maximization problem, we will need revenue. Revenue and profit maximization will be the focal points of the next section.

9.3   Revenue and Profit Maximization

This section starts with a discussion of revenue and then combines the revenue and cost concepts to address profit maximization. We confine our interest to the competitive case, where again we assume that competitive firms cannot affect the price of the product. Thus, as before, we expect that the MR will equal price. In this case, we need not distinguish between the long-run and short-run revenue curves as they are the same. See Figure 9.5 for the details.

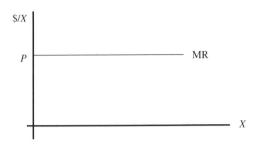

Figure 9.5 Here we show the MR for the competitive firm, which is the same for both the long and short run.

We can now put together the costs and revenues to obtain the profit maximization proposition. It will contain no surprises!

Proposition 9.9: Long-Run Profit Maximization

Suppose that LRATC and LRMC are derived as shown above, and that we have a competitive firm. If LRMC is continuous and there is a profit-maximizing output between 0 and infinity, then at the profit maximum, LRMC = LRMR.

Proof 9.10: The proof is standard and should be a straightforward matter for you at this point. □

Exercise 7. Prove proposition 9.9.

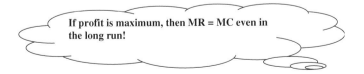

If profit is maximum, then MR = MC even in the long run!

We are now in a position to see what is going on in the long run and then also see how the short run fits in. So suppose that we have a competitive firm that has been given the price P. The firm has two choices to make. One is the scale of plant, which short-run average total cost to use; and then, second, what output to produce.

Given the price, we know that the price is the same as MR under the competitive assumption, so we also have the LRMR. What happens next is that we put the LRMR together with the LRMC to determine the output to produce. Once we have the output, in the long run, the firm will also choose a scale of plant. The scale of plant will be the scale of plant that provides the minimum cost of all possible scales of plant to produce the output in question.

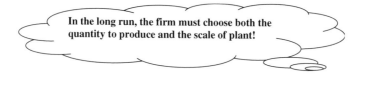

In the long run, the firm must choose both the quantity to produce and the scale of plant!

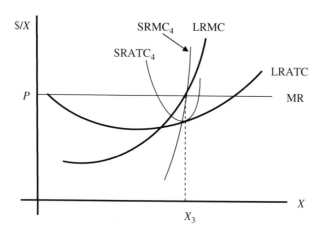

Figure 9.6   Given a price of P, the firm chooses to produce X_3 in the long run. They will also choose a scale of plant yielding SRATC$_4$. You can see that the firm is also maximizing profit in the short run as well as the long run.

Exercise 8. In Figure 9.6, assume that the firm uses SRATC$_4$ and show the amount of profit that the firm makes in the long run. How much profit does the firm make in the short run?

In Figure 9.6, we have the firm facing a price of P. The first step is to choose a level of output for long-run profit maximization. Using proposition 9.9, the firm chooses to produce X_3. The firm then chooses a scale of plant by looking for the scale of plant that minimizes the SRATC for the output X_3. In this case, it would be the scale of plant that yields SRATC$_4$. Note now that when we draw in the SRMC associated with that scale of plant, SRMC$_4$, we would have the SRMC going through the minimum point on SRATC$_4$, and because SRATC$_4$ is tangent to the LRATC at X_3, SRMC$_4$ has to be equal to LRMC at X_3. This is a second point on the SRMC$_4$ curve. Thus, the firm is also maximizing profit in the short run as well as the long run. What happens if the price changes?

Section Summary:
In this section, we have established the profit maximization proposition that would hold in the long run. We have also found the profit-maximizing choice in both the short and long run for the competitive firm. In the next section, we will look at how the firm might have to adjust in the long run.

9.4 Long-Run Adjustment

We wish to now examine what happens if the price changes. How will the firm adjust? The basic idea is that there is a short-run and a long-run adjustment that will be made. In the short run, the firm is stuck with the scale of plant from the long run. Thus, the firm can adjust output in the short run, but not the scale of plant. We show this in Figure 9.7.

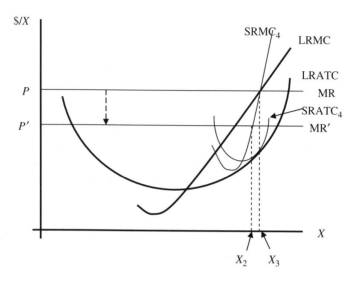

Figure 9.7   In this graph, we start with the price P. In the long run, the firm chooses to produce X_3 with a scale of plant SRATC$_4$. The firm is maximizing profit in both the short and long run. Now if the price falls to P', in the short run the firm can only adjust output, and moves along the SRMC$_4$ curve to the new output, X_2, which maximizes profit in the short run. The firm is not maximizing profit in the long run as it cannot, yet, change the scale of plant.

In the long run, the firm has another change to make: it will alter the scale of plant. In this case, we see that the firm would like a smaller scale of plant. In Figure 9.8, we continue the argument and show the smaller scale of plant the firm would choose. Here, at the lower price P', in the long run the firm will want to choose the output X_1 and the scale of plant associated with SRATC$_0$. They will also produce so that they are maximizing profit in the short run if they do this.

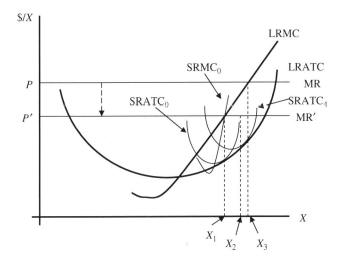

Figure 9.8 In this graph (same as Figure 9.7 except that we have removed SRMC$_4$ and added SRMC$_0$ and SRATC$_0$), we show the scale of plant the firm would choose in the long run to maximize profit. They end up with SRATC$_0$. In so doing, they also maximize profit in the short run as well as the long run.

Note that in both the long run with price equal to P and with price equal to P', the profit-maximizing firm has a positive profit. What are the forces that will cause some natural long-run adjustment?

Assumption 9.11: *If profits are positive, then new firms will enter the industry. If profits are negative, then firms will exit the industry.*

Recall that when we compute profit, we include a normal return as part of the cost (see Chapter 4, Section 4.6). That is, if the firm were to make zero profit, they would still manage to stay in business earning a normal rate of return. Using assumption 9.11, we can see the dynamics of the firm.

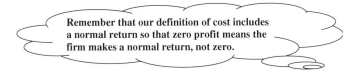

Remember that our definition of cost includes a normal return so that zero profit means the firm makes a normal return, not zero.

If profits are positive in the long run, we expect firms to enter the industry. If profits are negative, we expect firms to leave the industry.

Definition 9.12: *We say the firm is in* **long-run equilibrium** *if there are no forces causing the firm to wish to change output or scale of plant.*

Proposition 9.13: *The long-run equilibrium for the competitive firm maximizing profit will be where the firm earns zero profit (but a normal return).*

Proof 9.14: We prove this by arguing that if profit is not zero, then there will be forces in the market that will cause output and price to change so the firm is not in long-run equilibrium (recall that equilibrium is the balance of force). There are two cases. If the profit is positive, then we are not in long-run equilibrium; and if profit is negative, then we are not in long-run equilibrium. We will take the first case and leave the second to the student.

If profit is positive, then by assumption 9.11, we know that firms will enter the market. If so, the increase in the number of firms will cause the market supply to increase (shift right), and the price will fall. This will cause the firm to reduce output and scale of plant, and profit will fall. The fact that either output or scale of plant automatically falls in this case means that we are not in long-run equilibrium.   □

Exercise 9. Prove that if profit is negative, then the firm is not in long-run equilibrium.

Exercise 10. Draw the market supply and demand, and show what happens to price as the number of firms in the industry increases.

We can now see where the firm ends up in the long run. This is shown in Figure 9.9.

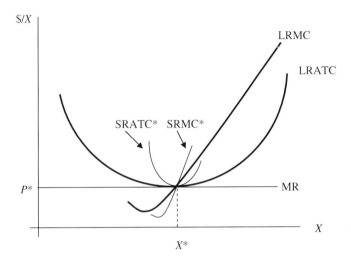

Figure 9.9   In this graph, we show the long-run equilibrium for the firm. Here price has been pushed to P^* and the firm chooses scale of plant X^* with SRATC* and produces X^*. This is a profit maximum for both the short run and the long run. Profits are zero, and there is no force on price or quantity. This is the long-run equilibrium.

Definition 9.15: *We say a firm is **productively efficient** if it produces at the minimum cost per unit, the minimum of the average total cost.*

We can see that competitive firms in the long run achieve productive efficiency. This is a reason to prefer the competitive outcome. Note that competitive firms achieve productive efficiency by allowing free entry to the market. In a monopoly, even when profits are positive, no firms can enter the market. Hence in monopoly, price will not be pushed down, and the firm will not be pushed to the lowest point on their average total cost curve. Monopoly will not automatically end up in a productively efficient outcome.

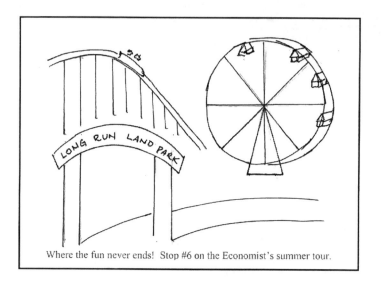

Where the fun never ends! Stop #6 on the Economist's summer tour.

Section Summary:
In this section, we have examined the long-run adjustment process for the competitive firm. The outcome is that in the long run, the firm always ends up at the lowest point on its average total cost curve. It should be pointed out that this outcome has a desirable property, namely that in the long run, the competitive firm provides its output with the smallest average expenditure which is an efficient outcome. Thus, competitive firms achieve two desirable outcomes not achieved by monopoly: $P = MC$ and price at the lowest ATC.

9.5   A Numerical Example[1]

In this section, we will approach the problem of the long run with a numerical example. We will start with a family of short-run average total cost curves and find the long-run total cost. Once we have long-run total cost and given the price of output, we can find the

---

[1] Essential to the example in this section is the cost curve. I assumed that the short-run average total cost is parabolic and that as the capacity of the firm grows, the vertex of

profit-maximizing choice. We can also examine what happens when the price changes.

We start with the SRATC. Suppose we have the following SRATC, where X_c is the capacity of the firm, the output where the SRATC has its minimum, and X_m is the output where the LRATC will have its minimum. X measures output.

$$\text{SRATC} = 10 + (X_c - X_m)^2 + (X - X_c)^2.$$

For given values of X_c and X_m, we can plot this curve, and we will get a U-shaped curve with its minimum at X_c.

Exercise 11. By using the derivative, find the minimum value for the SRATC. That is, find the X so that SRATC is minimum while treating both X_c and X_m as constants.

FIND LRATC

The LRATC is the lower envelope of the SRATC curves. Thus, to find LRATC, we need to minimize the SRATC with respect to X_c, the scale of plant, to find the scale of plant at each X. To do this, we will find the derivative of SRATC with respect to X_c, set the derivative equal to zero, and solve for X_c. This process will give us the scale of plant, X_c that minimizes our SRATC. To ease the computation, assume that $X_m = 150$. That means that the LRATC will have its minimum at

---

the SRATC will follow a parabolic shape. If the vertex of the short-run ATC is (z, X_c), and the parabola of these vertices has its minimum at X_m with a value of k, then $z - k = a(X_c - X_m)^2$. The SRATC (with vertex (z, X_c)) is parabolic with equation $SRATC - z = (X - X_c)^2$. We can replace the z in the second equation with the z in the first to obtain the SRATC: $SRATC = k + a(X_c - X_m)^2 + (X - X_c)^2$. If we minimize this expression with respect to X_c, we get the long-run scale of plant, which we can substitute back into the SRATC to get LRATC.

One has to choose k so that the MC > 0. The problem is that this SRATC does not have a fixed cost, and to include a fixed cost makes the outcome messy.

$X_m = 150$. We have the following SRATC for a firm with a scale of plant equal to X_c:

$$\text{SRATC} = 10 + (X_c - 150)^2 + (X - X_c)^2.$$

The derivative with respect to X_c is as follows:

$$\text{SRATC}' = 2(X_c - 150) - 2(X - X_c) = 0.$$

Solve for X_c:

$$2X_c - 300 - 2X + 2X_c = 0$$

$$4X_c = 2X + 300$$

$$X_c = (1/2)X + 75.$$

This tells us that the scale of plant so that SRATC is minimum at X is the scale of plant $X_c = (1/2)X + 75$. Thus, if $X = 50$ were to be the profit maximum output, then our scale of plant would be $X_c = (1/2) \times 50 + 75 = 100$. To produce 50 units with the smallest short-run cost (and thus be on the LRATC), we choose a scale of plant of 100, meaning that the minimum SRATC for this plant would be at 100.

To find LRATC, we put this term back in the SRATC equation. Hence, our LRATC is as follows:

$$\text{LRATC} = 10 + (75 + (1/2)X - 150)^2 + (X - (1/2)X - 75)^2$$
$$= 10 + ((1/2)X - 75)^2 + ((1/2)X - 75)^2$$
$$= 10 + 2((1/2)X - 75)^2.$$

We now have the equation of the LRATC.

FIND LRTC

Hence, we will have the LRTC as shown next:

$$\text{LRTC} = 10X + 2X((1/2)X - 75)^2.$$

We can now work on the profit-maximizing problem. Suppose that the price is \$1660 per unit. Our long-run profit function will be as shown:

$$\pi = 1660X - \{10X + 2X((1/2)X - 75)^2\}$$
$$= 1650X - 2X\{(1/4)X^2 - 75X + 75^2\}$$
$$= 1650X - (1/2)X^3 + 150X^2 - 2X \times 75^2.$$

FIND THE LONG-RUN PROFIT-MAXIMIZING OUTPUT

We will maximize profit in the usual way:

$$\pi' = 1650 - (3/2)X^2 + 300X - 11250$$
$$= -(3/2)X^2 + 300X - 9600 = 0.$$

We solve for X using the quadratic formula:

$$X = \frac{-300 \pm \sqrt{(-300)^2 - 4(-3/2)(-9600)}}{2(-3/2)}$$

$$= \frac{-300 \pm \sqrt{90000 - 57600}}{-3} = \frac{-300 \pm \sqrt{32400}}{-3}$$

$$= \frac{-300 \pm 180}{-3} = 160 \text{ or } 40.$$

The second derivative is $\pi'' = -3X + 300$. So $\pi''(160) = -180$; hence, $X = 160$ is a maximum. Check to see that $X = 40$ is a minimum.

FIND THE SCALE OF PLANT

We can compute the scale of plant the firm would use in the long run. We use the formula for the capacity developed above, $X_c = (1/2)X + 75$. Here the output the firm actually produces is $X = 160$, so $X_c = 80 + 75 = 155$. Thus, the firm in the long run would choose a capacity of 155 (the SRATC would have its minimum at $X = 155$), and would choose to produce 160 units. At $X = 160$, the SRATC should be equal to the LRATC. We can check on that condition:

$$SRATC(160) = 10 + (155 - 150)^2 + (160 - 155)^2$$
$$= 10 + 5^2 + 5^2 = 60.$$
$$LRATC(160) = 10 + 2((1/2)X - 75)^2$$
$$= 10 + 2((1/2) \times 160 - 75)^2$$
$$= 10 + 2(80 - 75)^2$$
$$= 10 + 2 \times 25 = 60.$$

FIND THE AMOUNT OF PROFIT THE FIRM MAKES

We can also see the amount of profit the firm is making. We know that the average cost is $60 and the price is $1660, so that means that each unit generates $1600. The firm produces 160 units, so they have a profit of $256,000. In this case, we would expect that the price would fall as firms enter the industry. In summary, we have the following outcomes.

When the price is $1660 per unit, the long-run equilibrium output is 160 units, and the capacity of the firm, X_c, is 155 units. The firm also maximizes profit in the short run with this combination. The firm's profit is $256,000, suggesting that firms would enter the industry and price would fall. What would happen if the price were to fall to $316 per unit?

FIND THE SHORT-RUN ADJUSTMENT

In the short run, the firm would, of course, reduce output. But they would be stuck with the initial scale of plant, $X_c = 155$. We pursue the short-run profit maximum based on that assumption.

We start with the short-run average total cost curve with $X_c = 155$:

$$SRATC = 10 + (155 - 150)^2 + (X - 155)^2$$
$$= 35 + X^2 - 310X + 24025.$$

Now SRTC will be as follows:

$$\text{SRTC} = 35X + X^3 - 310X^2 + 24025X.$$

The short-run profit is:

$$\pi = 316X - X^3 + 310X^2 - 24060X = -X^3 + 310X^2 - 23744X.$$

The derivative of profit is shown next:

$$\pi' = -3X^2 + 620X - 23744 = 0.$$

Solve for X:

$$X = \frac{-620 \pm \sqrt{620^2 - 4 \times (-3) \times (-23744)}}{2 \times (-3)}$$

$$= \frac{-620 \pm \sqrt{384400 - 284928}}{-6} = \frac{-620 \pm \sqrt{99472}}{-6}$$

$$= \frac{-620 \pm 315.39}{-6} = 155.89 \text{ or } 50.76.$$

You should see that the second derivative is negative for $X = 155.89$, meaning that we have a maximum.

The firm's short-run profit is found as follows, where $X = 155.89$:

$$\pi = 316 \times X - (10 + (155 - 150)^2 + (X - 155)^2) \times X$$

$$= 316 \times 155.89 - (35 + 0.89^2) \times 155.89$$

$$= (316 - 35.79) \times 155.89 = 280.21 \times 155.89 = 43681.61.$$

Thus, in the short run, given a scale of plant of 155 and a price of \$316, the firm would produce 155.89 units and make a profit of \$43,681.61. We know, though, that the firm will also have to make a long-run adjustment to the scale of plant. How can we see what will happen? We need the long-run cost curve. Above, we found the LRTC; it is

$$\text{LRTC} = 10X + 2X((1/2)X - 75)^2.$$

FIND THE NEW LONG-RUN EQUILIBRIUM

When price is \$316, we will therefore have this profit function in the long run:

$$\pi = 316X - \{10X + 2X((1/2)X - 75)^2\}$$
$$= 306X - 2X((1/4)X^2 - 75X + 5625)$$
$$= 306X - (1/2)X^3 + 150X^2 - 11250X$$
$$= -(1/2)X^3 + 150X^2 - 10944X.$$

We find the profit maximum by taking the derivative, setting the derivative equal to zero, and solving for X:

$$\pi' = -(3/2)X^2 + 300X - 10944 = 0.$$
$$X = \frac{-300 \pm \sqrt{300^2 - 4 \times (-3/2) \times (-10944)}}{2 \times (-3/2)}$$
$$= \frac{-300 \pm \sqrt{90000 - 65664}}{-3} = \frac{-300 \pm \sqrt{24336}}{-3}$$
$$= \frac{-300 \pm 156}{-3} = 152 \text{ or } 48.$$

Exercise 12. Is $X = 152$ or $X = 48$ the profit maximum? How do you know?

Exercise 13. Suppose the price is \$10. Find the short-run and long-run profit maximum in this case.

Exercise 14. Suppose that SRATC $= 10 + 10(X_c - 150)^2 + (X - X_c)^2$.

    a. Take the derivative of SRATC with respect to X_c (treat X as a constant); set it to zero. Solve the resulting expression for X_c and replace X_c in SRATC with that X_c (X_c will depend on X; you will not get a number for this outcome). This is LRATC.

    b. Find the LRTC.

c. Suppose that $P = 3010$ and find the long-run profit-maximizing output.
d. Find the short-run scale of plant for this case.
e. Find the SRATC and SRTC at the profit maximum.
f. How much profit will the firm make? What do you think will happen as a result?

Section Summary:
In this section, we have used an example to show what happens in the long run and how the adjustment occurs from the long to the short and back to the long. In the next section, we examine a factor that will determine the shape of the long-run average total cost: returns to scale.

9.6   Increasing and Decreasing Cost Industries

One might wonder why the family of short-run average total costs has the shape we have drawn. Is there some reason to think that this shape is appropriate? What are the forces that might determine the shape? In this section, we examine one of the primary factors determining the shape of the long-run curves: returns to scale.

Definition 9.16: *A production function displays* **constant returns to scale** *if at all combinations of inputs, a doubling of inputs exactly doubles output.*

Definition 9.17: *A production function displays* **decreasing returns to scale** *if at all combinations of inputs, a doubling of inputs less than doubles output.*

Definition 9.18: *A production function displays* **increasing returns to scale** *if at all combinations of inputs, a doubling of inputs more than doubles output.*

Exercise 15. Suppose that we double output but need less than twice as much of each input. Do we have increasing or decreasing returns to scale? Explain how you know. What if we double output and need more than twice as much of each input? Do we have increasing or decreasing returns to scale? Explain how you know.

A couple of points. First, the question we started with had to do with the shape of the average total cost. We then said an important concept that would be a factor in determining this shape is returns to scale, which is about the production function. How is the production function related to the average total cost?

It is pretty easy to see that there is a relationship between the production function and total cost. Recall that we are in the long run, and there are no fixed costs, so total cost starts at the origin as shown in Figure 9.10.

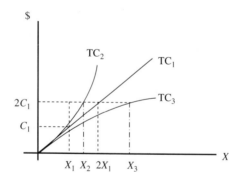

Figure 9.10   Along TC_1, as output doubles (goes from X_1 to $2X_1$), cost doubles (goes from C_1 to $2C_1$). Along TC_2, as cost doubles, output less than doubles, to X_2, due to decreasing returns to scale. Along TC_3, as cost doubles, output more than doubles, to X_3, due to increasing returns to scale.

Start with some combination of inputs. There is a cost associated with that combination of inputs, C_1, and also an output, X_1. We have one point on the total cost curve. If we double inputs, we have doubled the cost, $2C_1$. If we then double output as a result, we have a second point on the total cost curve, $2X_1$. And the total cost must be linear. If we double the inputs, we double the cost, but if output more than doubles (increasing returns), then the total cost must bend down as shown by TC_3. If output less than doubles (decreasing returns), then the long-run total cost must bend up as shown with TC_2. If the total cost bends down, then the average total cost must also slope down.

How do we know? Recall our work from Chapter 4, Section 4.7, where we found the average cost from the total cost using the slope of the straight line from the origin. If the total cost bends down, then the average cost will have a negative slope. If the total cost bends up, the average cost will have a positive slope. Recall that total fixed cost is zero, so the long-run total cost starts at the origin. Thus, the returns to scale do determine the shape of the average cost.

Which shape of the production function makes the most sense? Is there evidence that constant returns are more likely than increasing or decreasing returns? On the face of it, constant returns seem the most likely. Suppose we have a firm making 300 bicycles every day. If we wanted to produce 600 bicycles per day, what would we do? We would simply build a second plant exactly like the first, doubling inputs. So we double inputs to double output. Now you might argue that because of the experience of using the plant to build 300 bicycles per day, you have some information about a better way to build the new plant, or that building a brand new plant might allow double output with less than double input. At the very least, you might not need all of the staff in the second plant. For example, you buy aluminum for the bicycle frame so you have an employee whose job is to make the purchase. Do you need two such employees when you have the second plant? Can't the first employee simply order twice as much aluminum? Why have two people ordering when one could do the job? So we could double output with fewer than double our original inputs. This is an argument for increasing returns to scale and a downward-sloping average cost. On the other hand, at some point, it may be important to increase the management. Suppose we have 10 plants making 300 bicycles per day. Now we add 10 more plants. Each plant has a plant manager overseeing the operations of that plant. We had 10 plant managers before the change, and have 20 after the change. The 10 plant managers reported to a Vice President. We have doubled inputs, so we have doubled the Vice Presidents as well. But now these Vice Presidents cannot both report to the President; it is too much for the President. But because we doubled inputs, we now have two Vice Presidents. So now we need one person to whom both Vice Presidents report. Hence, we have another layer of management to oversee the production process. This is an argument for decreasing returns to scale and an upward-sloping average cost.

The discussion given above provides a rationale for the shape of the long-run average total cost that we have drawn. As output increases from small levels, we expect that some increasing returns to scale elements will cause the long-run average total cost to fall. As output gets larger and larger, eventually we would expect that the decreasing returns to scale forces would prevail and the long-run average total cost would rise. This would yield the long-run average total cost we have drawn above.

The shape of the total cost also determines the marginal cost. We generally know (see proposition 4.19 — the Average Marginal Fact) that if the average cost is rising, the marginal must be above the average. If the average is falling, the marginal must be below the average. Hence, we also know what the long-run marginal cost must look like.

Exercise 16. What does proposition 4.19 say and how does it apply here?

Exercise 17. Suppose that we have increasing returns to scale. What will the LRATC and LRMC look like? Explain how you know.

Exercise 18. Suppose that we have constant returns to scale. What will the LRATC and LRMC look like? Explain how you know.

In the case of a firm selling output competitively, we could have either decreasing or constant returns to scale. Increasing returns to scale are incompatible with competition.

Exercise 19. Suppose that we have a competitive firm. What will the MR look like? Suppose we have increasing returns to scale. What will the MC look like? At what output is profit maximum? How do you know? Why is competition incompatible with increasing returns?

In the case that every firm in an industry has decreasing returns to scale, we say that the firm is in an increasing cost industry. In this case, we have that the LRATC slopes upward, and the LRMC will be above the LRATC. The graph will look as shown in Figure 9.11. Suppose that all firms in the industry have the same cost curves. The firm in Figure 9.11 earns positive profits and in the long run we know that price will be bid down to the bottom of the LRATC. Thus, capacity of the individual firm will approach zero and the number of firms in the industry will become very large, exactly what we would expect for competition.

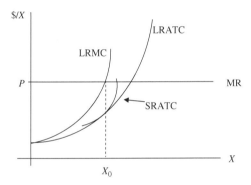

Figure 9.11   Here we have the case of decreasing returns to scale. The LRATC rises for all output and the LRMC is above the LRATC. Profit maximization occurs at X_0. This is a short-run outcome, not the final long-run equilibrium.

If all firms in an industry have constant returns to scale and the same cost curves, then the LRMC will equal the LRATC and both will be horizontal. In this case, with a constant MR, MR must equal MC and every output will generate the same profit, so the amount of output that any firm will produce will not be determined. This is both a long-run and a short-run equilibrium, and is shown in Figure 9.12.

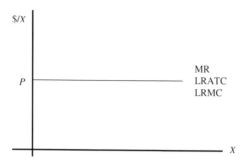

Figure 9.12   Here we have the firm with constant returns to scale. The result is that every output maximizes profit in the long and short run.

There is an important point to be learned from the case of decreasing and constant returns to scale. In the long run, the price in the market falls to the lowest point on the LRATC and stays there. The outcome is that in the long run for these two cases, price is determined by costs, not by demand. Second, the long-run supply in both cases will be horizontal at the lowest price on the LRATC. That is, there is only one price that is consistent with long-run equilibrium in the world of decreasing or constant returns to scale. The quantity will be determined by the demand in these situations.

FROM THE LITERATURE

Is there evidence that some industries face increasing returns to scale? How would we know if some industry did? We would look at the average total cost curve to see if it is falling as output rises. There are a number of problems with putting this rather simple concept into practice, but there are economists who have looked at this issue for particular industries. One industry of interest is dairy farming, and there is some evidence of increasing returns to scale in the dairy industry. This means that the cost per unit may well fall as the herd size rises. Here is the citation: Roberto Mosheim and C.A. Lovell, "Scale Economies and Inefficiency of U.S. Dairy Farms," *American Journal of Agricultural Economics*, Vol. 91, No. 3, August, 2009, pp. 777–794.

Section Summary:

In this section, we have discussed returns to scale and the impact of returns to scale on the shape of the cost curves with a resulting impact on the long-run supply. What we discovered is that increasing returns to scale are not compatible with competition and that with either decreasing or constant returns to scale, we have a horizontal long-run supply curve. Many firms selling goods competitively may not exhibit either of these scale characteristics, but some mixture or no scale characteristics at all.

This section ends our discussion of the long run. However, it should be apparent to you that there is a significant flaw in this approach. We assume that we know the price in the future. But what can we know in the long run? Can we know, with certainty, the price? It would make sense to at least examine the problem with some uncertainty about the prices, and we will undertake that in Chapter 13.

9.7   Summary

In this chapter, we have examined the behavior of the firm in the long run:

A. We have developed a method to find the long-run average total cost based on the short-run average total costs.
B. We introduced the revenue for the competitive firm and found the profit maximum in the long run.
C. We also examined what would happen if the price would change in both the short and long run.
D. We concluded that in the long run, the competitive firm would produce at an output where the LRATC has its minimum, signifying an efficient outcome.

Terms Defined:

• Scale of plant
• Long-run average total cost

- Long-run total cost
- Long-run marginal cost
- Long-run equilibrium
- Productively efficient
- Constant returns to scale
- Decreasing returns to scale
- Increasing returns to scale

Chapter 10

Hiring Labor

Key Concepts:

- Profit maximization yields demand for inputs
- Demands for inputs are consistent with profit-maximizing output choices

Goals:

- Profit-maximizing firms hire labor so that MRP = MIC.
- Demand for labor in the competitive case of one variable input is the MRP.
- Diminishing returns determine the slope of demand for labor in the competitive case.
- The profit-maximizing quantity of labor produces the profit-maximizing output.

Our efforts so far have been aimed at finding the supply of output from the firm's decision process. But in fact, the firm also acts to demand inputs. Of course the firm will be a profit maximizer in its choice of inputs. We now take up this demand for inputs and work toward an understanding of how the two profit maximization problems (one choosing a level of output and another choosing a quantity of an input) are really the same problem.

10.1   Introduction

Suppose that you are the basket maker still working in the garage. Your business is booming with more work than you can produce. You want to hire another person, or maybe two. How do you go about deciding what to do? What factors will play into your decision?

In the process of making the decision to hire labor, the firm is essentially confronted with the same information as when it determines its output. That is, the firm has information about the cost, namely the wage it has to pay its labor, and the revenue, the price it will charge for its output. The firm is also constrained by the technology (no matter how hard we try, we cannot produce something from nothing). What changes is the way the firm combines this information to approach the problem of hiring inputs. It would be wise for you to go back to Chapter 4 to review Section 4.4, where the firm's technology was discussed.

In Chapter 4, we made the following assumptions about the firm:

Assumptions 4.1:

a. *The firm produces one output, $X \geq 0$.*
b. *The firm uses two variable inputs, labor, $L \geq 0$, and capital, $K \geq 0$.*
c. *There is a fixed factor (this is a short-run analysis).*
d. *The inputs and output are infinitely divisible.*
e. *The firm is given the input prices, w (wage) for labor, $w > 0$, and r (rental rate) for capital, $r > 0$. The firm cannot affect the input prices by its own effort.*
f. *The technology for producing the output is known and does not change.*
g. *There are no externalities.*

In this chapter, we will start by altering assumption b and only consider one variable input (but we will return to the world of two variable inputs later in this chapter). We start with the assumption that the firm buys inputs competitively, and later in the chapter we will also relax this assumption. However, the other assumptions will be maintained. We return now to the topic of technology, which we first examined in Chapter 4. We aim to develop the appropriate revenue and cost concepts so that we may proceed to profit maximization and the demand for labor.

10.2 Marginal Product

The primary concept we need from our earlier work is the marginal product. You will find the marginal product defined in definition 4.7. It is the slope of the total product curve (see definition 4.6). We obtain the total product from the production function and the marginal product from the total product. The production function represents the technology the firm has available, so the marginal product (MP) is also a representation of the technology. We generally expect that the MP will have a particular shape, eventually sloping downward. This is the Law of Diminishing Returns, which we state next (a repeat of definition 4.8).

Definition 10.1: *The **Law of Diminishing Returns** states that as we add more of a variable factor to fixed factors, eventually the marginal product of the variable factor will begin to decrease as the variable factor is increased.*

Note what the law says. It says that the MP will eventually fall. It does not say that the MP will eventually become zero, nor does it say that output will fall as the input increases. And the law is particularly vague about when this falling MP will start to happen. All the law says is that at some point, the MP will begin to fall. One might wonder why we think this law is likely to be true.

> The Law of Diminishing Returns says that as a variable input increases, other inputs not changing, eventually the MP of that input will fall.

The Law of Diminishing Returns is set in the short run where there is a fixed factor, and the fixed factor is the problem. When the firm wants to increase (or decrease) its output, it can do so by adjusting labor, but not the fixed factor, say the scale of plant. Consider this example. I have a basket-making business in my garage. I go out and collect reeds from the ditches by the road, bring them home, and dry them in the sun. I then take the reeds and weave them into a basket using no staples or other fastening devices. My labor is the variable input. My garage is the scale of plant. In my garage, I have a long bench where I weave the baskets. By myself, I make four baskets a day. Suppose that for some unknown reason, my baskets start to sell, and I hire someone else to help. This may be a really good thing. Now, there is someone to collect reeds most of the day, bring them back, and set them out to dry, while the other person weaves the reeds into baskets. So production rises by a lot; we more than double output. What happens when we hire a third person? If we had more space in the garage to assemble the baskets, the third person would be able to increase production by a large amount. But we do not have the space in the garage for both people to work. Hence, we gain some output, but the third worker does not add as much output as the second, and diminishing returns sets in.

Exercise 1. What does the Law of Diminishing Returns say?
Exercise 2. Why do economists think that the Law of Diminishing
Returns is true?

We now have a reason for diminishing returns, so we know the shape of the MP. We can now move toward connecting the amount of labor hired to the revenue of the firm.

Exercise 3. How is the Law of Diminishing Returns different from
decreasing returns to scale?

Section Summary:
In this section, we reviewed the concept of marginal product and introduced the idea of diminishing returns, which provides a shape for the marginal product. We are now ready to move forward to integrating the marginal product concept with the marginal revenue to generate our revenue concept — the marginal revenue product.

10.3   Marginal Revenue Product

In this section, we will define the primary concepts we need for the firm to decide how much labor to hire. In this case, we are looking at a world where there is only one variable input: labor. For example, imagine a person gathering reeds and weaving baskets from the reeds. The only input is the individual's labor. To decide how much labor to hire, we will need both revenue and cost concepts. We start with the revenue.

At first, it seems a bit hard to imagine how inputs are related to output. In our example, as the person works more, they will produce more baskets. When they sell the baskets, they will generate more income. Thus, we have a relationship between the labor provided and the revenue that the firm generates. More labor yields more output, which yields more revenue.

Definition 10.2: *Total revenue product* (TRP) *is a relationship between labor and dollars showing the total revenue the firm generates from the quantity of labor hired at each quantity of labor with the quantity of all other inputs held constant.*

Recall that the relation between the inputs used and the output produced is the production function (see definition 4.3), which we could write in this case as $X = f(L)$, where X is the output produced and L is labor. The notation $f(L)$ stands for the production function. If we also assume that the firm sells its output in a competitive market, then the firm sells its output for a price determined by the market, and the firm cannot change the price. Denote the price by P. Now we can write a formula for the TRP:

$$\text{TRP} = P \times f(L).$$

Things are a bit more complicated if we have a monopoly. In that case, we know that the price is determined by the demand for the firm's good (actually, the firm's AR):

$$P = P(X).$$

Now $X = f(L)$, so to get TRP only in terms of L, we have $P = P(f(L))$. This notation says that P is a function (average revenue) of a function, $f(L)$, the production function. Now we have

$$\text{TRP} = P(f(L)) \times f(L).$$

We also know that for profit maximum, it is not the total that is crucial, but the marginal. We define that concept next.

Definition 10.3: *Marginal revenue product* (MRP) *is a relationship between labor and dollars per unit of labor showing the change in total revenue that occurs when an added unit of labor is hired at each quantity of labor with the quantity of all other inputs held fixed.*

What formula can we write for MRP? Of course it will depend (at least a little) on whether the firm sells output as a competitive firm or as a monopoly. We take up these cases one by one, starting with the competitive case.

If a firm hires another unit of labor, that unit of labor generates added output, the MP. If the firm is competitive in the sale of output, each unit of output sells for the price of output, P. Hence, the added revenue from the added unit of labor is $P \times MP$. Therefore, $MRP = P \times MP$. Because P appears constant to the firm, the shape of MRP is the same as the shape of MP, and we know that MP eventually has a negative slope due to diminishing returns.

If the firm is a monopoly, and hires another unit of labor, then output rises by MP, but now each added unit of output brings in MR added revenue. Hence, MRP $= MR \times MP$. Of course, if a firm is competitive, $P = MR$, so we can use this formula, MRP $= MR \times MP$, for both the firm selling output competitively and the firm selling output as a monopoly.

Exercise 4. Draw the MP on one graph and, on a separate graph, the MRP for the competitive firm. What are the labels on the axes for MRP? Explain how you know the shape of MRP.

How do we find the MRP for the monopoly? We know that we need both the MR and the MP, but how are these connected? The MR depends on output, X, while the MP depends on the input, L. To be able to match up the MR and the MP, we need to know the X that goes with the L we are using to find MP. Once we know the X, we can then find the MR. Hence, we need a relation between the input, L, and output, X — the total product. Figure 10.1 shows the process utilizing the steps listed below.

Steps to find MRP:

1. Choose a level of labor, L_1. Mark L_1 on the horizontal axis of the marginal product graph, the total product graph, and the MRP graph, as shown below.
2. In the marginal product graph (Figure 10.1, Panel A), find the corresponding MP, MP_1. Hold this number.
3. In the total product graph (Figure 10.1, Panel B), find the output corresponding to L_1, X_1. Use that X_1 in the MR graph (Figure 10.1, Panel C) to find the corresponding MR, MR_1.
4. Now multiply the MP you found in the marginal product graph by the MR you just found to get the MRP at L_1. $MRP(L_1) = MP(L_1) \times MR(X_1) = MP_1 \times MR_1$, and graph this at L_1 in Figure 10.1, Panel D.
5. Change L and go to step 2.

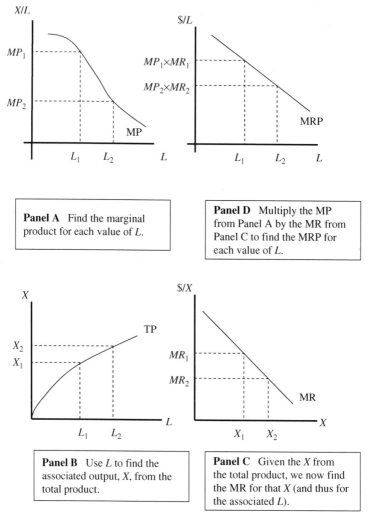

Figure 10.1   In Panel A, we use L to find MP. In Panel B, we use the same L and TP to find the output, X. In Panel C, we use the X to find MR. In Panel D, we show MR times MP, MRP, at the original L.

It turns out that in this case, we have a downward-sloping MRP. This is because both MP and MR have a negative slope and X rises as L rises (why is this last fact critical?).

Exercise 5. Why do we need to find quantity of output using TP for monopoly, but not for competition?

Exercise 6. While the definition of MRP does not explicitly say it, it is true that the MRP is the slope of the TRP. Thus, the MRP is the derivative of the equation TRP $-$ $P(f(L)) \times f(L)$. Find the MRP by finding the derivative of this equation.

Observe that the MRP for both the firm selling output as a competitor as well as the firm selling output as a monopoly is downward-sloping. So if we draw an MRP, we cannot know, just by looking, whether we have a firm selling output as a monopoly or a firm selling output as a competitor.

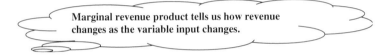

Marginal revenue product tells us how revenue changes as the variable input changes.

Section Summary:
In this section, we have developed the revenue concepts we will need for the profit maximization argument for the firm. As you know, the revenue is half the issue! We now turn to the cost side.

10.4 Marginal Input Cost

In this section, we will examine the cost side of hiring inputs. We start with the central definitions and examine how alternative market structures affect the costs.

Definition 10.4: *The **total input cost** (TIC) relates a variable input and dollars, and shows the cost of the input at each quantity of the input with all else held fixed.*

Definition 10.5: *The **marginal input cost** (MIC) relates a variable input and dollars per unit of variable input, and shows the change in cost associated with hiring an additional unit of the variable input, all else held fixed.*

Note that, as is usually the case, the marginal input cost is the slope of the total input cost. Also note that this total input cost assumes that there is only one variable input, but the idea can be extended to more than one variable input.

We now need to examine the market structure of the input market. Just as with output, there are two major possibilities. The first is that the firm buys the inputs in a competitive fashion. Recall that we have a special meaning for competition, and here we mean that the firm buying the input cannot affect the price of the input. Similarly, the seller of the input cannot affect the price of the input; rather, the price is determined by market forces. From the point of view of the firm, the buyer of the input, the price of the input seems constant and equal to the MIC. For the case of one variable input, labor, the price of labor is the wage, which we will denote by w. For the firm buying labor competitively, the price of labor seems constant to the firm and is equal to the wage, w. In this case, the MIC is a horizontal line equal to the wage as shown in Figure 10.2.

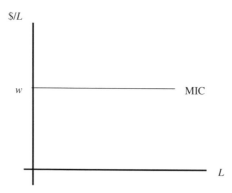

Figure 10.2   Here we see the MIC for the firm buying labor competitively and the MIC equals the wage.

> Exercise 7. In the case that the firm buys labor competitively, we write $TIC(L) = wL$. Find the MIC by finding the derivative of this expression. What do you get?

There is another case where the buyer of the labor has some market power. This is the case of monopsony, or a single buyer of the labor. This is where we are changing assumption 4.1e. In this case, the firm faces the market supply of labor. The classic case used to be the coal company hiring coal miners in a valley where little other employment was available. Here the buyer of the labor has some power. We examine this case now.

Look at Figure 10.3. Here we show the market supply of labor. The operative assumption is that all units of labor receive the same wage. So if L_1 units of labor are hired, then the wage is w_1. If the quantity of labor rises by one unit to $L_1 + 1$, then all units of labor will receive a wage of w_2. We can compute the MIC for the new unit of labor, the $L_1 + 1^{st}$ unit of labor:

$$MIC(L_1 + 1) = \frac{(\text{cost of labor for } L_1 + 1) - (\text{cost of labor for } L_1)}{\text{change in labor}}$$

$$= \frac{w_2(L_1 + 1) - w_1 L_1}{L_1 + 1 - L_1} = \frac{w_2 L_1 + w_2 - w_1 L_1}{1}$$

$$= w_2 + (w_2 - w_1)L_1.$$

We can conclude that $MIC(L_1 + 1) > w_2$ because $w_2 > w_1$. That is, $MIC(L_1 + 1) = w_2$ plus some positive number $(w_2 - w_1)L_1$. Thus, the MIC must lie above the supply at $L_1 + 1$. But this argument holds for all L, so MIC is above the supply as shown in Figure 10.4.

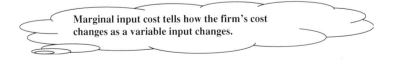

Marginal input cost tells how the firm's cost changes as a variable input changes.

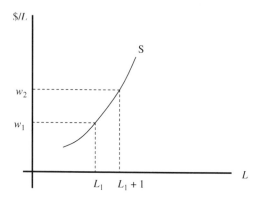

Figure 10.3   Here we have the market supply of labor. If L_1 units of labor are hired, the wage is w_1. If we hire one more unit of labor, the wage for all units of labor rises to w_2.

Exercise 8. Does the formula for MIC we developed above for the monopsony also work for a firm buying inputs competitively? How do you know?

Exercise 9. In our work above, we proved the following proposition. Use the information given above and write out a proof. Proposition: If the labor supply is positively sloped, then the MIC will lie above the supply.

Exercise 10. In the case that the firm buys labor as a monopsony, we have $TIC(L) = Lw(L)$, where $w(L)$ is the supply curve. Find MIC by finding the derivative of TIC. What do you get? How does this expression relate to the MIC expression we found above for the monopsony?

Exercise 11. How is this argument, $MIC > S$, related to the proposition saying that $MR < D$ for the monopoly?

Exercise 12. How does this argument, MIC > S, relate to the average marginal fact?

Exercise 13. In Figure 10.3, find $w_1 L_1$ and $w_2(L_1+1)$. The difference between them is the MIC. Find the area repre-
senting MIC in Figure 10.3. In the area representing
MIC, where is the area w_2?

Hence, we have that the MIC would look as shown in Figure 10.4
for the case of monopsony.

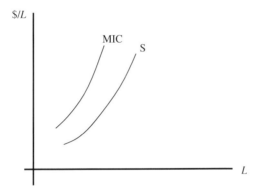

Figure 10.4   Here we show the market supply of labor and the associated MIC in
the case of monopsony. In this case, the MIC lies above supply.

Section Summary:
In this section, we have found the MIC for both the case where the
firm buys labor in a competitive market and for the case where the
firm buys labor as a monopsony, a single buyer. In the competitive
case, the MIC is horizontal. For the monopsony, the MIC is above
the market supply.

10.5   Profit Maximization in Terms of Labor

Now that we have the cost and revenue for the firm hiring one variable input, labor, we can find the profit-maximizing output. This next step will not be much different than what we have seen before.

Proposition 10.6: Profit Maximization for One Variable Input

If   a. *there is one variable input, L,*
      b. *technology is given,*
      c. *the* MRP *and* MIC *are continuous,*
      d. *profit is maximum at* $L_0, 0 < L_0 < \infty,$
Then e. *at* L_0, MRP $=$ MIC.

Proof 10.7: We will approach the problem by the contrapositive. So we will show that if MRP $\neq$ MIC, then profit is not maximum. There are two cases: MRP $>$ MIC and MRP $<$ MIC. We will provide a proof for the first case, and you should prove the second.

Suppose MRP $>$ MIC. An increase in labor will increase total revenue by the MRP. Total cost will rise by the MIC. Because MRP $>$ MIC, the increase in total revenue will be greater than the increase in total cost, so profit will rise. Because profit rises, profit could not have been maximum at the initial quantity of labor.   □

If profit is maximum, then MRP = MIC.

Exercise 14. Prove the other half of proposition 10.6.

Note that in this proposition, we have not distinguished the possible cases for the market structure of the output market (competition or monopoly) or the market structure of the input market (competition or monopsony). Thus, all cases are covered by this proposition. This proposition is useful for two reasons. First, we can use it to find the demand for labor, which we will do in the next section. Second, we can use this proposition to link back to the profit maximization proposition for output, which we do in Section 10.7.

> Exercise 15. Draw graphs showing the four cases: the firm selling output competitively and buying labor competitively, the firm selling output competitively and buying labor as a monopsony, the firm selling output as a monopoly and buying labor competitively, and the firm selling output as a monopoly and buying labor as a monopsony. How are these graphs the same? Different?

While the above proposition deals with the case where there is only one input, the proposition is true for each input if there were more than one. So if there are two inputs, L and K, we would have the following:

If a. there are two variable inputs, L and K,
   b. technology is given,
   c. the MRP and MIC are continuous for each input,
   d. profit is maximum at L_0, $0 < L_0 < \infty$, and K_0,
      $0 < K_0 < \infty$,
Then e. at (L_0, K_0), $\text{MRP}_L = \text{MIC}_L$ and $\text{MRP}_K = \text{MIC}_K$.

The key difference is that we now have an MRP for each input, which will depend on both inputs, and an MIC for each input. But because we can adjust the inputs independently, the above proof will hold for each input independently. We note this for future reference.

There is one question remaining: the wage the firm pays. It should be clear that the wage will be given to the firm by the market in the case that the firm buys labor competitively. In this case, the firm has no choice but to pay w. Only in the case of the monopsony do we have to worry about what the wage will be. Examine Figure 10.5.

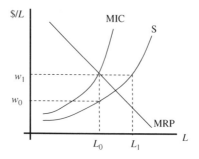

Figure 10.5   Here we see that the only wage that will induce L_0 units of labor is w_0.

In Figure 10.5, we see the MRP, the market supply of labor, and the MIC. We know that the profit maximum occurs at the quantity of labor so that $MRP = MIC$, L_0. What wage would the firm have to pay? If they pay wage w_1, where MIC and MRP intersect, we see that workers will supply more labor, L_1, than the firm wants to hire. Thus, there would be downward pressure on the wage. How far will the wage fall? It would fall to the point where the profit-maximizing quantity of labor, L_0, intersects the market supply of labor curve, w_0. At this wage, the quantity of labor the firm wants to hire will be available to work. If the firm offers a lower wage, they will not attract the profit-maximizing quantity of labor. Hence, the wage has to be where the profit-maximizing quantity of labor hits the market supply of labor, w_0.

Section Summary:
In this section, we have examined the profit maximization proposition for the firm hiring one variable input. This proposition applies to the cases where the firm sells output either as a competitor or as a monopoly and to the cases where the firm buys labor either as a competitor or as a monopsony. We also found the wage that would be paid under monopsony. We can use proposition 10.6 to find the firm's demand for labor.

10.6 The Demand for Labor

In this section, we will find the demand for labor for the firm hiring one variable input. We will later see that the outcome we get here will not generalize to more than one variable input. We start with the definition of the demand for labor.

Definition 10.8: *The **demand for labor** relates the quantity of labor with dollars per unit of labor, and shows the quantity of labor the firm would hire at each wage with all other prices and technology held fixed.*

In Figure 10.6, we show the process of finding demand (note that we have ignored the shutdown condition) for the case that the firm buys inputs competitively. In this case, the MIC is equal to the wage.

In the graph on the left, we have the profit maximization graph. When the wage is w_1, the profit-maximizing firm hires L_1 units of labor according to the profit maximization proposition. Thus, we have one point on the demand for labor, the point (L_1, w_1), which we show in the right graph. If the wage were to fall to w_2, the firm would adjust the quantity of labor to L_2 to maximize profit according to the profit maximization proposition. Thus, the point (L_2, w_2) is also a point on the labor demand as we show in the right graph.

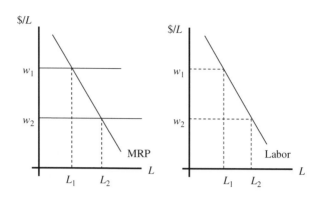

Figure 10.6   In the left graph, we show profit maximization for wages w_1 and w_2. In the right graph, we bring the wage over and mark off the corresponding quantity of labor to get labor demand. Observe that the labor demand is the same as the MRP.

Now compare the two graphs. They have the same axes, so we can lay one graph on top of the other. If we put the labor demand graph on top of the profit maximization graph, how will the labor demand line up with the MRP? They will be the same. They have to be, as each point of profit maximization lies on the MRP curve. Therefore, at each wage, the MRP will be the demand for labor in the case of one variable input and the firm buying inputs competitively.

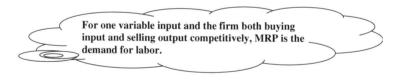

For one variable input and the firm both buying input and selling output competitively, MRP is the demand for labor.

This outcome, that the demand for labor and the MRP are the same, only holds for the case of one variable input. We will examine the case of two variable inputs shortly (Section 10.8). You can see that in general, we would not expect the two curves to be the same by comparing their definitions. Focus on what is held fixed in each case. Hence, in general, we do not expect that these two curves should be the same.

Exercise 16. State the definition of MRP and of the demand for labor. How are these two definitions different? How are they the same? Is there reason to think that generally they will not be the same curve? Explain!

Now we can ask some interesting questions. Why does the labor demand have a negative slope? Well, in the case of the firm buying inputs competitively, the demand is the MRP and MRP is the price of output times the marginal product. The price is held fixed in finding the demand for labor, so the negative slope comes from the negative slope of the marginal product — the Law of Diminishing Returns.

What factors make the demand for labor shift? Because the demand for labor in this one-variable case is the MRP and MRP is price of output times the marginal product, anything that changes either of these will make the demand for labor shift. Here a change in the price of output or a change in technology will make the demand for labor change. If there is a fixed factor, say capital, then changes in capital will cause the marginal product to shift and the demand for labor will also shift.

This pretty much covers the demand for labor in the one-variable-input, competitive case. We can look at the situation now for a monopsony. This case is a bit easier. In this case, similarly to the monopoly, the firm only has a point for the demand. The only quantity that the firm will want to hire is the quantity where the MRP crosses the MIC. The wage they pay will be the wage on the supply curve. Hence, the only point on the monopsonist's demand for labor is the profit-maximizing quantity of labor and the associated wage.

Exercise 17. What makes the monopsonist's demand for labor shift?

FROM THE LITERATURE

We have only looked at the profit-maximizing decision in terms of output, but for some firms, there may be a host of other alternative choices that must be made. Of course, these firms will not be competitive firms as we have defined competition. So consider firms who have a field sales force to sell their product. There are a number of decisions these firms must make, including how many sales people to hire and what size the sales territory should be (both in terms of area covered and number of customers or potential customers). What rules would the firm use to make these decisions? For whether or not to hire another sales person, they would want to look at the costs associated with hiring that person, and then compare that to the expected increase in sales that would occur (they would have to account for the change in sales by other sales persons if the new person got part of an existing sales territory). For the question of how to divide up the region among sales people, they would want to compare the possible change in sales if the regions were changed assuming that the total number of sales persons stayed the same. A methodology for pursuing the latter computations is given in: Leonard Lodish, "Sales Territory Alignment to Maximize Profit," *Journal of Marketing Research*, Vol. 12, No. 1, February, 1975, pp. 30–36.

Section Summary:

In this section, we found the demand for labor in the one-variable-input case, and where the firm bought inputs in a competitive market. The demand turned out to be the MRP. This is a very special result that does not generally hold. In the next section, we will more carefully examine how the purchase of inputs is related to the sale of output.

10.7   Connecting Profit Maximization for Output and Labor

So far in this chapter, we have examined how the firm chooses a quantity of labor to maximize profit. In earlier chapters, we looked at how the firm chooses an amount of output to maximize profit. Surely these two computations are related, and it ought to be true that the profit-maximizing quantity of labor will produce the profit-maximizing quantity of output. In this section, we will examine this issue more carefully in the case of one variable input and where the firm is competitive in both the sale of output and the purchase of labor.

Here is the situation. We have a production function where output, X, depends essentially on one variable input, L. The price of output, P, appears to be a constant to the firm, and the price of labor, w, also seems constant to the firm. Thus, we could write the profit function as follows:

$$\pi = PX - wL.$$

But this ignores the relationship between X and L, $X = f(L)$, the production function. So if we replace X with $f(L)$, we would have this expression:

$$\pi = Pf(L) - wL.$$

To find the maximum for this expression, choose L to maximize profit, we would have the following:

$$\pi' = Pf'(L) - w = 0.$$

Because $f'(L)$ is MP, we can write this as

$$\text{MRP} = w,$$

which we also derived in Section 10.5 as the profit-maximizing outcome.

To find the profit maximization outcome in terms of X, we would need to rewrite the production function to get an expression so that we can replace L in the profit function. What we would do would be to find the inverse production function:

$$L = f^{-1}(X).$$

Now plug into the profit function to obtain this expression:

$$\pi = PX - wf^{-1}(X).$$

Find the maximum by taking the derivative with respect to X and setting the outcome to zero. Here is what we get:

$$\pi' = P - wdf^{-1}(X)/dX = 0.$$

Now in a fabulous turn of events, $df^{-1}(X)/dX = 1/f'(L)$. So we have

$$\pi' = P - w\{1/f'(L)\} = 0.$$

How can we interpret $w/f'(L)$? This is $w/\{dX/dL\} = wdL/dX$. Because total input cost is wL, the change in cost when one more unit of labor is utilized is wdL (assume w does not change). The denominator, dX, is the change in output. Therefore, $wdL/dX = d\text{TC}/dX = \text{MC}$! Hence, we may write the above expression as follows:

$$\pi' = P - \text{MC} = 0.$$

This is the profit maximization requirement for the competitive firm.

Hence, we get the standard results depending on how we write the profit function. But the two equations we have are the same. Here are the two equations:

$$\pi' = Pf'(L) - w = 0.$$
$$\pi' = P - w\{1/f'(L)\} = 0.$$

We can obtain the first equation from the second by multiplying the second equation by $f'(L)$. Thus, the L that satisfies the first profit maximization condition must produce an X that satisfies the second. So profit maximization in one case yields profit maximization in the other case.

There is another matter that we can see now as well. Because MC = $w/f'(L)$, and because the MC is the supply for a competitive firm, the slope of MC and hence supply is determined by $w/f'(L)$. w is a constant, and the shape of $f'(L)$ is determined by diminishing returns. Hence, once diminishing returns set in, $f'(L)$, MP, falls; and the MC (and hence supply) must rise, have a positive slope.

It should be clear that diminishing returns plays a big role in micro and, in the case of a firm selling output competitively and buying inputs competitively with one variable input, dictates the shape of both the firm's demand for labor and the firm's supply curve.

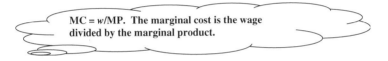

MC = w/MP. The marginal cost is the wage divided by the marginal product.

Section Summary:
In this section, we have established that in the case of one variable input where the firm is competitive in both the sale of output and the purchase of inputs, the profit-maximizing quantity of labor and the profit-maximizing quantity of output are closely related. The profit-maximizing quantity of labor must produce the profit-maximizing quantity of output. As a bonus, we found that MC = $w/f'(L)$ in this case. Now we have a reason for the positive slope of the firm's supply curve as well as the negative slope of the demand for labor in this competitive, one-variable-input case. In the next section, we look at what happens if we have more than one variable input. Some things will change!

10.8   Two Variable Inputs and the Demand for Labor

In this section, we allow the possibility of more than one variable input. Our objective will be to find the demand for the inputs in this case, and also to see some of the interaction among inputs. We start with the demand for labor. We will stick with the case where the firm sells output competitively and buys inputs competitively. The search for the demand for labor will require us to put together information from a number of the previous chapters.

To start the process of finding the demand for labor when there are two variable inputs, we begin by recalling that the firm is given the price of output as well as the prices of both inputs, capital and labor. So the firm knows P, r, and w, where P is the price of output, r is the price of capital, and w is the wage rate, the price of labor. Because the firm is competitive in both the purchase of inputs and the sale of output, the prices P, r, and w seem constant to the firm.

To start the problem, we use the price of labor and the price of capital together with the technology, also given, to find the total variable cost. This is done by employing the least cost combination proposition (proposition 4.11), and is shown in Panels A and B of Figure 10.7. Once we have the TVC, we can find its slope which will be the marginal cost, MC. We can then combine the MC with the price of output, P, to find the profit-maximizing output as shown in Panel C of Figure 10.7. Given that output, we can then go back to the least cost graph and find the amount of capital and labor the firm would use. This quantity of labor is the quantity of labor demanded given the wage, the price of capital, the price of output, and the technology. We have one point on our labor demand, as shown in Panel D of Figure 10.7.

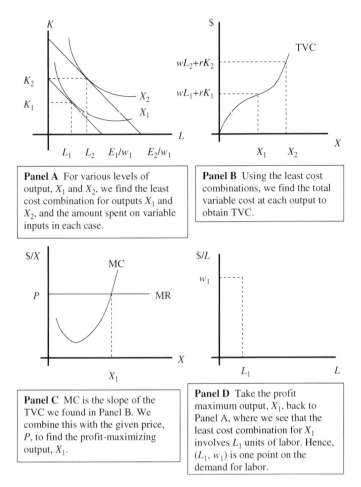

Panel A For various levels of output, X_1 and X_2, we find the least cost combination for outputs X_1 and X_2, and the amount spent on variable inputs in each case.

Panel B Using the least cost combinations, we find the total variable cost at each output to obtain TVC.

Panel C MC is the slope of the TVC we found in Panel B. We combine this with the given price, P, to find the profit-maximizing output, X_1.

Panel D Take the profit maximum output, X_1, back to Panel A, where we see that the least cost combination for X_1 involves L_1 units of labor. Hence, (L_1, w_1) is one point on the demand for labor.

Figure 10.7 The information from Panel A, least cost, is used to draw the TVC in Panel B. The slope of TVC is MC, which is used in Panel C to find the profit maximum, which is then taken back to Panel A to find the quantity of labor. We thus have one point on the labor demand curve in Panel D.

To find a second point on the demand for labor, we need to change the wage and find what happens to the TVC, MC, profit-maximizing output, and quantity of labor. Suppose that the price of labor falls from w_1 to w_2 while holding the price of capital, r, constant. What will happen? Start with the least cost graph as shown in Figure 10.8.

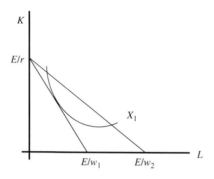

Figure 10.8   The price of labor fell from w_1 to w_2. For a given expenditure of E on variable inputs, the isocost swings out as shown. That means that output X_1 can be produced for less than E, and TVC falls.

The impact is that the isocost (holding expenditure on variable inputs constant) will swing out. That means that output X_1 can now be produced for fewer than E dollars spent on variable inputs. Hence, TVC falls, as shown in Figure 10.9.

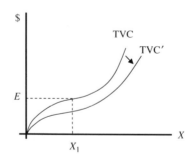

Figure 10.9   Because of the lower price of labor, the TVC shifts down.

Now that TVC shifts down, TVC must have a lower slope, and the slope is MC, so MC must also fall, as shown in Figure 10.10. Given the price of output, the profit-maximizing output must rise. We take this information back to the least cost graph to find the quantity of labor. This is shown in Figure 10.11.

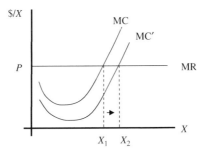

Figure 10.10 The MC shifts right because of the lower price of labor. The quantity of output that maximizes profit increases to X_2.

In Figure 10.11, we show the initial output the firm produces, X_1, along with the original isocost with the price of labor at w_1. Also shown is the new, higher level of output, X_2, and the isocost with the new lower price of labor, w_2. We see that as the price of labor falls, the profit-maximizing firm will increase its use of labor, resulting in a downward-sloping demand for labor, also in Figure 10.11.

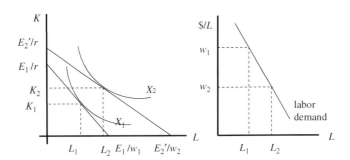

Figure 10.11 The left graph shows the impact of the lower wage, the isocost is flatter, and the greater output; we are on a higher isoquant. The outcome is that as the wage falls, the firm hires more labor, which is summarized in the right graph.

We have now found the demand for labor in the case of two variable inputs. You may have some questions. For example, when the wage falls, and MC shifts right, how did we know that we would end up at X_2 output? We did not. What we know is that we end up at some larger output, and we just used X_2 without knowing what the new output would be. As long as we choose some output larger than X_1, it does not matter which one it is or what we call it.

It is a bit tedious to see how the demand for labor would change if there were a change in the price of capital or the price of output. We may approach the problem with mathematics to obtain the results.[1]

Suppose that the production function for the firm is a Cobb–Douglas form as shown:

$$X = L^\alpha K^\beta,$$

where $\alpha + \beta < 1$ and are constants. We can write the profit function for the firm as follows:

$$\pi = PL^\alpha K^\beta - wL - rK.$$

We will take the derivative of this function, first for L and then for K. Here is what we get (these are the $MRP_L = MIC_L$ and $MRP_K = MIC_K$ conditions we discussed in Section 10.5):

$$\frac{\partial \pi}{\partial L} = P\alpha L^{\alpha-1} K^\beta - w = 0. \tag{1}$$

$$\frac{\partial \pi}{\partial K} = P\beta L^\alpha K^{\beta-1} - r = 0. \tag{2}$$

Suppose that we solve each equation for K and then graph the result. For $\alpha = \beta = 1/3$, here is what we get:

$$K = \left(\frac{3w}{P}\right)^3 L^2. \tag{1$'$}$$

$$K = \left(\frac{3r}{P}\right)^{-3/2} L^{1/2}. \tag{2$'$}$$

---

[1] What follows requires calculus of two variables. The partial notation may be something new for many students.

We can either set the equations equal to each other and solve for L, which would give the demand for labor, or we could graph these. The latter strategy will be pursued and the outcome is shown in Figure 10.12.

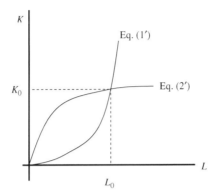

Figure 10.12 We show the intersection of our two K equations, which gives the values of K and L the firm would choose to maximize profit.

We can now see what would happen to the optimal value of L if w or r or P would change. Note that these equations both go through the origin, and a change in w, r, or P will not change that point. Hence, changes in w, r, or P will cause these curves to swing around the origin.

If w were to rise, equation (1′) would swing up. Thus, the optimal value of L would fall. Similarly, if r increases, equation (2′) will swing down and the optimal value of L will fall. Note that in this case, the optimal value of K would also decrease, which makes sense as we would be moving along the K demand curve. What if P rises? Then equation (1′) swings down, and equation (2′) will swing up. Both of these movements cause the optimal value of both L and K to increase. This makes some sense. As P rises, the firm will produce more output so that the need for both L and K will rise.

Exercise 18. In Figure 10.12, show what happens if w falls. What will happen to the optimal value of L? Of K?

Exercise 19. In Figure 10.12, show what happens if r falls. What will happen to the optimal value of L? Of K?

Exercise 20. In Figure 10.12, show what happens if P falls. What will happen to the optimal value of L? Of K?

Exercise 21. How is the computation of the two equations (1) and (2) similar to a best reply function from Chapter 8? Does equation (1) tell the firm's best reply for L given the value of K? Does equation (2) tell the firm's best reply for K given the value of L? Use equations (1′) and (2′) to support your answer.

Section Summary:

In this section, we have examined how to find the demand for an input when there are two variable inputs. We have also seen what happens to the demand for labor when there is a change in the price of output or the price of capital in the case of the Cobb–Douglas production function. In the next section, we return to the one-variable-input case and work through the process using calculus.

10.9   The Demand for Labor Using Calculus — One Variable Input

In this section, we will have a look at the problem of hiring inputs by using calculus in the case of one variable input. The relevant information for this problem is the production function. Here we will use the following form:

$$X = L^{1/2}.$$

Thus, for the firm selling output competitively and buying inputs competitively, we have

$$\pi = PL^{1/2} - wL.$$

To find the maximum for profit, we take the derivative, set it to zero, and solve for L:

$$\pi' = P(1/2)L^{-1/2} - w = 0.$$

Before going on to find L, we should be sure we have a maximum, not a minimum. We can do this by checking the second derivative of profit. Here is what we get:

$$\pi'' = P(-1/4)L^{-3/2}.$$

This expression is less than zero for all positive L. So we can be sure we will obtain a maximum from our computations. Let us find L now!

$$L^{-1/2} = 2w/P$$
$$L^{1/2} = P/2w$$
$$L = (P/2w)^2.$$

This is the demand for labor. You can see that the slope of the labor demand is negative, and that the labor demand will shift if P changes.

Exercise 22. Draw a graph of the price times the production function (L on the horizontal axis and $\$$ on the vertical axis). On the same axis, draw a graph of $TC = wL$. Now find the difference between these two curves. What do you have? Where is profit maximum?

Exercise 23. Suppose we solve the production function for L, and, in the profit function, replace L with this expression. What do you get? Now maximize this profit function, finding the X that maximizes profit. How is this X related to the L we found above? Does the L that maximizes profit produce a level of X that also maximizes profit?

Exercise 24. Suppose that $X = L^\alpha$, where α is a constant and between 0 and 1. Find the demand for labor in this case, and explain why the demand for labor has a negative slope.

We can extend the analysis to the case of the monopsony. Suppose that we have the same production function as before, $X = L^{1/2}$, and the price is $192. Suppose that the supply of labor is $w = L^2$. We have the following profit function:

$$\pi = 192L^{1/2} - L^2L = 192L^{1/2} - L^3.$$

Again, find the derivative and set it to zero:

$$\pi' = 192(1/2)L^{-1/2} - 3L^2 = 0.$$

Hence, we get the following result:

$$(96/3)L^{-1/2} = L^2$$

$$32 = L^{5/2}$$

$$L = (32)^{2/5} = (2^5)^{2/5} = 4.$$

We can then find the wage, $w = L^2 = 16$.

Exercise 25. Using the data from the monopsony case, find the MRP and graph it. Find the MIC and graph it on the same graph as the MRP. Graph the supply of labor on the same graph as the other two. In the graph, find the profit-maximizing quantity of labor and the wage the firm will pay.

Section Summary:
In this section, we have found the demand for labor using calculus in the case that we have one variable input and competition on both sides of the market. We also examined the case of the monopsony.

10.10 Summary

In this chapter, we have examined the firm's decision to hire labor. What are the big lessons from this chapter?

A. Profit-maximizing competitive firms hire labor so that $MRP = MIC$.
B. The demand for labor is MRP for one variable input, but MRP is no longer demand when there are more variable inputs.
C. Diminishing returns determine the shape of the demand for labor and the supply of output for the competitive firm in the case of one variable input.
D. The profit-maximizing choice of labor is the amount of labor needed to produce the profit-maximizing output.

This pretty much completes our discussion of the behavior of the firm.

Up to this point, we have been looking at models of how the consumer and firm actually behave — models describing behavior, not models prescribing behavior. One of the claims of the competitive model is that resources are allocated well by the competitive process. To assess this claim, we need to look at how resources should be allocated — models that prescribe. This is our next task.

Terms Defined:

- Law of Diminishing Returns
- Total revenue product
- Marginal revenue product
- Total input cost
- Marginal input cost
- Demand for labor

Chapter 11

General Equilibrium

Key Concepts:

- Edgeworth box
- Competitive equilibrium
- How do we know where the equilibrium is for the following models?
  - o Robinson Crusoe model
  - o Pure trade model
  - o Trade with production model

Goals:

- Establish where competitive equilibrium occurs in each of the three models: Robinson Crusoe model, pure trade model, and trade with production model.
- Equilibrium in Crusoe requires a tangency of an indifference curve with the production function.
- Competitive equilibrium for consumers is characterized by tangency of indifference curves in an Edgeworth box.
- Equilibrium for firms is characterized by the tangency of isoquants in an Edgeworth box.
- Competitive equilibrium also requires that the slope of the production possibilities is the same as the slope of the indifference curves.

Up to this point, we have looked at the world pretty much one actor at a time. That is, we looked at each consumer by himself or herself, and each firm by itself. The one exception was when we discussed oligopoly, and we considered two firms at the same time. We could think of those models as being descriptive of the world as the economist sees it. But how do these pieces fit together?

11.1 Introduction

In this chapter, we wish to look at both consumers and producers at the same time and ask a different kind of question. It is a question of logical consistency. In our earlier work, the consumer maximized utility given prices and chose quantities of the goods X and Y. From this we would get a market demand for each good. Each firm (the X firms and the Y firms) is given prices and, from profit maximization, chooses an amount to produce. From this we would get the market supply of these goods. If we intersect the market demand and supply for each good, we would obtain the market price and the quantity of each good (the market-clearing prices and quantities). Here is the question we wish to address. Are the market-clearing prices consistent with the quantities chosen by consumers maximizing utility given those prices and with the quantity firms produce by maximizing profits given those prices? Suppose that at the prices that clear the markets, consumers, upon maximizing utility, do not choose the market-clearing quantities or that firms, given prices, do not supply the market-clearing quantities of the goods. Then utility maximization and profit maximization would be inconsistent with the clearing of markets. We want to know if this happens. To address this question, we will need to establish a model.[1]

---

[1]To completely establish the consistency, we would have to prove the existence of prices that do what we want. This would take us into mathematical regions considerably beyond what we know. We will characterize the equilibrium, but not prove its existence.

11.2 Robinson Crusoe

Imagine a really simple world in which there is only one person; we will call him Robinson Crusoe. Robinson has a split personality. Robinson is both a producer and a consumer. As a producer, Robinson buys his labor which he uses to collect and process coconuts. Sometimes Robinson can find coconuts on the ground, while at other times he has to climb a tree. He always has to find a way to get the coconuts open. He then sells the finished, ready-to-consume coconuts to Robinson the consumer. In this process, Robinson the producer chooses the amount of labor to hire and the number of coconuts to harvest and open so that his profit is maximum given the wage and price of coconuts. Then Robinson the consumer maximizes his utility as a supplier of labor and a demander of coconuts given the price of labor (which determines his income) and the price of coconuts. We assume that Robinson is not allowed to set the prices, but that the prices arise from some process (but what?). Because Robinson does not determine the prices, he is acting as a competitor both as a consumer and as a producer. The question is: Are there prices that will allow this split-personality Robinson to do both maximization problems at the same time and so that the quantity of labor and the quantity of coconuts are the same for both of his persons, i.e., so that markets clear (quantity supplied equals quantity demanded)?

We begin with the assumptions of the model.

Assumptions 11.1 (Robinson Crusoe):
a. *There is one good, coconuts, C, and one input, labor, L.*
b. *Robinson has differentiable indifference curves and BT_W is strictly convex for each W.*
c. *Bundles to the northwest are preferred (given that C is on the vertical axis).*
d. *The production function for coconuts is differentiable and diminishing returns hold.*
e. *Both coconuts and labor are infinitely divisible.*
f. *There are no externalities in consumption or production.*

We have met most of these assumptions before. The one that is new is about externalities. Externalities in consumption would be where Robinson likes having the coconuts picked up from the ground; it makes the island look neater. He gets satisfaction from both the consumption of the coconuts and from the tidiness of the island. An externality in production would be where opening the coconuts produces a pile of spent husks that interferes with finding the unopened coconuts. In any case, we have none of these effects in our model world.

We begin with the production side of the problem. Robinson's profit function is the first matter of interest. The price of coconuts is P, and the price of labor is w. Robinson demands L_d amount of labor and supplies C_s coconuts (the subscripts are either d for demand or s for supply). The profit is $PC_s - wL_d$, which Robinson will maximize subject to the production function $C_s = f(L_d)$. We will start with a graphical approach, and we need to be able to graph profit. The problem is that profit depends on both C_s and L_d, which makes a three-dimensional relation that is not so easy to draw. One way to proceed is to form the isoprofit function; this function is all the combinations of C_s and L_d that leave profit exactly the same. This is the profit function with w, P, and π held fixed. For the moment, treat π as a constant:

$$\pi = PC_s - wL_d.$$

The isoprofit can be graphed on an axis with L on the horizontal axis and C on the vertical axis, so we solve this equation for C_s:

$$C_s = (\pi/P) + (w/P)L_d.$$

This is a straight line with intercept of (π/P) and slope (w/P). Each point on the line provides Robinson with the same profit. Lines that are higher on the C axis represent higher levels of profit. Given Robinson's production function, we can find the profit-maximizing choice. This is shown in Figure 11.1. The profit maximum occurs where the isoprofit is tangent to the production function.

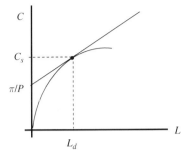

Figure 11.1 Robinson the producer maximizes profit by choosing L_d and C_s given the prices w and P.

Exercise 1. Draw an isoprofit line. Suppose that w rises. What happens to the line? What if P rises? Now suppose that π rises. What happens to the line? In which of these cases does the slope change? When does the intercept change?

Exercise 2. Prove the following proposition:
If Robinson's production function is differentiable and looks as shown in Figure 11.1 and profit is maximum at (L_d, C_s), then the isoprofit is tangent to the production function at (L_d, C_s).

We now turn to Robinson's utility maximization problem. Robinson the consumer wants to maximize $U(L_s, C_d)$ subject to his budget, where L_s is the quantity of labor supplied and C_d is the quantity of coconuts demanded. The budget has one unusual (for us) feature. If Robinson the producer makes a profit, where do the profits go? To the owner of the firm, Robinson! Thus, the profit that Robinson earns as a producer becomes income to Robinson the consumer. Robinson the consumer's budget will be $\pi + wL_s = PC_d$. We solve for C to obtain the following:

$$C_d = (\pi/P) + (w/P)L_s.$$

We can now graph Robinson the consumer in Figure 11.2. Robinson's utility maximum will be where an indifference curve is tangent to the budget line.

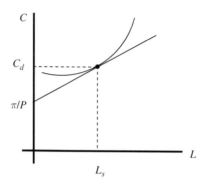

Figure 11.2   Robinson the consumer is shown here choosing L_s and C_d according to utility maximization subject to the budget.

Exercise 3. How is Robinson's budget line related to the isoprofit line?

Exercise 4. In Figure 11.2, where are the preferred bundles, the "better than" bundles? Provide a rationale for your answer.

Exercise 5. Assume that π is a constant and graph Robinson's budget line. What happens to the line if w rises? If P rises? What about a change in profit? Which changes affect the slope? The intercept?

Exercise 6. Prove the following proposition:
If Robinson's indifference curves are differentiable, the preferred bundles are to the northwest, the "better than" set is strictly convex, and (L_s, C_d) maximizes utility subject to the budget, then an indifference curve is tangent to the budget line at (L_s, C_d).

Section Summary:
In this section, we have set up the Robinson Crusoe model and then examined isoprofit lines, profit maximization, budget lines, and utility maximization. We have done this to set up for the idea of a competitive equilibrium. We take up this issue in the next section.

11.3 Equilibrium for Robinson Crusoe

In both profit maximization and utility maximization, the prices, P and w, were given. We want to see if there are prices so that not only can Robinson be both a profit maximizer and a utility maximizer, but so that it is also true that $C_s = C_d$ and $L_s = L_d$; this latter condition is the market-clearing condition. In other words, the question we are asking is if there are prices w and P so that $C_d = C_s$ and $L_d = L_s$ while (L_s, C_d) solves Robinson's utility maximization problem and (L_d, C_s) solves Robinson's profit maximization problem all at the same time.

Definition 11.2: *A competitive equilibrium (Crusoe economy) is a set of prices, P^* and w^*, and quantities, C^* and L^*, so that*

a. *Robinson maximizes utility at (L^*, C^*) given P^* and w^*, subject to the budget.*
b. *Robinson maximizes profit at (L^*, C^*) given P^*, w^*, and the production function.*
c. *at P^* and w^*, both the L market and the C market clear.*

In the case we have here, it is easy to see that we can get a solution. By choosing w and P, we determine the slope of both the isoprofit line and the budget constraint, which are the same line. So the question is: Can we find a budget/isoprofit line so that $C_d = C_s$ and $L_d = L_s$ and so that both Robinsons maximize their objectives? We show the outcome in Figure 11.3. We start by ignoring prices and ask Robinson to maximize utility subject to the production function. In so doing, Robinson chooses C^* and L^*. They are our candidates for both the utility-maximizing choice and the profit-maximizing choice, so $C_d = C_s = C^*$ and $L_d = L_s = L^*$; this choice makes the markets clear. What would the prices have to be to get Robinson to this point?

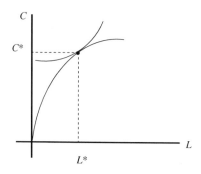

Figure 11.3 Here Robinson maximizes utility subject to the production function and determines C^* and L^*. Are there prices that will induce Robinson to choose these both as a profit maximizer and as a utility maximizer?

Note now a crucial fact. It is only the relative prices — w/P, the slope of the budget line and the slope of the isoprofit line — that matter. If we can choose w/P properly, Robinson will end up at C^* and L^*, and we will be done. You might wonder what happened to profit in this computation. Given the prices, the profit will be maximum, and the profit is owned by Robinson, so the budget line for Robinson the consumer has the same intercept as the profit line. The formal statement of this proposition follows.

Proposition 11.3: *If* (P^*, w^*, C^*, L^*) *is a competitive equilibrium in the Crusoe economy, then an indifference curve for Robinson must be tangent to the production function at* (L^*, C^*), *and the tangency has slope* w^*/P^*.

Proof 11.4: If we have a competitive equilibrium, we know that Robinson the consumer maximizes utility subject to the budget given prices P^* and w^*, so will choose a bundle (L_s, C_d) so that (L_s, C_d) is the point of tangency of the budget line with an indifference curve. At the same time, Robinson the producer maximizes profit given P^* and w^*, and chooses a bundle (L_d, C_s) where (L_d, C_s) is the point of tangency of the isoprofit line with the production function. Because both the producer and consumer face the same prices, the budget line and the isoprofit will be the same line. Because the competitive equilibrium requires that markets clear, we have $C^* = C_d = C_s$ and $L^* = L_d = L_s$, and the indifference curve must be tangent to the production function at (C^*, L^*). Thus, we are done.   □

For a competitive equilibrium, the slope of the straight line that is mutually tangent to both the production function and the indifference curve at (L^*, C^*) is w^*/P^*. With this ratio of prices, we would have Robinson acting as both a utility maximizer and a profit maximizer and both markets would clear. It turns out that given the differentiability and convexity assumed here, there is exactly one such line; hence, we can find such prices in this simple case. Thus, we have a competitive equilibrium in the Crusoe economy. Note what this says. By acting to maximize utility and profit, Robinson creates prices, which if they prevailed would also cause both the market for coconuts and labor to clear. These prices are not chosen by Robinson, but come from his actions as a maximizer.

Proposition 11.5: *If in the Crusoe world we have an indifference curve for Robinson tangent to the production function at (L^*, C^*), and the tangent has slope w^*/P^*, then (P^*, w^*, C^*, L^*) is a competitive equilibrium.*

We have essentially proved this proposition above. You should fill in the details!

Exercise 7. How are propositions 11.3 and 11.5 related?

Exercise 8. Suppose that the prices w and P generate a competitive equilibrium in this economy. Show that kw and kP, for k a positive constant, also provide a competitive equilibrium.

HINT: How do the budget line and the isoprofit function change when we multiply the prices by k?

Thus, in the case of Robinson Crusoe as shown here, yes, there are prices so that Robinson the consumer maximizes utility given the budget, so that Robinson the producer maximizes profit, and so that markets clear, but this result depends on the production function looking as drawn above, the indifference curves looking as we have drawn, and with sufficiently differentiable curves. If these technical conditions are not met, we may fail to find a competitive equilibrium in the Crusoe economy, as the next exercise shows.

Exercise 9. Suppose that the production function looks as shown below (why do we think this production function is unlikely?). Where would the profit maximum be in this case? Now assume that Robinson has indifference curves as shown in Figure 11.2. Can we find a set of prices so that Robinson maximizes both utility and profit and so that markets clear? Explain!

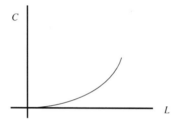

Section Summary:
In this section, we have found that we can find an equilibrium in the Robinson Crusoe model. What would happen if the economy became more complicated with the addition of another person? We take up this case next.

11.4   Pure Trade

Suppose now that Robinson, upon searching the island, finds another person, Zelda![2] And suppose that a second good is introduced into

---

[2]The traditional second person, in keeping with the novel, is Friday. But with fish in the story, coming next, adding Friday made the notation too confusing.

the problem, fish. Both Robinson and Zelda can either fish (F) or harvest coconuts (C). To ease the discussion further, assume that both Robinson and Zelda work eight hours a day and split their time equally between fishing and harvesting coconuts. Because of this latter assumption, we ignore the choice of how much time is spent working and how much of each good is produced. The only economic activity that matters in this world is trade. Robinson ends each day with some coconuts and some fish, as does Zelda. Robinson has (C_R^0, F_R^0) and Zelda has (C_Z^0, F_Z^0). If either of them has a surplus of either good, or if either one wants more of a good than they have, then they will trade. The question here is as before. Are there prices so that both the fish market and the coconut market clear? We start with the assumptions of the pure trade model (so named because the only activity of interest is trade).

Assumptions 11.6 (pure trade):

a. *There are two consumers, Robinson (R) and Zelda (Z).*
b. *There are two goods, fish (F) and coconuts (C).*
c. *Each consumer has preferences represented by differentiable indifference curves, and BT is strictly convex for each consumer.*
d. *More is preferred to less by both consumers.*
e. *Each consumer starts with an initial endowment of the two goods. R's initial endowment is (C_R^0, F_R^0) and Z's is (C_Z^0, F_Z^0). The subscripts refer to the person, R for Robinson and Z for Zelda.*
f. *Both goods are infinitely divisible.*
g. *There are no externalities.*
h. *Each consumer's preferences depend only on what that consumer consumes.*

We have met these assumptions before, but it would pay to go back to Chapter 2 where these assumptions are discussed to review what they mean and how they can be used. The one assumption that is new is the assumption concerning the endowment. We have discussed the origin of the endowment above, and will accept that assumption for now. The endowment is what each person produces, which we assume is determined by some force outside the model. The second assumption that we have not explicitly made up to now is the assumption that the consumer's preferences (and hence their choices) do not depend on what other consumers do. That is, when my neighbor comes home with a new car, in no way does that influence my interest in having a new car. If my neighbor says that, after examining the alternatives, she would never own a particular brand of TV, that information does not change the process I would use to evaluate televisions. In truth, this is not an assumption grounded in fact. While we want to be independent of others, too often we emulate the behavior of our parents or neighbors. However, we will maintain this assumption because to alter it to reflect reality more correctly would be a very difficult task.

In any case, each consumer is provided with an endowment. The combined endowment will provide the total resources for the economy. Our objective is, at this moment, to decide which distribution of these endowments would maximize utility for each of the two consumers.

"If the only things we can do are fish and gather coconuts, why do we have this Frisbee?"

Section Summary:
In this section, we have provided the assumptions we will need for the pure trade model. In the next section, we will develop some additional apparatus that will be useful in our quest for the competitive equilibrium economic outcomes — the Edgeworth box.

11.5 Edgeworth Box

In this section, we will develop an important tool that we will use in most of the rest of this chapter and the next: the Edgeworth box.[3] To begin this construction, we note the total resources available to the economy. The total amount of C available to the economy is $\bar{C} = C_R^0 + C_Z^0$. Similarly, $\bar{F} = F_R^0 + F_Z^0$. We have two consumers; we draw the axis system for each in Figure 11.4.

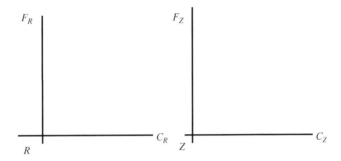

Figure 11.4 Here we have the axis systems for consumers R and Z.

We now rotate Z's axis system $180°$ so that we have the situation as shown in Figure 11.5.

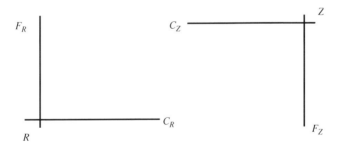

Figure 11.5 The axis systems for consumers R and Z with Z's axis rotated $180°$.

---

[3]The Edgeworth box is named for the British economist of the 19th century, Francis Edgeworth.

Now we move the axis systems together to form a box. The box will be $\bar{C}$ wide and $\bar{F}$ high. Thus, the box shows the existing quantities of the goods C and F. We show this outcome in Figure 11.6; it is the Edgeworth box.

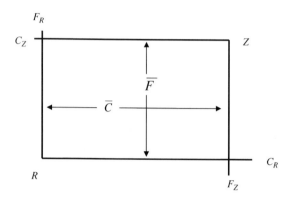

Figure 11.6   Here is the Edgeworth box of dimension $\bar{C}$ by $\bar{F}$.

Before moving on, observe that if we put the initial endowment in the box, we will have the situation shown in Figure 11.7.

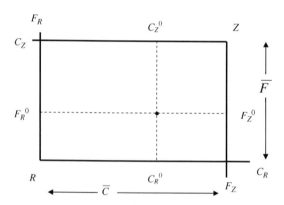

Figure 11.7   The initial endowment is (C_R^0, F_R^0) for R and (C_Z^0, F_Z^0) for Z. You should see the relationship to $\bar{C}$ and $\bar{F}$.

The question we wish to examine is: How do we divide $\bar{C}$ and $\bar{F}$ between R and Z so that we get an equilibrium outcome? One more definition is needed before we move forward toward that issue. We begin with definitions of the possible distributions in the economy.

Definition 11.7: *A **pure trade economic state** (PTES), S, is a division of C and F between the two consumers, $S = \{(C_R, F_R), (C_Z, F_Z)\}$. We require that $C_R + C_Z \leq \bar{C}$ and $F_R + F_Z \leq \bar{F}$.*

A pure trade economic state tells how much of each good each consumer gets. Most often, a PTES is a point in the Edgeworth box. Any point in the box divides the two goods between the two consumers. Thus, any point in the Edgeworth box is a PTES, including the initial endowment. One PTES is identified in Figure 11.8.

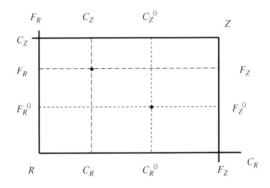

Figure 11.8 The initial endowment is (C_R^0, F_R^0) for R and (C_Z^0, F_Z^0) for Z. The point $\{(C_R, F_R), (C_Z, F_Z)\}$ is a pure trade economic state, as is any other point in the Edgeworth box.

Notice that there are some limits on what consumers can have. It cannot be that $C_R + C_Z > \bar{C}$ or $F_R + F_Z > \bar{F}$. On the other hand, we can have PTESs that do not exhaust $\bar{C}$ or $\bar{F}$. That is, we could have either $C_R + C_Z < \bar{C}$ or $F_R + F_Z < \bar{F}$, or both.

Exercise 10. Show a PTES so that both $C_R + C_Z < \bar{C}$ and $F_R + F_Z < \bar{F}$ hold.

Exercise 11. Suppose that we allow a PTES so that either $C_R + C_Z > \bar{C}$ or $F_R + F_Z > \bar{F}$ holds. What would this look like?

Section Summary:
In this section, we have developed the primary tool of analysis for finding an equilibrium — the Edgeworth box. We now need to define equilibrium and see if it exists, and if so, what an equilibrium might look like.

11.6   Budget Lines in the Edgeworth Box

In this section, we will define our equilibrium concept, and then see what happens when prices are announced.

Definition 11.8: *Excess demand for good X (ED_x) relates price and quantity of the good X, and shows the quantity demanded of the good X minus the quantity supplied of X at each price with other factors held fixed.*

Note that excess demand is a curve, just as demand is. Furthermore, we refer to excess demand even if the quantity supplied is greater than the quantity demanded at some price. Such a situation would make excess demand negative.

Exercise 12. Draw a standard demand and supply. Now draw an axis system with price on the vertical axis and quantity on the horizontal axis to the right of your demand and supply. For several prices, find the quantity demanded and the quantity supplied and then the quantity demanded minus the quantity supplied, and mark them on the new axis system. This would be the excess demand.

> Exercise 13. Go back to the Robinson Crusoe model (Section 11.2) and find excess demand for both L and C.

Definition 11.9: *A **pure trade competitive equilibrium** (PTCE) is a set of prices, P_C and P_F, and a pure trade economic state, $\{(C_R^*, F_R^*), (C_Z^*, F_Z^*)\}$, so that the following three conditions are true:*

a. *Robinson maximizes utility at (C_R^*, F_R^*) given the prices and his initial endowment.*

b. *Zelda maximizes utility at (C_Z^*, F_Z^*) given the prices and her initial endowment.*

c. *The quantity of coconuts demanded by Robinson and Zelda equals $\bar{C}$ at P_C (i.e., $C_R^* + C_Z^* = \bar{C}$), and the quantity of fish demanded by Robinson and Zelda equals $\bar{F}$ at P_F (i.e., $F_R^* + F_Z^* = \bar{F}$). Markets clear, and excess demand is zero.*

Again, this concept is really one of internal consistency. Can we find prices so that both consumers maximize utility and at the same time the prices clear the markets? To move toward the answer to this question, we need to understand how the prices enter the Edgeworth box. We take up that matter next.

To move forward, we will introduce the auctioneer. The auctioneer has the role of yelling out prices. Once the prices are given, either consumer can sell their endowment to the auctioneer at those prices and then use the income generated by the sale to purchase the combination of goods they want from the auctioneer at these prices. The process stops once the auctioneer sees that a pure trade competitive equilibrium is achieved. The process mimics the competitive process in that neither Robinson nor Zelda can affect the prices. To see what happens when prices are announced, we will start with Robinson, but exactly the same process holds for Zelda.

Suppose that the auctioneer yells out prices P_C and P_F. Robinson's income will be as follows:

$$\text{Robinson's income} = P_C C_R^0 + P_F F_R^0.$$

If Robinson buys C_R coconuts and F_R fish, then Robinson's expenditure will be the following:

$$\text{Robinson's expenditure} = P_C C_R + P_F F_R.$$

If Robinson spends all his income, then we would have the following budget constraint:

$$P_C C_R^0 + P_F F_R^0 = P_C C_R + P_F F_R.$$

In this equation, the following are given quantities: P_C, P_F, C_R^0, and F_R^0. The variables are C_R and F_R.

Exercise 14. Write Zelda's budget constraint.

Suppose we wish to graph Robinson's budget. What will we get? To easily graph the budget line, we will put it in slope-intercept form (and hope that the equation is linear). So we solve for F_R (not F_R^0). Start by subtracting $P_C C_R$ from both sides of the equation:

$$P_F F_R = P_C C_R^0 + P_F F_R^0 - P_C C_R.$$

Now divide by P_F to get the following:

$$F_R = \frac{P_C C_R^0 + P_F F_R^0}{P_F} - \frac{P_C}{P_F} C_R.$$

The term $\frac{P_C C_R^0 + P_F F_R^0}{P_F}$ is made up only of constants and so is a constant. This term is the intercept of the line. In addition, the term $-\frac{P_C}{P_F}$ is a constant and is the slope of the line. So we have a straight line and the slope is negative. You should see that the point (C_R^0, F_R^0) is on the line.

Exercise 15. Show that (C_R^0, F_R^0) is on the line. Where does the budget line cross the C_R axis? Where does it cross the F_R axis?

Exercise 16. What happens to the line when P_C rises? What about P_F?

We have the outcome for Robinson as shown in Figure 11.9.

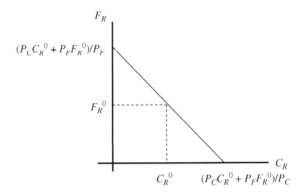

Figure 11.9 This is the graph of R's budget line. It has a slope of $-P_C/P_F$, and goes through (C_R^0, F_R^0), R's initial endowment.

Exercise 17. Draw Zelda's budget constraint and label the end points of the budget line.

We now combine both Robinson's and Zelda's budget lines in an Edgeworth box. Remember that Zelda is turned $180°$. We know that the budget line for Robinson goes through his initial endowment, and the budget line for Zelda goes through her initial endowment, and that these initial endowments are a PTES. Thus, both budget lines go through the initial endowment. Furthermore, both lines have the same slope, so they must be the same line.[4] Hence, when the auctioneer yells out the prices, we have the outcome as shown in Figure 11.10.

As Figure 11.10 shows, the budget line essentially divides the Edgeworth box into R's part and Z's part. R cannot get over the budget

---

[4]The fact that the slope is the same is almost enough — the problem is that we need to be standing at the same origin when we measure the slope for this argument to work. You can convince yourself that from Robinson's origin, the slope of Zelda's line is the same as the slope of Robinson's line, so the lines are the same.

line, nor can Z. Thus, Robinson can choose any point on the budget line or any point below (toward R's origin). Zelda can choose any point on the line or any point below (toward Z's origin).

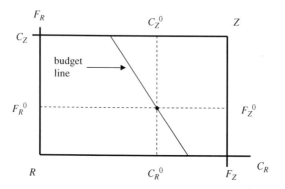

Figure 11.10   The auctioneer yells out prices and a budget line appears in the Edgeworth box. R cannot get on the other side of the budget line, nor can Z.

> **Section Summary:**
> We have introduced prices into the Edgeworth box, which yield a budget line for each consumer. The budget line divides the box into a portion for Robinson and a portion for Zelda. What point will each consumer choose? To address that question, we need to introduce the consumer's preferences, which we do in the next section.

11.7   Preferences and Choice in the Edgeworth Box

In this section, we will bring in the preferences of each consumer. This discussion should then remind you of Chapter 2. Once we have the preferences, we can combine them with the budget line and discuss consumer choice.

Recall that we represent a consumer's preferences by indifference curves. Each consumer has a whole set of indifference curves with the general properties that indifference curves for a given consumer do not cross. If more is preferred to less, then the indifference curves also display a negative slope and generate more utility as we move further from the origin. We can draw such indifference curves for each consumer. We start by drawing only one curve for each consumer, as shown in Figure 11.11.

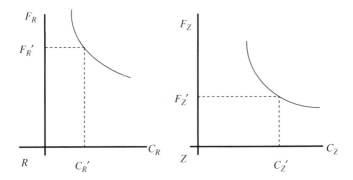

Figure 11.11 Indifference curves through the point (C_R', F_R') for R and (C_Z', F_Z') for Z.

Now when Z's axis system is rotated $180°$, Figure 11.12 will result. We denote the PTES $\{(C_R', F_R'), (C_Z', F_Z')\}$ by S.

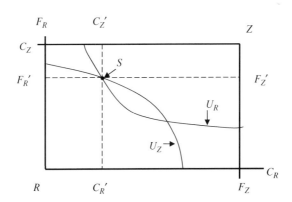

Figure 11.12 This is the Edgeworth box with an indifference curve for R (U_R) and an indifference curve for Z (U_Z) through the PTES S, $\{(C_R', F_R'), (C_Z', F_Z')\}$.

Exercise 18. In Figure 11.12, which way does Z want to move (where are Z's preferred bundles)? Which way does R want to move? How do you know?

We now bring the budget lines back along with the indifference curves for both R and Z. To ease the graph, we will only draw in one indifference curve for each consumer, but remember that there are an infinite number of such curves for each. Where will each consumer end up? It is easy to see what must happen; each consumer must choose so that their indifference curve is tangent to the budget line.

Proposition 11.10: *If assumptions 11.6 hold and if, for R, (C_R^*, F_R^*) is utility maximum given the budget, then an R indifference curve must be tangent to the budget line at (C_R^*, F_R^*).*

Proof 11.11: By contrapositive. R will choose a bundle on the budget line because more is preferred to less. If the budget line is not tangent to an indifference curve at (C_R^*, F_R^*), then the budget line crosses that indifference curve. Hence, there are bundles preferred to (C_R^*, F_R^*) in the budget set (on or below the budget line), so (C_R^*, F_R^*) cannot be utility maximum. □

Exercise 19. Prove proposition 11.10 for Zelda.

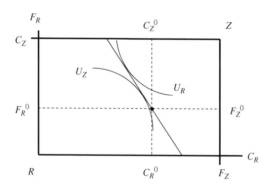

Figure 11.13 An indifference curve for each consumer is shown tangent to the budget line.

It now appears that the solution shown in Figure 11.13 is nearly what we need. We have both consumers maximizing utility given the budget, which is required by the definition of a PTCE. But do the markets clear? We turn to that issue next.

> **Section Summary:**
> In this section, we have brought in the preferences of each consumer and placed the indifference curves in the Edgeworth box. In addition, we have brought the budget lines into the discussion, and looked at having each consumer choose. In the next section, we will complete the discussion of equilibrium by imposing the last condition for equilibrium — that markets clear.

11.8   Excess Demand and Equilibrium in Pure Trade

In this section, we build on what we learned in the last section by discovering what must happen when we require both consumers to maximize utility given their budget and that markets clear. This will be equilibrium in the pure trade model. We will also examine a case where equilibrium does not exist.

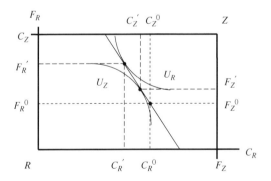

Figure 11.14 R starts with (C_R^0, F_R^0) and wants (C_R', F_R'). Robinson would give up some C to increase consumption of F. He is a supplier of C and a demander of F.

We turn now to finding excess demand for each good. In Figure 11.14, we repeat Figure 11.13 and mark the amounts each consumer chooses. R chooses (C'_R, F'_R) and Z chooses (C'_Z, F'_Z). Note that Robinson starts with (C^0_R, F^0_R). We see that $C^0_R > C'_R$ and $F^0_R < F'_R$. Hence, Robinson is a supplier of C and a demander of F. Furthermore, Robinson supplies $C^0_R - C'_R$ amount of coconuts and demands $F'_R - F^0_R$ amount of fish.

> Exercise 20. Compare the bundle Z chooses with her initial endowment. Which good does Z demand and in what quantity? Which good does Z supply and in what quantity?

Using the data from Figure 11.14, we can find one point on the excess demand for C and one point on the excess demand for F. We show the outcome in Figure 11.15. Start with coconuts. One way to proceed is to find the total amount of coconuts demanded by both R and Z, $C'_R + C'_Z$. This is the quantity demanded. The quantity supplied is the initial endowment, $C^0_R + C^0_Z$. We see that $C'_Z + C'_R < C^0_R + C^0_Z$. Thus, the excess demand at the price P_C is $C'_R + C'_Z - (C^0_R + C^0_Z)$. This amount is negative.

For fish, the amount demanded is $F'_R + F'_Z$, and the amount supplied is $F^0_R + F^0_Z$. Thus, the excess demand is $F'_R + F'_Z - (F^0_R + F^0_Z)$. Here, $F'_R + F'_Z > F^0_R + F^0_Z$, so this amount is positive.

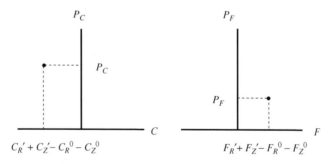

Figure 11.15   The left panel shows the quantity of excess demand for C at the price P_C, and the right panel shows the quantity of excess demand for F at the price P_F.

To get the whole excess demand for either good, we have to change the price of that good. If we want the excess demand for coconuts, we would vary the price of coconuts and see what happens to the excess demand for coconuts. We can see in Figure 11.15 that the price of C must fall if we are to eliminate the negative excess demand. Suppose this happens. We show the result in Figure 11.16 (which is nearly the same as Figure 11.14 with some lines removed).

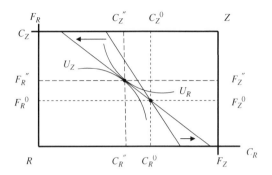

Figure 11.16 When P_C falls, the budget line swings counterclockwise around the initial endowment. R starts with (C_R^0, F_R^0) and wants (C_R'', F_R''). Robinson would give up some C to increase consumption of F. He is a supplier of C and a demander of F.

If P_C falls, then the budget line gets flatter, but still goes through the initial endowment. Now both R and Z maximize utility (not the same indifference curves as before — we have to draw new curves consistent with the original curves) and we seek the tangency. In Figure 11.16, we see that the number of coconuts that R wants to give up, $(C_R^0 - C_R'')$, exactly equals the number of coconuts that Z wants, $(C_Z'' - C_Z^0)$. In this case, the excess demand for coconuts is zero, and the coconut market is in equilibrium. At this point, the auctioneer stops yelling out prices, and trade between Robinson and Zelda occurs.

Exercise 21. Find the point on the excess demand for fish at this new price of coconuts. What has happened to the excess demand for fish? What is held fixed when we find the excess demand for fish? What changes?

Exercise 22. Suppose that we multiply both P_C and P_F by a positive constant, k. What impact will this have on the budget line for both consumers? What impact does it have on the budget line in the Edgeworth box? What is the lesson from this exercise?

In fact, both markets are in equilibrium, and both consumers have maximized utility, so we have a PTCE. We have, then, the following proposition.

Proposition 11.12: *If assumptions 11.6 hold, and if the prices (P_C, P_F) together with the PTES $\{(C_R^*, F_R^*), (C_Z^*, F_Z^*)\}$ form a pure trade competitive equilibrium on the inside of the Edgeworth box, then an indifference curve for R must be tangent to an indifference curve for Z at $\{(C_R^*, F_R^*), (C_Z^*, F_Z^*)\}$ and this point must also be on the budget line.*

Proof 11.13: We already know that if we have a PTCE, one of R's indifference curves must be tangent to the budget line at (C_R^*, F_R^*) and one of Z's indifference curves must be tangent to the budget line at (C_Z^*, F_Z^*) by proposition 11.10. For a PTCE, we also need the excess demand for all goods to be zero, so we know that $C_R^* + C_Z^* = C_R^0 + C_Z^0$ and $F_R^* + F_Z^* = F_R^0 + F_Z^0$ must hold. Hence, the tangencies must exhaust the initial endowment. $\qquad\square$

This characterization of the PTCE is important. It says that the ratio of prices must be the same as the slope of both consumers' indifference curves. In a sense, the ratio of prices is determined by the mutual tangency of the indifference curves. The other restriction is that the mutual tangency line must also pass through the initial endowment. Note that because the BT sets are strictly convex for both consumers, there is at least a chance that such a line exists.

Once the equilibrium is achieved, we then allow the two consumers to trade at the equilibrium prices. We see that the amount of added F that R wants is exactly equal to the amount of F that Z is willing to give up. And the amount of C that Z wants is equal to the amount of C that R is willing to give up. Furthermore, the amount of coconuts given up by Robinson exactly generates the appropriate amount of fish from Zelda. When the trade occurs, both consumers gain from the trade.

FROM THE LITERATURE

One of the outcomes of this chapter is that the competitive process has an equilibrium. One outcome of the equilibrium is that trade is generated. We can apply this idea to the case of international trade. After all, we could consider Robinson as one country and Zelda as another. There is a long tradition in economics arguing that free trade (essentially trade under competitive conditions) yields good outcomes. There is a very nice piece by Paul Samuelson on the conditions where trade does yield good outcomes and conditions where it may not. One part of the argument is that if consumers can purchase commodities at lower prices, they gain. At the same time, some producers may lose as they are unable to compete in the marketplace. Is it true that the move to free(er) trade will benefit the society? Samuelson addresses the question with some numerical examples and some cogent (and pithy) observations! See: Paul Samuelson, "Where Ricardo and Mill Rebut and Confirm Arguments of Mainstream Economists Supporting Globalization," *Journal of Economic Perspectives*, Vol. 18, No. 3, Summer, 2004, pp. 135–146. You can find this online at http://www.ejep.org/, then look down the right-hand side of the webpage for previous issues.

The one thing we have not done is to examine whether a PTCE exists or not. This is not an easy matter. You can see that there are cases where an equilibrium may not exist. Figure 11.17 shows one case, called Arrow's exceptional case. Suppose that the initial endowment is on R's horizontal axis at the PTES S, and that Zelda has indifference curves that look as shown. Zelda has an indifference curve tangent to Robinson's C axis at the initial endowment. Robinson's indifference curves look more normal. Here is the problem. At any positive prices, Zelda will maximize utility at S, the initial endowment. She already has all the fish, but wants more. She does not want any more coconuts.

Robinson wants more of both. There is an excess supply of coconuts and an excess demand for fish. We would expect the price of fish to rise (the price of coconuts to fall). The slope of the budget line is $-P_C/P_F$, so the budget line flattens. But as long as the price of coconuts is positive, there will be an excess supply of coconuts, forcing the budget line to flatten further. Once the price of coconuts goes to zero, then Zelda maximizes utility by choosing S, but Robinson wants to move to buying all the coconuts. So now there is an excess demand for coconuts. There is no way out of this problem. There are no prices so that, with those prices and both consumers maximizing utility, markets clear. There is no PTCE in this case.

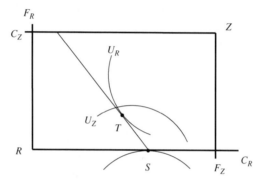

Figure 11.17   Given the budget line shown, Zelda maximizes utility at S, the initial endowment, while Robinson maximizes utility at T. There is an excess demand for fish, and the price of fish will rise, causing the budget line to flatten. At a zero price of coconuts, Zelda stays at S, but Robinson moves to only buy coconuts so there is an excess demand for coconuts. No equilibrium exists in this case.

Section Summary:

In this section, we examined a model where trade is the only economic activity. The point of the section was to find a competitive equilibrium, which we were able to do. Though we are not able to establish the existence of an equilibrium, it does exist under a wide variety of conditions. We did see one set of circumstances where the equilibrium does not exist.

11.9 Competitive Equilibrium with Production

In this section, we continue to build on what we did in the previous section, and we introduce production to the problem. Once we have production, we can then utilize what we have just done to see how the goods are distributed.

The problem we wish to address now is how to allocate resources in an economy with production and trade among the participants of the economy. The economy is still composed of Robinson and Zelda. They each have an endowment of labor and capital, (L_R^0, K_R^0) for Robinson and (L_Z^0, K_Z^0) for Zelda. They use these resources to produce the goods, coconuts and fish. Note that Robinson and Zelda can trade resources so that in their production process, they are not constrained to use only their labor and capital, but they could trade labor for the other's capital or vice versa. We will assume that Robinson produces only coconuts and Zelda only produces fish, though this assumption is not essential to the outcome.

Definition 11.14: *An **input state** is a division of capital and labor between the two producers, $\{(L_C, K_C), (L_F, K_F)\}$.*

We state more fully the assumptions of this model and then define an allocation of resources in this economy.

Assumptions 11.15 (trade with production):

a. *There are two producers, Robinson for coconuts and Zelda for fish.*
b. *Each producer has an endowment of labor and capital, (L_R^0, K_R^0) for Robinson and (L_Z^0, K_Z^0) for Zelda.*
c. *The isoquants for each good are differentiable, and the set of input combinations producing at least X_0 output is strictly convex for each quantity of output for each producer.*
d. *There are two consumers, Robinson and Zelda. Each has indifference curves that are differentiable, and the BT_W sets are strictly convex for each W.*
e. *More is preferred to less by both consumers.*
f. *All goods are infinitely divisible.*

g. *There are no externalities in consumption or production.*
h. *Each consumer makes decisions independently of the other consumer.*

We have met these assumptions before, so they need little comment.

Definition 11.16: *An allocation of resources is*

a. *the quantity of coconuts and fish produced, C^* and F^*.*
b. *the division of coconuts and fish between Robinson and Zelda,* $(C_R^*, F_R^*), (C_Z^*, F_Z^*)$.
c. *a division of the labor and capital devoted to the production of each good,* $(L_C^*, K_C^*), (L_F^*, K_F^*)$.

Again, we will use a price system to allocate resources. The auctioneer will yell out prices for coconuts, fish, labor, and capital. Given these prices, Robinson and Zelda, as consumers, will maximize utility and choose an amount of coconuts and fish they demand. As producers, Robinson and Zelda will, given the prices as well as the initial endowment of labor and capital, maximize profit to determine the quantity of goods to produce. As part of the profit-maximizing choice, Robinson and Zelda will also choose a quantity of labor and capital to use in the production of coconuts and fish. The supply of resources for both capital and labor is inelastic at the total of the endowment amounts. Again, the auctioneer will stop yelling out prices once the excess demand for all goods goes to zero. Again, this system is competitive in that neither Robinson nor Zelda can affect the prices the auctioneer yells out. This is the competitive equilibrium.

Definition 11.17: *A competitive equilibrium with production is a set of prices,* (P_C^*, P_F^*, w^*, r^*), *and an allocation of resources,* $\{(C^*, F^*), (C_R^*, F_R^*), (C_Z^*, F_Z^*), (L_C^*, K_C^*), (L_F^*, K_F^*)\}$, *so that the following conditions are met:*

a. *Robinson maximizes utility at* (C_R^*, F_R^*) *given the prices,* (P_C^*, P_F^*), *and his endowment of labor and capital,* (L_R^0, K_R^0).
b. *Zelda maximizes utility at* (C_Z^*, F_Z^*) *given the prices,* (P_C^*, P_F^*), *and her endowment of labor and capital,* (L_Z^0, K_Z^0).
c. *Robinson, producing C, maximizes profit at C^* while using* (L_C^*, K_C^*) *resources at the given prices,* (P_C^*, P_F^*, w^*, r^*).

d. *Zelda, producing F, maximizes profit at F* while using (L_F^*, K_F^*) resources at the given prices, (P_C^*, P_F^*, w^*, r^*).*

e. *At (P_C^*, P_F^*, w^*, r^*), the excess demand for each good and each resource is zero, so $C^* = C_R^* + C_Z^*$, $F^* = F_R^* + F_Z^*$, $L_R^0 + L_Z^0 = L_C^* + L_F^*$, and $K_R^0 + K_Z^0 = K_C^* + K_F^*$.*

Section Summary:
In this section, we introduced the model with production and defined a competitive equilibrium for this model. We would like to have a geometrical way to proceed toward a characterization of the competitive equilibrium. Fortunately, we have developed the techniques that will help us toward this end. We will use the Edgeworth box for dividing C and F between the two consumers, but we can use this same construct for another purpose, although some adjustments will have to be made. Here we go!

11.10 Edgeworth Box for Production

In this section, we will develop the geometrical tools needed to represent production and the choice of input combinations. We rely on what we have done earlier, and extend the Edgeworth box to this purpose.

Recall from Chapter 4 that we represented the technology for a firm by isoquants. Here we have a set of isoquants for Robinson, the producer of coconuts, and a set of isoquants for Zelda, the producer of fish. These are shown in Figure 11.18.

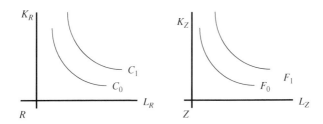

Figure 11.18 Some of Robinson's isoquants for producing coconuts are shown on the left. On the right are some of Zelda's isoquants for producing fish.

Recall that both Robinson and Zelda have an endowment of labor and capital, (L_R^0, K_R^0) for Robinson and (L_Z^0, K_Z^0) for Zelda. The total amount of labor and capital they have together is $(L_R^0 + L_Z^0, K_R^0 + K_Z^0)$. We can now form an Edgeworth box using the isoquants with dimensions equal to the total resource endowment. The R origin reflects Robinson the producer. The Z origin represents Zelda the producer. This is shown in Figure 11.19.

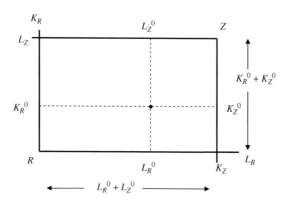

Figure 11.19   The initial resource endowment is (L_R^0, K_R^0) for R and (L_Z^0, K_Z^0) for Z.

We may now introduce the isoquants into the box, as shown in Figure 11.20.

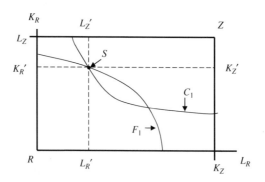

Figure 11.20   This is the Edgeworth box for production with an isoquant curve for R (C_1) and an isoquant curve for Z (F_1) through the input state S, $\{(L_R', K_R'),$ $(L_Z', K_Z')\}$.

Exercise 23. Given the price of labor and capital, w and r, find the income that Robinson can generate from his initial endowment, (L_R^0, K_R^0). Now write an expression for Robinson's expenditure on these inputs. Suppose that income equals expenditure. Graph this line in the Edgeworth box for inputs.

Exercise 24. Repeat the above exercise for Zelda. When the auctioneer yells out w and r, what happens in the Edgeworth box for inputs?

Exercise 25. In this setting, we could view Robinson and Zelda as demanders of inputs. For a given set of input prices, w and r, they would each try to maximize the output they produce from those inputs (this choice would also put the firm on its TVC). If Robinson and Zelda behave this way, what combination of inputs would each choose? You should be able to state and prove a proposition.

Exercise 26. Suppose that Robinson and Zelda choose as discussed in the previous exercise. Find the excess demand for labor by having the auctioneer yell out several prices for labor while holding the price of capital and the price of both outputs constant. What do you get? What would make the excess demand shift?

Section Summary:
In this section, we have used an Edgeworth box to represent the production choices facing the society. We can summarize these choices with a new graph, production possibilities, which we develop in the next section.

11.11   Production Possibilities

In this section, we will summarize the tradeoff of output combinations facing the society: production possibilities. We start with the definition of production possibilities.

Definition 11.18: *Production possibilities relates coconuts and fish and tells, for each quantity of fish, the maximum quantity of coconuts that can be produced in this economy given resources and technology.*

We can also define production possibilities as the maximum quantity of fish for each given quantity of coconuts given resources and technology. How do we find the production possibilities? We need to know the maximum quantity of coconuts at each quantity of fish. To find these combinations of coconuts and fish, we rely upon the following proposition.

Proposition 11.19: *For the quantity of fish, F_1, the maximum quantity of coconuts that can be produced will be the quantity of coconuts of the coconut isoquant tangent to the F_1 fish isoquant in the production Edgeworth box.*

Proof 11.20: Choose a point on the F_1 fish isoquant. Draw the coconut isoquant through that input state. Assume that the coconut isoquant, C_1, is not tangent to the F_1 fish isoquant. Then there are input states that will produce more coconuts and still produce F_1 fish, so the initial input state cannot provide a point on the production possibilities.   □

Exercise 27. Prove the proposition when we start with a quantity of coconuts and find the maximum fish we can produce.

The outcome could look as shown in Figure 11.21. Note that we can obtain a number of points of tangency, one for each possible quantity of fish produced.

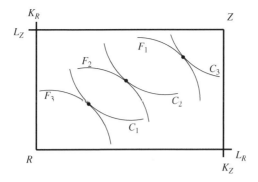

Figure 11.21 Here we show combinations of use of capital and labor that maximize the production of coconuts for each quantity of fish.

To find production possibilities, choose an output for fish, F_1. Now find the maximum quantity of coconuts that could be generated with the remaining resources, C_3. We have one point on production possibilities. We can find others by looking for other tangencies. The outcome is shown in Figure 11.22.

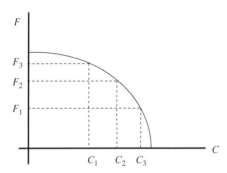

Figure 11.22 Choose a level of fish output in Figure 11.21 and find the corresponding profit-maximizing quantity of coconuts.

We can find the slope of the production possibilities in the following way. Suppose we take a dollar from Zelda's expenditure on L and K. Zelda reduces her use of L and K, and her output would go down. Now take the dollar's worth of labor and capital, and transfer them to Robinson. His output rises. The fall in Zelda's output is $1/MC_F$.

How do we get this? Note that we are reducing the amount spent on inputs and looking for the change in output, so it seems natural to think about the marginal cost. Start with Zelda.

Zelda's marginal cost, $MC_F, = \frac{\Delta TC}{\Delta F}$. If we solve for ΔF, we get $\Delta F = \Delta TC / MC_F$. Because we changed expenditure by 1, $\Delta TC = 1$. Hence, fish production changes by $1/MC_F$. By similar reasoning, Robinson's increase in output is $1/MC_C$. Thus, the slope of production possibilities is the change in fish over the change in coconuts, which turns out to be $\frac{\Delta F}{\Delta C} = \frac{-\frac{1}{MC_F}}{\frac{1}{MC_C}} = \frac{-MC_C}{MC_F}$.

We are now ready to proceed to the characterization of the competitive equilibrium in a model with production.

Section Summary:
In this section, we have derived the production possibilities curve from a production Edgeworth box. We can use this tool to take the next step and characterize the competitive equilibrium for the economy with production.

11.12   Competitive Equilibrium with Production

In this section, we again build on the previous work. We seek a description of the conditions which follow from the assumption that we have a competitive equilibrium. This will require an examination of both production and consumption, and will utilize production possibilities and the Edgeworth box for both production and for consumption. We are ready to state and prove a central proposition.

Proposition 11.21: *If assumptions 11.15 hold and if prices (P_C^*, P_F^*, w^*, r^*) and an allocation of resources $\{(C^*, F^*), (C_R^*, F_R^*), (C_Z^*, F_Z^*), (L_C^*, K_C^*), (L_F^*, K_F^*)\}$ are a competitive equilibrium with production, then:*

a. *the (negative of the) slope of the production possibilities at (C^*, F^*) is equal to the (negative of the) ratio of the price of coconuts to the price of fish, (P_C^*/P_F^*).*

b. *at* $(C_R^*, F_R^*), (C_Z^*, F_Z^*)$, *an indifference curve for R must be tangent to an indifference curve for Z, and* $C_R^* + C_Z^* = C^*, F_R^* + F_Z^* = F^*$.

c. *at* $(L_C^*, K_C^*), (L_F^*, K_F^*)$, *the* C^* *isoquant is tangent to the* F^* *isoquant and* $L_R^* + L_Z^* = L_C^* + L_F^*, K_R^* + K_Z^* = K_C^* + K_F^*$.

Proof 11.22: We are assuming that we have a competitive equilib rium. Hence, we assume that both Robinson and Zelda maximize profits in their role as producers. We also assume that both Robinson and Zelda maximize utility given the budget in their role as consumers. We start by proving part a of the proposition.

a. For proposition 11.21a, we will use profit maximization. Recall from Chapter 5 that, in the case of competition, firms produce so that $P = MC$. Hence, we would have the following conditions:

$$P_C = MC_C.$$

$$P_F = MC_F.$$

If we form the ratio, and take the equilibrium prices, we would get the following condition:

$$\frac{P_C^*}{P_F^*} = \frac{MC_C(C^*)}{MC_F(F^*)}.$$

We have argued above that $-\frac{MC_C}{MC_F}$ is the slope of the production possibilities. In short, under competition, the ratio of output prices must be equal to the negative of the slope of the production possibilities. A line with the slope of the negative of the ratio of prices must be tangent to the production possibilities at the profit-maximizing outputs, in this case C^* and F^*. Figure 11.23 shows the outcome.

Note that once we choose a point on the production possibilities, namely (C^*, F^*), we have answered the first resource allocation question: what quantity of each good to produce. Once we have answered that question, we will construct an Edgeworth box of that size (C^* wide and F^* high), and address the question of how to divide the goods between the two consumers — part b of proposition 11.21.

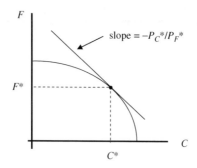

Figure 11.23   The line with slope $-P_C^*/P_F^*$ is tangent to the production possibilities at (C^*, F^*), the output produced under competition.

b. We already know that proposition 11.21b must be true by the proof of proposition 11.12. Again, we assume for the competitive equilibrium that both consumers maximize utility given prices. This yields the tangency.

　　The combined outcome of parts a and b of proposition 11.21 is shown in Figure 11.24.

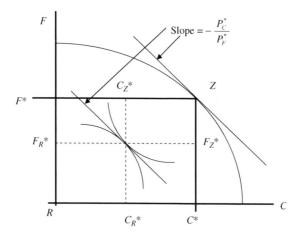

Figure 11.24   Use the output prices to determine a point on the production possibilities, (C^*, F^*), and construct an Edgeworth box of that size. Using the same prices, find an allocation of C^* and F^* between Robinson and Zelda, (C_R^*, F_R^*), (C_Z^*, F_Z^*).

We know from the proof of proposition 11.12 that, under competitive conditions, Robinson and Zelda will end up so that they each have an indifference curve tangent to the other's indifference curve and the mutual slope will be the negative of the ratio of output prices. Thus, we will have a division of C^* and F^* between Robinson and Zelda. Note that the slope of the budget lines and the slope of production possibilities are the same.

c. For proposition 11.21c, once we have chosen a point on the production possibilities, (C^*, F^*), we go back to the Edgeworth box with isoquants, and find where the C^* and F^* isoquants are tangent to divide the inputs between the two goods. Because the graph of production possibilities was constructed from tangent isoquants, we have the third condition, proposition 11.21c, satisfied as well. In short, we have allocated resources by the competitive mechanism, and we are done. □

In short, selecting a point on the production possibilities allocates resources in the economy. By selecting a point on the production possibilities, we determine the quantities of output to produce, how to distribute the inputs between the production of the goods, and how to distribute the goods between the consumers.

Note that we have that the competitive process achieves allocative efficiency (Chapter 7), $\frac{P_x}{MSC_x} = \frac{P_y}{MSC_y}$. This follows from part a of proposition 11.21.

There is an added question to examine: the role of the input prices. If both Robinson the producer and Zelda the producer act to maximize profit, then we know from Chapter 10 that the following conditions for hiring inputs must hold. For Robinson, who produces coconuts, we would have two conditions: one for labor and one for capital. Here MP_L^C is the marginal product of labor, L, in the production of coconuts, C.

$$P_C^* \bullet MP_L^C = w^*.$$

$$P_C^* \bullet MP_K^C = r^*.$$

Similarly, for Zelda, who produces fish, we would have

$$P_F^* \bullet MP_L^F = w^*.$$
$$P_F^* \bullet MP_K^F = r^*.$$

Working with Robinson's first, we could divide the top equation by the bottom to get the following condition:

$$\frac{MP_L^C}{MP_K^C} = \frac{w^*}{r^*}.$$

A similar condition would hold for Zelda. Because w/r will be the same for both Robinson and Zelda, we conclude that the following condition must hold due to profit maximization:

$$\frac{MP_L^C}{MP_K^C} = \frac{MP_L^F}{MP_K^F}.$$

Thus, from Chapter 4, we see that the slope of the coconut isoquant, $\frac{MP_L^C}{MP_K^C}$, must be equal to the slope of the fish isoquant, $\frac{MP_L^F}{MP_K^F}$. Therefore, under profit maximization, we have that the isoquant for the production of coconuts must have the same slope as the isoquant for the production of fish. We now have a complete characterization of the economy by the prices that we have chosen.

There may be a few questions that you might have. For example, note that we have pretty much ignored the initial endowment of resources, (L_R^0, K_R^0) and (L_Z^0, K_Z^0). Yet we know that when the auctioneer yells out the prices for capital and labor, the isocost must go through the initial endowment. Can we be sure that the C^* and F^* isoquants could be chosen for any positive input prices? What if we have the situation shown in Figure 11.25?

What has to happen in this case? Obviously, the prices of inputs as well as the prices and quantities of both coconuts and fish must change so that the optimal quantities of coconuts and fish can be generated from the initial endowment of resources. If the input prices change, the quantities of both fish and coconuts produced will also change, along with the prices of those goods.

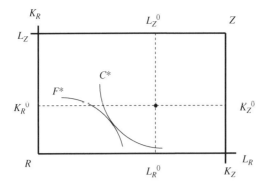

Figure 11.25 There is no isocost with positive input prices that will allow C^* and F^* to be optimal choices.

Second, we have not written out the budget constraints for the consumers. If we did, we would have to include the profit generated by the firms as part of the consumer's income. To complete that matter, which we will not pursue, one would need to identify how much profit from each firm each consumer would receive. There are several possible ways to proceed. One would be to assume that one consumer owns one firm, as we have done here. A second possibility is to assume the consumers own shares of stock in the firms. In any case, the ownership issue will have to be faced before we can properly write the consumer's budget.

There is another way to obtain the result that the ratio of prices for coconuts and fish must be equal to the slope of the production possibilities. The value of the output of the economy is $P_C C + P_F F$, gross domestic product (GDP). Then we have GDP $= P_C C + P_F F$. If we graph this line for a fixed value of GDP, we would obtain all combinations of C and F that yield that amount of GDP given the prices. If we take a larger GDP, the line will move out parallel to itself. If we maximize GDP subject to the production possibilities, we would end up with the GDP line tangent to the production possibilities. You will recognize this tangency condition as the condition we obtained in proposition 7.9, where we argued that the ratio of price to marginal social cost has to be the same for all goods if we are to maximize social satisfaction.

Exercise 28. Graph the line GDP $= P_C C + P_F F$ for fixed values of GDP, P_C, and P_F. What happens to the line if GDP rises?

Exercise 29. Show that, if production possibilities is differentiable and looks as shown in Figure 11.22, if GDP is maximum at (C_1, F_1), then the GDP line must be tangent to the production possibilities at (C_1, F_1).

It is not easy to see whether the equilibrium actually exists. With the previous model, we had a case where equilibrium did not exist: Arrow's exceptional case (see Section 11.8). This example can be stretched to a world with production as well.

The only situation we have not directly discussed is the case where the supply of labor is determined by utility maximization. Geometric treatment of this case is hard, and few new insights arise from this case.

Section Summary:
In this section, we have examined the implication of having a competitive equilibrium with production. The conclusion we reached is that if we have a competitive equilibrium with production, then the slope of the production possibilities and the indifference curves must be equal to the negative of the ratio of the price of coconuts to the price of fish. Furthermore, for the outputs produced, the slope of the isoquants for those outputs must be equal to each other and equal to the ratio of input prices.

11.13   Summary

This chapter has been devoted to the idea of a competitive equilibrium. We have looked at this concept in three models: the Robinson Crusoe model, the pure trade model, and the model with production. The important ideas you should take from this chapter are the following:

A. Equilibrium in Crusoe requires a tangency of an indifference curve with the production function.

B. Competitive equilibrium for consumers is characterized by tangency of indifference curves in an Edgeworth box.

C. Equilibrium for firms is characterized by the tangency of isoquants in an Edgeworth box.

D. Overall equilibrium also requires that the slope of the production possibilities is the same as the slope of the indifference curves.

One important question is whether these outcomes have any desirable properties. The next chapter is devoted to this issue.

Terms Defined:

- Competitive equilibrium (Crusoe economy)
- Pure trade economic state
- Pure trade competitive equilibrium
- Excess demand
- Input state
- Allocation of resources
- Competitive equilibrium with production
- Production possibilities

Chapter 12

Welfare Economics

Key Concepts:

- Pareto optimality
- Efficiency
- Does the competitive process yield Pareto optimal and efficient outcomes?

Goals:

- Characterize Pareto optimal outcomes.
- See if the competitive process achieves Pareto optimal outcomes.
- Characterize efficient outcomes.
- See if the competitive process allocates resources efficiently.
- Is it possible to develop social preferences from individual preferences?

The previous chapters have been primarily devoted to models that describe how the world looks to an economist. There is also a rich tradition of saying that there is something good about the way the competitive process allocates resources. We address this issue in this chapter.

12.1   Introduction

Among the first to espouse the value of the competitive process was Adam Smith, who wrote in 1776 about how competitive markets yield desirable outcomes, and how they do this without explicitly trying to do so. We quote him now:

> ... directing that industry in such a manner as its produce may be of the greatest value, he intends only his own gain, and he is in this, as in many other cases, led by an invisible hand to promote an end which was no part of his intention. Nor is it always the worse for the society that it was no part of it. By pursuing his own interest he frequently promotes that of the society more effectually than when he really intends to promote it.[1]

The question is whether we can replicate this result in the models we have developed. Does the competitive process as we understand it lead to any desirable outcomes? If so, what? We can also ask what failings competition has as well.

In this chapter, we examine a model that details one aspect of how resources should be allocated and look to see if the competitive process fulfills this objective. We start with the essential definitions of optimality we will use in the pure trade world. We will also use the Edgeworth box construction from Chapter 11. After we examine the case of pure trade, we will turn to the world including production. We will amend our definition of optimality to include production issues at that point, and we will examine whether the competitive process achieves our requirements for a desirable allocation of resources.

12.2   Pareto Optimality and Pure Trade

In this section, we will begin the process of trying to identify the best outcome for the pure trade economy. We repeat the assumptions for pure trade here (and maintain the 11.6 number from the previous chapter).

---

[1] Smith, Adam, *An Inquiry into the Nature and Causes of the Wealth of Nations*, edited by Edwin Cannan, The Modern Library, Random House, New York, 1937, p. 423.

Assumptions 11.6 (pure trade):

a. *There are two consumers, Robinson (R) and Zelda (Z).*
b. *There are two goods, fish (F) and coconuts (C).*
c. *Each consumer has preferences represented by differentiable indifference curves, and BT is strictly convex for each consumer.*
d. *More is preferred to less by both consumers.*
e. *Each consumer starts with an initial endowment of the two goods. R's initial endowment is (C_R^0, F_R^0) and Z's is (C_Z^0, F_Z^0). The subscripts refer to the person, R for Robinson and Z for Zelda.*
f. *Both goods are infinitely divisible.*
g. *There are no externalities.*
h. *Each consumer's preferences depend only on what that consumer consumes.*

The key question is: What do we mean by the best outcome for the economy? Whatever we mean, the idea of "best" should be one that is responsive to the participants of the economy. In other words, whatever is "best" must somehow reflect the tastes and preferences of the individuals in the society. No individual should be left out, and at the same time, it should not be true that one person (or a small subgroup of the economy) dictates the best outcome to the others. In addition, we would like for the process of determining the best to somehow rank the alternative PTESs. The following definitions will help us move in the desired direction. These definitions attempt to satisfy the requirement that both consumers count in the decision about what is best, and no consumer is allowed to dictate to another what is best. This is accomplished by allowing each consumer to indicate his or her preferences. As before, we will use the consumer's indifference curves to represent preferences. Before coming to the definitions, we review the Edgeworth box.

In Figure 12.1, we start with a particular PTES, S. To ease the burden, we will start by only showing one indifference curve for each consumer. We will not show the initial endowment as it does not bear on the argument (except to define the size of the box).

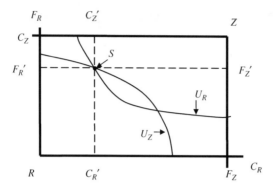

Figure 12.1   This is the Edgeworth box with an indifference curve for R (U_R) and an indifference curve for Z (U_Z) through the PTES S, $\{(C_R', F_R'), (C_Z', F_Z')\}$.

We now define the key concepts for this section.[2]

Definition 12.1: *Let S and S' be two PTESs. We say that S is **Pareto superior** (PS) to S' if both consumers like S at least as much as S' and at least one consumer likes S strictly better than S'.*

Definition 12.2: *Let S and S' be two PTESs. We say that S' is **Pareto inferior** (PI) to S if both consumers like S' no better than S and at least one consumer is strictly worse off at S'.*

Exercise 1. If S is Pareto superior to S', must S' be Pareto inferior to S? If S is not Pareto superior to S', must S' be Pareto superior to S? Explain how you know.

To better understand these definitions, have a look at Figure 12.2. Here, we wish to find all the PTESs that are Pareto superior to S. For Pareto superior, we know that both consumers, Robinson and Zelda, must like these bundles at least as much as S. This suggests the idea of "better than" (BT) from Chapter 2. So for each consumer, find the bundles the consumer prefers to S, the bundles on or above

---

[2] Pareto is the name of the Italian economist/sociologist, Vilfredo Pareto.

the indifference curve through S — better than S, BT_S. Thus, for Robinson, the bundles R prefers to S, BT_S^R, are to the northeast of U_R. For Zelda, the bundles BT_S^Z are to the southwest of U_Z. The intersection of BT_S^R and BT_S^Z is all the bundles that both prefer to S (the indifference curves are also part of that set except for the point where they cross again). The intersection of BT_S^R and BT_S^Z is, then, the set of bundles Pareto superior to S. This intersection is shown in gray in Figure 12.2.

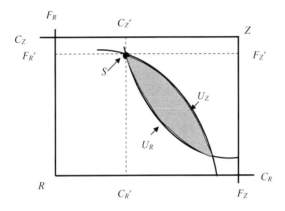

Figure 12.2 R's preferred bundles are northeast of U_R and Z's preferred bundles are to the southwest of U_Z. The intersection, the area in gray, gives the bundles both prefer to S, the bundles Pareto superior to S.

Exercise 2. Use the logic provided above to find the bundles that both find inferior to S, the Pareto inferior bundles.

Exercise 3. Consider a bundle to the northeast of S. Call it S'. Is S' Pareto superior to S? Is S Pareto superior to S'? Is S' Pareto inferior to S? Is S Pareto inferior to S'? Explain how you know.

The last exercise should give you some concern. You should have found that there is no relation between S and S' from that exercise. That means that some combinations of PTESs cannot be ranked by the Pareto process. Remember that one of our hopes was that we would be able to rank alternative PTESs so we could decide which one or ones are the best. But apparently there are some pairs of states that cannot be compared using Pareto. Pareto is an example of a ranking that is not complete. Check back in Chapter 2 for a discussion of complete rankings. But even with this observation, we can determine some PTESs that seem to dominate others.

Definition 12.3: *A PTES S is **Pareto optimal** if there is no state Pareto superior to S.*

Where are the Pareto optimal PTESs? Look back at Figure 12.2. The presence of an area like the gray area means that S cannot be a Pareto optimum. Somehow we need to find a state where no such gray area exists. Where might we find such a state? The following proposition gives the condition.

Proposition 12.4: *If assumptions 11.6 hold and S is a Pareto optimum on the inside of the Edgeworth box, then an indifference curve for R is tangent to an indifference curve for Z at S.*

Proof 12.5: By contrapositive. If an indifference curve for R is not tangent to an indifference curve for Z at S, then the two indifference curves must cross at S. Hence, BT_S^R must intersect BT_S^Z. The bundles in that intersection are Pareto superior to S, so S is not Pareto optimal.   □

Exercise 4. What does it mean to be on the inside of the Edgeworth box? Why is that restriction important here?

In Figure 12.3, we show a Pareto optimal PTES, S. Here there are no PTESs that both R and Z prefer to S. Hence, S is Pareto optimal.

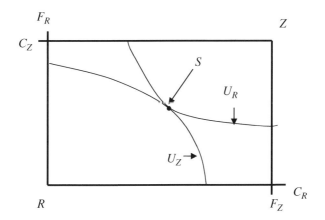

Figure 12.3 Here, BT_S^R and BT_S^Z do not intersect, so there are no PTESs that both R and Z prefer to S. S is Pareto optimal.

In fact, all Pareto optimal points pretty much have to look as shown in Figure 12.3.

Proposition 12.6: *If assumptions* 11.6 *hold and at S an indifference curve for R is tangent to an indifference curve for Z, then S is Pareto optimal.*

Proof 12.7: If at S, an indifference curve for R is tangent to an indifference curve for Z, and BT_S^R and BT_S^Z are both strictly convex, then BT_S^R cannot intersect BT_S^Z. Hence, there are no bundles Pareto superior to S, and S is Pareto optimal. □

In a pure trade world (see assumptions 11.6), the tangency (at least on the inside of the Edgeworth box) is a complete characterization of Pareto optimality. The bad news is that the Pareto optimal outcomes are not unique. In fact, there are a lot of them. Figure 12.4 shows how this happens.

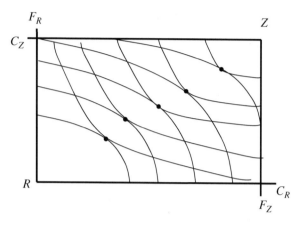

Figure 12.4   A number of Pareto optimal PTESs have been identified in this graph. In fact, there are an infinite number.

It should be clear that we want at least to get to a Pareto optimum outcome if we can. If you look back at Figure 12.2, if we were at the PTES S, then we would be able to improve the outcome for both consumers without hurting anyone by moving into the shaded area. Once we get to a Pareto optimum, we cannot help one consumer without hurting the other.

I'm trying to get this rap going. What do you know that rhymes with Pareto? Tomato? Potato?

Definition 12.8: *The contract curve (conflict curve) is the set of all Pareto optimal outcomes.*

It should now be clear to you that if we have a competitive equilibrium in the pure trade case, we also have a Pareto optimum.

Proposition 12.9: *If $\{(P_C^*, P_F^*), (C_R^*, F_R^*), (C_Z^*, F_Z^*)\}$ is a pure trade competitive equilibrium on the inside of the Edgeworth box and assumptions* 11.6 *hold, then* $(C_R^*, F_R^*), (C_Z^*, F_Z^*)$ *is Pareto optimal.*

Proof 12.10: According to proposition 11.12, we know that if $\{(P_C^*, P_F^*), (C_R^*, F_R^*), (C_Z^*, F_Z^*)\}$ is a pure trade competitive equilibrium, then an indifference curve for R must be tangent to an indifference curve for Z at $(C_R^*, F_R^*), (C_Z^*, F_Z^*)$. Hence, $(C_R^*, F_R^*), (C_Z^*, F_Z^*)$ must be Pareto optimal according to proposition 12.6, and we are done. □

You might wonder if proposition 12.9 has a converse. In fact it does, sometimes called the Second Welfare Theorem. Here is the statement and proof.

Proposition 12.11: *If $\{(C_R^*, F_R^*), (C_Z^*, F_Z^*)\}$ is Pareto optimal on the inside of the Edgeworth box and assumptions* 11.6 *hold, then there is a set of prices* (P_C^*, P_F^*) *and an initial endowment* $\{(C_R^0, F_R^0), (C_Z^0, F_Z^0)\}$ *so that* $\{(P_C^*, P_F^*), (C_R^*, F_R^*), (C_Z^*, F_Z^*)\}$ *is a pure trade competitive equilibrium.*

Proof 12.12: Suppose we have a Pareto optimum at $\{(C_R^*, F_R^*), (C_Z^*, F_Z^*)\}$. Then we know that an indifference curve for Robinson must be tangent to an indifference curve for Zelda at $\{(C_R^*, F_R^*), (C_Z^*, F_Z^*)\}$. Take the price ratio as the mutual slope of the indifference curves, and the initial endowment equal to the point $\{(C_R^*, F_R^*), (C_Z^*, F_Z^*)\}$. Then we have $\{(P_C^*, P_F^*), (C_R^*, F_R^*), (C_Z^*, F_Z^*)\}$ as a competitive equilibrium. □

This proposition is a very powerful statement that points out the importance of the initial endowment. The lesson is that if we do not like the Pareto optimal distribution that the competitive system ends up at, we need to change the initial endowment and allow prices to be determined by a competitive process.

The above theorems give support to the argument often made by economists that free trade is a good thing, that all countries gain from free trade. What is the link? Suppose that R and Z are countries and that we can represent the desires of the countries by indifference curves (you will find reason later in this chapter to doubt this possibility). Then if we allow a competitive mechanism to work (free trade) between the countries, both parties will end up on indifference curves at least as high as when they started. Both sides gain from the trade. If, however, the trade is not free, then the result is not so clear. Some country could be forced to an indifference curve lower than where they started, if the other country is powerful enough. This is only one way to approach this important debate.

It should be clear to you that Pareto optimality is a weak criterion, and in this model, the equilibrium may not be very good depending on the initial endowment. So if Z has a large initial endowment and R has a small endowment, then the outcome will favor Z. The outcome from the competitive process is at least as good for both consumers as the initial endowment, but may not be a desirable outcome. What are the policy implications of this outcome? First, we want at least a Pareto optimum. If the Pareto optimum we end up at is not desirable for some reason, then the way out is to redistribute the initial endowment in a way that allows a more desirable outcome. This is the alternative offered by the Second Welfare Theorem. What we do not want to do is keep the initial endowment the same, and then alter prices so that we end up at a state that is not Pareto optimal.

Note the complication that is introduced. First, we have assumed that the consumers reveal their preferences through their indifference curves. Then after we find the Pareto optimal outcome, we somehow decide that this outcome is not desirable. On what grounds? Shouldn't the preferences reveal this lack of desirability? There is no easy way out. If we do impose some added preferences in addition to the indifference curves, then we should try to specify them in some way and find analytical ways to include them in the analysis. We return to this matter in a later section.

Section Summary:
In this section, we have found that the competitive process in a pure trade world yields Pareto optimal outcomes. In this limited sense, the competitive process works well. Without centralized decision making, we manage to get a desirable outcome. The market is indeed an impressive institution. Does this result extend to worlds with production? We examine this matter in the next section.

12.3 Pareto Optimum and Efficiency in Worlds with Production

The question is: How do we extend the Pareto technique to worlds with production? The model is now the model with production, and the assumptions of that model, assumptions 11.15, are presented again.

Assumptions 11.15 (trade with production):

a. *There are two producers, Robinson for coconuts and Zelda for fish.*

b. *Each producer has an endowment of labor and capital, (L_R^0, K_R^0) for Robinson and (L_Z^0, K_Z^0) for Zelda.*

c. *The isoquants for each good are differentiable, and the set of input combinations producing at least X_0 output is strictly convex for each quantity of output for each producer.*

d. *There are two consumers, Robinson and Zelda. Each has indifference curves that are differentiable, and the BT_W sets are strictly convex for each W.*

e. *More is preferred to less by both consumers.*

f. *All goods are infinitely divisible.*

g. *There are no externalities in consumption or production.*

h. *Each consumer makes decisions independently of the other consumer.*

The main concern is that we somehow get the "right" combination of inputs to produce the desired levels of output. The following definitions are what we need.

Definition 12.13: *An input state S is **more efficient** than the input state S' if, under S, the output of at least one good is greater than under S' and the output of no good is smaller than under S'.*

Definition 12.14: *An input state S' is **less efficient** than the input state S if, under S', the output of at least one good is less than under S and the output of no good is more than under S.*

Exercise 5. How is the concept of more efficient related to the concept of Pareto superior?

Definition 12.15: *An input state S is **efficient** if there is no input state more efficient than S.*

We characterize the efficient states with the following proposition.

Proposition 12.16: *If assumptions 11.15 hold, and S is an efficient input state on the inside of the Edgeworth box, then at S, an isoquant for the coconut producer will be tangent to an isoquant for the fish producer.*

Proof 12.17: By contrapositive. Suppose that S is an input state and that an isoquant for F is not tangent to an isoquant for C at S. Because the isoquants are differentiable, the isoquants must cross, and there are input states that will increase the output of at least one good without decreasing the output of the other, so S cannot be efficient. □

We also have a sort of converse to this proposition which is true.

Proposition 12.18: *If assumptions 11.15 hold and at S, an isoquant for fish is tangent to an isoquant for coconuts, then S is efficient.*

Proof 12.19: If the isoquants are tangent, then there is no place where they intersect. Hence, there are no input states that provide more output for both producers at the same time. Thus, S is efficient. □

Exercise 6. Draw an Edgeworth box to illustrate proposition 12.18 and its proof.

At least on the inside of the Edgeworth box, the tangency is a complete characterization of efficiency in a world with production (see assumptions 11.15).

Note what this means. Because we obtain the production possibilities curve from the tangencies of the isoquants, every point on the production possibilities is efficient.

So far we have argued that both the tangency of indifference curves and tangency of isoquants are required if we have a Pareto optimum and efficient allocation of resources. One other matter must be considered: whether we have the right combination of the two goods. Note that once we have the production possibilities, once we choose a point on the production possibilities, not every Pareto optimal distribution of that combination of output will be equally good. It could be that some distributions that are Pareto optimal could be dominated by a different combination of outputs. We define the concept we need now.

Definition 12.20: *An **efficient mix of outputs** is a combination of goods on the production possibilities (C^*, F^*) and a Pareto optimal division of that combination, $\{(C_R^*, F_R^*), (C_Z^*, F_Z^*)\}$, so that there are no other combinations of goods that could make at least one consumer better off without harming the other.*

To see what this condition entails, we will look at proposition 12.21.

Proposition 12.21: *Given assumptions* 11.15, *if* $\{(C_R^*, F_R^*), (C_Z^*, F_Z^*)\}$ *is a Pareto optimal combination of coconuts and fish, and* (C_1, F_1) *is a point on the production possibilities where* $C_1 = C_R^* + C_Z^*$ *and* $F_1 = F_R^* + F_Z^*$, *and* (C_1, F_1) *is an efficient mix of outputs, then the slope of production possibilities at* (C_1, F_1) *is exactly equal to the slope of R and Z's indifference curves at* $\{(C_R^*, F_R^*), (C_Z^*, F_Z^*)\}$.

Proof 12.22: We will argue by contrapositive. We already know that for a Pareto optimal distribution, we need R and Z to have tangent indifference curves, so the slope of their indifference curves must be the same at that distribution. Assume that the indifference curves for R and Z are tangent, but that the slope of the tangency is different from the slope of the production possibilities. The graph would look as shown in Figure 12.5.

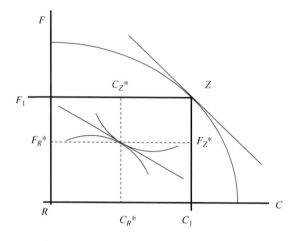

Figure 12.5   Here the slope of production possibilities is different from the mutual slope of the tangent indifference curves for R and Z.

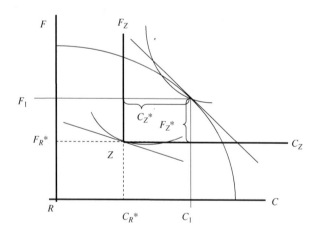

Figure 12.6   Here the slope of production possibilities is different from the mutual slope of the tangent indifference curves for R and Z.

We now turn Zelda's axis system back around and put the origin down at (C_R^*, F_R^*), Robinson's consumption of coconuts and fish. This would result in Figure 12.6. It must be true that Zelda's indifference curve now cuts the production possibilities. Hence, there are combinations of fish and coconuts that would provide greater satisfaction for at least one consumer without decreasing the satisfaction of either. Thus, the quantities of output produced, (C_1, F_1), are not a combination that provides the best outcome for the consumers, and we are done. □

Here, then, are the conditions we need satisfied for a good allocation of resources:

A. The slope of Robinson's indifference curve must be equal to the slope of Zelda's indifference curve at the combination of goods each consumes.
B. The slope of the production possibilities at (C^*, F^*) must be equal to the slope of indifference curves for both Robinson and Zelda at the combination of goods they consume.
C. The slope of the fish isoquant must be equal to the slope of the coconut isoquant at the input combination used by the two firms.

Using the concepts we have developed, Pareto optimality and efficiency, we can now assert the goodness of the competitive system.

Proposition 12.23: *Given assumptions* 11.15, *if we have a competitive equilibrium with production, then the resulting input state and pure trade economic state constitute a Pareto optimum, an efficient allocation of resources, and an efficient mix of outputs.*

Proof 12.24: Look back at proposition 11.21. We know that if we have a competitive equilibrium, we have the indifference curves for the consumers tangent to each other at the pure trade economic state, thus satisfying Pareto optimality. Second, we know that at a competitive equilibrium, then we have the slope of the production possibilities equal to the slope of the indifference curves for both consumers at the Pareto optimal distribution of goods. Furthermore, we know we will be on the production possibilities, so the input state must also be efficient, and we are done.   □

Exercise 7. Draw a production possibilities curve, an Edgeworth box for consumption, and an Edgeworth box for production illustrating proposition 12.23 and its proof.

Thus, the competitive process satisfies the weak conditions of Pareto optimality and efficiency. What is not addressed are questions of the equity of the initial distribution of inputs. We might hope that we could somehow address these issues. We consider that matter next.

Section Summary:
In this section, we have seen that a competitive economy with production yields outcomes that satisfy both Pareto optimality and efficiency. By these criteria, the competitive process yields an excellent outcome. In the next section, we see if we can find ways to examine the fairness of the distribution of output.

12.4   Arrow's Theorem

The question is: Can we find a way to examine income distribution issues? Recall from Chapter 11 that, if we choose a point on the production possibilities, we effectively choose an allocation of resources. By choosing a point on production possibilities, we have decided on the quantities of both goods to produce. Furthermore, given the ratio of prices that determined that combination of goods, we can find a Pareto optimal distribution of goods between the two consumers. Finally, given the combination of goods we wish to produce, we have an efficient division of inputs between the two firms that is consistent with those quantities of goods. Can we find the "right" place on the production possibilities to choose?

That discussion, together with the observation that we want a price ratio tangent to the production possibilities, suggests an idea. What if we had some kind of social indifference curves representing the society's preferences? What if we then tried to maximize that social utility? We would end up with a tangency of the social indifference curve to the production possibilities. That tangency would determine the ratio of prices that would then allocate the goods. Figure 12.7 shows what might happen.

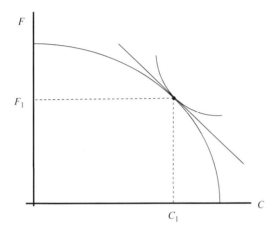

Figure 12.7 If we had social indifference curves so that we could maximize social utility, we could then find the optimal quantities of each good to produce, C_1 and F_1, and also the prices, the slope of the tangent line determined by this maximization. Resources would be fully allocated by this process.

The idea in Figure 12.7 is this. If we had social indifference curves, we could maximize social welfare subject to the production possibilities. We know that the outcome would be a combination of coconuts and fish, and also, if we use the slope of the mutual tangency as a price ratio, we would fully allocate resources by the competitive process. A reasonable question at this point is: Is there something like social welfare, social indifference curves?

Before moving to an answer to this question, we need to set the stage. What we want is a ranking of combinations of coconuts and fish by the society so that all citizens contribute to the ranking, and so that no one citizen dictates to the other. Another reasonable condition is that if there is an alternative that all agree is not the best, the presence of that bundle in the choice set does not alter the outcome. There are some technical conditions as well.

In a rather astonishing piece of analysis, Kenneth Arrow argues that there is no aggregation device that will allow us to take an arbitrary set of consumers and find the social utility function satisfying the above properties.[3] Arrow's argument is roughly that in any group, there is a decisive subgroup, so that when the winners are chosen by the full group, we could have replaced the full group with the decisive subgroup. But if this is true, we can then replace the decisive subgroup with a decisive subgroup of itself, and the process continues until we have a subgroup of only one — a dictator.

The bad news is that individual preferences alone cannot, in general, be aggregated to allocate resources to maximize the society's satisfaction. We are thus stuck with political processes and other means for finding ways to allocate resources. In short, if we go back to the discussion in Section 12.2 (see p. 380), we see that the decision to reallocate the initial distribution to improve the welfare of the society can be done, but it has to be done with mechanisms that are somewhat arbitrary.

Note that if economists were willing to make comparisons of utility between individuals, this issue would move toward a solution. So if the economist were willing to argue that the losses suffered by Robinson (when we take some of his initial endowment away and give it to Zelda) are smaller than the gains that Zelda enjoys in this reallocation, then we could make these trades with less difficulty. But because economists have been traditionally reticent to say that the utility lost by one is more or less than the utility gained by another, this mode of argument is out of bounds for the economist.

---

[3] Arrow, Kenneth, *Social Choice and Individual Values*, John Wiley & Sons, New York, 1951. This work set off a whole industry of efforts not only in economics, but in a variety of other areas as well.

FROM THE LITERATURE

One consequence of Arrow's theorem is that we cannot use mechanisms like majority voting to reveal the true winner. An article where this point is made simply is by Donald Wittman, "Parties as Utility Maximizers," *American Political Science Review*, Vol. 67, No. 2, June, 1973, pp. 490–498. In this paper, Wittman goes on to argue that rather than look at political parties as being only interested in winning elections, we should model their behavior as utility-maximizing where the objective is to implement specific policies consistent with their values. His models include a model where parties are competitive, and a model where parties collude. Check it out!

Section Summary:
In this section, we have presented a brief discussion of whether it is possible to obtain social preferences from individual preferences, and have concluded that in general it is not possible. Thus, to reallocate requires some kind of arbitrary decision process. Some consumers may well be hurt in the process of helping others.

12.5   Summary

In this chapter, we have examined criteria for allocation of resources: Pareto optimality and efficiency. We have looked at the competitive process to see if the competitive process satisfies these criteria. We have these results:

A. In a pure trade world, tangency of indifference curves yields Pareto optimal outcomes.
B. A pure trade competitive equilibrium is Pareto optimal.
C. In a world with production, tangency of indifference curves, tangency of isoquants, and a point on the production possibilities with the same slope as the tangent indifference curves yield Pareto optimal and efficient outcomes.

D. A competitive equilibrium in a world with production satisfies Pareto optimality and efficiency.
E. It is not possible in general to aggregate individual preferences into social preferences.

Terms Defined:

- Pareto superior
- Pareto inferior
- Pareto optimal
- Contract curve
- More efficient
- Less efficient
- Efficient
- Efficient mix of outputs
- Arrow's theorem

Chapter 13

Uncertainty

Up to this time, we have assumed that the world is ruled by certainty. Suppose you are in the business of making baskets. You are thinking about adding a new stapler to your production process, but wonder if the machine will pay for itself or not. You have information from the maker of the stapler that it will last for five years with regular maintenance, and you have talked to others who use it and they agree with that assessment. Should you buy this stapler? The problem is that you cannot predict what the demand for baskets will be for the next five years to know whether the stapler will have enough use to pay for itself. How do you proceed?

13.1   Introduction

When uncertainty arises, we have to take into consideration that the choice problem is now more complicated. There is some factor bearing on a decision that is uncertain and outside the control of the decision maker. It is pretty clear that the decision maker will not end up at the same outcome as when there is no uncertainty. In this chapter, three applications will be discussed. First, we will discuss consumer behavior in the presence of uncertainty, and follow with an application to insurance. We then turn to the firm and look at a particular aspect of choice under uncertain conditions. Finally, we look at uncertainty in the Cournot model.

13.2   Consumer Choice under Uncertainty

In our previous discussion of the consumer, we assumed that the consumer acted to maximize utility subject to a budget. We would like to maintain that methodology to the extent we can. To move forward, we will consider a particular problem and see how we can use the ideas we have already developed.

Suppose that a consumer is confronted with the opportunity to participate in a game of chance. The consumer will have to pay a fee to play the game, but will win $100,000 with the probability of P or will win $60,000 with the probability of $1 - P$. How much would a consumer be willing to pay to play this game? Rather clearly, a consumer could not expect to be allowed to play the game if the price were less than $60,000. Nor would the consumer play if the price were more than $100,000. In some sense, the price has to be between these two amounts. One answer would be that the consumer would pay what the game is worth, on average — the expected value of the game. We define the expected value next.

Definition 13.1: *Suppose that we have n different possible outcomes,* $Z_1, Z_2, \ldots, Z_n$. *Suppose that outcome* Z_i *occurs with probability* P_i, *where* $P_1 + P_2 + \cdots + P_n = 1$. *The **expected value** of* $Z_1, Z_2, \ldots, Z_n$ *is*

$$EV = P_1 \times Z_1 + P_2 \times Z_2 + \cdots + P_n \times Z_n.$$

In the case we are considering here, the expected value of the game is

$$EV = P \times 100{,}000 + (1 - P) \times 60{,}000.$$

If $P = 0.9$, then $EV = 0.9 \times 100{,}000 + 0.1 \times 60{,}000 = \$96{,}000$.

Exercise 1. Find the expected value of a prize worth \$200,000 with probability 0.2 and a prize worth \$15,000 with a probability of 0.8. What if the probabilities change to 0.8 for \$200,000 and 0.2 for \$15,000?

Before moving to whether this price is the right choice for the price of entering the game, it will be useful to look at the expected value as a function of probabilities.

If we are given values for the prizes (income) but are unsure of the probabilities, then we can treat EV as a function of the probability values. In the case of two different income values, the probability of one alternative is one minus the probability of the other. So if P is the probability of the first alternative, \$100,000, then $(1 - P)$ is the probability of the other alternative, \$60,000. We can write the following equation:

$$EV = P \times 100{,}000 + (1 - P) \times 60{,}000 = 60{,}000 + P \times 40{,}000.$$

Suppose that we want to graph this equation with the values of income on the horizontal axis and values of EV on the vertical axis. What will we get? First, we can plot two points, when $P = 0$ and when $P = 1$. The resulting graph is shown in Figure 13.1.

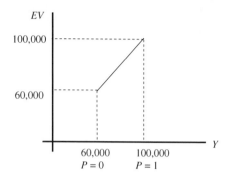

Figure 13.1   The graph of *EV* for values of *P* between 0 and 1.

When $P = 0$, $EV = 60,000$. When $P = 1$, $EV = 100,000$. As P moves from 0 to 1, we move in a linear fashion between the two points. For example, if $P = 1/2$, then $EV = 80,000$, and the corresponding value of Y is also at 80,000. This straight line is the expected value line.

Exercise 2. Show that as P goes from 0 to 1, EV is a straight line.
Exercise 3. Find the expected value for the following gambles:
   a. Prize 1 = $40,000 with probability 0.5, prize 2 = $20,000 with probability 0.5.
   b. Prize 1 = $60,000 with probability 0.6, prize 2 = $0 with probability 0.4.
   c. Prize 1 = $40,000 with probability 0.8, prize 2 = −$20,000 with probability 0.2.

The question is whether this amount, the expected value, is the appropriate choice for the price of the game. Is there reason to think that maybe the expected value is not a good choice?

One powerful example suggests that there is some danger here. The example is the St. Petersburg paradox; here is how it works. The player pays a fee to enter the game. Our job is to find the fee a player would pay; would the consumer pay the expected value of the game? Here is the game. A fair coin is flipped. If it comes up heads, you win $1 and the game is over. If the coin comes up tails, it is flipped again. If, on the second flip, a heads is revealed, you get $2 and the game is over. If the outcome is tails, the coin is flipped again. If it comes up heads, you get $4 and the game is over. If tails, there is another flip. In short, if the first heads appears on the kth flip, you will get 2^{k-1}.

To find the expected value, we need to know the probability of each outcome and the dollar value of each outcome. The probability of winning on the first flip is $1/2$ and the prize is $1. The probability of winning on the second flip is $1/4$ and the prize is $2. The probability of winning on the third flip is $1/8$ and the value of the prize is $4. You can see that the probability of winning on the kth flip is $(1/2)^k$. The value of the prize on the kth flip is 2^{k-1}. To find the expected value of the game, we find the sum of all these values. Hence, the expected value of the game is:

$$EV = \frac{1}{2} \times 1 + \left(\frac{1}{2}\right)^2 \times 2 + \left(\frac{1}{2}\right)^3 \times 2^2 + \cdots$$

$$= \frac{1}{2} + \frac{1}{2} + \frac{1}{2} + \cdots.$$

The expected value is infinite! Would you pay an infinite amount to play this game? I bet not! No one would! So what is the problem here? The problem is that we have used the dollar value of the prizes to measure the value to the player. As the prize doubles, the value of the prize doubles. But often we think that there are diminishing returns (more properly, diminishing marginal utility) so that if the prize doubles, the value of the prize does not double, but increases by a factor less than two. As the number of flips increases, the value of the prize grows more slowly than the actual dollar prize. What matters to the consumer is not the dollar amount, but some measure of the value of the dollar amount, say utility.

We can think of utility in the following way. Suppose we have some income numbers. The income can be spent on goods and services which provide utility. If the consumer has $100,000 in income, there is some utility associated with that level of income, $U(100,000)$. If the income is \$60,000, then there is some utility associated with that income, $U(60,000)$.

Definition 13.2: *Diminishing marginal utility occurs when the marginal utility falls as income (or the value of the prize) rises. If marginal utility is differentiable, then $MU'(\Upsilon) < 0$ is necessary and sufficient for diminishing marginal utility.*

Exercise 4. Does $U(X) = \sqrt{X}$ satisfy diminishing marginal utility? To find marginal utility, find the derivative of U. Now find the slope (derivative) of marginal utility. Is it negative or not? What do you find in this case?

Rather than look at expected value, perhaps we should look at expected utility. We turn now to that concept.

Definition 13.3: *Suppose that we have n different possible outcomes, $Z_1, Z_2, \ldots, Z_n$. The utility of each outcome is $U(Z_i)$. Suppose that outcome Z_i occurs with probability P_i, where $P_1 + P_2 + \cdots + P_n = 1$. The* **expected utility** *of $Z_1, Z_2, \ldots, Z_n$ is*

$$EU = P_1 \times U(Z_1) + P_2 \times U(Z_2) + \cdots + P_n \times U(Z_n).$$

Suppose that utility is the curved line shown in Figure 13.2, and that we have two levels of income possible, Υ_1 and Υ_2. The utilities associated with these incomes are $U(\Upsilon_1)$ and $U(\Upsilon_2)$, respectively. Where do we find expected utility? The answer depends on the values of the probabilities. In the graph below, $EU = (1-P) \times U(\Upsilon_1) + P \times U(\Upsilon_2)$. If $P = 0$, the consumer gets income Υ_1 with certainty. If $P = 1$, the consumer gets income Υ_2 with certainty. As P goes between 0 and 1, the consumer moves from Υ_1 to Υ_2. If $P = 1/2$, then the consumer would have expected income of $0.5 \times \Upsilon_1 + 0.5 \times \Upsilon_2$, halfway between Υ_1 and Υ_2. The expected utility would be $0.5 \times U(\Upsilon_1) + 0.5 \times U(\Upsilon_2)$, halfway between $U(\Upsilon_1)$ and $U(\Upsilon_2)$. Thus, the expected utility will lie on the straight line connecting the points $(Y_1, U(Y_1))$ and $(Y_2, U(Y_2))$; call this the expected utility line.

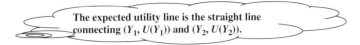

The expected utility line is the straight line connecting $(Y_1, U(Y_1))$ and $(Y_2, U(Y_2))$.

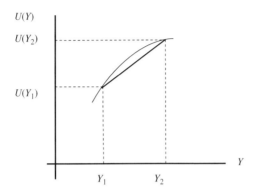

Figure 13.2 Expected utility is $(1 - P) \times U(Y_1) + P \times U(Y_2)$. If $P = 0$, we get Y_1 with certainty. If $P = 1$, we get Y_2 with certainty. If $P = 0.5$, expected Y is halfway between Y_1 and Y_2. Expected utility will be halfway between $U(Y_1)$ and $U(Y_2)$. In short, expected utility is on the straight line between $(Y_1, U(Y_1))$ and $(Y_2, U(Y_2))$.

In the case of St. Petersburg, the consumer determines the price to pay by paying a price equal to the expected utility. Suppose that we use the square root of income as the utility so that diminishing marginal utility of income holds. We would have the following value for this game:

$$EU = \frac{1}{2} \times \sqrt{1} + \frac{1}{4} \times \sqrt{2} + \frac{1}{8} \times \sqrt{4} + \frac{1}{16} \times \sqrt{8} + \frac{1}{32} \times \sqrt{16} + \frac{1}{64} \times \sqrt{32} + \cdots.$$

It may not be apparent to you that this sum is less than infinity. After all, there are an infinite number of terms to add. Suppose that we break the sum into two pieces. One piece is all the odd-numbered terms (the first term plus the third term plus the fifth term, and so on), and the other piece is the even-numbered terms (the second term plus the fourth term plus the sixth term, and so on). Focus on the first piece. If we take the odd-numbered terms, we get the following sum, S_1:

$$S_1 = \frac{1}{2} \times \sqrt{1} + \frac{1}{8} \times \sqrt{4} + \frac{1}{32} \times \sqrt{16} + \cdots = \frac{1}{2} + \frac{1}{4} + \frac{1}{8} + \cdots = 1.^1$$

Exercise 5. Use the formula in footnote 1 to show that S_1 adds up to 1.

If we take the even terms, we get the sum S_2:

$$S_2 = \frac{1}{4} \times \sqrt{2} + \frac{1}{16} \times \sqrt{8} + \frac{1}{64} \times \sqrt{32} + \cdots$$

$$= \frac{1}{4} \times \sqrt{2} + \frac{1}{8} \times \sqrt{2} + \frac{1}{16} \times \sqrt{2} + \cdots.$$

S_2 is almost the same as S_1. In fact, we can get S_2 from S_1 by multiplying S_1 by $(1/2)\sqrt{2}$. Thus, we can find S_2:

$$S_2 = S_1(1/2) \times \sqrt{2} = 1 \times (1/2)\sqrt{2} = (1/2) \times \sqrt{2}.$$

Hence, $EU = S_1 + S_2 = 1 + \frac{\sqrt{2}}{2} = 1.707$.

Exercise 6. Show that $S_2 = S_1 \times (1/2)\sqrt{2}$ by multiplying each term of S_1 by $(1/2)\sqrt{2}$. Do you get S_2 by this process?

Thus, the consumer would be willing to pay \$1.71 (in round terms) for the privilege of playing this game. That makes a lot more sense than an infinite payment! Would you pay \$1.71 to play this game? Obviously, the amount one would pay depends on one's utility function. Choose another utility function and get a different price for the game.

We see that by using expected utility rather than expected value, we have found a more reasonable answer to the St. Petersburg paradox. If we account for diminishing marginal utility of income, the expected

---

[1] S_1 is a geometric series. $S_1 = a + a^2 + a^3 + a^4 + \cdots$, where $a = 1/2$. It is well known that for $a < 1, a + a^2 + a^3 + a^4 + \cdots$ adds up to $a/(1-a)$. For $a = 1/2$, $S_1 = (1/2)/(1-1/2)$. What does S_1 turn out to be?

utility is a finite number compared to the infinite expected value. This suggests that we should focus on expected utility rather than expected value, at least in some settings.

What we need is some kind of utility function for the consumer. In the above example, we used the square root function for our utility function. Is that always the best choice? A lot depends on the particular consumer. What we know is that a linear function will not be successful in this setting; the linear function that we used for the original version $(U(Y) = Y)$ of St. Petersburg did not work.

It is also true that a lot depends on the value of the prizes. If the value of the prizes grows very quickly — say the prizes are 1, 2, 4, 16, 256, and so on, where the next term is the square of the previous term — then the square root utility function will not generate a finite expected utility for St. Petersburg. In that case, a different utility function would be needed if we hope to get a finite expected utility.

We argued in the St. Petersburg case that the utility should display diminishing marginal utility of income. Are there consumers for whom this is not a good representation of their preferences? Should the utility function bend up or bend down? Two possible cases are shown in Figure 13.3.

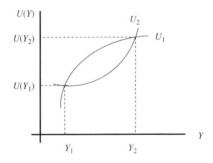

Figure 13.3 Is U_1 or U_2 a more reasonable choice for the utility function? Under U_2, we see that for levels of Y between Y_1 and Y_2, the utility is less than the expected utility.

Exercise 7. In Figure 13.3, which of the utility functions, U_1 or U_2, displays diminishing marginal utility? How do you know?

These two different shapes reveal two different kinds of behavior. How can we see the difference in behavior these two curves represent? Suppose that the consumer has a choice between income Y_1 with 50% probability and Y_2 with 50% probability, or the income of $(1/2)(Y_1 + Y_2)$ with certainty. How do we compare these two alternatives? The second is easy to represent. We find the utility of the income $(1/2)(Y_1 + Y_2)$. The income $(1/2)(Y_1 + Y_2)$ is halfway between Y_1 and Y_2, and we can find the utility of that amount from the utility function. This is shown in Figure 13.4 as $U\left(\frac{Y_1}{2} + \frac{Y_2}{2}\right)$. What about the alternative when the income is uncertain? We would use expected utility, $\frac{1}{2}U(Y_1) + \frac{1}{2}U(Y_2)$. We find this value on the straight line connecting $(Y_1, U(Y_1))$ with $(Y_2, U(Y_2))$, as shown in Figure 13.4. What does this U-shape tell us? We see in Figure 13.4 that $\frac{1}{2}U(Y_1) + \frac{1}{2}U(Y_2) > U\left(\frac{Y_1}{2} + \frac{Y_2}{2}\right)$. That means that if offered the choice between the two, this consumer would choose to gamble rather than take the certain outcome. This consumer is a risk lover. Note too that this utility function does not bend down as Y rises. That is, the second derivative of U is positive, not negative as required by diminishing marginal utility. Look now at Figure 13.5 where the other case is shown.

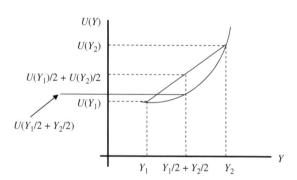

Figure 13.4 The values of utility are below the expected utility line, the straight line connecting the points $(Y_1, U(Y_1))$ and $(Y_2, U(Y_2))$. This consumer would rather take a gamble on whether he or she gets Y_1 or Y_2 than take income with certainty. This consumer is a risk lover.

In Figure 13.5, we show a utility function with diminishing marginal utility. To start the process of understanding, we construct the straight line between the points $(Y_1, U(Y_1))$ and $(Y_2, U(Y_2))$. This line shows the values of expected utility as we move from Y_1 to Y_2. In this case, the expected utility line lies below the utility curve. Thus, the expected utility is less than the utility of the middle income with certainty. This consumer would not choose to take the gamble, if offered, if the alternative is the expected income with certainty. This consumer is risk-averse. The diminishing marginal utility is the signature of risk aversion.

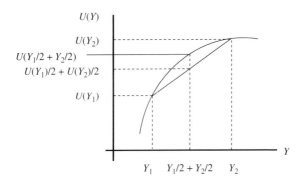

Figure 13.5 Here the values of utility are above the expected utility line, the straight line connecting the points $(Y_1, U(Y_1))$ and $(Y_2, U(Y_2))$. This consumer would rather take income with certainty than a gamble on the incomes Y_1 and Y_2. This consumer is a risk avoider, risk-averse.

Definition 13.4: *We say a consumer is **risk-averse** if for every pair of incomes, the utility function lies above the expected utility line.*

Definition 13.5: *We say a consumer is a **risk lover** if for every pair of incomes, the utility function lies below the expected utility line.*

Exercise 8. Suppose we have the following utility function: $U(Y) = Y^4$. Does it represent risk aversion or risk loving? How do you know?

Exercise 9. It was asserted above that in Figure 13.5, the utility
function displays diminishing marginal utility. How do
we know that? Where do you see marginal utility in the
graph? Does it diminish as Y rises?

Up to this point, we have pretty much assumed that a consumer
would act to maximize expected utility. We have done this based on
our earlier work where the consumer was a utility maximizer. It is easy
to assign utility to the various levels of income (or whatever the bundles
may be). But the question is: Will the consumer then act to maximize
expected utility? Will that action bring about the greatest satisfaction,
or is there some other process that the consumer should pursue? Perhaps the consumer should choose the alternative with the least risk or
possibly the one with the highest median utility. Von Neumann and
Morgenstern have provided an axiom system where choosing by maximizing expected utility provides the best outcome.[2]

Suppose we have a set of individual prizes, $Z_1, Z_2, \ldots, Z_n$. The consumer associates utility with each of these prizes, $U(Z_i)$. If the consumer is offered a set of prizes with probabilities associated with each
prize (a lottery ticket), what will the utility of this lottery ticket be?
The process used by Von Neumann and Morgenstern essentially con-
structs a utility function for each possible lottery ticket, and the utility
of the lottery ticket is expected utility. Hence, the consumer maximizing utility as constructed here will also be maximizing expected
utility.

We will maintain the assumption that consumers maximize expected
utility despite the fact that there are serious issues with the model,
and evidence that consumers do not behave as this assumption
requires.

---

[2]Von Neumann, John and Oskar Morgenstern, *Theory of Games and Economic Behavior*, Princeton University Press, Princeton, 1944. A readable introduction can be found
in R. Duncan Luce and Howard Raiffa, *Games and Decisions*, John Wiley & Sons,
New York, 1957.

> **Section Summary:**
> In this section, we have introduced the problem of consumer choice under uncertainty and have developed the basic framework of maximizing expected utility. We have also distinguished risk-averse from risk-loving utility functions. In the next section, we will apply the above to the case of insurance.

13.3 Insurance

In this section, we will look at consumers buying insurance. This is an application of the techniques we developed in Section 13.2.

Suppose that a consumer has an income of $64,000. The consumer also faces a 10% chance of serious illness in the next year, which would reduce income by $15,000 (the $15,000 is the reduction in income due to lost work plus medical expenses), leaving $49,000 of income to spend. Would the consumer be willing to buy insurance to protect against this possible loss? How would the insurance work? What would the insurance cost?

Suppose the consumer is offered full insurance, that is, insurance that pays for all of the loss; in this case, $15,000. If the consumer buys no insurance, then they have a 0.9 chance of income of $64,000 and a 0.1 chance for $49,000. The expected income is $0.9 \times \$64,000 + 0.1 \times \$49,000 = \$57,600 + \$4,900 = \$62,500$. Suppose now that the consumer purchases insurance and that the price of the insurance is the expected value of the loss. The loss would be $15,000, and occurs with a probability of 0.1. The expected loss is therefore $1,500. So the consumer pays $1,500 for insurance that pays $15,000 if the illness occurs. What does the consumer get for $1,500? If the consumer has no illness, then the income would be $62,500. If the consumer has the illness, then the income is $62,500. How did we get these? In the case of no illness, the income is what one would earn minus the cost of insurance, so $64,000 − $1,500 = $62,500. If the consumer has the illness, the income is what one would earn, $64,000, minus the cost of the insurance, $1,500, minus the cost of the illness, $15,000, plus the amount that the insurance pays because of the illness, $15,000. Thus, the consumer's income is $62,500 regardless of what happens. The uncertain situation has been converted to a certain situation, where the certain income is equal to the expected income in the uncertain situation.

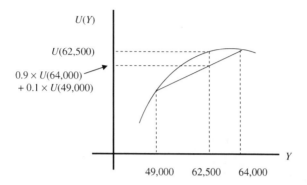

Figure 13.6   If the consumer is fully insured and pays $1,500 in insurance premium, then the consumer will get $62,500 income no matter what. The utility of that certain outcome lies above the expected utility line, so the consumer gains by buying insurance.

Again, in either case, the consumer would have an income of $62,500 with certainty. They would get utility of $U(62,500)$, as shown in Figure 13.6. If they do not buy insurance, they would have an expected utility of $0.9 \times U(64,000) + 0.1 \times U(49,000)$, which is on the straight line directly above $Y = 62,500$. The expected utility would be less than the certain utility with insurance, so the consumer would be willing to buy the insurance.

If we use the square root utility function, we can carry out some computations. In the case the consumer does not choose insurance, they would have expected utility as follows:

$$EU = 0.9 \times \sqrt{64,000} + 0.1 \times \sqrt{49,000}$$
$$= 0.9 \times 252.98 + 0.1 \times 221.36$$
$$= 227.68 + 22.14$$
$$= 249.82.$$

If the consumer chooses insurance, they would be in the certain situation with income of $62,500, and the utility would be 250 (the square root of 62,500). You can see that the utility with insurance beats the utility without insurance. Buying insurance makes sense in this setting.

We can see from Figure 13.7 that the consumer is willing to buy insurance that provides a certain income at least as large as Y'. Why is that? If the consumer does not buy insurance, they get $0.9 \times U(64,000) + 0.1 \times U(49,000)$ as shown on the $U(Y)$ axis. The consumer would be better off with a certain income of at least Y'. As long as the certain income provides as much utility as expected U, the certain income is preferred.

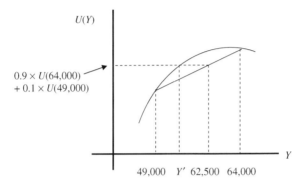

Figure 13.7 The consumer would pay an insurance premium up to $\$64,000 - Y'$ for full insurance. A higher premium would make their utility fall below the expected utility with no insurance and would not be chosen.

Exercise 10. What if the consumer (with a square root utility function) faces a situation where they either have an income of $\$100,000$ with probability 0.8 or income of $\$80,000$ with probability of 0.2? They could buy full insurance for $\$4,500$. Would the consumer be willing to do this?

Using the square root utility again, we can compute Y'. We know the consumer gets an expected utility with no insurance of 249.82. Thus, we would have $249.82 = \sqrt{Y'}$. To find Y', we would square both sides. Hence, $Y' = \$62,410$.

> Exercise 11. What is the most the consumer in Exercise 10 would pay for insurance?

The one problem with insurance as we have described it here is that there is some moral hazard. You might wonder what this is. In this case, once the insurance is purchased, the consumer has no incentive to do anything that might keep them from getting sick. They will have the same income whether they are sick or not. And the consumer might even be sicker than expected because they will get the same income, $62,500, regardless of what happens to them. How might the insurance company protect itself?

One way to protect itself would be for the insurance company to not offer full insurance, but to require a co-payment. Thus, the consumer pays, say, $1,000 for the insurance, but then the insurance company pays, say, 80% of the cost and the consumer pays the other 20%. In this scenario, the consumer then may have an incentive to avoid seeking too much health care and the incentive encourages the consumer to take better care of themselves.

Consider this example. Suppose that the consumer again has an income of $64,000 and that there is a 10% chance of an illness costing $15,000. Suppose that the consumer can get insurance that costs $1,000, but only covers 80% of the bill. Would the consumer be willing to buy this insurance?

If the consumer buys no insurance, we know that expected utility is $0.9 \times U(64,000) + 0.1 \times U(49,000)$. What if the consumer buys insurance? If the consumer is not sick, then the consumer would have $64,000 income minus the $1,000 for insurance, or $63,000 income. If the consumer is sick, they would have to pay $1,000 for insurance and 20% of the $15,000 that the illness costs. The consumer would have $64,000 - $1,000 - $3,000 = $60,000$. The consumer would have an uncertain income, and an expected utility of $0.9 \times U(63,000) + 0.1 \times U(60,000)$.

Using the square root utility function, we can compute the expected utility of each alternative to see which the consumer would choose.

If no insurance:

$$EU = 0.9 \times \sqrt{64{,}000} + 0.1 \times \sqrt{49{,}000}$$
$$= 0.9 \times 252.98 + 0.1 \times 221.36 = 249.82.$$

If insurance with co-pay:

$$EU = 0.9 \times \sqrt{63{,}000} + 0.1 \times \sqrt{60{,}000}$$
$$= 0.9 \times 251.00 + 0.1 \times 244.95 = 250.40.$$

The expected utility of income with the insurance is higher than the expected utility of income without insurance. Hence, the consumer buys insurance.

You can see in Figure 13.8 that the expected utility line with insurance is above the expected utility line without insurance.

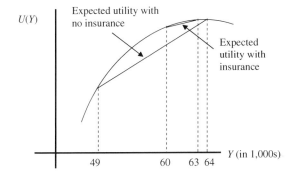

Figure 13.8   The expected utility with insurance is above the expected utility without insurance. Hence, the consumer would buy this insurance policy.

Section Summary:
In this section, we have examined the possibility that insurance could help to offset uncertainty. At the same time, we recognized that if there was full insurance, there would be an incentive for the consumer to behave badly. An alternative type of insurance was examined to help offset the bad incentive. In the next section, we examine the behavior of a firm facing a particular uncertainty.

13.4   The Firm under Uncertainty

We wish to consider how uncertainty can affect the firm's choices. You may recall that in the chapter on the long run, Chapter 9, one criticism of the model presented there was that the real problem in the long run is uncertainty. We wish to begin to address how a firm facing uncertainty would choose and how the results for the firm would be different than when uncertainty is not present.

Consider this world of two periods. The firm has to purchase capital in the first period, but it is not delivered until the second period. The firm pays for the capital in the first period, so the price of capital, r, is certain. What is uncertain is the price of output in the second period.[3] Suppose, though, that the firm is sure that the price of output will either be high (big), P_B, or low (tiny), P_T. The probability that the price is high is s and the probability that it is low is $(1 - s)$.

We will proceed using a rather standard game theory approach of solving the problem of maximizing profit in the second period if the price is high. In this setting, we pretend we know the amount of capital the firm has in the second period, and denote that amount by K. The firm then chooses the profit-maximizing value of labor, L; call it L_B. This L_B depends on the price of output, P_B, the wage, w, and the amount of capital the firm employs in the second period, K. However, this L_B only occurs s percent of the time. By the same process, we maximize profit in the second period if the price of output is low, P_T, by choosing the profit-maximizing quantity of labor, L_T. This quantity of labor depends on the price of output, P_T, the price of labor, w, and the amount of capital in the second period, K. This L_T would only occur $(1 - s)$ percent of the time. Now to determine the amount of capital, we maximize expected profit in the second period. In this expected profit, we know that s percent of the time we would have a high price yielding a quantity of labor L_B, which depends on the price of output, the wage, and the quantity of capital. We replace L in the

---

[3]What is uncertain is the price of output relative to the price of labor in the next period. But to keep things simple, we will assume that the price of labor in the next period is known with certainty, but the price of output is not.

profit function with this L_B function. We also know that $(1-s)$ percent of the time, the firm faces a low price and would want an amount of labor optimal for that price, L_T. This L_T is a function that depends on the price of output, the wage, and the quantity of labor. Expected profit will be

$$E\pi = s \times (\text{revenue if the price is } P_B \text{ as a function of } K - wL_B)$$
$$+ (1-s) \times (\text{revenue if the price is } P_T \text{ as a function of}$$
$$K - wL_T) - r \times K.$$

We then maximize expected profit by choosing K.

We can begin to approach the problem graphically using tools we developed in Chapter 10. There we learned that if profit is maximum, then the MRP must be equal to the price of the input. In the case the firm buys labor competitively and sells output competitively, the condition is $P \times MP_L = w$ where MP_L is the marginal product of labor. When the price of output is high, if profit is maximum, we would have $P_B \times MP_L = w$. Again, the marginal product of labor, MP_L, depends on the quantity of capital, K. If K changes, then MP_L would shift. We show the profit maximization outcome in Figure 13.9.

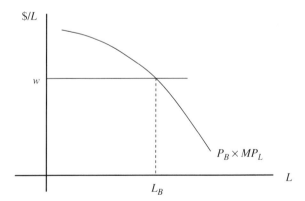

Figure 13.9   If the price of output is P_B, the MRP is $P_B \times MP$. Given the wage of w, the firm hires L_B. This quantity depends on the wage, w, and the amount of capital, K, which affects the position of the MP curve.

Exercise 12. In Figure 13.9, show what happens if there is an increase in the quantity of K. Assume that increases in K enhance labor productivity. How does this assumption bear on your answer?

Exercise 13. Suppose that P_B rises. Show what happens as a result in Figure 13.9.

In the case that the firm faces a low price of output, we have a similar graph, except that we are multiplying MP_L by P_T rather than P_B. The MP is the same curve, so $P_T \times MP_L$ will shift to the left as shown in Figure 13.10.

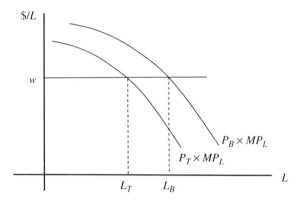

Figure 13.10 If the price of output is P_T, the MRP is $P_T \times MP$. Given the wage of w, the firm hires L_T. This quantity depends on the wage, w, and the amount of capital, K, which affects the position of the MP curve. Note that the change in price causes $P \times MP$ to shift, which changes the quantity of L.

Exercise 14. In Figure 13.10, should $P_T \times MP_L$ and $P_B \times MP_L$ be parallel? How do you know?

Exercise 15. In Figure 13.10, what happens to L_T and L_B if w rises?

What we have determined in the above are two functions, one for L_B and one for L_T. In each case, the L variable depends on w, K, and the price of output:

$$L_B = g_B(w, P_B, K).$$

$$L_T = g_T(w, P_T, K).$$

These are the profit-maximizing choices of L_B and L_T, given values of w, K, and the output prices. We now find expected profit by putting these expressions into the profit function. Suppose the production function is $X = f(L, K)$. We can now write profit as follows:

$$\pi_B = P_B \times f(L_B, K) - w \times L_B - rK$$

$$= P_B \times f(g_B(w, P_B, K), K) - w \times g_B(w, P_B, K) - rK.$$

$$\pi_T = P_T \times f(L_T, K) - w \times L_T - rK$$

$$= P_T \times f(g_T(w, P_T, K), K) - w \times g_T(w, P_T, K) - rK.$$

We can write expected profit as follows:

$$E\pi = s\{P_B \times f(g_B(w, P_B, K), K) - w \times g_B(w, P_B, K) - rK\}$$
$$+ (1-s)\{P_T \times f(g_T(w, P_T, K), K) - w \times g_T(w, P_T, K) - rK\}.$$

If we maximize this expression now for K, we get an expression that is essentially the following: expected price which also depends on the wage, w, $E(P, w)$, times marginal product of capital, MP_K, equals the price of capital, r.

$$E(P, w) \times MP_K = r.$$

You should be aware that $E(P, w)$ can be a very complicated function and not just the standard expected value. We show the outcome in Figure 13.11.

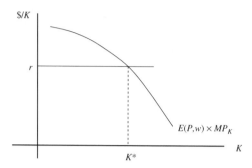

Figure 13.11   The firm chooses the quantity of capital based on the expected price and the marginal product of capital. This MP has had labor replaced by our expressions for labor in terms of output price, wage, and the quantity of capital.

Exercise 16.[4]   Suppose that the production function is $X = L^{1/3}K^{1/3}$ and that w is a constant.

a. Suppose that the price of output is P_B. Write out the profit for the firm in this case (assume that L is the only variable input). Find the profit-maximizing choice of L, L_B, by taking the derivative of profit with respect to L. Solve the resulting derivative for L_B.

b. Repeat part a using the price of output as P_T to obtain L_T. Solve the resulting expression for L_T.

c. Form profit using P_B and replace L in the production function with L_B that you found in part a; the variable input is K, whose price is r. Call this profit π_B. Now form profit using P_T and replace L in the production function with L_T obtained in part b; again, the variable input is K, whose price is r. Call this π_T. Expected profit is s times π_B plus $(1 - s)$ times π_T.

---

[4]This problem requires the use of partial derivatives, which may be an issue for some students. This problem can be skipped in that case.

d. Find the maximum of expected profit with respect to the variable K (i.e., take the derivative of expected profit with respect to K, set the derivative equal to zero, and solve for K). What do you get? This is the amount of capital the firm hires for the second period.

The outcome is that we have a solution to the problem. The firm will choose K^* units of capital in the first period. That quantity of capital will be in place in the second period so that when the price of output in the second period is revealed, the firm then hires the profit-maximizing quantity of labor. Note that K^* will not be the quantity the firm would choose if it knew with certainty that the price would be P_B or P_T. This is the main difference between the case of certainty and that of uncertainty.

It is hard to see what else the results say, but it is clear that if either output price rises, the firm will want to hire more capital. If the price of capital increases, the firm will want to reduce the amount of capital it hires. If the probability of the high-price outcome increases, the firm will want to hire more capital. Thus, many of the same kind of results hold under this model of uncertainty as would without uncertainty. But at the same time, the firm's choices will be different when uncertainty arises than if there were none.

This is not the only way we can approach uncertainty, and the results we obtain will depend on the particular way we model the uncertainty. But this model should give you a view different from the model we studied in Chapter 9, where the scale of plant was introduced as a variable in the long run, and we were certain about the future. In the model of this chapter, the fixed factor can be adjusted, only a period in the future, and here, uncertainty about the future plays a role where it did not in our earlier chapter.

> **Section Summary:**
> In this section, we have proposed a model where the firm faces uncertainty. In this case, the firm has to choose the amount of capital it will have before it knows the price of the output it will be selling. We have used the ideas we developed in Chapter 10 to aid in our discussion.

13.5 Cournot with Uncertainty

In this section, we will return to the case of Cournot (see Chapter 8) and ask what happens if there is some asymmetric information. Recall the case of Cournot, where each firm knows the market demand and the cost of production for both firms. We then proceeded to find the profit-maximizing choice for each firm, the best reply function, and then used those two best replies to find the optimal output choice for each firm. What if one firm knows both costs, but the other firm knows its own cost and is uncertain about the cost of the other firm's production? How will this change the problem? We attack that problem now.

For ease of exposition, we will assume that the demand is linear. Thus, we would have (the AR form of demand):

$$P = A - B(X_1 + X_2),$$

where X_1 is the amount firm 1 produces and X_2 is the amount firm 2 produces. Both A and B are positive constants, and P is the price. Firm 1 computes its revenue as $P \times X_1 = (A - B(X_1 + X_2)) \times X_1$. Firm 2 does a similar computation.

Suppose that each firm has a constant marginal cost, and that firm 2 knows the cost that it faces and the cost of firm 1. Firm 1 knows its own cost, but is uncertain about the cost that firm 2 faces. Firm 2 could have a high cost, C_{2H}, with probability s or a low cost, C_{2L}, with probability $1 - s$. We also assume that fixed costs are zero. If firm 2 has high costs, then it will produce output X_{2H}. If firm 2's costs are low, it will produce X_{2L}.

We can now write the profit for each firm. For firm 1, there is uncertainty about which X for firm 2 will show up in the revenue function. So firm 1 has an expected profit equation as shown:

$$\pi_1 = s\{(A - B(X_1 + X_{2H})) \times X_1 - C_1 X_1\}$$
$$+ (1 - s)\{(A - B(X_1 + X_{2L})) \times X_1 - C_1 X_1\}.$$

From the point of view of an outsider, we would not know which cost firm 2 actually had. We show the computation firm 2 would do for each possible cost, C_H and C_L. Hence, we would have the following:

$$\pi_{2H} = (A - B(X_1 + X_{2H})) \times X_{2H} - C_{2H} X_{2H}.$$
$$\pi_{2L} = (A - B(X_1 + X_{2L})) \times X_{2L} - C_{2L} X_{2L}.$$

We would have the following first-order conditions for these profit functions:

$$\frac{\partial \pi_1}{\partial X_1} = s\{(A - B(X_1 + X_{2H})) - BX_1 - C_1\}$$
$$+ (1 - s)\{(A - B(X_1 + X_{2L})) - BX_1 - C_1\} = 0.$$

$$\frac{\partial \pi_{2H}}{\partial X_{2H}} = (A - B(X_1 + X_{2H})) - BX_{2H} - C_{2H} = 0.$$

$$\frac{\partial \pi_{2L}}{\partial X_{2L}} = (A - B(X_1 + X_{2L})) - BX_{2L} - C_{2L} = 0.$$

We have, now, three equations with three unknowns. Solving the second and third for X_{2H} and X_{2L}, respectively, we obtain the following:

$$X_{2H} = \frac{A - BX_1 - C_{2H}}{2B}.$$
$$X_{2L} = \frac{A - BX_1 - C_{2L}}{2B}.$$

We may plug these into the first equation and solve for X_1:

$$X_1 = \frac{A - 2C_1 + (sC_{2H} + (1-s)C_{2L})}{3B}.$$

We could continue and find the values for X_{2H} and X_{2L}, but X_1 is a term of interest. Compare this with the result without uncertainty. In Chapter 8, we found

$$X_1 = \frac{A - 2C_1 + C_2}{3B}.$$

Now, C_2 is replaced by expected $C_2, sC_{2H} + (1-s)C_{2L}$. We can see there is a pretty simple alteration in the outcome for this model. The point is that when we have some uncertainty, the outcomes will be different, and the actors need to take into consideration the uncertainty. The simple replacement of C_2 with its expected value works in this case, but is not always the appropriate way to proceed. If the objective function, utility, cost, or the production function is essentially linear, the replacement by expected value will work as in the case of Cournot, where the cost function was linear. If cost had been $C_1 X_1^2$, then a simple replacement by expected value would not work. You saw in the last section that in the case of the firm hiring capital under uncertainty, the outcome was not a simple replacement by the expected value, but something more complicated due to the nature of the production function.

Section Summary:
In this section, we have looked at how the Cournot model is affected by the possibility that one firm is uncertain of the cost of the other firm. In this case, we see that the firm's decision is changed by replacing the certain output of the other firm with the expected output. Replacing the certain variable is not always the correct way to proceed, but it works in this case.

13.6   Summary

This chapter has dealt with the possibility that some uncertainty arises in an economic actor's decision process. We have looked at the case of the consumer, the firm, and also the Cournot duopoly. Much more has been done in this area than is reported here. Here is what we learned:

A. Consumers may maximize expected utility.
B. Expected utility can be used in the choice of insurance.
C. For the firm's choices under uncertainty in the choice of capital, the result is different from what we would get in the long-run analysis.
D. When uncertainty enters the Cournot case, we end up with a solution different from the case with certainty.

Terms Defined:

- Expected value
- Expected utility
- Diminishing marginal utility
- Risk-averse
- Risk lover

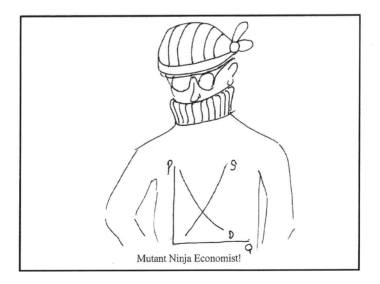

Mutant Ninja Economist!

"That's the thing about economists. They <u>look</u> like normal people!"

Glossary

A

An ***allocation of resources*** is

a. the quantity of coconuts and fish produced, C^* and F^*.
b. the division of coconuts and fish between Robinson and Zelda, $(C_R^*, F_R^*), (C_Z^*, F_Z^*)$.
c. a division of the labor and capital devoted to the production of each good, $(L_C^*, K_C^*), (L_F^*, K_F^*)$.

Allocative efficiency occurs when $\dfrac{P_x}{MSC_x} = \dfrac{P_y}{MSC_y}$.

Average revenue (AR) is a relationship between output and dollars per unit of output showing total revenue per unit of output.

The ***average total cost*** (ATC) is a relationship between output and dollars per unit of output showing the total cost per unit of output at each output.

B

The ***best reply function*** (BRF) (sometimes called a reaction function or best response) tells the optimal (profit-maximizing) output to produce for a firm, given the output of the other firm.

The set of all commodity bundles V so that $V \, R \, W$ is called the ***better than W*** set and is noted BT_W.

The *budget set* (or choice set) is the set of alternatives that the consumer can afford, the set bounded by the budget line and the two axes.

C

A *commodity bundle* is an amount of X and an amount of Y, written as (X, Y). A commodity bundle is an ordered pair.

By *competitive*, we mean that the chooser, whether buyer or seller, cannot affect the price.

A *competitive equilibrium (Crusoe economy)* is a set of prices, P^* and w^*, and quantities, C^* and L^*, so that

a. Robinson maximizes utility at (L^*, C^*) given P^* and w^*, subject to the budget.
b. Robinson maximizes profit at (L^*, C^*) given P^*, w^*, and the production function.
c. at P^* and w^*, both the L market and the C market clear.

A *competitive equilibrium with production* is a set of prices, (P_C^*, P_F^*, w^*, r^*), and an allocation of resources, $\{(C^*, F^*), (C_R^*, F_R^*), (C_Z^*, F_Z^*), (L_C^*, K_C^*), (L_F^*, K_F^*)\}$, so that the following conditions are met:

a. Robinson maximizes utility at (C_R^*, F_R^*) given the prices, (P_C^*, P_F^*), and his endowment of labor and capital, (L_R^0, K_R^0).
b. Zelda maximizes utility at (C_Z^*, F_Z^*) given the prices, (P_C^*, P_F^*), and her endowment of labor and capital, (L_Z^0, K_Z^0).
c. Robinson, producing C, maximizes profit at C^* while using (L_C^*, K_C^*) resources at the given prices, (P_C^*, P_F^*, w^*, r^*).
d. Zelda, producing F, maximizes profit at F^* while using (L_F^*, K_F^*) resources at the given prices, (P_C^*, P_F^*, w^*, r^*).
e. At (P_C^*, P_F^*, w^*, r^*), the excess demand for each good and each resource is zero, so $C^* = C_R^* + C_Z^*$, $F^* = F_R^* + F_Z^*$, $L_R^0 + L_Z^0 = L_C^* + L_F^*$, and $K_R^0 + K_Z^0 = K_C^* + K_F^*$.

A production function displays *constant returns to scale* if at all combinations of inputs, a doubling of inputs exactly doubles output.

Consumer surplus is the value the consumer places on the good, the demand price, minus the price the consumer pays for the good for all units consumed.

We say a function is *continuous* if the curve can be drawn without lifting our pencil from the paper.

The *contract curve* (*conflict curve*) is the set of all Pareto optimal outcomes.

Suppose that we have a logical statement "If A, then B." The *contrapositive* of this statement is a logical statement "If not B, then not A."

Suppose that we have a logical statement "If A, then B." The *converse* of this statement is a logical statement "If B, then A."

We say a set is *convex* if the straight-line segment connecting any two points in the set stays within the set, possibly on the boundary.

D

A production function displays *decreasing returns to scale* if at all combinations of inputs, a doubling of inputs less than doubles output.

Demand is a relationship between price and quantity, and shows the number of units of a good an individual would choose at each price with all else not changing.

The *demand for labor* relates the quantity of labor with dollars per unit of labor, and shows the quantity of labor the firm would hire at each wage with all other prices and technology held fixed.

If a function has a slope at a point, we say the slope is the *derivative* of the function at that point, and we note the derivative as $f'(X)$.

We say a curve is *differentiable at X_0* if the curve has a slope at X_0. Furthermore, if a curve has a slope at each point, we say that the *curve is differentiable*.

Diminishing marginal utility occurs when the marginal utility falls as income (or the value of the prize) rises. If marginal utility is differentiable, then $MU'(Y) < 0$ is necessary and sufficient for diminishing marginal utility.

E

An input state S is *efficient* if there is no input state more efficient than S.

An *efficient mix of outputs* is a combination of goods on the production possibilities (C^*, F^*) and a Pareto optimal division of that combination, $\{(C_R^*, F_R^*), (C_Z^*, F_Z^*)\}$, so that there are no other combinations of goods that could make at least one consumer better off without harming the other.

We say that demand is *elastic* if $\varepsilon > 1$. We say that demand is *inelastic* if $\varepsilon < 1$. We say that demand is of *unitary elasticity* if $\varepsilon = 1$.

By an *equilibrium*, we mean a value of a variable at which there is no force acting on the variable to cause it to change.

Excess demand for good X (ED_x) relates price and quantity of the good X, and shows the quantity demanded of the good X minus the quantity supplied of X at each price with other factors held fixed.

Suppose that we have n different possible outcomes, $Z_1, Z_2, \ldots, Z_n$. The utility of each outcome is $U(Z_i)$. Suppose that outcome Z_i occurs with probability P_i, where $P_1 + P_2 + \cdots + P_n = 1$. The *expected utility* of $Z_1, Z_2, \ldots, Z_n$ is

$$EU = P_1 \times U(Z_1) + P_2 \times U(Z_2) + \cdots + P_n \times U(Z_n).$$

Suppose that we have n different possible outcomes, $Z_1, Z_2, \ldots, Z_n$. Suppose that outcome Z_i occurs with probability P_i, where $P_1 + P_2 + \cdots + P_n = 1$. The *expected value* of $Z_1, Z_2, \ldots, Z_n$ is

$$EV = P_1 \times Z_1 + P_2 \times Z_2 + \cdots + P_n \times Z_n.$$

F

A *function* is a relationship between two sets of variables — X, the domain, and Y, the range — where, for each element in the domain, there is one and only one corresponding element in the range. We write $Y - f(X)$.

G

A good is *Giffen* if the demand for the good is positively sloped.

I

The *income effect* is that part of the movement along demand due to a change in real income with relative prices held fixed. We denote the income effect as $\frac{\Delta X}{\Delta I}|$ *relative prices fixed*.

A production function displays *increasing returns to scale* if at all combinations of inputs, a doubling of inputs more than doubles output.

The set of all commodity bundles the consumer finds indifferent to W is called the *indifference curve* through W.

Let W and V be commodity bundles. We say that a consumer is *indifferent* between W and V if $V\,R\,W$ and $W\,R\,V$, and we write $W\,I\,V$ (or $V\,I\,W$).

A good is *inferior* if the income effect is negative.

We say that demand is *infinitely elastic* if ε is infinite.

We say that demand is *infinitely inelastic* if ε is zero.

An *input combination* is a quantity of labor and a quantity of capital. We denote the input combination as an ordered pair, (L, K).

An *input state* is a division of capital and labor between the two producers, $\{(L_C, K_C), (L_F, K_F)\}$.

The *intersection* of two sets A and B is a set whose elements are all the elements that are in both set A and set B.

The *isocost* is all combinations of L and K that cost exactly E dollars.

The X_0 *isoquant* is all combinations of L and K that produce X_0 units of output.

L

The **Law of Diminishing Returns** states that as we add more of a variable factor to fixed factors, eventually the marginal product of the variable factor will begin to decrease as the variable factor is increased. [See also definition 4.8 in Chapter 4.]

An input state S' is **less efficient** than the input state S if, under S', the output of at least one good is less than under S and the output of no good is more than under S.

Let W and V be two commodity bundles. We say V is **less than** W if V has no more of any good than W and less of some good.

Let $W = (X_1, Y_1)$ and $V = (X_2, Y_2)$. We say that W is **lexicographically preferred** to V if $X_1 > X_2$ and we write $W L V$. We say that V is lexicographically preferred to W if $X_2 > X_1$ and we write $V L W$. If $X_1 = X_2$, we say that W is lexicographically preferred to V if $Y_1 > Y_2$ ($W L V$) or V is lexicographically preferred to W if $X_1 = X_2$ and $Y_2 > Y_1$ ($V L W$).

A **logical statement** (*or a statement, or a proposition*) means a statement that starts with "If ..." and has a following "then ...."

At each output, the **long-run average total cost** (LRATC) is the minimum, for all possible scales of plant, of the short-run average total costs.

We say the firm is in **long-run equilibrium** if there are no forces causing the firm to wish to change output or scale of plant.

The **long-run marginal cost** (LRMC) relates output and dollars per unit of output, and shows the change in LRTC due to a change in output at each output.

The **long-run total cost** (LRTC) relates output and dollars, and shows long-run average total cost times output at each output.

M

The *marginal cost* (MC) is a relationship between output and dollars per unit of output showing the change in total cost due to a change in output at each level of output.

The *marginal input cost* (MIC) relates a variable input and dollars per unit of variable input, and shows the change in cost associated with hiring an additional unit of the variable input, all else held fixed.

The *marginal product* of a variable input is a relationship between a variable input and output showing the change in output due to a change in the variable input with all other inputs held fixed. We denote the marginal product by MP_L when L is the variable input.

Marginal revenue (MR) is a relationship between output and dollars per unit of output showing the change in total revenue due to a change in output at each level of output.

Marginal revenue product (MRP) is a relationship between labor and dollars per unit of labor showing the change in total revenue that occurs when an added unit of labor is hired at each quantity of labor with the quantity of all other inputs held fixed.

Marginal social cost (MSC) is the cost to society of producing an added unit of output.

The *marginal social willingness to pay* of a given quantity is the sum of the willingness to pay for that quantity plus the value of the externality of that quantity.

The *marginal utility* relates the consumption of a good, X, and utility, and shows the change in utility when X changes, with the consumption of all other goods held constant. We denote marginal utility by MU_x, where the subscript X is the good whose consumption is changing, or by $\frac{\Delta U}{\Delta X}$.

The *marginal willingness to pay or demand price* of quantity X_1 is the price on the demand curve at quantity X_1.

Market demand is the sum of the quantities demanded by all consumers at each price, with all else not changing.

Market supply is a relationship between price and quantity, and shows the number of units of a good all firms would produce at each price with all else fixed.

We say that a function $f(X)$ has a ***maximum*** at the point X_0 if for all X near X_0, $f(X_0) \geq f(X)$. We say that a function $f(X)$ has a ***minimum*** at the point X_0 if for all X near X_0, $f(X_0) \leq f(X)$.

An input state S is ***more efficient*** than the input state S' if, under S, the output of at least one good is greater than under S' and the output of no good is smaller than under S'.

When we say that ***more is preferred to less***, we mean that for any bundle W that is more than a bundle V, W is strictly preferred to V.

Let W and V be two commodity bundles. We say W is ***more than*** V if W has at least as much of every good as V and more of some good.

N

A ***Nash equilibrium*** is a combination of outputs, one for each firm, so that once we have the Nash equilibrium, neither firm has an incentive to change output. That is, each firm is maximizing profit given the output of the other firm.

P

Let S and S' be two PTESs. We say that S' is ***Pareto inferior*** (PI) to S if both consumers like S' no better than S and at least one consumer is strictly worse off at S'.

A PTES S is ***Pareto optimal*** if there is no state Pareto superior to S.

Let S and S' be two PTESs. We say that S is ***Pareto superior*** (PS) to S' if both consumers like S at least as much as S' and at least one consumer likes S strictly better than S'.

Let W, V, and S be commodity bundles. Let R be a relationship between two commodity bundles. R is read as "is at least as preferred as." If R satisfies the following three properties, we say R is a **preference relation**:

a. Completeness — For any two bundles, W and V, either $W\ R\ V$ or $V\ R\ W$ or both.
b. Transitivity — For any three bundles, W, V, and S, if $W\ R\ V$ and $V\ R\ S$, then $W\ R\ S$.
c. Reflexivity — For each bundle W, $W\ R\ W$ must hold.

The **price elasticity of demand** is the percentage change in quantity demanded divided by the percentage change in price; we will use ε to stand for elasticity.

Price/MSC is the change in value to society due to changing the spending by one dollar on the resources devoted to the production of the good. We will call this the change in social satisfaction.

Producer surplus is the price the producer receives for the good minus the value the firm places on the good for all units sold.

The **production function** tells the maximum output that can be produced at each input combination.

Production possibilities relates coconuts and fish and tells, for each quantity of fish, the maximum quantity of coconuts that can be produced in this economy given resources and technology.

We say a firm is **productively efficient** if it produces at the minimum cost per unit, the minimum of the average total cost.

Profit (π) is a relationship between output and dollars showing the total revenue minus the total cost at each output.

A **pure trade competitive equilibrium** (PTCE) is a set of prices, P_C and P_F, and a pure trade economic state, $\{(C_R^*, F_R^*), (C_Z^*, F_Z^*)\}$, so that the following three conditions are true:

a. Robinson maximizes utility at (C_R^*, F_R^*) given the prices and his initial endowment.
b. Zelda maximizes utility at (C_Z^*, F_Z^*) given the prices and her initial endowment.

c. The quantity of coconuts demanded by Robinson and Zelda equals $\overline{C}$ at P_C (i.e., $C_R^* + C_Z^* = \overline{C}$), and the quantity of fish demanded by Robinson and Zelda equals $\overline{F}$ at P_F (i.e., $F_R^* + F_Z^* = \overline{F}$). Markets clear, and excess demand is zero.

A *pure trade economic state* (PTES), S, is a division of C and F between the two consumers, $S = \{(C_R, F_R), (C_Z, F_Z)\}$. We require that $C_R + C_Z \leq \overline{C}$ and $F_R + F_Z \leq \overline{F}$.

Q

The *quantity demanded* is the quantity all consumers together would choose at a specific price given all determinants.

The *quantity supplied* is the quantity all firms together would produce at a specific price given all determinants.

R

We say that the *ratio of relative prices* (the relative price ratio or relative prices) is the ratio of the price of X to the price of Y, P_x/P_y.

We say a consumer is *risk-averse* if for every pair of incomes, the utility function lies above the expected utility line.

We say a consumer is a *risk lover* if for every pair of incomes, the utility function lies below the expected utility line.

S

We say that two bundles represent the *same real income* if they are on the same indifference curve, have the same utility.

The *scale of plant* for a firm is the choice of a particular short-run capacity for production, X_c, which is the output where the SRATC has its minimum.

Suppose $f(X)$ is a function. The *second derivative of $f(X)$*, denoted $f''(X)$, is the derivative of the first derivative of $f(X)$.

A *set* is a collection of elements with a common feature.

We say a curve has a *slope* at the point X_0 if there is a straight line tangent to the curve at X_0, and the slope of the curve at X_0 is the slope of the straight line.

The *slope of a straight line*, m, is the rise over the run.

The *slope of demand* is the amount that the quantity demanded changes when there is a change in the price of the good. We denote the slope as $\frac{\Delta X}{\Delta P_x}$.

A set is *strictly convex* if the straight-line segment connecting any two points stays strictly inside the set except possibly at the end points.

We say that W is *strictly preferred* to V if $W\,R\,V$ and not $V\,R\,W$. We write $W\,P\,V$.

The *substitution effect* is that part of the movement along demand due to a change in relative prices with real income held fixed. We denote the substitution effect as $\frac{\Delta X}{\Delta P_x}\big|_{real\ income\ fixed}$.

Supply is a relationship between price and quantity showing the number of units of a good a firm would supply at each price with all else not changing.

The firm's *supply curve* is a relationship between output and dollars per unit of output showing the number of units a firm would choose to produce and sell at each price with input prices and technology not changing.

T

We say a straight line is *tangent* to a curve at a point where that straight line is the only straight line that touches the curve at the point, but does not intersect the curve at that point.

When we say that two curves (or a line and a curve) are *tangent*, we mean that the curves (the line and the curve) touch at a point and have the same slope at that point.

We say a firm is *technologically efficient* if they are producing on their production function.

Total cost (TC) is a relationship between output and dollars showing the sum of total fixed cost and total variable cost at each output.

Total fixed cost (TFC or FC) is a relationship between output and dollars showing the cost of the fixed factors at each output.

The *total input cost* (TIC) relates a variable input and dollars, and shows the cost of the input at each quantity of the input with all else held fixed.

Total product is a relationship between a variable input and output, and shows the output that can be produced at each quantity of the variable input with the other variable input held fixed. We denote total product of the variable input L when K is held fixed at K_0 as $TP_L(K = K_0)$.

Total revenue (TR) is a relationship between output and dollars showing price, P, times quantity sold, X.

Total revenue product (TRP) is a relationship between labor and dollars showing the total revenue the firm generates from the quantity of labor hired at each quantity of labor with the quantity of all other inputs held constant.

The *total variable cost* (TVC) is a relationship between output and dollars showing the minimum expenditure on variable inputs for each level of output with input prices and technology not changing.

The *total willingness to pay* for units up to X_1 is the area under the demand between the origin and X_1.

U

The *union* of two sets A and B is a set whose elements include all the elements of set A and all the elements of set B.

Utility is the assignment of real numbers, U, to commodity bundles so that the following rules are satisfied:

a. $U(W) \geq U(V)$ if $W\ R\ V$.
b. $U(W) = U(V)$ if $W\ I\ V$.

W

The set of all commodity bundles that W is at least as good as (all V so that $W\ R\ V$) is called the *worse than* W set and is noted WT_W.

Answers to Selected Exercises

Some Building Blocks

3.

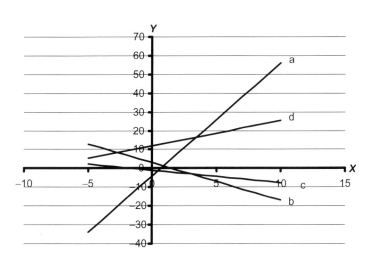

8. a. $f'(X) = 2X$.
   b. $f'(X) = 5X^4$.
   c. $f'(X) = \frac{1}{2}X^{\frac{-1}{2}}$.
   d. $f'(X) = 0$.
   e. $f'(X) = 2\pi X$.

9. a. $f'(X) = 7(100 - 5X)^6(-5) = -35(100 - 5X)^6$.

   b. $f'(X) = \frac{1}{2}(1.5 - 3X)^{-0.5}(-3) = \frac{-3}{2}(1.5 - 3X)^{-0.5}$.

   c. $f'(X) = \frac{-1}{2}(22 - 7.2X)^{-1.5}(-7.2) = (3.6)(22 - 7.2X)^{-1.5}$.

   d. $f'(X) = \frac{2}{3}(143 - 9.2X)^{\frac{-1}{3}}(-9.2)$.

12. a. $f''(X) = -210(100 - 5X)^5(-5) = 1050(100 - 5X)^5$.

   b. $f''(X) = \frac{-3}{2}\left(\frac{-1}{2}\right)(1.5 - 3X)^{-1.5}(-3)$

          $= \frac{-9}{4}(1.5 - 3X)^{-1.5}(-3)$.

   c. $f''(X) = (3.6)\left(\frac{-3}{2}\right)(22 - 7.2X)^{-2.5}(-7.2)$

          $= (38.88)(22 - 7.2X)^{-2.5}$.

   d. $f''(X) = \left(\frac{-1}{3}\right)\left(\frac{-18.4}{3}\right)(143 - 9.2X)^{\frac{-4}{3}}(-9.2)$

          $= \left(\frac{-169.28}{9}\right)(143 - 9.2X)^{\frac{-4}{3}}$.

15. The two propositions are essentially converses. Proposition A.13 says if $f(X)$ is maximum at X_0, then $f'(X_0) = 0$. Proposition A.15 says if $f'(X_0) = 0$ and $f''(X_0) < 0$, then $f(X)$ has a maximum at X_0. Note that in A.15, we need to add an additional condition to make the proposition true, so it is not an exact converse of A.13.

20. a. Contrapositive: If it does not rain, then I did not wash the car.

        Converse: If it rains, then I washed the car.

   b. Contrapositive: If I do not catch fish, then I did not go fishing.

        Converse: If I caught a fish, then I went fishing.

   c. Contrapositive: If I did not catch a fish and it was raining, then I did not go fishing.

        OR If I did not catch a fish and I went fishing, then it was not raining.

        Converse: If I catch a fish, then I went fishing and it rained.

d. Contrapositive: If I did not sprain my ankle, then I did not dance.

   Converse: If I sprained my ankle, then I went dancing.

Chapter 1

3. There are two ways to think about this problem, but they come to the same conclusion. One way is to see the cash award as an increase in income, so the demand for housing shifts right, to D'. As shown below, the price rises from P_1 to P_2 and quantity rises from Q_1 to Q_2. Note that the total price the consumer pays has gone up, but out of pocket, the consumer pays the price minus the $8,000, shown as P_3 in the graph. If the supply of housing is not vertical, then the price P_2 is not $8,000 higher than P_1. This has to be true: if the difference between P_2 and P_3 is $8,000, the difference between P_1 and P_2 cannot be $8,000.

   The second way to think about this problem is to see the cash award as a decrease in the price of the good, so we move along the original demand curve. This appears to the consumer to be an increase in supply, so the supply shifts down vertically by $8,000. In that case, we will end up at a price P_3 and quantity Q_2. The amount the consumer pays is P_3, but the amount the seller receives is $P_3 + \$8,000$. You can see we have the same outcome in either case.

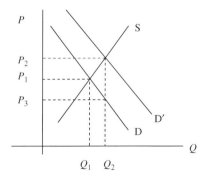

Chapter 2

1. Start with the budget equation, $M = P_x X + P_y Y$. We want to know the value of X when the line crosses the X-axis. To be on the X-axis, $Y = 0$ must hold. Put $Y = 0$ into the budget equation and solve for X:

$$M = P_x X + P_y 0$$
$$= P_x X$$
$$X = M/P_x.$$

4. Write the budget line in slope-intercept form:

$$Y = \frac{M}{P_y} - \frac{P_x}{P_y} X.$$

Income only appears in the intercept of the budget line, so a change in income affects the intercept, but not the slope. The budget line moves out parallel to itself.

6. The slope of the budget line is $-P_x/P_y$. The units of slope can be determined from the units of the prices. The price of X has units of $\$/X$, and the price of Y has units of $\$/Y$. Hence, the slope has units of $(\$/X)/(\$/Y) = \frac{\$}{X}\frac{Y}{\$} = \frac{Y}{X}$. This should not be a surprise as the slope is rise over run, and in our case, the graph is on an axis system with Y on the vertical axis and X on the horizontal axis. So rise is in units of Y, and run is in units of X.

9. To say that W is not indifferent to V, we mean that either $W\ R\ V$ and not $V\ R\ W$, which means $W\ P\ V$. Alternatively, "W is not indifferent to V" could mean $V\ R\ W$ and not $W\ R\ V$. But this is exactly $V\ P\ W$.

13. We need to show: If $W\ P\ V$ and $V\ P\ S$, then $W\ P\ S$. This requires showing $W\ R\ S$ and not $S\ R\ W$. We start with $W\ R\ S$. Because $W\ P\ V$ means $W\ R\ V$, and $V\ P\ S$ means $V\ R\ S$, then by the transitivity of R, we thus have $W\ R\ S$. We now need to show that if not $V\ R\ W$ and not $S\ R\ V$, then not $S\ R\ W$. The hint says try the contrapositive. The form suggested is: If not $V\ R\ W$ and $S\ R\ W$, then $S\ R\ V$. Not $V\ R\ W$ means $W\ R\ V$. So if we have $W\ R\ V$ and $S\ R\ W$, by the transitivity of R, we must have $S\ R\ V$, which is what we have to prove!

16. The only bundle that is both BT_W and WT_W is W. Thus, the indifference curve through W is exactly W and only W.

18.

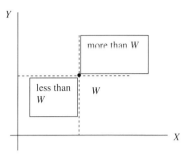

19. If W is not more than V, then W could be less than V (southwest of V), but W could also be northwest of V or southeast of V. In either of those cases, W would not be less than V. Hence, to say that W is not more than V does not mean that W is less than V.

24.

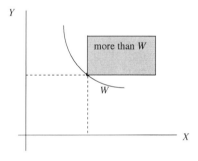

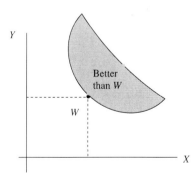

The bundles more than W are the bundles to the northeast of W. "More" means more of both commodities. The bundles better than W are those to the right of the indifference curve. So the "better than W" bundles are the "more than W" bundles and the bundles above the indifference curve that are not more than W.

26. The change in utility would be $MU_x \times \Delta X = 5 \times 0.3 = 1.5$.

29. To find the marginal utility of X, we hold Y constant at Y_1, and then ask how much utility changes if X changes by 1. In our graph, the marginal utility is $U_2 - U_1$ for the $X_1 + 1$ unit of X (given $Y = Y_1$).

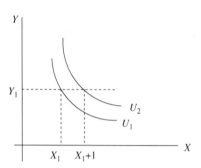

36. The converse is as follows:

If   a. assumptions 2.1 hold,
      b. the consumer has differentiable indifference curves,
      c. BT_W is strictly convex for each W,
      d. more is preferred to less,
      e. an indifference curve is tangent to the budget line at (X_0, Y_0),

Then f. utility is maximum given the budget at (X_0, Y_0).

Note that in e, we are assuming that (X_0, Y_0) is on the budget line, which accounts for why that statement does not appear in our discussion.

Normally, we do not expect the converse to be true, but in this case it is true. The key assumption is c, that BT_W is strictly convex.

To prove this, we would argue directly. We have (X_0, Y_0) with an indifference curve tangent to the budget line. The bundles preferred to (X_0, Y_0) are the bundles above the indifference curve, all of which are outside the budget set. Hence, there are no bundles preferred to (X_0, Y_0) in the budget set, so (X_0, Y_0) maximizes utility given the budget.

It should be clear that if assumption c does not hold, then the proposition need not be true.

43. a. Solve the budget constraint for Y to obtain $Y = \frac{M}{P_y} - \frac{P_x}{P_y}X$. Substitute this expression into the utility function to obtain this expression:

$$U = X^{\frac{1}{2}} + \left(\frac{M}{P_y} - \frac{P_x}{P_y}X\right)^{\frac{1}{2}}.$$

The derivative of this expression is as follows, which we set to zero.

$$U' = \frac{1}{2}X^{\frac{-1}{2}} + \frac{1}{2}\left(\frac{M}{P_y} - \frac{P_x}{P_y}X\right)^{\frac{-1}{2}}\left(\frac{-P_x}{P_y}\right) = 0.$$

We now use the rules of algebra to solve this. First, put the right-hand term on the other side of the equal sign, and multiply both sides by 2. Here is the result:

$$X^{\frac{-1}{2}} = \left(\frac{M}{P_y} - \frac{P_x}{P_y}X\right)^{\frac{-1}{2}}\left(\frac{P_x}{P_y}\right).$$

Multiply both sides by $X^{\frac{1}{2}}\left(\frac{M}{P_y} - \frac{P_x}{P_y}X\right)^{\frac{1}{2}}$, and we obtain the following:

$$\left(\frac{M}{P_y} - \frac{P_x}{P_y}X\right)^{\frac{1}{2}} = X^{\frac{1}{2}}\left(\frac{P_x}{P_y}\right).$$

Now square both sides:

$$\left(\frac{M}{P_y} - \frac{P_x}{P_y}X\right) = X\left(\frac{P_x}{P_y}\right)^2.$$

Solve for X:

$$\left(\frac{M}{P_y} - \frac{P_x}{P_y}X\right) = X\left(\frac{P_x}{P_y}\right)^2$$

$$\frac{M}{P_y} = \frac{P_x}{P_y}X + X\left(\frac{P_x}{P_y}\right)^2 = \left(\frac{P_xP_y + P_x^2}{P_y^2}\right)X$$

$$X = \frac{MP_y}{P_xP_y + P_x^2}.$$

That's it, the demand for X!!

44. Neither of these equations satisfies the requirement of homogeneity of degree zero in prices and income, which is what Exercise 41 requires. Multiply each price and income by k, and see that the value of X changes. This cannot happen if demand is derived from utility maximization given the budget.

Chapter 3

1. The relative price ratio is exactly the (negative of the) slope of the budget line.

5. If, in the time period from 1955 through 2005, we stayed on the same demand, then we might have a case. But because the demand and supply are both shifting, we cannot tell from this evidence whether housing is Giffen or not. Most likely housing is not a Giffen good.

6. The formula for elasticity can be restated as $\varepsilon = $ *slope of demand* $\times \frac{P_x}{X}$. If elasticity is exactly 1, then the formula says that the absolute value of the elasticity must be 1. Is there always such a point where this happens? As long as the slope is not infinite or zero, then there is. Our formula would become $1 = (-1) \times$ *slope of demand* $\times \frac{P_x}{X}$ or $\frac{X}{P_x} = (-1) \times$ *slope of demand*. The slope of demand is negative, so $(-1) \times$ *slope* is positive. The ratio X/P_x takes every value between 0 (if $X = 0$ and P_x is not zero, then X/P_x is zero) and infinity as X increases at some point ($P_x = 0$ and X is not zero, so the ratio X/P_x goes to infinity). Hence, there

is some point (X, P_x) on the demand so that demand is unitarily elastic.

9. $P_x X = M/2$. $X = M/(2 \times P_x)$. Because expenditure is constant along this demand, the demand must be unitarily elastic.

10. If the consumer's expenditure on X is the same for all prices of X, then $P_x X$ is constant. Given that M is constant, and $P_y Y = M - P_x X$, $P_y Y$ must also be constant, and therefore the demand for Y is also unitarily elastic.

Chapter 4

3. The equation of the isocost is $E = wL+rK$, where we are currently treating E, w, and r as constants. When put in slope-intercept form (solve for what is on the vertical axis!), we get $K = (E/r)-(w/r)L$. The terms E/r and w/r are constants in this formulation, and E/r is the K-intercept and w/r is the slope. Both are constant, so we have a straight line. To find the L-intercept, the point where the line crosses the L-axis, set $K = 0$ in the original equation to obtain $E = wL$. Solve for L so that $L = E/w$, the point where the line crosses the L-axis. Now if w falls, the K-intercept does not change but the L-intercept increases, so the isocost swings out around the K-intercept. If E rises, the slope of the isocost does not change but both the L- and K-intercepts do, so we know the isocost moves out parallel to itself.

5. In the graph, we cannot tell what happens to the expenditure by looking at the two points (L_1, K_1) and (L_2, K_2) because here K falls while L rises. But if we look at the intercept of the two lines, given that w and r did not change, we know that the higher intercept signifies higher expenditure on inputs. The intercepts tell the tale.

8. As long as MC is positive, the fact that MC falls only means that the TC rises at a slower rate.

9. If MC is constant, then the TC has a constant slope and is a straight line. If the TFC is zero, then TC starts at the origin and has a constant positive slope. The equation of TC is $TC = MC \times X$. If the TFC > 0, then the TC starts at the TFC and is a positively

sloped straight line from that point. The equation of TC would be $TC = MC \times X + TFC$ in this case. The ATC will be equal to the MC if TFC is zero (you can see this using the geometrical tools we have developed or by finding ATC from the formula of TC in this case). If $TFC > 0$, then the ATC will be decreasing for all X. Again use the geometrical tools to see this or compute ATC from the formula of TC in this case. You should get that $ATC = MC + (TFC/X)$.

17. The AFC is TFC/X. Because TFC is fixed, the AFC must fall as X rises.

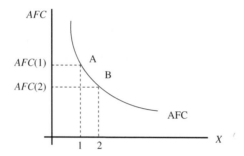

The area of the rectangle formed by going from the origin to 1 to A on the curve to $AFC(1)$ and back to the origin is the same as the area of the rectangle formed by going from the origin to 2 to B to $AFC(2)$ to the origin. Both rectangles have the area TFC. You can see this from the definition of AFC.

19. If $A(X_0)$ has a minimum, then $A'(X_0) = 0$ holds (see proposition A.13). The average marginal fact says $M(X_0) = A'(X_0) \times X + A(X_0)$. Because $A'(X_0) = 0$, $M(X_0) = A(X_0)$. Thus, $M(X_0)$ cuts $A(X_0)$ at the minimum of $A(X_0)$.

Chapter 5

1. The area under MR between X_1 and X_2 is $TR(X_2) - TR(X_1)$.
3. $TR(X) = P \times X$. The slope-intercept form would be $TR(X) = P \times X + 0$, where P is the constant price. So the line is straight with slope P.

6. The proposition we are trying to prove attempts to link the level of profit and how MR is related to MC. If we assume profit is maximum, how do we proceed? There is no obvious relationship between MR and MC. If we use the contrapositive — if MR and MC are not equal, then profit is not maximum — we cannot now assume that profit is maximum when MR equals MC; that is the proposition we are trying to prove.

9. The converse is:

If   a. least cost holds,
       b. MR and MC are continuous,
       c. MR = MC,
Then d. profit is maximum.

This statement is not generally true. In Figure 5.3, look at the output X_4 where MR = MC. If we increase output from this point, we see that MR > MC. Hence, we add more to total revenue than to total cost, and profit rises. Therefore, profit is not maximum at X_4.

10. In the short run, the firm has to pay its fixed cost no matter what it does. Hence, the fixed costs are irrelevant to its decision of whether to produce or not. Thus, the firm only need worry about covering its variable cost.

11. Well, this one is a surprise! We can tell. The shutdown condition says we need $P >$ AVC. Alternatively, we need $P \times X >$ AVC $\times X$ or TR > TVC. We can clearly see TR at X_0 from this graph; it is the rectangle $P \times X_0$. Where is TVC? By the fundamental theorem, the area under MC between X_1 and X_2 is $TC(X_2) - TC(X_1)$. Let $X_1 = 0$ and $X_2 = X_0$. By the fundamental theorem, then, the area under MC between 0 and X_0 is $TC(X_0) - TC(0)$. But $TC(0) =$ TFC. So we have the area under MC between 0 and $X_0 = TC(X_0) - $ TFC $= TVC(X_0)$. Hence, the area under MC between 0 and X_0 is $TVC(X_0)$. In Figure 5.4, because $P >$ MC for all X up to X_0, the area of TR must be greater than the area under MC, which is TVC. Therefore, this firm should not shut down.

15. To find the profit maximum, we set $MR = MC$. In this case, $MR = 79$ and $MC = X^2 - 50X + 655$:

$$79 = X^2 - 50X + 655$$
$$X^2 - 50X + 576 = 0$$
$$(X - 32)(X - 18) = 0.$$

$X = 32$ and $X = 18$ are the choices. To use the second derivative, we need to find the second derivative of profit. The derivative of profit is $MR - MC$. Hence, the second derivative of profit will be $MR' - MC'$:

$$\pi'' = MR' - MC' = 79' - (X^2 - 50X + 655)'$$
$$= 0 - (2X - 50)$$
$$= -2X + 50.$$

At $X = 32$, $\pi'' = -2(32) + 50 = -64 + 50 = -14$. At $X = 18$, $\pi'' = -2(18) + 50 = -36 + 50 = 14$. Hence, $\pi'' < 0$ when $X = 32$, so $X = 32$ is the maximum; and $\pi'' > 0$ when $X = 18$, so $X = 18$ is the minimum.

Chapter 6

2. If the consumer pays P_1 for the first unit, the MR is P_1. If the consumer pays P_2 for the second unit (the first unit still sells for P_1), the MR is P_2. Think about it this way: The total revenue of the second unit is $P_1 + P_2$. The total revenue of the first unit is P_1. Thus, the change in revenue when the second unit is sold is $P_1 + P_2 - P_1 = P_2$. For the third unit, the total revenue would be $P_1 + P_2 + P_3$. To find the marginal revenue, subtract the total revenue of the first two units, $P_1 + P_2$, and we are left with P_3. If we continue in this way, the marginal revenue is always equal to the price of the next unit, the AR. Hence, in this case, MR and AR are the same.
3. $TR = P \times X = (100 - 5X) \times X = 100X - 5X^2$.
$MR = TR' = 100 - 10X$.

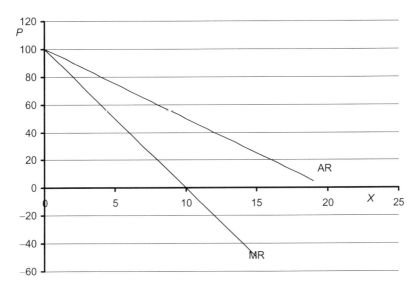

MR < P = AR at all X > 0.

4. If demand is elastic, expenditure rises as we move down demand. If demand is inelastic, expenditure falls as we move down demand. In this case, consumer expenditure is the firm's total revenue (because the firm is a monopoly). Therefore, if demand is elastic, we have that total revenue rises as X rises (we move down demand). Thus, MR > 0. If demand is inelastic, TR falls as X rises, and MR < 0 must hold. Hence, if MR > 0, demand is elastic. If MR < 0 (MR is below the X-axis), demand is inelastic.

9. As the answer to Exercise 4 suggests, the key factor is whether MR < 0 or MR > 0. If MR > 0, then as X rises, total revenue rises. If MR < 0, then total revenue falls as X rises. We can see this from the definition of MR:

$$MR = \frac{\Delta TR}{\Delta X}.$$

Because we move down demand, that is, we are moving to the right on the demand curve, X must increase. That means $\Delta X > 0$. So if MR > 0, $\Delta TR > 0$ must also hold, and TR rises. If MR < 0, $\Delta TR < 0$, and TR falls.

13. The iron laws of algebra!! Solve $P = 96 - 2X$ for X:

   Add $2X$ to both sides: $P + 2X = 96$.
   Subtract P from both sides: $2X = 96 - P$.
   Divide both sides by 2: $X = 48 - (1/2)P$!

14. a. We start by re-writing the demand as AR. $3X = 135 - P$, so $P = 135 - 3X$. Now write TR $= P \times X = 135X - 3X^2$. We can write profit as TR – TC:

$$\pi = 135X - 3X^2 - (1/3)X^3 + 10X^2 - 175X - 50.$$

   To find the profit maximum, we find the derivative of profit and set it to zero:

$$\pi' = 135 - 6X - X^2 + 20X - 175 = 0$$
$$= -X^2 + 14X - 40 = 0$$
$$(-X + 10)(X - 4) = 0$$
$$X = 10 \text{ or } 4.$$

   To find which one is the maximum, we find $\pi'' = -2X + 14$. When $X = 10$, the second derivative of profit is -6, which means $X = 10$ is a profit maximum. When $X = 4$, the second derivative of profit is 6, which means $X = 4$ is a profit minimum.
   Note that when $X = 10$, $P = 135 - 3 \times 10 = 135 - 30 = 105$.

   c. As in the previous case, we first re-write demand as AR. First multiply both sides by 5 and then add P to both sides of the equation. We get $5X + P = 625$. Now subtract $5X$ from both sides to get AR, $P = 625 - 5X$. Find TR $= 625X - 5X^2$. We can find profit as TR – TC:

$$\pi = 625X - 5X^2 - (1/3)X^3 + (15/2)X^2 - 601X - 30.$$

Find the derivative of profit and set it to zero to find the possible maximum values:

$$\pi' = 625 - 10X - X^2 + 15X - 601 = 0$$

$$-X^2 + 5X + 24 = 0$$

$$(-X + 8)(X + 3) = 0$$

$$X = 8 \text{ or } -3.$$

The second derivative of profit is

$$\pi'' = -2X + 5.$$

When $X = 8$, the second derivative is negative, so we have a maximum when $X = 8$. When $X = -3$, the second derivative is positive, which means $X = -3$ is a profit minimum.
    When $X = 8$, $P = 625 - 5 \times 8 = 625 - 40 = 585$.

15. In Exercise 14c, MC is the derivative of TC. Hence, MC $= X^2 - 15X + 601$. AR $= 625 - 5X$. If we set these equal to each other, we can solve for X:

$$X^2 - 15X + 601 = 625 - 5X$$

$$X^2 - 10X - 24 = 0$$

$$(X - 12)(X + 2) = 0$$

$$X = 12 \text{ or } -2.$$

So we have the quantity where the MC = demand, and we can take $X = 12$ as the relevant answer (a negative X does not make sense). If $X = 12$, $P = 625 - 5 \times 12 = 625 - 60 = 565$. This is the competitive solution. We find that the competitive quantity is 12, whereas the monopoly quantity is 8. The competitive price is 565, while the monopoly price is 585. So competition produces more and has a lower price than we would have under monopoly.

Chapter 7

2. This question is most easily addressed with a graph. Here is the situation:

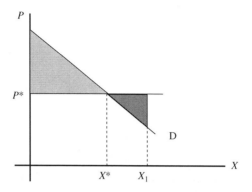

The consumer is paying P^* and consuming X_1. If we stopped at X^*, the consumer surplus would be, as always, the area above P^* and below the demand from the origin to X^*; this is shown in the light gray area. But now we have to make an adjustment. The consumer is forced to buy units worth less than the price the consumer must pay. The units between X^* and X_1 have a value less than P^*. Thus, we have to subtract the area below P^* and above demand between X^* and X_1 from the original consumer surplus; this is the dark gray area. Hence, the consumer surplus is the net of the light gray area minus the dark gray area.

5. Again, this question is most easily approached with a graph:

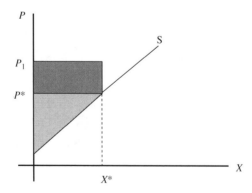

In this case, the firm gets the usual producer surplus, the triangle above the supply and below P^* up to X^*. This is shown in light gray. But the firm also gets a price above P^*, and therefore also gets the surplus in the area from P^* up to P_1 from zero output to X^*, shown in dark gray.

7. If assumptions 7.7 hold and for each pair of goods X and Y we have $\frac{P_x}{MSC_x} = \frac{P_y}{MSC_y}$, then the satisfaction to society is maximum.

10. Here is the argument. Suppose that $\frac{P_x}{MSC_x} > \frac{P_y}{MSC_y}$. Reduce expenditure on inputs for Y by \$1. Output of Y falls by $1/MSC_y$. The satisfaction of society falls by P_y/MSC_y. Take the \$1 of resources and apply to X. The output of X rises by $1/MSC_x$, and the satisfaction of society rises by P_x/MSC_x. Because $\frac{P_x}{MSC_x} > \frac{P_y}{MSC_y}$, we gain more satisfaction than we give up, so total satisfaction rises.

When Y falls, MSC_y falls and now, because the slope of demand is negative, smaller quantities of Y mean that the price of Y rises. So the ratio P_y/MSC_y has to rise as the numerator rises and the denominator falls. Similarly, as X rises, MSC_x rises and now the price of X falls. Hence, the ratio P_x/MSC_x falls because the numerator falls and the denominator rises. Thus, the two sides move toward equality.

14. Again, graphs are the key.

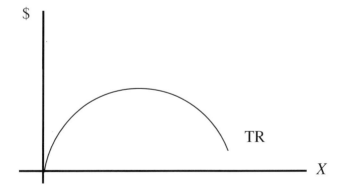

This is the shape of TR for a monopoly. If we now look at the total revenue with only the price ceiling, we would have the following graph:

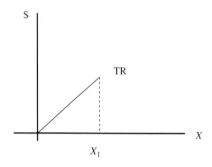

Because the price is constant under the price ceiling, TR is a straight line from the origin up to X_1, when the price ceiling is no longer effective. If we combine the two graphs, we end up with the following:

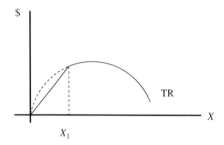

Thus, total revenue is now a straight line up to X_1 and then follows the original TR for output greater than X_1.

20. In this case, TR $= 176X - 5X^2$. Thus, profit is as follows:

$$\pi = 176X - 5X^2 - (1/3)X^3 + 5X^2 - 140X - 100.$$

Find the derivative of profit and set it to zero to find the possible profit-maximizing outputs:

$$\pi' = 176 - 10X - X^2 + 10X - 140 = 0$$
$$-X^2 + 36 = 0$$
$$X = 6 \text{ or } -6.$$

To distinguish the maximum from the minimum, look at the second derivative of profit:

$$\pi'' = -2X.$$

So $X = 6$ is the maximum and $X = -6$ is the minimum.

21. MC for this firm is $X^2 - 10X + 140$. Set this equal to $176 - 5X$ and solve for X:

$$X^2 - 10X + 140 = 176 - 5X$$
$$X^2 - 5X - 36 = 0$$
$$(X - 9)(X + 4) = 0$$
$$X = 9 \text{ or } -4.$$

In this case, we can reject $X = -4$ as a possible answer. If $X = 9$, $P = 176 - 5 \times 9 = 176 - 45 = 131$.

24. a. TR $= 200X - 10X^2$. MR $= 200 - 20X$.
    b. MR $=$ MC requires the following:

$$200 - 20X = 180/X.$$

Multiply both sides by X:

$$200X - 20X^2 = 180.$$

Divide by 20:

$$10X - X^2 = 9.$$

Solve for X:

$$-X^2 + 10X - 9 = 0$$
$$(-X + 9)(X - 1) = 0$$
$$X = 9 \text{ or } 1.$$

Check the second derivative of profit:

$$\text{MR} - \text{MC} = 200 - 20X - 180X^{-1}$$
$$(\text{MR} - \text{MC})' = -20 + 180X^{-2}.$$

For $X = 1$, the second derivative of profit is

$$-20 + 180/1^2 = -20 + 180 = 160.$$

This is positive, so $X = 1$ is a profit minimum.
When $X = 9$, the second derivative of profit is

$$-20 + 180/9^2 = -20 + 2.222.$$

This is negative, so $X = 9$ is a profit maximum.
$P = 200 - 10X = 200 - 10 \times 9 = 200 - 90 = 110$. So the profit-maximizing output and price are $(9, 110)$.

c. Here we want $200 - 10X = 180/X$. Solve for X:

$$200X - 10X^2 = 180.$$

Divide both sides by 10:

$$20X - X^2 - 18 = 0$$
$$-X^2 + 20X - 18 = 0.$$

To solve this, we need the quadratic formula:

$$X = \frac{-20 \pm \sqrt{400 - 72}}{-2} = \frac{-20 \pm \sqrt{328}}{-2}$$
$$= \frac{-20 \pm 18.11}{-2}$$
$$= 19.055 \text{ or } 0.945.$$

So if we use $X = 19.055$, the corresponding price will be $200 - 10 \times 19.055 = 9.45$.

Chapter 8

1. $TR_2 = P \times X_2 = (A - B(X_1 + X_2)) \times X_2.$
3. $\pi_2 = (A - B(X_1 + X_2)) \times X_2 - C_2 X_2.$

7. We have $X_1 = \frac{A - 2C_1 + C_2}{3B}$ and $X_2 = \frac{A - 2C_2 + C_1}{3B}$. Profit for firm 2 is the formula in the answer to Exercise 3. We need to find $X_1 + X_2$; this computation follows.

$$X_1 + X_2 = \frac{A - 2C_1 + C_2}{3B} + \frac{A - 2C_2 + C_1}{3B}$$
$$= \frac{2A - C_1 - C_2}{3B}.$$

We now find $A - B(X_1 + X_2)$:

$$A - B(X_1 + X_2) = A - B\left(\frac{2A - C_1 - C_2}{3B}\right)$$
$$= A - \left(\frac{2A - C_1 - C_2}{3}\right)$$
$$= \left(\frac{A + C_1 + C_2}{3}\right).$$

We now find profit for firm 2:

$$\pi_2 = (A - B(X_1 + X_2)) \times X_2 - C_2 X_2$$
$$= \left(\frac{A + C_1 + C_2}{3}\right) X_2 - C_2 X_2.$$

Now factor X_2:

$$\pi_2 = \left(\frac{A + C_1 + C_2}{3} - \frac{3C_2}{3}\right) X_2.$$

Complete the algebra in the bracketed term, and put in our formula for X_2 to complete the computation:

$$\pi_2 = \left(\frac{A + C_1 - 2C_2}{3}\right) \frac{A - 2C_2 + C_1}{3B} = \frac{(A + C_1 - 2C_2)^2}{9B}.$$

8. We know that firm 2's BRF is the following:

$$X_2 = \frac{A - C_2 - BX_1}{2B}.$$

There is hardly any algebra to do, as we have already solved for the variable on the vertical axis, X_2. But to see that we have a straight line, we will try to put the equation in slope-intercept form:

$$X_2 = \frac{A - C_2}{2B} - \frac{X_1}{2}.$$

The intercept would be $\frac{A-C_2}{2B}$ which is a constant, and the slope would be $-1/2$ which is also constant. So we have a straight line with slope $-1/2$.

11. In this graph, firm 2 can choose only X_2, and the firm chooses X_2 given the value of X_1. So at A, $X_1 = X_1^0$. Firm 2 wants to move to its BRF, so X_2 must fall.

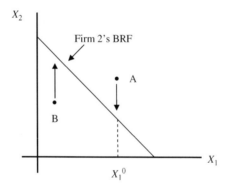

By a similar argument, at B, firm 2 is below its BRF and wants to get back to the BRF, so X_2 will increase.

15. In this case, $\pi = (A - BX)X - CX$. We find the derivative of profit and set this to zero to find the profit-maximizing output:

$$\pi' = (A - BX) - BX - C = 0$$

$$= A - 2BX - C = 0$$

$$X = \frac{A - C}{2B}.$$

We find the price by putting X into the price equation:

$$P = A - BX = A - B\left(\frac{A - C}{2B}\right)$$

$$= A - \left(\frac{A - C}{2}\right) = \frac{A + C}{2}.$$

$$\pi = P \times X - C \times X = (P - C) \times X$$

$$= \left[\left(\frac{A + C}{2}\right) - C\right]\frac{A - C}{2B}$$

$$= \left(\frac{A + C}{2} - \frac{2C}{2}\right)\frac{A - C}{2B} = \frac{(A - C)^2}{4B}.$$

19. If $C_1 = C_2 = C$, then we have the following comparisons of Cournot and Stackelberg:

	Cournot	Stackelberg
X_1	$\dfrac{A - C}{3B}$	$\dfrac{A - C}{2B}$
X_2	$\dfrac{A - C}{3B}$	$\dfrac{A - C}{4B}$
π_1	$\dfrac{(A - C)^2}{9B}$	$\dfrac{(A - C)^2}{8B}$
π_2	$\dfrac{(A - C)^2}{9B}$	$\dfrac{(A - C)^2}{16B}$

Firm 1 produces more under Stackelberg than it would under Cournot, but firm 2 has the opposite result and produces less under Stackelberg than under Cournot. Similarly, profit will be higher for firm 1 under Stackelberg than under Cournot, but firm 2 will have less profit under Stackelberg than under Cournot.

Chapter 9

1. We find SRTC by multiplying SRATC by output, X_1.
3. If SRTC cuts LRTC at X_1, then for that X_1, SRATC = LRATC. For $X < X_1$, SRTC is either smaller or larger than LRATC.

Suppose SRTC < LRTC. The SRATC for those X's will be less than LRATC because we find the average cost by dividing the total cost by output. So if SRTC < LRTC, then SRATC < LRATC must hold. For outputs where SRTC > LRTC, then SRATC > LRATC must hold. Since SRTC cuts LRTC at X_1, on one side of X_1 SRTC < LRTC, and therefore SRATC < LRATC must hold. On the other side of X_1, we have SRTC > LRTC, and therefore SRATC > LRATC must hold. Hence, SRATC cuts LRATC at X_1, which cannot be. LRATC lies on or below all SRATCs.

5. Because we are on LRTC, SRTC must not cut LRTC (otherwise we violate the definition of LRTC). So if $SRTC_1$ and LRTC are equal at X_0, and both are differentiable, and given that they cannot cut, they must be tangent. We can do this by contrapositive. If $SRTC_1$ is not tangent to LRTC at X_0, but they touch at X_0, then $SRTC_1$ must cut LRTC at X_0. But then $SRTC_1$ would go below LRTC, which cannot happen as the LRTC must be the smallest of all possible SRTCs.

10. If the number of firms rises, then the market supply will shift right; price will fall and quantity will rise.

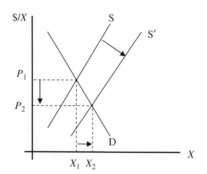

11.

$$\text{SRATC} = 10 + (X_c - X_m)^2 + (X - X_c)^2.$$
$$\text{SRATC}' = 2(X - X_c) = 0.$$

Therefore, to have the minimum SRATC given X_m and X_c, $X = X_c$ must hold.

15. If we can double output with fewer than double inputs, we have increasing returns to scale. That is because if we doubled all inputs, we would get more than double output. If we need more than double inputs to double output, then we have decreasing returns to scale.

18. If we have constant returns to scale, then when we double all inputs, costs double, and output exactly doubles. Suppose that the cost to produce one unit is C. So if we produce 2 units, the cost is $2C$. If we compute the LRMC, we get the following:

$$\text{LRMC} = \frac{LRTC(2) - LRTC(1)}{2 - 1} = \frac{2C - C}{2 - 1} = \frac{C}{1} = C.$$

What if output goes from 2 to 4? LRTC goes from $2C$ to $4C$. LRMC will be $(4C-2C)/(4-2) = 2C/2 = C$. Hence, MC $= C$.

If we compute LRATC at each output, here is what we get:

$$LRATC(1) = \frac{LRTC(1)}{1} = \frac{C}{1} = C.$$

$$LRATC(2) = \frac{LRTC(2)}{2} = \frac{2C}{2} = C.$$

In short, LRMC $=$ LRATC $= C$.

Chapter 10

5. In the case of competition, the MR does not depend on the level of output; the MR is constant. Hence, to find MRP, we multiply a constant MR by the MP. For monopoly, MR depends on the level of output. As output rises, the MR falls. Now when we find MRP, we need to know the output so we can multiply by the right MR. The output depends on the amount of the variable input used, so we need to use the total product to find the output associated with each quantity of the variable input to find the right MR.

8. The formula for MIC is $MIC(L_1 + 1) = w_2 + (w_2 - w_1)L_1$. In the case the firm buys inputs competitively, then the wage is constant and $w_2 = w_1$. The formula for MIC is then $MIC(L_1 + 1) = w_2$, which is exactly the formula we get for the competitive case. Remember that $w_2 = w_1 = w$ in the competitive case.

10. $TIC(L) = L \times w(L)$; to find the MIC, we find the derivative. We will need the product rule:

$$MIC(L) = TIC'(L) = w(L) + L \times w'(L).$$

This expression is essentially the same as the formula we got above. $w(L)$ plays the role of w_2, and $L \times w'(L)$ plays the role of $(w_2 - w_1)L_1$.

11. The argument for MR < D and MIC > S are essentially the same argument:

$$MR(X) = P(X) + X \times P'(X).$$

$$MIC(L) = w(L) + L \times w'(L).$$

The difference is that $P'(X)$, the slope of AR or demand, is negative; whereas the slope of labor supply, $w'(L)$, is positive.

16. The **demand for labor** relates the quantity of labor with dollars per unit of labor, and shows the quantity of labor the firm would hire at each wage with all other factors held fixed.

   Marginal revenue product (MRP) is a relationship between labor and dollars per unit of labor showing the change in total revenue that occurs when an added unit of labor is hired at each quantity of labor with the quantity of all other inputs held fixed.

   Both relate quantity of labor and the wage. The demand for labor holds all other factors, wages (and prices), constant. The MRP holds the quantities of all other inputs constant, not the prices. Just because the price of other inputs is constant does not mean that the quantity of the other inputs is constant (when the wage changes). Think back to the least cost combination proposition: when the wage changes, both the quantity of labor and the quantity of capital change.

22. In this case, the firm is competitive in both the sale of output and the purchase of inputs. So the price of output, P, and the wage, w, are constants. The production function has the standard shape, so if we multiply it by a constant, P, the shape will stay the same. This curve is labeled PX in the graph. The cost line is wL, which is a straight line from the origin with slope w. This

line is labeled wL in the graph. In the lower graph, we show the difference between the two, which is profit. Profit is maximum where the slope of PX is the same as the slope of wL. Hence, $Pf'(L) = w$ must hold, which is L^*.

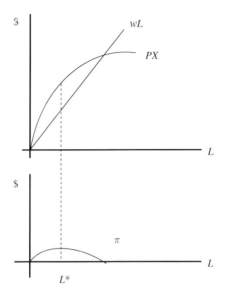

23. We have $X = f(L)$. So if we solve for L, we have $L = f^{-1}(X)$. We can then write profit as

$$\pi = PX - wL = PX - wf^{-1}(X).$$

Now find the derivative and set it to zero to find the profit maximum:

$$\pi' = P - w[f^{-1}(X)]' = 0.$$

In an astounding turn of events, $[f^{-1}(X)]' = 1/f'(X)$. So we can write the derivative as follows:

$$\pi' = P - w1/f'(X) = 0.$$

If we multiply through by $f'(X)$, we get the standard result!

$$Pf'(X) = w.$$

Chapter 11

1. The equation of isoprofit is $\pi = PC_s - wL_d$. We have C on the vertical axis, so solve for C_s:

$$PC_s = \pi + wL_d$$
$$C_s = (\pi/P) + (w/P)L_d.$$

Now we have assumed that π, P, and w are constants (for the moment). Thus, π/P is constant and so is w/P. That means we have a straight line with slope w/P and intercept π/P. The slope is positive, and the sign of the intercept depends on whether profit is positive or negative. If profit is positive, we have the following graph:

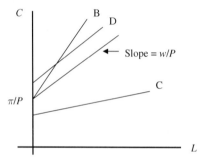

If w rises, the slope gets bigger, but the intercept does not change, so the line swings up still going through the initial intercept. This line is labeled B. If P rises, the intercept falls and the slope also falls. The line shifts down and becomes flatter. This line is labeled C. If profit rises, the line shifts up parallel to itself as the slope, w/P, does not change. This line is labeled D.

3. The budget line and the isoprofit line are the same. Because Robinson gets all the profit from the firm, and P is a constant to Robinson, the intercept of his budget line is the same as the intercept of the isoprofit. Because w and P are the same for both Robinson the buyer and Robinson the seller, the slope of the two lines are the same.

5. The answer to this question is the same as the answer to Exercise 1! The equation of the budget line is $\pi = PC_d - wL_s$. We have C on the vertical axis, so solve for C_d:

$$PC_d = \pi + wL_s$$

$$C_d = (\pi/P) + (w/P)L_s.$$

Now we have assumed that π, P, and w are constants (for the moment). Thus, π/P is constant and so is w/P. That means we have a straight line with slope w/P and intercept π/P. The slope is positive, and the sign of the intercept depends on whether profit is positive or negative. If profit is positive, we have the following graph:

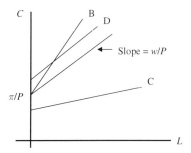

If w rises, the slope gets bigger, but the intercept does not change, so the line swings up still going through the initial intercept. This line is labeled B. If P rises, the intercept falls and the slope also falls. The line shifts down and becomes flatter. This line is labeled C. If profit rises, the line shifts up parallel to itself as the slope, w/P, does not change. This line is labeled D.

8. If we multiply all prices by the same constant, k, profit is multiplied by k. Then because P is multiplied by k, the intercept, profit divided by P, is not changed. Also, the slope w/P is not changed, as both w and P are multiplied by k. Thus, multiplying all prices by k does not change the budget or isoprofit line. Hence, if w and P provide a competitive equilibrium, then kw and kP also provide a competitive equilibrium. We conclude that it is the ratio of prices that matters, w/P.

14. $P_C C_Z^0 + P_F F_Z^0 = P_C C_Z + P_F F_Z.$

15. One way to show that (C_R^0, F_R^0) is on the budget line is to put C_R^0 into the equation of the budget line and find the corresponding value of F_R on the line. If we do this, we get the following:

$$P_C C_R^0 + P_F F_R^0 = P_C C_R^0 + P_F F_R.$$

Now $P_C C_R^0$ is on both sides of the equation and can be canceled. We are left with the following:

$$P_F F_R^0 = P_F F_R.$$

P_F is not zero, and we can divide by it which leaves $F_R = F_R^0$. Thus, (C_R^0, F_R^0) is on the budget line.

16. Suppose we write Robinson's budget line in slope-intercept form:

$$F_R = \frac{P_C C_R^0 + P_F F_R^0}{P_F} - \frac{P_C}{P_F} C_R.$$

   Now if P_C rises, the slope gets more negative, and the line gets steeper. At the same time, the intercept also rises. Note that it is easy to see that even with the new price, the point (C_R^0, F_R^0) is still on the line. After all, the argument of Exercise 15 will also apply to the new prices as well as the original prices. Hence, the line rotates about the point (C_R^0, F_R^0) and gets steeper.

   If P_F rises, then the slope of the line gets less negative and the intercept gets smaller. You can see that the intercept gets smaller because we can rewrite the intercept as follows:

$$\frac{P_C C_R^0}{P_F} + F_R^0.$$

   As P_F gets larger, the intercept gets smaller. Thus, the line rotates about the point (C_R^0, F_R^0) and gets flatter.

22. You should be getting used to this question by now! As the budget lines for the two consumers are symmetric, if we look at Robinson, we can also see what happens to Zelda. If both prices are multiplied by k, then Robinson's income, $P_C C_R^0 + P_F F_R^0$, is multiplied by k. At the same time, Robinson's expenses, $P_C C_R + P_F F_R$, are also

multiplied by k. Thus, the set of coconuts and fish Robinson can afford does not change! There is no impact on Robinson's budget line!

The lesson is that it is the ratio of prices that matters, not the level of prices.

28. We have fish on the vertical axis, so we solve for F:

$$GDP = P_C C + P_F F$$

$$GDP - P_C C = P_F F$$

$$F = \frac{GDP}{P_F} - \frac{P_C}{P_F} C.$$

Because GDP, P_F, and P_C are constants, this is the equation of a straight line with intercept GDP/P_F and slope of $-P_C/P_F$. If GDP rises, the line moves out parallel to itself as the slope, $-P_C/P_F$, does not change, but the intercept, GDP/P_F, gets larger.

29. By contrapositive. If the GDP line is not tangent to the production possibilities at (C_1, F_1), then the GDP line must intersect the production possibilities at (C_1, F_1). In that case, there are combinations of C and F on the production possibilities that yield higher levels of GDP, so GDP cannot be maximum.

Chapter 12

3. For the PTES S', northeast of S, R is better off at S', but Z is worse off at S' compared to S. Thus, S' cannot be Pareto superior to S as Pareto superior requires that both consumers prefer S' to S. Similarly, S is not Pareto superior to S' as Zelda likes S better than S', but Robinson likes S less than S'. For S to be Pareto superior to S', both consumers must like S better than S'.

For S' to be Pareto inferior to S, both consumers must like S' less than S, but Robinson likes S' more, so S' is not Pareto inferior to S. Finally, S is not Pareto inferior to S' because Pareto inferior requires that both consumers like S less than S', but Zelda likes S more than S'. The outcome is that there is no Pareto relationship between S and S'!

4. To be inside the Edgeworth box means that we are not on the edge. That is, we are not on the axis for either commodity for either consumer. Thus, positive quantities of both commodities are consumed by both consumers.

5. These are essentially the same concept. Pareto (as we have defined it) is applied to the case of pure trade economic states and "efficient" is applied to input distributions.

Chapter 13

3. a. Expected value $= 0.5 \times (\$40,000) + 0.5 \times (\$20,000)$
$$= \$20,000 + \$10,000 = \$30,000.$$

   b. Expected value $= 0.6 \times (\$60,000) + 0.4 \times 0 = \$36,000.$

   c. Expected value $= 0.8 \times (\$40,000) + 0.2 \times (-\$20,000)$
$$= \$28,000.$$

4. $U(X) = \sqrt{X}$, so $U'(X) = \frac{1}{2} X^{\frac{-1}{2}}$. The second derivative is $U''(X) = \frac{-1}{4} X^{\frac{-3}{2}} < 0$. Thus, this utility function exhibits diminishing marginal utility.

8. $U(Y) = Y^4$, so $U'(Y) = 4Y^3$, and $U''(Y) = 12Y^2 > 0$. This is the utility function of a risk lover.

10. Find expected utility if there is no insurance:

$$0.8\sqrt{\$100,000} + 0.2\sqrt{\$80,000}$$
$$= 0.8 \times 316.2277 + 0.2 \times 282.8427$$
$$= 252.9822 + 56.5685 = 309.55.$$

If there is full insurance, the consumer ends up with $100,000 minus the cost of the insurance, $4,500, or $95,500. The utility of this outcome is 309.03. The utility of insurance is less than the utility without insurance, so the consumer would choose to not take insurance.

11. Given that the consumer has full insurance, the utility to the consumer with insurance would be $\sqrt{\$100,000 - premium}$. This would have to be at least as much as the consumer would get without insurance, 309.55 (from Exercise 10). So set $\sqrt{\$100,000 - premium} = 309.55$ and solve for the premium.

Square both sides to get the following:

$100,000 − premium = $95,821.20

Premium = $100,000 − $95,821.20 = $4,178.80.

Thus, the maximum premium the consumer would pay would be $4,178.80.

13. Figure 13.9 is reproduced below. In this graph, if P_B rises, then the MRP curve will shift to the right, $P'_B \times MP_L$, and the profit-maximizing quantity of labor, L_B, will rise to L'_B.

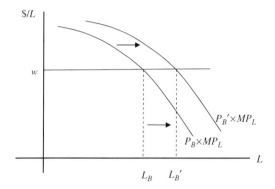

Index